A CAPTAIN'S PORTRAIT

Witold Pilecki – Martyr for Truth

Adam J. Koch

FREEDOM
PUBLISHING BOOKS

FREEDOM
PUBLISHING BOOKS

Published in Australia by
Freedom Publishing Books
33 Scoresby Road
Bayswater Vic. 3153
Australia

ISBN 9781922589026

Copyright © Adam J. Koch 2018

All rights reserved. Other than for the purposes and subject to the conditions prescribed under the *Copyright Act*, no part of this publication may be reproduced, stored in a retrieval system, or transmitted in any form or by any means, electronic, mechanical, photocopying, recording or otherwise, without the prior permission of the publisher.

Every effort has been made to acknowledge and contact copyright holders for permission to reproduce material contained in this book. Any copyright holders who have been inadvertently omitted from acknowledgements and credits should contact the publisher and omissions will be rectified in subsequent editions.

Cataloguing-in-Publication entry is available from the National Library of Australia
http://catalogue.nla.gov.au/.

Text and cover design by Filmshot Graphics (FSG)

Printed in Australia by Brougham Press

ACKNOWLEDGEMENTS

This biography would never have been able to be completed and published had it not been for the critically important support and ongoing encouragement provided to me by Witold Pilecki's children. I am immensely grateful for it, and take this opportunity to once again thank Zofia Optułowicz and Andrzej Pilecki for trusting me with matters of greatest importance to them.

I am also indebted to the author of one of Witold Pilecki's Polish language biographies, Dr. Adam Cyra, for his untiring assistance and advice, particularly when it comes to describing the Auschwitz, and other episodes of Pilecki's life.

I am beholden to Professor Tracey Rowland for her warm words of support, and for her appreciation of the timeliness of my initiative. Heartfelt thanks go to my Melbourne publisher, Freedom Publishing Books, for making it possible for this book to appear in time for the 100th anniversary of Poland regaining its statehood.

Author's gratitude is extended here to all those who, in one way or another, supported me, strengthened my motivation, and helped me complete this project.

Last but not least, I wish to express special thanks to my spouse Krystyna, without whose understanding, unfailing support and unmatched magnanimity it would simply have not been possible to complete this book within just eight months of commencing it.

Photographs and other illustrative material presented in this book come from:

Auschwitz-Birkenau Memorial and Museum, Oświęcim, Poland,

Cambridge University Press,

Euratlas Nüssli, Switzerland

Fathers Missionaries' Museum of History and Mission in Cracow, Poland,

Institute of National Remembrance, Warsaw, Poland,

Jasna Góra Monastery, Częstochowa, Poland

Ryszard Maceikianec,

Museum of 1944 Warsaw Uprising, Warsaw, Poland

National Museum at Wroclaw, Poland,

Pilecki family,

Museum of Polish Army, Warsaw, Poland and

Republic of Poland's Department of Foreign Affairs.

All these contributions are gratefully acknowledged by its author.

*'Starałem się tak żyć, abym
w godzinie śmierci mógł
się raczej cieszyć, niż lękać.'*

Witold Pilecki

*'I strove to live such a life that at the hour of my
death I would rather rejoice than be fearful.'*

CONTENTS

Acknowledgements	iii
Foreword	ix
Introduction	13
The reward for fidelity	21

PART I – THE PORTRAIT'S BACKGROUND — 27

Discovering tradition inside a man	28
What shaped Witold Pilecki	30
Defining events from Poland's history (966-1920)	39
The baptism of Poland	39
Safe haven for many	43
Poland united	45
Lithuanian Grand Duke on the Polish throne	48
Wars against the Teutonic Knights Order	51
Poland's *Age of Golden Liberty*	56
Polish-Russian strategic opposition – how it came about	59
Election of kings and *liberum veto* – have they served Poland well?	69
Triggers of decline	72
The relief of Vienna	73
Neighbours' conspiracy renders the Commonwealth helpless	76
Three attempts at regaining statehood	83
Poles rise to the occasion	86

PART II - HIS JOURNEY OF DUTY — 91

A few words on Pilecki's ancestry	93
Childhood in Karelia	95

Return home	101
In war's turmoil	104
Poland exists again!	107
His peacetime service commences	119
His life at Sukurcze	133
Harbingers of World War II	149
Poland attacked by Hitler's Germany and the Soviet Union	157
Let down by its allies	166
The gallant defence	167
Defeated - yet unyielding	168
Going underground	170
A volunteer to KL Auschwitz	179
An Auschwitz inmate	184
At Auschwitz	188
His escape from the camp	231
Pilecki's *Report W* from KL Auschwitz	239
From the translator of *Report W*	239
Report W	243
Introduction to *Report W*	243
End notes to *Report W*	316
His Kedyw Service	319
The 1944 Warsaw Uprising	324
A German war prisoner	336
The Italian episode	340
In the bear's den	344
His arrest and trial	354
Epilogue	376
Index of Persons	381
Bibliography	394
Endnotes	411

FOREWORD

In a world obsessed with individualism, self-assertion and even self-idolatry, as well as gender ideology, a world where concepts like chivalry, manliness, self-sacrificial love and heroism, are no longer immediately understood or even seen to be socially worthwhile qualities, Adam Koch's work on the life of Witold Pilecki, a Polish hero of the first half of the twentieth century (13 May 1901 – 25 May 1948), is more than timely.

Koch approaches his work with an understanding that Pilecki's biography is incomprehensible if taken out of the context of the Polish culture which moulded him. A brief oversight of Poland's history provided by the author not only helps the reader better understand the motives behind Witold's many decisions, but also serves as an explicatory background to Pilecki's interest in the Polish cavalry, his commitment to Polish independence and the various knightly virtues associated with both.

Pilecki was born when Poland was not even on the map of Europe though as a seventeen year old scout he already fought for Poland's independence, the independence his country regained on November 11, 1918. He also served his country in peacetime (1918-1939). This historical context is covered in the sections *Peacetime Service Commences* and *His Life in Sukurcze*.

Amidst his many sacrifices for the common cause, Pilecki was also a loving father to his son Andrzej and his daughter Zofia. One of my favourite stories in the book, told by Zofia, is that he tried to persuade her to eat porridge by noting that horses eat oats and they have beautiful glossy coats. He clearly knew something about how the feminine soul works.

Pilecki is best known as a Polish cavalry officer, WWII Polish underground intelligence agent and resistance leader. In late 1939 after Poland's loss of the September campaign it fought against the invading German army, a loss which was expedited by the invasion on September 17 by the Soviet Army which were allied with the Wehremacht, he co-founded the Secret Polish Army (*Tajna Armia Polska*). He later became a member of the largest Polish WWII underground movement, the Home Army (*Armia Krajowa*), with which he later fought in the 1944 Warsaw Uprising.

Earlier, in September 1940, he volunteered for a mission which required getting himself imprisoned in the German concentration camp of Auschwitz, so as to gather intelligence on that camp's operations, and to organize resistance there.

Once at KL Auschwitz, he went beyond his original mission. He found extra food and clothing for fellow inmates, smuggled medicines across barbed wire fences, found lighter work for those weaker than others, and helped those who got into trouble with the camp's authorities by getting them hospitalized until the storm passed. Most of all, he would sustain fellow inmates' hope, which was most important for everyone's survival.

The section of the book dealing with Pilecki's experience of Auschwitz is based mainly on Pilecki's own reports which were passed on to the allied high command during the war.

After the main objectives of his Auschwitz mission had been achieved, together with two fellow inmates, he escaped from the camp. He then worked with the Polish wartime underground military intelligence and took part in the 1944 Warsaw Uprising, as a commander of a platoon, later a company. In this capacity he achieved many successes against an enemy that was numerically superior and far better armed.

In 1948, having survived both Auschwitz and the Warsaw Uprising, he was executed by Communists on trumped up charges of supporting "foreign imperialism". The sub-text here is that he was an officer with the Second Corps of the Polish Army stationed in Italy which answered to the legal Polish Government-in-Exile in London. He chose to serve the legal government rather than the Communist thugs, who with Soviet help, under Soviet strict control, took over the reins of power in July 1944. The Communists feared the non-Communist leaders like Pilecki, so he had to be killed and his heroism erased from public memory.

Ultimately, however, the Communists failed. In post-1989 free Poland Pilecki was posthumously awarded membership of the Order of the White Eagle, the highest honour bestowed by the Polish government.

For some reason, this being perhaps some spiritual mystery, Poland often finds herself fighting on the front lines in the wars against the Christian West. In the seventeenth century, it was Ottoman Turks, in the 20th, first Soviet Marxism, then German Fascism, then Soviet Marxism again.

In the 21st century Poland is yet again under attack, this time from proponents of a totalitarian liberalism, many of them highly placed within the bureaucracies of the European Union. To achieve their aims they want to suppress the history of Polish heroism and of the staunch defence of the Catholic faith underlying Poland's traditional culture. Indeed, there are some who would want surnames like Sobieski, Sikorski, Pilecki and Wojtyła air-brushed out of the history books. They would also gladly have the names of so many great Polish battlefield victories forgotten. These would include the victory over the Teutonic Knights at Grunwald (1410), the relief of the siege of Vienna (1683) by King Jan Sobieski and his defeat of the Ottoman army there, the defeat of the Red Army on the outskirts of Warsaw in August 1920 (otherwise known as the miracle on the Vistula) which saved Western Europe from further Bolshevik expansions, the crucial part Polish airmen played in saving Great Britain in 1940 from German invasion, and the greatest bravery shown by the Polish Second Corps at Monte Cassino (1944). Each of these victories is forever a part of the tapestry of Polish national identity. Young people who read about these victories will come to understand that Poland is not simply a 'telephone company' to use Alasdair MacIntyre's metaphor. MacIntyre has observed that in contemporary liberal political theory the state is presented as having no moral authority or responsibilities. It is merely the provider of social utilities like electricity and communication networks. MacIntyre then asks, 'who would want to die for a telephone company?' The Poland for which Pilecki died had a moral dimension and carried moral responsibilities.

It was against the backdrop of the ideological battles of the 20th century that St John Paul II, in a speech delivered to the scholars of Lublin University (KUL), remarked:

> The human person must in the name of the truth about himself stave off a double temptation: the temptation to make the truth about himself subordinate to his freedom and the temptation to subordinate himself to the world of objects; he has to refuse to succumb to the temptation of both self-idolatry and of self-subjectification: *Positus est in medio homo: nec bestia—nec deus.*

Witold Pilecki got it right precisely because of his strong Catholic faith and knowledge of Polish history. In times such as our own when new ideologies and forces of social engineering seek to denigrate the divine element in humanity, one would hope that stories such as the one told in this book will inspire new generations to walk the tight-rope between self-idolatry and self-subjectification.

Professor Tracey Rowland
(ODM) (Poland), PhD (Cantab), STD (Lateran).
St. John Paul II Chair of Theology, University of Notre Dame (Australia)

INTRODUCTION

Of books that portray and reflect on lives of eminent people there seem to be several categories. One of them, is eulogies. Another one concentrates on unknown details and anecdotes about the person. Still another, is serious works written by historians. Then, there are books that challenge popular impressions of a person within the society and aim to disabuse its readers of what their authors regard as fallacies about character, motives, or deeds of the person in question. Those best versed in the categories of literature may add one, or perhaps even more categories of such literature to this list.

This book may ill fit any of the acknowledged types of biography, in that it consists of two distinct parts. The first one presents Poland's rich historical background, the role of which is to help readers from all over the world better understand its hero's world view which, to a very considerable degree, has been a product of particular Polish nation's experiences over the centuries.

This biography was written for people all over the world to make it possible for them to learn about one very remarkable person, a person whose entire life could serve as an example of a life well spent, a life of sacrifice and service to all those in need, a life the best-known episode of which is its most fitting metaphor. That episode was a voluntary undercover mission undertaken to provide comprehensive help and at the same time upheld human dignity in extreme circumstances of self-immolating trial: one inside a Nazi German death camp, a place of most horrendous human suffering. That place's name was KL Auschwitz.

Those who have any idea of the ghastly realities of a German World War II death camp must wonder: what could have moved someone to get Germans to lock him up in a camp where his chances of survival were very slim indeed, where he could expect to suffer extreme maltreatment and hunger, and see inmates deprived of their dignity and human rights?

This book seeks to answer this question. It presents a person whose life of self-denial and unconditional service to others had the quality of a flawless diamond. It also invites the reader to reflect on the significance of that life as a source of salutary inspiration to the entire world, the world many of us find today very deeply troubled.

This book is about Captain Witold Pilecki[1], a Pole who lived through, arguably, one of the most turbulent, tragic and transforming periods of human history: the first half of the twentieth century.

Witold Pilecki's life has certainly been most remarkable: it is also emblematic in the sense of the type and intensity of his response to the very demanding circumstances of his life. His is a life of a man of many heroic virtues and talents, all of which are well applied by him. His response to challenges of his life embodies the best qualities of Polish culture and tradition he upheld throughout his life.

All his childhood years he spends in Russia's northern province of Karelia. His patriotic family lived there as exiles. They were banished there by Tsarist Russia's government as a punishment for the role they played in the 1863 Uprising whose purpose it was for Poland to regain its independence from Russia. As a child, he learns a lot about the proud history of Poland: this, together with very traditional Catholic upbringing, forms his values and life aspirations. In his scouting years, he strengthens his motivation. In his early manhood he fights for, wins, and then successfully defends Poland's independence after World War I.

It is the combination of the truly dramatic circumstances of his life, of his unwavering defence of all values he stood for, his staunch service to fellow men, and his preparedness to sacrifice so much in his life that show the most remarkable strength of his character. Its exquisiteness demands that none of its qualities be omitted. After all, it is in its wholeness that the quality of his character can truly be revealed.

The hero of this book embodies many quintessential values of Polish tradition and culture: he is a freedom-loving patriot ready to lay his life for Poland if only the common good of his compatriots demands this. He is also a man of deep faith: he is guided in his actions and thoughts by the desire to remain true to all precepts of the Decalogue. He loves God above all. His hope in God's providence is unshakeable.

Witold Pilecki is most dedicated in his service to all those in need. He is compassionate and highly dependable. He is humble and never motivated by career prospects, or the pursuit of significance in this world. He is honest, sincere and discreet, never hateful of anyone and tolerant of differences of opinions between people. He suffers indignities and setbacks in his life without complaint, or a sense of injustice. He is diligent and untiring in the pursuit of his goals.

He is farsighted, reasonable, temperate and patient. He is level-headed, cheerful, resourceful and well-mannered. He never hesitates to express his gratitude to people. He is dedicated to the task of bringing people together, regardless of their differences. He is receptive to all beauty in God's creation, as he is to all beauty that transpires from human creation of true excellence.

Witold Pilecki not only respects all people, but he also staunchly defends their rights. In particular, he stands up for their dignity. There is no trace of a double-standard, or hypocrisy, in anything he does, or says. Being himself of a very generous mind, he always sets the bar very high for himself. He takes a great deal of care not to waste any opportunity to offer all his talents and capabilities to those around him, because he knows to whom he owes those gifts. He is also aware that they were given to him so that he could produce good in abundance.

Captain Pilecki is a person of unshakable rectitude, great courage, unwavering sense of responsibility, and – most of all – a person of great love for his fellow men. At the same time, he is a man of genuine humility[2]. The sources of his moral rectitude are: God, Honor and Fatherland.

Witold Pilecki's life witness will be looked upon by many with an admiration that cannot help but inspire.

While there certainly are not many people like him, we must never doubt all of us do have a capacity to become a little bit more like Witold Pilecki.

*

When I contacted Captain's daughter, Zofia Optułowicz, and his son, Andrzej Pilecki, to present this book's idea to them (this idea was conceived soon after I had completed my translation of Witold Pilecki's original report from KL Auschwitz (September 1940 – April 1943)[3], they wholeheartedly and gratefully approved of this initiative.

Zofia's expectation of this book was expressed very briefly: *'What I really wish for this book, is to say the truth about my father.'* What she meant was not just the obvious: that she would wish for the book to only contain confirmed facts about her father. She meant more: she was hopeful this book would say the whole truth about her father, that it would present him as she, her brother, and all those who knew him well, still remember him.

*

As the World War II hostilities in Europe ended on May 9, 1945, Poland and other countries of central Eastern and south-eastern Europe[4], together with three Baltic states[5], all found themselves either annexed by the Soviet Union, or fell under complete ideological, political and military control of the latter country's totalitarian regime. Nearly all private property in these countries was to be soon forcibly taken over by the state. Soviet-style non-market economy was introduced and about every aspect of political and social life in those countries became under control of its Soviet installed puppet government.

For nearly half a century, between 1944 and 1989, Polish underground independence fighters of World War II, such as Captain Pilecki, among them some of the finest Polish patriots of that time, had been besmirched by the communist propaganda machine as bandits, simply because they did not acquiesce in the presence of Soviet troops on Poland's territory, or the Soviet control of the country. During the first ten years of the *de facto* Soviet occupation, many soldiers from Polish underground military units who remained true to their oath of allegiance to the independent and legally appointed Polish government-in-exile, would be killed on the spot or executed after sham trials.

Not only were many thousands of those '*unbreakable soldiers*'[6] as they are called today in Poland, killed by the communist regime between 1944 and 1955, but their names were to be expurgated forever from the nation's memory. Soon after the war, many families of those soldiers were dispossessed, their members often struggled to find and hold a fitting job, and children, sometimes even grandchildren of the executed underground independence fighters were denied access to tertiary education, especially before 1956. They often suffered extreme hardship.

All those families shared also the sense of helplessness and humiliation induced by calumnies spread about their closest ones, heroes who had known their patriotic duty and were determined to carry it out, regardless of the price that would be demanded of them to pay for such valour in those grim years. One of those Polish families who suffered radical discrimination and injustice, and whose members for a very long time could do nothing about restoring the good name of their martyred father, husband, or brother, was the Pilecki family.

That is why telling the truth about this period of the Polish history is so highly valued by all those Polish families. That is why it is so valued by the Pilecki family.

*

Before the work on this book could start, it was necessary to ensure that a sufficiently detailed and authoritatively confirmed picture of Witold Pilecki as a person was obtained. To serve as a background for this picture, exhaustive research was undertaken. Access to archival sources included Pilecki's Report W from Auschwitz - using my translation - along with numerous other Polish language biographies of Captain Pilecki[7], his telephone reviews, and his correspondence with Zofia Optułowicz and Andrzej Pilecki. Taken together, these materials made it possible to come up with a detailed psychological profile of the Captain. The values Witold espoused, and the principles he stood by, were defined and confirmed by his children.

Once a sketch of this book's idea received, in June 2014, the approval of Captain Pilecki's children, the work on this book commenced.

*

The hero of this book is viewed from multiple perspectives. One of them focuses on his very deep Catholic spirituality, for it is only through these lenses that some of his life's decisions and thoughts he shared with others do acquire a deeper meaning.

My reliance on multiple perspectives presented a significant additional challenge as I worked on this biography; a switch between four hats was necessary. One was a historian's hat; another was a biographer's hat, still another was a hat of someone describing some aspects of the Catholic faith and its spirituality to readers less, or not at all familiar with the Catholic beliefs; the last one was a hat of someone offering an insider's understanding about various matters relating to the challenges faced by Polish society in the first half of the twentieth century.

*

Over more than ten centuries of its recorded history, Poland has produced quite a few people of noble greatness like Witold Pilecki. Many of them may still not be very well known outside, or even – inside their country. Yet, there only is one Witold Pilecki.

In his foreword to *The Auschwitz Volunteer: Beyond Bravery*, the Chief Rabbi of Poland, Michael Schudrich, had this to say: '*Pilecki is a shining example of heroism that transcends religion, race and time*' [...] *When God created the human being, God had in mind that we should all be like Captain Witold Pilecki, of blessed memory.*' And then the rabbi invokes: '*May the life of Witold Pilecki inspire us all to do one more good deed, of any kind, each and every day of our lives*'[8]. Is this not a call the entire world should heed today?

*

There is but one more thing that I feel I should disclose to the readers in this introduction: English is not my first language. The choice of English for this biography was hardly a matter of whim: it was the consequence of universal appeal and significance of Captain Pilecki's most remarkable life and of his heroic fight against evil.

'What is the secret of Pilecki's universal appeal?' I think, the answer to this question can be inspired, at least in part, by the observation made by Simone Weil, a French mystic of the twentieth century, when she juxtaposed the nature of good and evil:

> *'Imaginary evil is romantic and varied;*
> *real evil is gloomy, monotonous, barren,*
> *boring. Imaginary good is boring; real good*
> *is always new, marvelous, intoxicating.'*[9]

This book simply had to be written in the *lingua franca* of our time. It had to be written in English.

THE REWARD FOR FIDELITY

For I am already being poured out like
a libation, and the time of my departure
is at hand.

I have competed well; I have finished the
race; I have kept the faith.

From now on the crown of righteousness
awaits me, which the Lord, the just judge,
will award to me on that day, and not
only to me, but to all who have longed
for His appearance.

(2 Tm 4, 6:8)

It is May 25, 1948. The city at the dusk hour is falling silent. The quiet evening's air is filled with the delightful and unique perfume of Polish spring.

We are inside the Mokotów prison in Warsaw, a drab, grey complex of buildings at Rakowiecka Street. It was completed during the early twentieth century (1904) by the Tsarist government, when Russia still occupied most of the territory of the former Commonwealth of Poland and Lithuania.[10]

Only three years have passed since World War II ended. Many buildings around the prison are, in 1948, still in ruins or at least badly damaged. They bear testimony to the enormous destruction of Warsaw at the hands of Hitler's troops, who had methodically, and with a ruthlessness unknown in earlier centuries, exacted their revenge on the city. For on August 1, 1944, Warsaw's inhabitants had dared to challenge the strength of the Nazi occupier, in a battle against overwhelming odds for Polish freedom, independence, and the dignity of sovereign nationhood: blessings so dear to the Polish heart. It is this battle which people now call the Warsaw Uprising.

Suddenly, we hear voices inside the prison. Soon after, we see several men walking down the prison's corridors, heading towards the basement. One of them, in front of the group, has a white gag over his mouth. He is in fact carried by two prison warders, who hold him firmly, grabbing him under his arms so that his feet appear to be barely touching the ground. He is languid. His face and body carry the scars of torture. Both of his collar-bones seem to have been broken. His fingernails have been torn out. His name is Witold Pilecki. He is a Polish Army Captain.

THE COURTYARD OF RAKOWIECKA STREET PRISON, AS AT AROUND 1948

[a public domain photo]

A year earlier, he was arrested and accused of three things. First, of having illegally entered the territory of Poland in October 1945 on a secret mission from the transitional headquarters of the Second Polish Corps in Ancona, Italy. Second, of having engaged in activities against the government – a government installed and supported by the Soviets – by collecting information about (among other things) the persecution and sometimes murder of Polish patriots. The third charge against Pilecki is that of having passed such information to the London-based Polish government-in-exile. A military court, itself firmly under Soviet control, had found him guilty of spying for Western powers and sentenced him to death.

Hence the scene we now witness. Those who accompany Pilecki are: Major Stanisław Cypryszewski, Deputy Prosecutor at the Polish High Military Court; Lieutenant Ryszard Mońko, Mokotów's deputy governor; Lieutenent Kazimierz Jezierski, a military doctor; Captain Wincenty Martusiewicz, a Catholic army chaplain; and a military executioner.

The executioner has the rank of Company Sergeant. He is a seasoned professional. His services have been in demand in that prison ever since the Germans fled Warsaw in January 1945 and Soviets took over the control of Poland so ruthlessly ravaged by the war and the exceedingly cruel and bloody Nazi occupation. Tragically for this occupied nation, the Soviets believe that they have their own unsettled scores with Poles[11].

Piotr Śmietański is the executioner's name. Like Pilecki, he is a Pole. Unlike Pilecki, he loyally serves the communist regime, as do the military prosecutor and the deputy prison governor.

Very soon the men reach the execution cellar. Its ceiling is low, and already there are many bloodstains visible on the floor and walls, which are made of cement. On the steps leading into the cellar, Śmietański draws his pistol, and touching Pilecki's occiput with its barrel – this being the Soviets' favoured mode of execution – he pulls the trigger. Pilecki slumps lifeless to the ground. Śmietański leaves the cellar.

Before the dawn Pilecki's body, presumably wrapped up in a bag (as had been the custom of this prison in those grim years), is disposed of. Precisely how, we cannot say for certain. The likeliest conjecture is that it was loaded at night onto a horse-drawn wagon, taken to an unknown place,[12] and secretly buried in an unmarked grave. Yet it might just as well have been removed by some other means.

At any rate, until 1989 very few people even within Poland – let alone outside it – knew of Pilecki's remarkable life. Today, however, he is widely recognised as an Allied hero of World War II, 'with few peers,' as British historian Norman Davies has said[13]; as one of the finest Polish patriots; and an example to countless people all over the world.

Soon after the Soviet-controlled national Communist party – which called itself Polish United Workers' Party – formally relinquished its grip on Poland in June 1989, Pilecki is fully rehabilitated under the Polish law. The death sentence which he received in 1948 is on October 1, 1990 pronounced to have been an act of gross injustice, and a violation of law. Five years later, Pilecki receives another posthumous tribute: admission to the Polish Order of Polonia Restituta: this ceremony is witnessed by his widow Maria. On February 6, 2002, aged 96, Maria dies. In 2006, Pilecki receives another posthumous award, the highest Polish decoration of the Order of the White Eagle. On September 6, 2013, he is retrospectively promoted to the rank of Colonel.

By the time this book's final chapters are written, over forty Polish schools and other Polish organisations bear Pilecki's name. Since 1989, several monuments to Pilecki have been erected throughout the country, acts of homage to this most remarkable person.

Perhaps the most notable of all these monuments was unveiled on May 25, 2017. On the very same day on which, sixty-nine years before, Pilecki was executed. This monument was unveiled in the Warsaw suburb of Żolibórz, at 40 Aleja Wojska Polskiego, the very address where he spent his last night before being apprehended on the morning of September 19, 1940, during a massive SS street round-up. Two days later, he was transported to Auschwitz. There, his secret underground mission awaited him.

This Żolibórz location is a most fitting place for the monument to honour this humble hero. A hero who, alas, still has no formally recognised grave. His remains are yet to be found.

PART I – THE PORTRAIT'S BACKGROUND

DISCOVERING TRADITION INSIDE A MAN

Unexpectedly for a great Polish patriot and national hero, Witold Pilecki was not actually born in Poland. On the day he was born – May 13, 1901 – there was no Polish state. You could not actually find Poland on any of the maps current at that time. In 1901, Poland as a state had not existed for over one hundred years.

Notwithstanding this, Pilecki was raised in a family deeply imbued with Polish culture, a family very well familiar with, and proud of, Poland's rich and proud traditions, of the Polish nation's contributions to the world. As a result, values Pilecki espoused, his behaviour, and his life choices all reflected this rich history and tradition.

A hundred years later, we live in a world that differs a lot from one in which Pilecki was born. Most significantly perhaps, we live in a world which is becoming more and more uniform. As a result, many of us have perhaps already lost an acute sense of our cultural identity. We are apt to become gradually more and more removed from our cultural roots. Affinity with tradition is harder and harder to come by. Naturally, this makes it a lot more difficult to comprehend today, than it would have been decades back, the motivation and actions of someone so strongly influenced by his traditional culture as Pilecki always was.

If so, how overwhelming that challenge must therefore be today for those whose cultural heritages are very different from his, how big it must be for those who cannot rely on the shared awareness of cultural nuances, and on the significance of various events from another country's history, can easily be imagined. This bar could well be put too high unless adequate assistance is provided to the reader, by the way of historical background which would outline all events believed to be most formative of the biographee.

In recognition of the obvious needs of those readers who may not be very familiar with the history and culture of Poland, this book has an introductory chapter entitled: 'What Shaped Witold Pilecki'. It contains a brief account of selected events of Polish history believed to have had a particularly significant influence on the way Pilecki perceived and made sense of the world around him.

Like so many of his compatriots, Witold Pilecki was shaped by his country's often tempestuous history. He also encapsulated what was most valuable in the traditional Polish culture.

A famous saying goes: 'Sometimes people can't see the forest for the trees.' Let's hope that the considerable physical distance from which I cast my gaze on Poland and Europe as I worked on this book ensured that I saw the entire forest clearly enough.[14]

WHAT SHAPED WITOLD PILECKI[15]

Once a proud and powerful state which occupied vast territories in Central and Eastern Europe, the Commonwealth of Poland and Lithuania ceased to exist in 1795. In that year, its last king, Stanisław August Poniatowski, had to step down from Poland's throne and was then forced to hand over the entire territory he ruled over to three other monarchs: Empress Catherine II of Russia; King Friedrich Wilhelm II of Prussia; and Emperor Franz II of Austria.

Those three absolute monarchies, neighbours of the Commonwealth of Poland and Lithuania, had for most of the eighteenth century conspired to first put this freedom-loving country under their control. This they soon achieved. That control they were able to exercise through a relatively small group of Polish parliamentary deputies these foreign powers were able to corrupt. The main purpose of their control was to prevent the country from introducing certain reforms which it badly needed, most of all - a new tax so as to make it possible for the Commonwealth to form, and maintain, a large standing army. Only with such an army could the Commonwealth's once formidable military might be restored. In their punitive designs, the monarchies succeeded. They were hence able to overpower Poland on the battlefield. Then, in 1795, they finally divided the remainder of Poland's territory between them.

The three powers' rulers thought at that time that they had erased the Polish state from the map forever. Yet, they misjudged the tenacity of their victim: they underestimated the Poles' patriotism, their resolve to keep their language, culture and tradition, their determination to win back their freedom and independence. Poland did regain its independence in 1918, after 123 years of Russo-German-Austrian occupation.

Poles had not waited idly for all this time to have their statehood to be returned to them. Already in 1797, under Napoleon Bonaparte, Polish Legions had been formed in northern Italy. There, they commenced the struggle to bring Poland back on the map. The Legions' banners carried words of their famous pledge: 'For your freedom and ours'.[16]. They fought gallantly and, for a very brief time, achieved their objective (if only partially, and for a very short time), owing it to the 1807 Tilsit peace treaty. This treaty, signed by Napoleon and Tsar Alexander I, made it possible to form, mostly from some of those Polish territories that were annexed in 1772, 1792 and 1795 by the Kingdom of Prussia, a mini-state called Duchy of Warsaw. Its ruler was to be one of Napoleon's allies, Friedrich August I, King of Saxony.

The territory of Duchy of Warsaw was only about one-eighth the size of the Commonwealth of Poland and Lithuania's pre-1772 territory. And, it did not last long. It survived only until 1815, and perished after Napoleon decisively lost at Waterloo. Once again, another European coalition decided to erase the remnants of Polish sovereignty from the map of Europe. This time it was the anti-Napoleon coalition (Russia, Great Britain, Prussia and Austria-Hungary) that did so, at the Congress of Vienna (1814-1815).

Twice over the next fifty years, dozens of thousands of patriotic Poles took part in heroic attempts to overthrow the occupiers' rule, and to restore a Polish state. These attempts occurred in 1830-1831 (November Uprising) and in 1863-1864 (January Uprising). Vast numbers of Poles died then in battle, or else were deported by the Tsarist governments to remote places in Siberia, many thousands of kilometres away from their homes. Many of them never returned from their deportation.

Józef Pilecki, Witold Pilecki's grandfather, took part in the January Uprising, and was among those condemned – by Alexander II, Tsar of Russia since 1855 – to banishment in Siberia. Much of what had been Polish and Lithuanian territory fell under direct Russian rule, to be plundered and laid waste. The sheer cruelty of the Russian troops in quashing the January Uprising was something that Poles long and bitterly remembered. The toll was especially severe on the Polish nobility of Lithuania where the Pilecki family lived at that time: one in four of those nobles were killed during the January Uprising.

As additional punishment, many basic rights were denied to Poles by Tsarist governments for half a century. Poles were forbidden to have their own universities; they were even forbidden to speak the Polish language in their schools. Not surprisingly, in view of the oppression and exploitation to which the occupying powers had subjected the Polish people, it was impossible for Poland to develop its economy and infrastructure at the same pace as most European countries were able to throughout the nineteenth century. Thus, the wealth gap between those countries and Poland kept increasing at that time.

Given the odds, to be able to regain its independence the Polish nation needed some help from outside. And it obtained this help in 1914, when two of its occupying powers, the Austro-Hungarian Empire[17] and Germany,[18] proclaimed war on the third occupying power – Russia.

When your enemies fight among themselves, you are bound to gain from it. It was no different in this case. Poland finally had its long-awaited good chance to restore its statehood. And, it did not waste it.

The Great War ended in November 1918. Great Britain, France and the United States emerged victorious from the war. For Russia, this victory was very much overshadowed by the Bolshevik revolution of October 1917. An extremely bloody overthrow of Russian feudal monarchy and the subsequent ruthless, and a very messy installation of the so-called people's rule by Lenin and his Bolshevik helpers, together with the Treaty of Brest-Litovsk, by which Russia had to cede great swathes of territory to Germany have all plunged this vast country, for about three years, into the abyss of domestic war.

In 1921, Witold Pilecki was just twenty years old. Yet by that time he had already taken part in the fight for Poland's independence, and he had also defended the young Polish state against the mortal threat which it faced in 1920 from the army of Bolshevik Russia.

The next chapter of this book outlines a number of events, as well as crucial political, social and cultural trends from Poland's history that appear to have exercised the strongest influence on the consciousness, sensitivities and perceptions of the young Pilecki during the most formative years of his childhood and young adulthood.

THE MIRACULOUS ICON OF BLACK MADONNA FROM JASNA GÓRA

[© Jasna Góra Monastery, all rights reserved]

KING JAN II KAZIMIERZ VOWS, PAINTING BY JAN MATEJKO

(© The National Museum at Wroclaw, all rights reserved)

KING STEFAN BATORY, PAINTING BY MARCIN KOBER

[© Fathers Missionaries' Museum of History and Missions in Cracow, all rights reserved]

THE BATTLE OF KIRCHHOLM, PAINTING BY WOJCIECH KOSSAK

[© The Museum of Polish Army in Warsaw, all rights reserved]

DEFINING EVENTS FROM POLAND'S HISTORY (966-1920)

THE BAPTISM OF POLAND

Even before Prince Mieszko (pronounced *Myeshkoh*) I, the first historically confirmed ruler of Poland, was baptised on April 12, 966, (others hold that the ceremony took place two days later, on Easter Saturday[19]), and Catholicism became Poland's official state religion, the country had already been a well-recognised entity with a considerable military strength. This is confirmed, among others, in Abraham ben Jacob's memoirs from his journeys.[20]

It was on the grounds of political expediency that Mieszko I did not wish for Poland to be Christianised by Germans. At that period, Germanic rulers had already conquered territories previously controlled by west Slavic tribes, and were at that time continuing their eastward expansion. Soon, they reached the western boundary of the territory governed by Mieszko I.

Mieszko I preferred for Christianization to come from the south. His south-western neighbour was Bohemia, a state whose territory roughly corresponded with the western and central part of what makes up the Czech Republic today[21]. Bohemia was inhabited by Czechs who, like Poles, were Slavic people. Czechs were ethnically and culturally akin to Poles. Czech princes, according to the early medieval annals of the Benedictine monastery at Fulda in Germany, were baptised much earlier, in 845.

POLAND'S BOUNDARIES, AS AT 1000

(© Euratlas, Nüssli 2011, all rights reserved)

And so Mieszko I decided to marry Czech princess Dobrawa (pronounced *Dobrava*). He arranged for a Czech missionary to receive not only himself, but the whole Polish nation, into the

Christian fold. This alliance represented a conscious choice on the part of Mieszko to ally himself with Bohemia. Soon after that, the young Polish Church, which had earlier refused to subordinate itself to the German Catholic hierarch, won its defining battle. The Polish Church was to be subordinated directly to the Holy See.[22]

Mieszko's wisdom and foresight is evident, if one considers that other Slavic tribes who at that time inhabited territories between the Elbe and Oder rivers had by 966 already lost, or were about to lose their ethnic and cultural identity and statehood precisely because they had failed to get baptised at about the same time as Poles did. When those tribes finally got baptised, it was simply too late for them to establish their independent Catholic Church provinces. The result was that during the tenth and eleventh centuries, their territories were gradually being taken over by Germanic tribes. To this very day, these previously Slavic territories form part of Germany's territory.

Some Christians had lived on the Polish soil long before Catholicism became the official religion there. It is believed that in Poland's southernmost province at that time, known as Lesser Poland, there lived a number of Christians even before 880, and that these Christians had been baptised by missionaries who arrived from Lesser Poland's south-western neighbour, Great Moravia, which itself was formally Christianised by St Metody in 822.[23]

In adopting Christianity as his state's religion, Mieszko sought to achieve several objectives. First, he wanted to strengthen his grip on power and thus to help unify the Polish nation. Second, Christianisation would, he expected, strengthen the position and win the Polish state respectability on the European scene. Third, the Church's experience and the valuable support that it could provide to a monarch in running the state were things that he himself very much needed.[24]

Thus, Catholicism crossed over to Poland through its south-western border. Poland's first Catholic saint, and one of the two patron saints of early Poland, Saint Wojciech (pronounced *Voytsyeh*), was actually a Czech. A missionary, Wojciech eventually went north to Prussia, then inhabited by a heathen tribe. There, in April 997, he died a martyr's death. His body was brought back to Poland and buried in Gniezno (Ghneyeznoh), which soon became the site of the first Polish archbishopric.

Later, throughout the sixteenth and the seventeenth centuries, Catholic Poland formed a crucial, and very effective, barrier between the expanding Ottoman Empire and Central Europe. It was a barrier that Europe's Christian nations could rely on, since Poland's military strength at the time was a sufficient guarantee of European safety. The might of the Polish army at that time discouraged also Crimean Tartars from making incursions into the Christian territories of Eastern Europe. No wonder, Poland was regarded at that time as 'Bulwark of Christianity' (in Latin, *antemurale christianitatis*).[25]

Over centuries, Polish Catholics became very well known for their deep veneration of Mary, Jesus' Mother. Among particularly treasured expressions of this tradition are the Lvov Vows taken by King Jan II Kazimierz on April 1, 1656, when most of the Poland's territory was under control of invading Swedish and Russian armies, and only a few of the country's fortresses remained in Polish hands. One of them, the fortified Virgin Mary's monastery at Jasna Góra had, against all odds, managed to resist the siege laid by the enemy vastly superior in numbers and material.

In the dedicated ceremony at Lvov, conducted by the Papal Nuncio Pietro Vidoni, the King entrusted the Polish-Lithuanian Commonwealth (more about its Lithuanian component will be mentioned later in this chapter) to the protection of the Blessed Virgin, whom the King hailed as 'The Queen of the Polish Crown and of all countries under his rule.' King Jan II Kazimierz also swore 'to protect the Kingdom's folk from any impositions and unjust bondage.'[26]

Military formations of the Commonwealth of Poland and Lithuania's finally drove back the Swedish army in 1657, and the

Russian army four years later. To this day, the Blessed Virgin is acknowledged by Catholic Poles as the Queen of Poland.

Once introduced to Poland by Mieszko I, the Catholic Church, particularly during the period when Poland did not exist as a sovereign state (1795-1918), played a vital role in preserving Polish identity, Polish language, and the proud tradition of national sovereignty. The Catholic Church has certainly helped the Polish nation survive its most difficult trials.

SAFE HAVEN FOR MANY

A state whose written history spans more than a thousand years, Poland is not exclusively defined by its Christianisation, nor yet by the strong faith of its people and the traditional Catholic culture which it has developed over the centuries, vital though these factors have long been. It is not so defined, because from its very beginnings, Poland distinguished itself as a country which offered refuge to victims of persecution from other countries, and which frequently invited other nations to join their territories with that of Poland so that they could enjoy equal rights with those of ethnic Poles, could contribute to the development of Poland, and could defend the common territory against external enemies.

Examples of non-Catholic groups which have greatly benefited from Poland's hospitality include Jews. From the late eleventh century, Jews had become victims of oppression, and sometimes of extremely violent pogroms, in many other European lands. They were expelled from Kiev between 1113 and 1158 (some of those expelled from there were Khazar Jews); from England (1290), from Germany (1346), from Hungary (1349-1526, and then 1686-1740), from Austria (1420), from Spain (1492), and from Portugal (1497).

Not from Poland, though. Successive Polish kings provided to Jewish refugees not only safe haven, but also many special economic and religious privileges. From the fourteenth-century, under King Kazimierz III the Great, Jews obtained special legal protection; cases against them could only be heard before the monarch's own courts, and not before common courts.

Poland's Jewish communities flourished. No wonder, many Jews referred to Poland, in particular to the sixteenth-century Poland, as *Paradisus Iudaeorum*.[27] A sixteenth-century rabbi from Cracow, Moises ben Israel Isserles, wrote: '*Had God not provided Jews with Poland as a safe haven, Israel's fate would have been unbearable.*'[28]

By the time the Polish-Lithuanian Commonwealth was called into being (1569), Jewish communities in Poland had already grown strong in their numbers and their culture had likewise flourished.[29] The Golden Age in the history of Polish Jews lasted from the sixteenth century to the first half of the seventeenth (specifically, until the 1648 uprising by the Khmelnytsky Cossacks). During this period, Jews enjoyed a high degree of autonomy within Poland. They had a considerable level of self-government, including the so-called Council of Four Lands (in Hebrew, *Vaad Arba Aratsot*). This was something without parallel anywhere else in Europe.

The second half of the sixteenth century brought yet another change: encouraged by the nobility, Jews started settling down on vast estates in the east of the country. They engaged in new activities: they would lease inns, mills and breweries, as well as trade in grain and cattle.[30]

Jews' very propitious and safe situation deteriorated somewhat commencing from the mid-sixteenth century. Once Protestantism arrived in Poland and attained considerable strength there, it brought with it religious tension previously unknown to this country. Another harmful development was series of devastating wars that Poland had to fight in the seventeenth century. The situation of Polish Jews' deteriorated further once the Polish state had ceased its existence (1795). All those negative changes, however, had their origins outside Poland itself.

When the Lithuanian Grand Duke Władysław Jagiełło (pronounced *Vladislav Yaghelloh*) married the Polish Queen Jadwiga (pronounced *Yadveegah*), in 1386, the two countries of Poland and Lithuania commenced a period of peaceful coexistence and rapprochement which was to last four centuries. Before, they had often been involved in wars against one another.

Less than two centuries later (in 1569), they will formally unify to constitute the Polish-Lithuanian Commonwealth, a very powerful and prosperous state, at that time the second largest by territory in the entire Europe (the largest one was Russia). The Commonwealth's rulers would respect the rights of people of all religions and would guarant extensive freedoms to their citizens.

Within the boundaries of that Commonwealth, there lived many ethnic minority groups, the largest of which were Lithuanians, Byelorussians, Ruthenians, Tartars, Cossacks and Jews. For a long time, all these ethnic minorities lived, on the whole, in peace and relative prosperity. This picture started changing for the worse after two catastrophic events: the 1648 Khmelnytsky Cossack uprising, and the invasion and the ruthless plunder of Poland by Swedish troops (1655-1660).

POLAND UNITED

Like many other European countries during the Middle Ages (Germany and Italy are two best-known examples), Poland had for almost two hundred years (1138-1320) been composed of a number of small principalities. This situation had not been conducive to a fast development of trade, economy, or culture. Small states tend to be often at war with one another, and therefore find it hard to defend themselves against major external threats, of which the most formidable in medieval Poland's case consisted of Mongol armies. During the thirteenth, fourteenth, and fifteenth centuries, indeed until the early sixteenth century, Mongols (or Tartars, as some of these tribes were referred to) made regular incursions into eastern, central, and south-eastern Europe. They plundered vast territories, burning down in the process many cities and villages, often putting all local population to the sword, and, on top of that, imposing heavy annual taxes (protection money, as it were) on the territories they invaded.

From the second half of the thirteenth century, support for unification started to grow in these small Polish states (there were up to twenty of them). The divided Poland had proven to be simply incapable of keeping its boundaries safe from Tartar, Yotvingian[31] and Lithuanian incursions. To make things even more precarious, three of Poland's neighbours – the Czech Kingdom, the Kingdom of Hungary and the Margravate of Brandenburg[32] – kept gaining considerably in strength during the very same time.

The situation got even more complicated by the large numbers of German economic migrants settling down in the medieval Poland. This process commenced in the early thirteenth century and continued until the middle of the fourteenth. Most of these migrants would settle down in Lesser Poland (the main city of which was Cracow) and Greater Poland (the main city of which was Poznań). They were attracted by these regions' relative wealth, fertile land, and their location along major trade routes from eastern Europe, south-eastern Europe, and Asia. Faithful to Germanic legal codes and keeping the German language, they would often refuse to pay some local taxes. The German migrants were well organised, and certainly determined to become an economic and political factor to be reckoned with on Poland's territory.

All German settlements of the time were well planned, and were governed by contracts which had been signed both by the original owners of the lands, and by persons who represented the colonists. Each such contract spelled out, in a detailed fashion, the colonists' rights and obligations. These German settlements in Poland increased the overall density of population, introduced to the locals new agricultural systems which were more effective than those that prevailed before their arrival, and brought with them knowledge of new trades and modified commercial techniques. The so-called Magdeburg Rights they popularised on Poland's territory (a set of principles, based mainly on Flemish law which regulated the degree of internal autonomy within cities and villages), once granted by local rulers were a powerful factor which expedited overall economic progress of the relevant regions[33]. This progress, however, had a social cost: significant changes to the ethnic set-up of local populations would often lead to conflicts between native peoples and newer arrivals.

No wonder, some far-sighted Poles grew worried that if the above-presented combination of political, economic, and migratory factors remain uncorrected *'we may soon see the extinction of our nation'*.[34] In response to this concern, appropriate measures were put in place, including those which aimed to *'preserve and improve the Polish language'*.[35]

Fortunately for Poland, one of the Polish princes of that time, Władysław Łokietek (pronounced *Vladislav Lokyehtehk*), had the required political vision and wisdom. Coupled with his outstanding leadership and military capacity as well as his remarkable tenacity, these virtues sufficed to thwart the plans of neighbouring powers (most notably, of the formidable alliance of Czech Kingdom with the Teutonic Knights Order), who sought to conquer and subjugate Poland. The same qualities made it also possible for Władysław Łokietek (Łokietek means in Polish 'short' or, literally, 'elbow-high') to form an important alliance with Hungary while in temporary exile there. Eventually, he was able to unify Poland. On January 20, 1320, he was formally crowned Poland's King.[36]

Had it not been for this Łokietek's success, the separate Polish states (especially the smallest ones) would most likely have been unable to defend themselves against the Teutonic Knights and their other external foes. Without his success, Poland would very likely not have managed to become two centuries later the largest and strongest state of Central Europe. Without this Łokietek's success, Poland would have likely been wiped out from the map of Europe long before the 1795 erasure took place.[37] If so, restoration of Poland's sovereignty would have conceivably been more difficult than it was in 1918. Besides, a mere federation of loosely associated duchies would not have attained the economic strength of the sixteenth century Commonwealth of Poland and Lithuania.

Władysław Łokietek's only son, Kazimierz (pronounced *Kahzeemyes*h) III the Great (reigned 1333-1370), a very talented and dedicated ruler, followed into his father's footsteps and laid foundations for the Polish Kingdom's future greatness. Of him, a popular saying still runs: 'He inherited Poland built of timber, and he left it built of bricks.' Throughout his reign, Kazimierz the Great firmly stood for peace, truth and justice, and for protecting even the weakest of his subjects.[38]

LITHUANIAN GRAND DUKE ON THE POLISH THRONE

Kazimierz III died childless. Following this, a Hungarian monarch ascended the Polish throne. Louis (or, to give the Polish form of his name, Ludwik) the Great, was to reign between 1370 and 1382. Louis had close family connections with his immediate precursors on the throne: Władysław Łokietek had been his maternal grandfather, and Kazimierz III - his uncle. As early as 1364, Kazimierz III had signed with Louis a contract whereby, should the former's recent marriage fail to produce sons (as in fact, it did), Louis would become the next King of Poland.

After Louis' death, his young daughter Jadwiga became in 1384 the first Queen of Poland. A mere child at the time, she was only eleven years of age. Despite her extreme youth, she was already well educated and able to fluently communicate in Latin, Hungarian, and German. At that time, she had a limited knowledge of Polish, though. Very intelligent, she possessed excellent manners and had strikingly good looks. Louis, not long before his death, had arranged for Jadwiga to become the wife of the young Habsburg prince Wilhelm. This nuptial agreement had been strongly opposed by some Polish aristocrats: they warned that if it went ahead, they would do their best to deprive Jadwiga of the throne and elect, in her stead, Prince Siemowit (a remote cousin of Kazimierz III) as King Siemowit IV.

As their alternative candidate to marry Jadwiga, the aristocrats had in mind the Lithuanian Grand Duke of the Jagiełło family,[39] who was not only much older than Jadwiga, but also still a pagan. Their choice was dictated largely by the nobles' desire to put an end to all hostilities between Poland and Lithuania, and to win thereby an important ally for Poland along its eastern and south-eastern boundary. With such an ally, they believed, Poland would be much better able to defend itself against invasions by the Teutonic Knights (of whom more in a moment). The aristocrats hoped, in addition, to secure from the Lithuanian candidate significant economic benefits for themselves.

And so Jagiełło got baptised on February 12, 1386, assuming the Christian name of Władysław. Six days afterwards, he married Jadwiga. On March 4, he was crowned king of Poland. Thereafter, husband and wife kept their separate courts, and they were dual sovereigns in the legal sense: signatures of both of them were required to make each royal edict valid. In 1387, Lithuania formally became Catholic.

Such were the beginnings of the Polish-Lithuanian union, and of the Jagiellonian [*Yaghyellonyan*] dynasty which was to rule Poland for almost two centuries. Under this dynasty's governance, the country's power and significance in Europe has been continuously increasing. Various members of the dynasty married in that period into other European royal families, became even Czech and Hungarian monarchs, and co-ruled some European states.

**KINGDOM OF POLAND AND
GRAND DUCHY OF LITHUANIA, AS AT 1400**

(© Euratlas, Nüssli 2011, all rights reserved)

In 1410, Władysław Jagiełło defeated Teutonic Knights at the great battle of Grunwald (also known as the battle of Tannenberg). This spectacular victory presented Poland with a chance to regain all territories it had lost to this enemy over nearly two hundred years. Regrettably, this King wasted this opportunity, as did several of his successors. As it turned out, this failure was to beget most dramatic consequences for Poland more than three hundred and fifty years later.[40]

WARS AGAINST THE TEUTONIC KNIGHTS ORDER

The Teutonic Knights Order (its official name: Order of Brothers of the German House of Saint Mary in Jerusalem)[41] was invited to Poland in 1226 by one of the Polish dukes of the time, Konrad I of Masovia. Duke Konrad wanted the Order to subdue heathen tribes inhabiting territories to Masovia's immediate north. Those tribes would frequently make forays into Masovia. Not only did the Duke want these tribes to be subdued militarily, he also wanted them to be Christianised.

The Teutonic Knights Order was originally formed to aid Christians on their pilgrimages to the Holy Land, and to establish and run hospitals there. Subsequently, it had been transformed into an essentially military order, one which took part in the Crusades' actual fighting.[42] It had a core membership of regular soldiers, with volunteers and mercenaries augmenting this core whenever required.[43]

Following the decisive battle of Hattin in 1187, when the Egyptian Sultan Saladin crushingly defeated the Crusader Kingdom of Jerusalem,[44] the Teutonic Knights Order commenced looking for new missionary engagements in Europe. From the Holy Roman

Emperor (Henry VI of the Hohenstaufen family), the Order obtained a generous endowment a few decades before Konrad I invited it to Masovia. In 1211, the Hungarian King András II the Jerosolimitan'[45] invited the Knights for them to help him in the defence of his kingdom against incursions by nomadic Kipchaks, who lived to Hungary's south-east. The Order soon broke the terms of that contract, and sought to hand over some of the territory it conquered to Pope Innocent III, as part of the latter's fiefdom, rather than to the Hungarian ruler as had been agreed. This double-cross led to András expelling the Teutonic Knights in 1225.[46]

Following Konrad's invitation, Emperor Friedrich II, the ruler of the Holy Roman Empire of the German Nation[47], issued Gold Bulla of Rimini. The Bulla decreed that the Teutonic Knights would henceforth have the right to possess all Prussian territories it would be able to Christianise. Friedrich's decision conflicted however with Konrad I's documented intention, which was for the territories in question to be annexed to Masovia, once the bishop of Prussia had formally Christianised them.[48]

Konrad leased out to the Order two relatively small territories in the north-west of his Duchy. They were to be used by the Order as bases from which to launch its campaigns against the pagan tribes of Prussia.

After 1237, the Knights were not the only such order present in that area. In the same year, they were joined by the Livonian Brothers of the Sword, another order of warrior monks founded in 1202.[49] This has considerably strengthened the Knights' political and military position *vis-à-vis* Konrad. Together, the two Orders controlled at that time a long and wide swathe of land along the shore of the Baltic Sea, north of Polish duchies.

With the Christianisation of Prussia's territory nearing its completion, the Knights sought to assert their sovereignty over the area. The Order heavily fortified the territory it controlled. It governed it with a heavy hand. Essential supplies and new recruits from Germany were arriving by sea.

In 1308, the Teutonic Knights Order conquered a large part of the Polish sea-abutting province of Pomerania, including Gdańsk,[50] a port city of great strategic significance for Poland. The German monarch Albrecht I turned a blind eye to the forcible annexation of territory over which Poland had historical claims of sovereignty, and gave it his seal of approval. Following this annexation, the Order decided, in 1309, to move its headquarters from Venice to Malbork,[51] a place on the eastern bank of the Vistula River, just south of its delta. There, the Order started building what would become one of the world's strongest fortresses of that period.

To a number of new territories (the island of Gotland, then Livonia - in 1398; and also Samogitia, known also as Lower Lithuania), the Knights added, in 1402, a new significant acquisition - New March, a gift from King Sigismund of Luxembourg.[52] Owing to this acquisition, the Order's territory got contiguous with that of its crucial ally, the Margravate of Brandenburg. From that moment on, all of the Order's Baltic Sea neighbours will need to reckon with the Order's power.

The acquisition of Samogitia, a territory between Prussia and Livonia, connected the Teutonic Knights Order's own territory to that of their Livonian ally. Once the Order forced Lithuania to surrender Samogitia and persuaded the Polish rulers of Western Pomerania to accept the Order's supremacy, a situation emerged whereby the two Germanic above-mentioned military orders jointly controlled approximately 1,500 kilometres of Baltic coastline, right from the Oder River's estuary to the Bay of Riga. The portents of this development for Poland were quite menacing.[53]

The Teutonic Knights Order could count on its friendship with the Hanseatic League, a commercial confederation of merchant guilds and towns which dominated the trade along the coasts of Northern Europe, its activities extending from the Baltic to the North Sea and inland.[54]

Once the Lithuanian Grand Duke Jagiełło became Poland's king, and Lithuania became Christian, there was reason left for the Teutonic Knights's Order to remain in this region. A resurgent unified Poland was capable of forcing the Order to return the territories leased out to the Order by Konrad of Masovia two hundred years earlier to their rightful owner. If achieved, this could imperil the Order's very survival.

The Knights's first reaction was to maintain that Lithuania was still a heathen nation. Yet, Poland proved otherwise. Pope Boniface IX's issued, in 1403, his Bulla which forbade any further military incursions by the Knights into Lithuania itself. The Order then sought to drive a wedge between Lithuania and Poland. It offered military support to Lithuania to help it conquer certain Ruthenian territories. It made its offer conditional upon Lithuania handing back to the Order the crucial region of Samogitia.

With Samogitia in the Order's hands again, an uprising started there however, in 1409, against the Order's renewed occupation of this region. This made a war by Poland and Lithuania against the Order unavoidable. At Grunwald (July 15, 1410), following what was the largest Middle Ages battle in Europe, the Order suffered a crushing defeat.

The victorious Polish army took quite some time to lay the siege to the Teutonic Knights' main fortress of Malbork. This delay allowed the surviving Teutonic Knights to prepare themselves well for it. Consequently, Władysław was unable to capture Malbork.

In 1422, the Order finally relinquished its claims to Samogitia and handed over this territory to Lithuania. Free trade between the Teutonic Knights' state and Poland was reinstated. Still, it took more than forty years before Poland was able to retrieve its former access to the Baltic Sea. This came by the way of Eastern Pomerania, when the Polish crown regained in 1466 the crucial seaport of Gdańsk.[55] In 1510, the Order acquired a new leader in Albrecht von Hohenzollern.[56] Following his refusal to submit to the Crown of Poland, a war broke out in December 1519. It ended in a devastating defeat for the Order. Early in 1521, Albrecht was offered a four-year truce. Subsequently, he went to Wittenberg in Germany, where he fell under the spell of Luther's ideas. As a result, he turned not only against Poland, but also the entire Catholic Church and the Holy Roman Empire. He then converted the Teutonic Knights' state into a Protestant hereditary realm.

Albrecht did not break diplomatic relations with his former antagonists, though. In 1525, he journeyed to Cracow to pay formal homage to his mother's brother, King Zygmunt I (known as 'the Old', Poland's ruler since 1508), pledging there a personal oath of allegiance to the Polish sovereign. This act had a good deal of self-interest involved: it resulted in Albrecht's Duchy of Prussia becoming, with Polish acquiescence, the first Lutheran state in Europe.[57]

Until early in the seventeenth century, the Duchy of Prussia did not pose any particular military threat to the Polish-Lithuanian Commonwealth. This was to change in 1619, after Albrecht's grandson, the last Duke of Prussia, died issueless. In that year, in an act of extreme, and rather thoughtless generosity, the Polish parliament voiced approval for the late Duke's uncle, Georg Wilhelm of Brandenburg, to inherit the Duchy. This was in contradiction with the terms of the 1525 agreement between Zygmunt and Albrecht, whereby if the Prussian dynasty died out, the entire Ducal territory would be re-joined with Poland.

How big a strategic mistake the Polish parliament had made in countenancing this succession, Poland was to find out in 1657 when, under extreme duress caused by the Swedish invasion of Poland, the Kingdom of Poland was forced to renounce, by signing the Treaty of Bromberg[58], all its claims to sovereignty over Ducal Prussia. At the same time, Poland also relinquished two smaller but strategically important territories to the west of the City of Gdańsk[59]. Combined with the former Duchy territory, they laid foundations for a very strong future Prussian state. Its first capital city was Królewiec (Königsberg), its next one was - Berlin.

One could argue that the disappearance of Poland from the map of Europe between 1795 and 1918 would probably not have taken place, had it not been for two gigantic mistakes: that by King Zygmunt I in 1525, and that by the Polish parliament in 1619.

POLAND'S *AGE OF GOLDEN LIBERTY*

The 1569 union between Poland and Lithuania gave successive rulers of the Commonwealth access to vast territories to Poland's east and south-east. This greatly benefitted the national economy and stimulated foreign trade. The period from 1569 to 1648 was a very prosperous one for the Polish-Lithuanian Commonwealth. Despite wars against the Ottoman Empire, Russia and Sweden during that time[60], this period was often referred to as 'the Age of Golden Liberty.'

It was a period that witnessed great advances for those Polish nobles who held large rural estates. They took advantage of the large, and continuously growing, European demand for Polish grain. For a few days each week, owners of these large estates could rely on unpaid toil by workers who lived on small blocks of land leased out to them. Workers were obliged to pay to the nobles a fixed rent, which often was quite high.

At this stage, the Polish nobility's statutory rights were at their highest ever. Since 1493, they had made it impossible for any Polish king to rule without securing their consensual support. The nobles alone possessed the right to own large amounts of property; many of them owned more land than the Kings. Peasants were expressly forbidden to move to another village without their landlords formally granting them permission to do so. Landlords invariably prevailed in any legal disputes between them and the peasantry. The law prohibited peasants from initiating court action against landlords.[61]

BOUNDARIES OF THE COMMONWEALTH OF POLAND AND LITHUANIA, AS AT 1600

[©Euratlas, Nüssli 2011, all rights reserved]

Throughout that period, Polish grain did not cost much, and was of superior quality. Many businesses in Gdańsk were making fortunes from the grain trade. Unfortunately, these huge profits were seldom, if ever, invested in any sectors of the national economy outside agriculture. Instead, it was the rest of Europe that benefited from supplies of cheap Polish grain, notably the Dutch and the English, whose economic development this grain much assisted.

There was an increasingly urgent need for more of the vast income from the grain trade to be used, via taxes, to form a strong standing Polish army, so that the dangers which the Commonwealth of Poland and Lithuania faced from its aggressive neighbours could be averted. The all-powerful Polish *szlachta* (nobility) was however fearful that a strong, well-trained and permanent army would significantly reduce the nobility's leverage on monarch: in particular, they feared that such an army would eliminate the monarch's need to rely, almost exclusively, on the nobles' *pospolite ruszenie* (mass mobilisation)[62], whenever war was imminent.

The gap between the level of skill, discipline and efficiency of those involved in the Commonwealth's so-called *pospolite ruszenie*, and regular, professional, experienced, and well-trained troops whom most neighbouring countries could rely on, had been constantly widening ever since the mid-fifteenth century. Another comparative drawback for the *pospolite ruszenie* was the length of time that the mobilisation usually required: usually up to a month.[63] Nor were the numbers of *pospolite ruszenie* soldiers up to the requirements. During the mid-sixteenth century, the *pospolite ruszenie* could field a maximum of about 50,000 soldiers.[64]

In 1562, it was decided that one-quarter of the income from all Crown estates would need to be assigned to maintaining permanent military units (*wojsko kwarciane*). King Stefan Batory, whose reign began in 1576, saw the need for numerically strong infantry units; in 1578, he formed first such units. They relied exclusively on Crown estates peasants who were called *piechota łanowa*. Better trained than had previously been the norm, they would acquit themselves well in battles.

In the sixteenth and seventeenth centuries, the Polish military relied heavily on its very well trained, indeed formidable, heavy cavalry units (the so-called Winged Hussars). Gradually, also, Polish governments introduced artillery and engineering corps, as well as developing the nation's fleet of warships. By 1567 Poland had over thirty warships.[65]

How could these be paid for? The nobility successfully blocked all attempts to introduce higher taxes, and the national treasury found itself with less and less money available to keep up a standing army. This was an act of greatest irresponsibility: it finally cost the Commonwealth its existence. By 1795, the Commonwealth's army had shrunk to a mere 16,000 men, readily overpowered by neighbouring forces. The Imperial Russian Army numbers at the time were nearly 300,000, the Prussian and Imperial Austrian armies could each call upon 200,000 soldiers.[66]

The collapse of Commonwealth of Poland and Lithuania was a most painful lesson. It was so painful because the damage had been entirely self-inflicted.

POLISH-RUSSIAN STRATEGIC OPPOSITION – HOW IT CAME ABOUT

In 1572, the throne became vacant after the death, without issue, of Zygmunt II August. The powerful Jagiellonian dynasty which had ruled Poland for 186 years had come to an end in its male line. Poland's Sejm[67] was given the power to elect a new king. It chose a foreigner in Prince Henri of the French House of Valois, the younger brother of the childless French monarch Charles IX. Within months Charles IX died, and Henri forfeited the Polish throne to ascend the French one.

After a very heated debate and a change of the preferred candidate, it was finally decided that Anna Jagiellon, the sister of the deceased Zygmunt II, should be elected Queen of Poland and should marry a Hungarian prince, Stephen Báthory. On May 1, 1576, Báthory (thereafter to be known in Poland as Stefan Batory) married Anna and became, *jure uxoris*,[68] King of Poland

and Grand Duke of Lithuania. At the same time, he also assumed the title of the Prince of Transylvania.[69]

Already at his election, Báthory faced a formidable opposition, particularly in Lithuania. Most of this opposition was fostered by those loyal to another candidate, Austrian Emperor Maximilian II. Only when Báthory accepted leading Lithuanians' demands did the latter acquiesce in his rule.

Another part of Poland which initially opposed Báthory's election was Prussia. Whilst Maximilian's sudden and early death (in October 1576) improved Báthory's situation, the city of Gdańsk refused to recognise Báthory as the sovereign unless he agreed to grant the city's rulers significant concessions. The city mutinied. To crush this rebellion, Báthory's army laid siege to it. Eventually, forces loyal to the throne prevailed, and the King came to an agreement with the city fathers. In exchange for countenancing some of their demands, Báthory would be acknowledged by Gdańsk as the rightful ruler of Poland, and the city would have to pay reparations to the monarch. King Stefan received in 1578 a formal homage from the Duke of Prussia, Georg Friedrich. In turn, the King acknowledged Georg Friedrich as legitimate Duke, Prussia being still at this stage a Commonwealth's fiefdom.[70]

Showing great energy and determination, King Stefan reorganised the royal judiciary by establishing new tribunals (Crown Tribunal - in 1578, and the Lithuanian Tribunal - in 1581).[71] Suitably impressed, the Sejm finally allowed the King to raise taxes, and to introduce a number of reforms for the purpose of strengthening the armed forces. Those reforms included the establishment of the *piechota wybraniecka*, an infantry formation composed of peasants.[72] Aiming to modernise the Commonwealth's military formations, King Stefan intended for them to resemble the Hungarian troops from Transylvania in armor and fight tactics.[73]

A Catholic himself, King Stefan respected the traditional Polish policy of religious tolerance. He issued decrees that offered additional protection to Polish Jews, and made it clear that religion-based violence would not be allowed in his realm.[74]

In external relations, this King above all sought peace by forming strong alliances. For all his distrust of the Habsburgs, he managed to maintain good relations with the Commonwealth's south-western neighbour, Austria. Over a few years, he was also able to relieve the tension on the border with the Ottoman Empire, by signing with that empire two consecutive truces. In 1577, and again in 1579,[75] he persuaded the Sejm to grant him funds he needed for the imminent war against Russia.[76]

At that time, Russia was ruled by fearsome and energetic Ivan IV the Terrible. In 1547, he assumed the title of 'Tsar of All Russia' replacing with it his former title of 'Grand Duke of Moscow'. During his rule, Russia's territory grew more than twice its pre-1547 size. Ivan conquered large territories to the east and south-east of Russia (the Khanates of Kazan and Astrakhan, in 1552 and 1554, respectively). Then, he turned his attention to territories that lay to his west. He made several territorial gains at the expense of Lithuania, and of Livonia, the latter being still governed by the Order of the Brothers of the Sword. It was these losses of territory, and the increasing danger for Lithuania from Russia that finally brought the Grand Duchy of Lithuania to form, in 1569, a Commonwealth with the Kingdom of Poland.

When Ivan invaded Poland in 1577, he achieved some successes in Livonia. Then, he lost several major battles, was forced to retreat, and in 1582 had to sign a truce with King Stefan in the town of Jam Zapolski. The truce was to be observed for 10 years: time enough to give the Tsar the chance to concentrate on his expansionary efforts on Russia's eastern frontier. Tsar Ivan cultivated strong trading links with England, and strengthened Russia economically. He died in 1584.

His son and successor, Feodor, was devoid of his father's ambitions. He was shy rather than ruthless, unlike his father. Notwithstanding that, it was during his rule that the Russian army completed, in 1589, the most significant of Ivan's planned expansions to the east which saw Russia's rule extended onto the huge expanses of the Khanate of Siberia. These conquests marked the beginnings of the Russian Empire.[77]

With Feodor being far less formidable an opponent than his father, King Stefan saw a great opportunity for the Commonwealth to decisively beat Russia in a new war. This, however, was not the only of this King's parallel ambitious plans. He also planned a decisive war against the Ottoman Empire, which was at that time thinking of further conquests in Central and Eastern Europe. So, if the Ottomans were to be defeated, the King needed to first secure a lasting peace on the Commonwealth's eastern border. To achieve the latter, he sought to do all he could to remove the childless Feodor from the throne. King Stefan intented to replace him with someone who would accept the Commonwealth's military superiority over Russia, and would commit himself to an extended truce between the two countries.

All such schemes presuppose money, a lot of money. And that was what King Stefan did not have. The Sejm no longer showed willingness to allocate any further funds for wars. As a result, King Stefan found himself unable to implement his strategic ambitions. Worse still, his health started declining. He died on December 12, 1586.

King Stefan's relatively brief reign is today regarded as being among the most successful governments in Poland's entire history, particularly from the defence and foreign affairs policy points of view. That this King died at no great age (he was only fifty-three), and lacked the time needed to achieve his long-term objectives for the Commonwealth, will have long-term negative consequences for the country's future position and influence in Europe.

Had the Sejm not turned down King Stefan's requests to provide the funds that he needed to enlarge and modernise the Commonwealth's army, and had the King been able to persuade the Sejm of the merits of his grand strategy, the chances were that the scales of power, within central and eastern Europe, would have tipped in the Commonwealth's favour for a long time to come.

In 1587, the nobility elected a new sovereign: the Swedish Crown Prince Sigismund, then merely twenty-one years old. His claim to the throne came through his Jagellonian mother: Polish Crown Princess Katarzyna [Katherine], the daughter of Zygmunt I the Old.[78] This connection was enough to ensure Sigismund favourable consideration from the start, but no more than that. He had a strong rival in Habsburg Archduke Maximilian. At first, Maximilian had been quite effective in winning support: he even managed to get himself proclaimed King of Poland by a nobility faction opposed to Sigismund. His reign did not last long, though. In December 1587, Sigismund was crowned in Cracow, taking the name of Zygmunt III. Battle fought at Byczyna between military units loyal to Sigismund and those loyal to Maximilian resulted in a decisive victory of the former. The treaty which Sigismund signed (1589) with Austria's Emperor, Rudolf II (Maximilian's elder brother), had Habsburgs vow they would never meddle in the Commonwealth's internal affairs. To further neutralise the influence of the House of Habsburg's, Zygmunt got himself a Habsburg wife: the Austrian Archduchess Anna.

After his father, Swedish King Johan III, died in 1592, Zygmunt III received permission from the Sejm to become also King of Sweden. Conscious of the Swedish population's overwhelmingly Lutheran sympathies at that time, Zygmunt guaranteed Lutheranism complete legal protection in Sweden. This made possible his coronation as Swedish king in 1594.[79] With it, the personal union of the Kingdom of Sweden and the Polish-Lithuanian Commonwealth became a fact. His rule as a King of Sweden was relatively short-lived: it was ended in him being, in 1599, deposed by his Swedish Lutheran subjects. They developed distrust of his professed religious tolerance once he married a Catholic Austrian Archduchess.

King Zygmunt never accepted this deposition, and used the title of the King of Sweden for the remainder of his life. The monarch's ardent desire to regain his Scandinavian throne led him to plan to first subdue Russia, and become the next Russian Tsar. He reckoned, once he had amassed such power, this would make Swedes change their mind and promptly return his Swedish crown to him, the rightful successor of his father.

Unfortunately for him and, more significantly, for the Commonwealth of Poland and Lithuania, King Zygmunt's grand plan had three major drawbacks. First, the very idea of it entailed significant reorientation of Poland's foreign policy, including discarding the alliance system to which his two of his predecessors, King Zygmunt II and King Stefan had subscribed. Archduchess Anna was by no means Zygmunt III's sole link to the Habsburgs. After Anna died, the King married (1605) her sister Constance. This strengthened his alignment with Austria's dynasty. Such a change of alliances would prove in the future more burdensome than beneficial for Poland, especially after the relief of Vienna in 1683. Eventually, as already mentioned in this book, the House of Habsburg will feel unconstrained by any considerations of its friendship with Poland, and will collaborate with Russia and Prussia in the eighteenth century's partitions of the Commonwealth's territory.

The second drawback of King Zygmunt's plan followed from the first. He made no secret of his intentions, and these provided a strong pretext for Sweden – at the time, and long afterwards, a formidable military power in Northern and Central Europe – to launch a series of invasions against various Commonwealth territories. With all such invasions, Sweden's motive was the same: to force Zygmunt to give up his dreams of Swedish restoration, dreams which he passed on to his two sons, Władysław (pronounced *Vladislav*) and Jan II Kazimierz, who will in their turn also attempt, unsuccessfully, to re-gain the Swedish throne.

As a result, for no fewer than sixty years (with only a few brief armistices), the Commonwealth had to continuously fight the Kingdom of Sweden. Even though the Commonwealth did win some major battles in these wars (one of Poland's most spectacular victories of all time was achieved at Kirchholm in 1605), all these victories having largely been owed to the formidable strength of its Winged Hussars heavy cavalry formation (in short: *husaria)*, the ongoing military involvement and losses sustained in this warfare were to the detriment of the Commonwealth's military capacity.

The third drawback of Zygmunt III's grand plan was the economic factor. For its economic well-being and strategic power, Poland largely depended on its capacity to halt Russia's advance towards the Baltic Sea. As already mentioned, the Commonwealth was at that time the largest supplier in Europe of grain, as well as of various food and timber products. It was also the most important transit territory for the far East's trade to western (as well as to central and eastern) Europe. It was clear, that if Russia established a strong presence on the shores the Baltic Sea, it would become a significant competitor to the Commonwealth in terms of trade. Once Russia had built up some Baltic ports of its own, it would also be able to increase its own military strength, at the Commonwealth's expense. This would, in turn, make Russia a more attractive strategic ally to the Western powers, in particular - to land-hungry German states.

The Jagiellonian monarchy's foreign policy before 1587 had been to maintain friendly relations with Sweden, and forestall Russia's desire for Baltic access. This made much more sense, and was far more realistic, than the presented Zygmunt III's plan. Zygmunt's ambition to fight Russia *and* Sweden at the same time made it all too likely that he would fail to defeat either of these two countries.

In 1655, by which time Zygmunt had been dead for twenty-three years, the dreadful scenario he had courted by his recklessness was played out. First, Russia attacked the Commonwealth, which had already suffered serious depletion of its military strength through the need to quell the Khmelnytsky Cossacks' uprising in the country's south-eastern provinces (1648-1654). Sweden joined in, by invading the western part of the Commonwealth. The exact timing of Sweden's invasion

(July 19. 1655) was no accident: Russia had invaded the Byelarussian territories of the Commonwealth during early June.

Karl X Gustav, youthful and vigorous Swedish king, believed his attack would make it possible for Sweden to form a veritable Baltic empire, by annexing several territories controlled by the Commonwealth. He also hoped he could compel the Polish king (by this stage Jan II Kazimierz, after the death of his older brother Władysław in 1648), to renounce, once and for all, familial claims to the Swedish crown. The latter objective he did attain, the former one he did not, simply because Russia proved too strong for Swedes to overcome. In 1660, the Commonwealth managed to force the Swedish army to retreat from the Commonwealth's soil. This however came at a crippling cost, both economic and military. The Swedes had ruthlessly plundered and burnt numerous cities in the Commonwealth. With it, the chances of the Commonwealth to be able to resist in the future the growing menace from its two most dangerous neighbours, the absolute monarchies of Russia and Prussia, were greatly impaired.

Zygmunt III's plan to conquer Russia and make himself its new Tsar was a case of seriously over-inflated ambition, and a vast overestimation of the military and financial resources that the King had at his disposal. Zygmunt had placed his individual ambition ahead of the national interest, and the Commonwealth was to pay a very hefty price for his folly. This became all the more evident once Russia had re-calibrated its own outlook and national priorities, aiming to achieve and sustain its imperial status.

To complete this chapter's account of relevant developments, we must go back for a moment to the years after Tsar Feodor's death. He died childless in 1598: this meant that the Rurik dynasty came to its end. The Time of Troubles (Russian: Смутное время) commenced in Russia, a period marred by massive disarray and chaos, by fight for dominance between various factions of the Russian aristocracy (many of whom sought foreign aid), and by the great famine of 1601–1603. The losses to Russia's population during this period were huge: some put the figure as high as one-third of the total. Four Tsars ruled, or purported to rule, during this era. Two of them were impostors. Not surprisingly, many historians regard this disordered period as an interregnum which came to an end once the Romanov dynasty was established in 1613.

Both Sweden and Poland sought to benefit from this anarchic situation. Polish intervention in Russia took, in 1603, the unorthodox form of forays of mercenaries who were sponsored by some Commonwealth aristocrats. They achieved some success, albeit quite limited and transitional. They took Moscow in 1605, to make it possible for their protégé, Dmitry (who claimed to be Ivan the Terrible's lost son) to ascend the Russian throne later in the year, as Tsar Dmitry I.

Dmitry enjoyed only a very brief term in office. Before 1606 was over, he had been deposed and slain, at the behest of a Russian prince, Vasily Shuysky, who made himself a new Tsar. Determined to thwart growing Polish influence, Shuysky – now Vasily IV – concluded an alliance with Sweden, thus challenging Zygmunt III further and making him resolve to intervene. The result was the Polish-Muscovite War: it was to last until 1618.

In 1609, King Zygmunt III dispatched his army to besiege the crucial fortress of Smolensk. At the battle of Klushino (July 4, 1610), the Polish contingent comprehensively defeated the Russian army despite the latter's vast numerical superiority.[80] Hetman Żółkiewski (pronounced *Zhoolkevsky*) captured Vasily IV and his brothers, and brought them to Poland. On October 29, 1611, Vasily had to swear allegiance to Zygmunt III, in the latter's royal castle in Warsaw.

Having learned of Vasily's overthrow, Moscow surrendered to the Poles without even putting up a fight. *Boyars* (Russian aristocrats) consented to the coronation of Prince Władysław, only fifteen at that time, as the new Tsar; they however insisted he would have to abandon Catholicism, and convert to Orthodoxy. At first, Zygmunt rejected this offer. He did it for two reasons. First, he wanted the Russian imperial crown for himself. Second, he feared that his young and inexperienced son would be a mere puppet under *boyar* control. Later, he changed his mind, and agreed to having young Władysław crowned.[81]

The Polish rule over Russia did not last long. An anti-Polish uprising in Moscow broke out in 1611, threatening the Polish-held Kremlin itself. To make things even worse, in January 1612, units of the Polish army mutinied, in protest against unpaid wages. Another Polish hetman, Jan Karol Chodkiewicz (pronounced *Khodkyeveetch*), led a relief attempt. It failed. Demoralised and starving, the Commonwealth's Kremlin garrison was forced to surrender in November 1612, after a siege that lasted nineteen months.[82]

Six years later, Zygmunt III signed a peace treaty with Russia, now under the new Tsar, the young Mikhail Romanov. The treaty brought the Commonwealth certain territorial gains; but these were meagre enough, in view of how much Commonwealth blood had been shed on Russian soil. Besides, all plans to make Prince Władysław the next Tsar were now off the table.[83]

The acquisition by Russia of most of the Ukrainian territories in 1667 (they were at that time referred to as Kievan Rus) was a momentous turning-point in the history of Polish-Russian relations.[84] This acquisition secured Russia the status of European empire.

From then on, Russia never abandoned its plans to subordinate the Commonwealth through political control and, where possible, subversion. Russia simply did not regard the Commonwealth as a fully sovereign state; it considered it merely a part of Russia's European zone of interests.

Since then, there could only be two possible outcomes for the Commonwealth: either its disintegration under the combined pressure of its mighty neighbours; or its full recovery which would make it possible for it to permanently block Russia's westward expansion.

ELECTION OF KINGS AND *LIBERUM VETO* – HAVE THEY SERVED POLAND WELL?

When the last Polish king from the Piast dynasty, Kazimierz III the Great, died, the King of Hungary Louis became the next King of Poland, in accordance with the terms of the contract he and Kazimierz III had signed. This marked the first time any Polish sovereign acquired his sovereignty on a principle other than hereditary right.

King Louis (or Ludwik, if we use the Polish version of his name) appreciated the hereditary principle enough to want to secure the Polish throne for one of his daughters. In so seeking, he aroused however the ire of clergy, burghers, and nobility. He overrode this opposition only in 1374, after he issued the Koszyce Bill of Privileges for the Polish *szlachta* (the first Polish statute affecting the entire Polish nobility). The Bill reduced the land tax and abolished various other taxes.[85] It also imposed on the monarch the obligation to ensure that as a King of Poland he loses none of its territories.

From then on, each candidate aspiring to become the next King of Poland had to present to the nobility a proposed list of its privileges, and to promise that he would enact all these privileges on becoming monarch.[86] Generally, these privileges bore the Latin name *Pacta Conventa*.[87] And so, following the death of King Władysław III Warneńczyk in 1444, all subsequent Polish kings were to be elected at convocations of the nobility.

In 1505, the nobility increased its control over the monarchy by enacting the *Nihil novi nisi commune consensu* principle.[88] This act's task, briefly alluded to earlier, was to prevent Polish sovereigns from issuing laws that would not have consent of all deputies. Since the act augmented the power of the Chamber of Deputies, already controlled by nobility, it was regarded as commencing the age of so-called 'Nobles' Democracy.'

It needs to be stressed here that Polish nobility was very strong numerically: it accounted for about ten percent of the entire country's population, a higher figure than that in any other European country.[89] While *szlachta* benefited from these new acts, others suffered. An early XVIth century ruling abrogated most cities' voting rights in the Sejm. Peasants' freedom to change residence was, as mentioned before, severely restricted.

After 1573, an additional curb on the monarchy was imposed. Every king-elect had to swear fealty to the Henrician Articles,[90] which took their name from the brief tenure of France's Henri III.

These articles founded a permanent elective monarchy, prohibiting automatic succession rights for monarchs' children[91]. They also introduced: the requirement of the Senate's approval of all Polish monarch's intended marriages; six-week sessions of the Sejm at least once every two years, preferably more often; the prohibition of new taxes, tariffs, or levies unless the Sejm had approved of them; a permanent advisory council of sixteen senators (with regularly changing membership) to govern when the Sejm was not in session; a ban upon a monarch raising an army, declaring war, or declaring peace without the Sejm's permission; a ban on any national army serving outside the Commonwealth's borders without heavy compensation; a permanent guarantee of religious tolerance; and formal empowerment for the nobility to refuse to carry out the king's commands, if they infringed on nobles' rights.

Each king had to since affirm the following at his coronation: 'if anything be done by Us against laws, liberties, privileges, or customs of this Kingdom, all of Our subjects shall be freed from their vow of obedience to Us.'[92] Moreover, as of two statutes issued in 1530 and 1538, each member of the nobility had a separate vote.[93] This put an end to any hopes of an alternative system whereby a mere majority of representatives would prevail. The result, in conjunction with the *liberum veto*, ensured chronic governmental weakness, beginning in the mid-seventeenth century, enfeebling

Poland against its neighbours, and never being wholly overcome before the 1795 catastrophe.[94]

The *liberum veto* (Latin for 'the free veto') was a requirement by which all bills being voted on required not a mere majority, but a *unanimous* vote, for them to be passed. Any Sejm member could, if he wished, curtail the entire Sejm session and block any legislation by simply exclaiming '*Nie pozwalam!*' (meaning in Polish: 'I do not allow!'). This was happening at a time when other European countries – above all the France of King Louis XIV – increasingly accepted the value of a strong and efficient executive, as the only reliable method for preventing a repeat of the Thirty Years' War.

Liberum veto put Poland out of step with Europe's prevailing trends at that time. It had largely contributed to the collapse of the Commonwealth's collapse, as it frustrated all necessary reforms. Worse still, foreign powers would bribe Sejm deputies to use the *liberum veto* in such a way as to favour those powers' interests. A more pernicious means of wrecking the Commonwealth's sovereignty and enfeebling it than the *liberum veto* had been, could have hardly been devised. It remained in force until it was too late to salvage the Commonwealth.

Of the approximately 150 Sejm sessions between 1573 and 1763, one-third of them failed to pass any legislation whatsoever. This was mostly because of the *liberum veto* being employed. No wonder, the expression *Polish parliament* has since come to signify a legislative paralysis.[95]

Polish monarchs would, now and then, seek to change the Polish nobility's attitude. King Stefan – annoyed at endless Sejm debates over his requests for further funds, these funds having been urgently needed to strengthen the Polish army and to prepare it properly for the imminent wars – complained: 'I am your real king, not an imaginary, or a painted one... I will govern, and rule, and I will not suffer any one of you impede me. Be minders, if you will, of your privileges – I will not let you be my preceptors.' (His original Polish words were: *Jestem królem waszym, nie wymyślonym, ani nie malowanym ... Chcę panować i rządzić i nie ścierpię, aby ktoś z was mi w tym przeszkadzał. Bądźcie strażnikami waszej wolności, ale nie pozwolę, abyście byli moimi nauczycielami.'*).⁹⁶

Some suggest that 1578, the year in which King Stefan surrendered his prerogative to deal with appeals to the newly established Crown Tribunal, marks the end to the privilege accumulation by the Polish nobility.⁹⁷ Others believe 1611, when nobles alone were allowed to buy landed estates in the Commonwealth, was the true end of that process.⁹⁸ Such a strong domination of nobility over the monarchy, and the other classes, as *szlachta* exercised in Poland had no precedent, or parallel, anywhere in Europe.⁹⁹ Notably, it was *szlachta*'s control over tax rates, and its insistence on keeping them quite low that starved the Commonwealth of income.¹⁰⁰

TRIGGERS OF DECLINE

By the late seventeenth century, the Commonwealth had been grievously, indeed fatally, weakened. Not only did it have to face the threat of a resurgent Russia, but it endured the depredations of plundering Swedish armies, especially between 1655 and 1660. The population and material losses that Poland suffered during the years of Swedish occupation (referred to as 'the Deluge') seem to have been even worse, on a proportional basis, than those inflicted on Poland during the Second World War. Of all Poland's cities, only Lwów and Gdańsk were spared Swedish rapine. The Cossacks' uprising led from 1648 in the Commonwealth's east by Bohdan Khmelnytsky had resulted, following spectacular bloodshed, in Russia taking over much of Ukraine. The Treaty of Bromberg that the Commonwealth signed in 1657 with Brandenburg-Prussia was remarkably one-sided. It forced the Commonwealth to cede several of its territories to Prussia, and to acknowledge the Hohenzollerns in perpetuity as Prussia's rightful rulers, while not obliging Friedrich Wilhelm to anything but assurances of support in the event of further Russian military trouble.

In the early eighteenth century, some Poles formed a very naive view that the Commonwealth was safer when it was weak. Such weakness, they asserted, would reassure all its neighbours that it could not possibly present a danger to any one of them, and thus would be unlikely to attack it.

A few figures emerged then on the Polish political scene who sought a way out from the debilitating, self-inflicted feebleness of government. Two of them, Stanisław Dunin Karwicki (pronounced *Karvitsky*) and Stanisław Konarski, proposed to convert the Sejm into the equivalent of ordinary European legislature, where majority rather than unanimous votes would be sufficient to enact new laws. Karwicki advocated splitting the Sejm into three chambers and recommended denying voting rights to those nobles who had proven their lack of concern for the common good.[101] Sadly, by the time these serious Sejm reforms were applied (in 1792), and the *liberum veto* abolished, it was a case of 'too little, too late.'

THE RELIEF OF VIENNA

Meanwhile, the Ottoman menace continued. Memories concerning the Ottomans' siege of Vienna in 1529, and its eventual defeat, remained vivid in eastern Europe. The Ottoman Empire had never forsaken its hopes of gaining possession of Vienna, and with it the control over the upper Danubian basin as well as over many of Europe's overland trade routes.

In 1681, opportunity struck when a Protestant rebellion (bound to be useful for Ottoman purposes) against Habsburg Emperor Leopold I broke out. The leader of this rebellion, Imre Thököly, was against oppressive Habsburg policies towards his Hungarian co-religionists. Thököly obtained military assistance from the Ottomans, who formally recognised him as the 'King of Upper Hungary.'[102] The territory controlled by Thököly included the easternmost part of present-day Slovakia, as well as present-day Hungary's north-eastern region. It seemed very likely that the Ottomans would have their hopes realized of installing a Hungarian client-monarch in Vienna.[103]

The Ottomans were formally at war with Austria from August 1682, yet they could not contemplate capturing Vienna before spring of the following year. They knew they were most unlikely to hold out against the European winter. The resultant breathing-space gave abundant time for Austria to improve its defences, and for Pope Innocent XI to plead with Jan III Sobieski (Poland's king since 1674) for a defensive alliance with Austria and Venice. By the 1683 Treaty of Warsaw, Austria and Poland agreed to come to one another's aid, if the Ottomans attacked Cracow, or Vienna.[104]

In April 1683, the Ottoman army started its march towards Vienna. On its way, it was joined by Transylvanian and Hungarian anti-Habsburg forces. By the time the combined invading armies approached Vienna's outskirts, they numbered around 150,000. The siege of Vienna commenced on July 17, with at this stage only 15,000 men under Count Ernest Rüdiger von Starhemberg able to hold off the invaders.[105]

Poland's relief expedition left Cracow on August 15, among fears – which turned out to be wholly justified – that Thököly would take advantage of the drastic reduction of troops within Poland itself, and would aid the Turks.[106] Sobieski's warnings to Thököly that his disloyalty would be punished proved unavailing.

Eventually, the anti-Ottoman coalition at Vienna included 46,050 infantrymen, 38,350 cavalrymen and dragoons, and a total of 152 cannons. The Polish contingent alone (the Lithuanian one did not arrive in time to take part in the battle) comprised 16,450 infantrymen and – of particular importance – a 20,550-strong cavalry division, with its famously effective Winged Hussars formation of heavy cavalry.[107] As for the Ottomans, they only had 130 field guns and 19 medium-calibre cannons which was clearly insufficient.[108] The fortifications of Vienna were very robust indeed. They had recently been overhauled which forced the Ottomans to dig tunnels under the city walls, to be able to then blow them up using black powder.[109]

Early on the morning of September 12, just before the battle commenced, a Holy Mass was celebrated for the King of Poland and his army. At about five in the afternoon, Sobieski unleashed his most formidable device: a cavalry attack in four groups. Of these, three were Polish formations; the fourth consisted of Leopold I's cavalry. Altogether around 18,000 horsemen charged down the hills: the largest cavalry charge in history.[110] Sobieski led the charge himself, at the head of the Winged Hussars formation of approximately three thousand.[111] Within three hours, Vienna was saved. The Ottomans, having lost at least 20,000 men during the siege itself, lost a further 40,000 against Sobieski's forces.[112]

After the battle, when writing his brief victory message to the Pope, Sobieski made a deliberate allusion to Julius Caesar's famous message after his victory at Zela (47 BC) over King Pharnaces II of Pontus. Julius Caesar had said: *'Veni, vidi, vici'*: 'I came, I saw, I conquered.'[113]. Sobieski now wrote: *'Venimus, vidimus, Deus vicit'*: 'We came, we saw, God conquered.'[114]

The Ottoman Empire never really recovered from this blow and never again presented an overriding military danger to Europe. Yet the Commonwealth, so conspicuously fortunate on the field, proved less fortunate in the political aftermath. It secured no significant and lasting benefits from the great 1683 victory. Also, it wasted the chance to free the Balkans from the Ottoman yoke.

From then on, it was Austria, rather than the Commonwealth, that managed this task.

Sobieski (who died in 1696) could not even secure succession of his son Jakub to the throne. Even though, owing to the peace treaty of Karlowitz (1699), the Commonwealth had regained the Ukrainian territories to the west of the Dnieper River and Podolia, this gain did not prevent Austria from gradually increasing its own in Centro-eastern Europe at the Commonwealth's cost.

Unconstrained by any grateful memories of 1683, Austria joined Russia and Prussia in 1772 in the first partition of the once-mighty Commonwealth.

NEIGHBOURS' CONSPIRACY RENDERS THE COMMONWEALTH HELPLESS

As we have seen, the Commonwealth was badly served by the persistence of the *liberum veto* and its elective monarchy. One would think that after Sobieski died, this truth should have struck everyone as obvious.

Unfortunately for the Commonwealth, the *liberum veto* continued to be hailed by many from *szlachta* as the quintessence of nobility's freedoms (in Polish: *źrenica szlacheckiej wolności*). They would defend it with zeal. Along with the elective monarchy, it guaranteed that nobility would pay very little tax and would be able to keep on forcing new privileges from monarchs who were only their ostensible leaders.

Outsiders would also benefit from the status quo. Any Commonwealth weakness suited very well the interests of Russia, Prussia and Austria. If a proposed bill was likely to make the Commonwealth stronger and more independent, it was enough for foreign agents to bribe one Sejm member to exercise his veto over a bill to prevent such bill from being enacted. But the three great powers soon went further than that.

In 1732, representatives of all these powers signed a secret pact known as the Treaty of the Three Black Eagles[115]. In that pact, they formulated their joint policy regarding Polish monarchical succession. At the time the pact was signed, the Polish king was August II the Strong (from Saxony's House of Wettin), who had less than a year to live. The signatories were opposed to two most likely candidates to succeed him, and namely to his son, also August; and to the pro-French candidate, Stanisław Leszczyński (pronounced: *Leshtshynski*), father-in-law to France's Louis XV.[116]

The signatories wanted to entrust the Polish crown to either Prince Manuel, Count of Ourém (brother of the Portuguese king João V),[117] or to a descendant of the Piast House.[118] Both of those candidates – so the signatories believed – could be relied on to keep the Commonwealth weak and pliable. They also believed both of their candidates would avoid implementing any reforms that might strengthen the Commonwealth[119] and would maintain friendly relationship with the three powers.[120]

After the death of August II (February 1733), Russia and Austria signed yet another treaty, this time with Saxony. Known as the Löwenwolde Treaty, this agreement promised that Russian troops would, after all, countenance supporting August's son: in fact, that they would secure his election and coronation, provided however that he recognised Anna Ivanovna as Tsaritsa of Russia. It was this recognition that would compel August the Younger to relinquish the Commonwealth's claims to Livonia, and acknowledge Russian interests in Courland.[121] Meanwhile, August the Younger vowed to Austria he would renounce his own claim to the Austrian throne (it being quite a strong one, since the Habsburg emperor Karl VI had no sons).[122]

Before August could be enthroned with Russian aid, Stanisław Leszczyński struck. He had already served one term as king of Poland, from 1705 until his deposition in 1709. So, he made a comeback, being supported by King Louis XV of France. Prussia made certain that Leszczyński won the royal election on September 12, 1733.[123]

Russian troops arrived in Warsaw eight days later.[124] Their arrival inspired, at least with several electors, second thoughts about the wisdom of crowning Leszczyński. Helped in their decision-making by the Russian army, they moved to another suburb of Warsaw. There, they chose August the Younger as the King, and so, he became August III.[125]

The resultant War of the Polish Succession lasted until 1738, pitting the pro-August forces of Austria and Russia against the pro-Leszczyński forces of France and Prussia. Finally, Leszczyński gave up his claim to the Polish throne, and returned to France.[126] The real loser was, once again, the Commonwealth.

Nursing its wounds, the Commonwealth did not want to later become involved in the Seven Years' War of 1756-1763. It did, nevertheless, allow Russian troops access to its western region, from which they could launch attacks against Prussia. The brilliant and unscrupulous Prussian monarch, Friedrich II (Frederick the Great, as he is known in English), reacted to Russian incursions in an unusual way: he ordered wholesale counterfeiting of the Polish currency, a move which greatly harmed the Commonwealth's economy.

Not that Russia showed itself any more kindly disposed than Prussia had been towards Polish interests. In 1767 Catherine the Great – who had become Russia's monarch five years earlier after her husband perished in mysterious circumstances – was able to force upon the Commonwealth a new constitution, via Prince Nicholas Repnin, her ambassador to Warsaw. Repnin dictated its terms to the Sejm. Those Sejm members who dared to question his policies were apt to be sent on his orders to exile in the Russian outpost of Kaluga.[127]

At this point the Commonwealth still had a notionally independent monarch, Stanisław II (Catherine's former lover), who in 1764 had insisted on Sejm reforms. Those reforms were scrapped by the Repnin-sanctioned constitution. There could now be no more talk of junking the *liberum veto* and the nobility's privileges.[128]

Stanisław II did what he could. Between 1768 and 1772, Polish troops tried to force Russia out of the Commonwealth territory.[129] Yet, they were outnumbered and were soon overpowered. This led to the first partition of Commonwealth territory, the terms and the extent of which were agreed in 1772 between the three powers in Vienna.

To make sure this partition was ratified by the Commonwealth, Russia, Prussia and Austria all dispatched armies to control the Commonwealth territories concerned. Then, the partitioning powers insisted on Stanisław and the Sejm formally and humiliatingly endorsing the outcome. Once again, the occupiers sent soldiers in to Warsaw, to prevent undue delays in the process of Polish leaders making their minds up. Reluctantly, the Sejm signed on September 18, 1773 the statutory cession.

By the terms of this partition, the Commonwealth lost almost one-third of its territory and one-half of its population. It no longer had access to the Baltic Sea. It forfeited around eighty per cent of its foreign trade to Prussia. It suffered from ferocious customs duties imposed by the vengeful Prussia.[130]

On Poles themselves, these developments left an impact which was as much psychological as economic. Finally, the nobles were able to see how much danger the country was in. Drastic administrative reforms, once considered impossible, were now being considered. Some of them had even been put into practice.

The National Education Commission was established with the task to oversee the Commonwealth's education system, to modernise it, and to make it more rational.[131] It laid unprecedented stress on teaching both civic duties and hard sciences.[132] Stanisław II, for his part, had a meeting with Catherine at Kaniov (Ukraine) in 1787.[133] He pleaded there for a formal alliance between Russia and the Commonwealth. Predictably, Catherine refused.

As part of the Commonwealth government's belated attempt to prevent collapse, a new constitution came into effect on May 3, 1791. It enfranchised the bourgeoisie; it codified the separation of the three branches of government; and it eliminated the abuses that the Repnin-controlled Sejm had enshrined.

These measures prompted an aggressive response from Russia and Prussia. Neither of those powers wished to see any renaissance on the Commonwealth's part. Russia, with the dire example of the French Revolution before it, feared that the new statutes were the result of Jacobin influence. In 1792, Russia invaded the Commonwealth's territory. It soon found it could rely on pro-Russian Polish magnates, who had founded their own group known as the Targowica (pronounced *Targovitsa*) Confederation.

Targowica opposed the 1791 constitution in every respect. Eventually, the magnates who formed this Confederation succeeded, and in 1793 the Sejm – with Russian soldiers present at its session – agreed to discard the reforms. This time, Russia and Prussia annexed so much of the Commonwealth's territory that only one-third of the 1772 population was left within the country's borders.

However, The Targowica Confederates, with whom King Stanisław had decided to throw in his lot, started losing prestige and momentum. The reformers' party, on the other hand, kept gaining popular strength. And so, in March 1794, the Kościuszko (pronounced *Kostyushko*) Uprising against Russia broke out.[134] Tadeusz Kościuszko himself hoped, rather too optimistically, that Prussia and Austria would stay neutral in the face of this struggle. They did not.

In early May, a Prussian contingent, 11,000 strong, joined with the Russian army. After a long siege, Warsaw fell to a combined force of 25,000 Prussian and 16,000 Russian troops.[135] The former were so sure the Commonwealth monarchy would never be restored that they took all Polish royal insignia from the king's castle to Berlin, for them to be melted down for gold which Prussia very much needed after fifty years of warfare.

For the powers, this presented the perfect opportunity to erase the Commonwealth from the map altogether. On October 24, 1795, the monarchs of Russia, Prussia, and Austria signed a treaty which formally completed the work of partition that had commenced twenty-three years earlier.[136]

Two countries refused to acknowledge the legitimacy of the 1795 partition. They were Persia (today's Iran), and the Ottoman Empire (today's Turkey).

Broken in spirit, King Stanisław travelled under a Russian military escort to Grodno, a city in what is now known as Western Belarus. There, he abdicated on November 25, 1795. Two years later (Catherine having been succeeded by her son Paul), the hapless Polish ex-king was taken to St Petersburg, where he spent the remainder of his days in captivity.

Throughout the eighteenth century, the declining and increasingly weak Commonwealth offered three neighbouring powers an irresistible temptation.[137] They cared little for the fact that the Commonwealth, at its political and cultural peak, had offered its citizens levels of freedom, religious tolerance, and often prosperity which presented a stark contrast to what generally prevailed elsewhere in Europe.

We must wonder what the Commonwealth would have achieved if its nobility had been able to value the greater public good above their own privileges, and if the country had maintained, from the early seventeenth century on, a consistently sensible approach to foreign affairs.

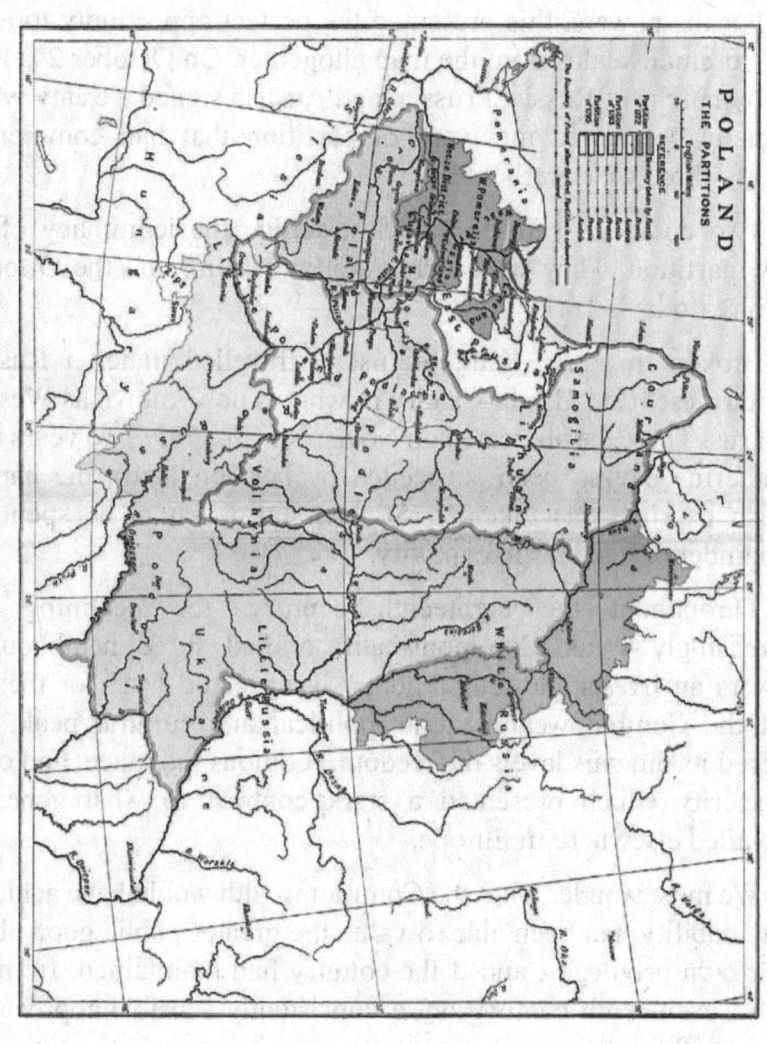

THE PARTITIONS OF POLAND IN THE PERIOD 1772-1795

(© *The Cambridge Modern History Atlas*, edited by Sir Adolphus William Ward, G.W. Prothero, Sir Stanley Mordaunt Leathes, and E.A. Benians, Cambridge University Press; London, 1912; the copyright permission obtained from Cambridge University Press, all rights reserved)

THREE ATTEMPTS AT REGAINING STATEHOOD

Having lost their own state, Poles started taking a very active part in uprisings elsewhere which aimed to change the balance of power in Europe.[138] With many of them banished to exile in Siberia to pay there for their love of freedom, many others would often migrate to Western Europe. They ensured that support for all freedom seeking movements would become a defining element of Polish nineteenth-century romanticism.[139]

The main dilemma confronting Poles after 1795 was where they should stay. Should they fight for liberty outside their former homeland, or should they do so within it? Both these policies would be tried out by turns over the next seventy years.

France seemed, initially, the likeliest source of help. Had not France been, since 1792, a declared foe of inherited despotism? Surely (many Poles reasoned), the nation that had first deposed and then guillotined the hereditary sovereign Louis XVI would come to the aid of Poland against hereditary sovereigns in Vienna, Berlin, and Moscow? Thousands of Poles went to live in France, hoping to win French backing for their own cause. Reference has already been made to the Polish Legions which were formed, under the leadership of Polish officers, during Napoleon's reign.[140]

After the Congress of Vienna, certain concessions were made to the Polish sentiment. Russian-controlled Polish territory was given some political autonomy in 1815, and the Russian Tsar acquired the courtesy title of Poland's king.[141] For the most determined

Polish patriots, however, these moves were not nearly generous enough to satisfy.

On November 29, 1830, an insurrection by Poles against Russian occupation erupted. The Polish insurgents were not numerous by Russian standards; they numbered around 57,000. Nevertheless, they fought valiantly and, at first, won several battles. Had the Lithuanian provinces managed to supply large numbers of fighting men as well organized and dedicated as those in Poland itself, the rebels would probably have attained their goals. Unfortunately, they did not. Uprising's weakness in Lithuania made it much easier for Russia to crush the rebellion. What came in its aftermath could have bene expected: confiscation of the rebels' property; Siberian banishment for many of the rebellion's leaders; closure of Polish-language universities thought to foment sedition.

Then, there were three waves of Polish exiles: in 1831, in 1833, and in 1835-1836. Many Poles went to France; others to Britain, Belgium, Italy, the Ottoman Empire, even the USA. In all these foreign lands, they kept alive national traditions, their cultural treasures, and their desire for independence.

During the 1848 Spring of Peoples[142] in Europe, Polish soldiers came again to the fore. Some led an uprising against Prussia; others took part in the Hungarian revolution led by Lajos Kossuth against Habsburg rule. A Polish general, Józef Bem, played a particularly important role as the pro-Kossuth forces' Transylvanian commander. Ultimately, though, all these uprisings failed. Yet again Russian Tsar (this time - Nicholas I) sent an army (this time 300,000 strong) to restore order.[143] By the end of 1849, so little permanent change could be discerned in European politics that it was almost as if the Spring of Peoples had never even happened.[144]

On January 22, 1863, yet another general uprising broke out in Poland against the Russian occupier. The immediate cause for the rebellion was a protest against enforced Polish service in the Tsar's army. This time the insurrectionists, though they formed a provisional government of their own, were severely outnumbered.

They were required – as the revolutionists of 1830 had not been – to resort to guerrilla warfare tactics more familiar to the twentieth century than to the nineteenth. The insurrections' leaders, despite their announcement that peasants loyal to their cause would be granted the ownership of the land that they already worked, had none of the sustained military success which had initially rewarded their forebears more than thirty years earlier.

Through yet another all-too-familiar undertaking, Prussia and Russia combined their resources to suppress the rebels. Prussia, in fact, put its railways at the disposal of the Russian military authorities, for the transportation of Tsarist troops through Prussian (formerly Commonwealth) territory. Fighting continued for more than a year, but the result was utterly disastrous. Some 25,000 Poles were killed, and the Russians – having imposed a scorched-earth policy of destroying entire towns – took a revenge. On August 5, 1864, five of the provisional government's ministers were executed in Warsaw itself. Approximately 80,000 other rebels were sent to Siberia.[145]

Russia abolished Polish monasteries and convents, turned Polish Catholic churches into Tsarist government departments offices, and made Russian the official language. The use of Polish in government bureaux was forbidden. Many civil servants of Polish background were dismissed from their posts, which were given to Russians instead.[146] In short, Russia withdrew the types of concessions that it had given to Poles earlier in the century. More than five decades would pass before Polish sovereignty became a practical program again. It would take a global conflict to bring this program about.

POLES RISE TO THE OCCASION

A mere few days into the Great War[147], on August 3, 1914, the first Polish military unit of the twentieth century, First Cadre Company, was formed in Cracow by Józef Piłsudski (pronounced: *Pilsoodsky*), the leader of the Polish independence movement and the future *de facto* ruler of the Second Republic of Poland.[148] The unit, established with the approval of Austria-Hungary, immediately crossed the border that separated Austria-Hungary from Russia, to engage the Russian army.

Piłsudski realized that if Austria-Hungary and Germany were fighting against Russia, Poles could, and should, benefit from it. Many other military units were formed by Poles soon afterwards. Some of these units were formed as far as France.

During this war, Poles could not avoid conscription into all three warring occupants' armies. As a result, they often, tragically and wastefully, faced each other in battle.

All three occupants of Poland: Russia, Germany and Austria-Hungary, knew of Polish soldiers' courage, so they tried very hard to gain their Polish subjects' loyalty. Soon, they all presented their individual offers of post-war Polish autonomy. Understandably, they were all offering territories each of them hoped to win from its enemy in this war.

A significant step towards restoration of Poland was made on September 12, 1917, when the Central Powers[149] (who by this stage had in their grasp most of the land belonging to the former Commonwealth) permitted Poles to set up a regency council. The idea was for this council to have a fair measure of independence until a monarch ascended the vacant Polish throne. Three months later, Poland's first local administration since 1795 took office.

In October 1918, competing quasi-governmental entities emerged in Cracow and Lublin, which complicated this situation. To make things worse, a fight between Poles and Ukrainians commenced in November over control of Lvov and Eastern Galicia, which neither party wished to give up. The province of Silesia likewise witnessed conflict between Poles and Czechs.[150]

Poland regained its statehood on November 11, 1918.

A very important role in keeping Poland safe in its early years was one played by General Józef Haller's Blue Army. Alarmed by the Treaty of Brest-Litovsk signed by Russia and Germany on March 3, 1918, General feared this treaty would prove a major obstacle to Poland gaining independence. He briefly entered Russia and then, via Murmansk, went to France. There, in October 1918, he set up an independent Polish Army (its popular name was the Blue Army), which consisted of Poles previously fighting for France, former Polish POWs from the Central Powers' armies, even Poles from the United States, Canada, and Brazil. The Blue Army kept on increasing in numbers, even after Armistice Day. Eventually it surpassed 100,000. Unlike many older forces, it was well equipped: it even had aeroplanes and Renault FT-17 tanks.

During the latter part of the war, when Kaiser Wilhelm's government could no longer afford to be generous towards Poles, Piłsudski had been confined to a prison in Magdeburg. On November 10, he emerged from gaol, to become within twenty-four hours the Polish army's commander-in-chief. Four days later, all executive authority within the new Polish state was transferred to him.

On January 16, 1919, Piłsudski concluded an agreement with the Polish National Committee, still based in Paris, regarding the formation of a new and sovereign government. Events proceeded to move with extraordinary rapidity. Elections for a new Sejm were held on January 26. On February 20, Piłsudski resigned as interim head of state, only to be re-installed in this capacity until such time that a president could be formally elected.[151]

In April 1919, Haller's Blue Army all transferred to Poland.

The re-emergence of Poland as a sovereign state was confirmed by all participating powers on June 28, 1919, as they signed the Treaty of Versailles. This Treaty defined the post-war order for the entire continent.

In late 1919, the new Bolshevik government in Russia proclaimed the need for the worldwide 'dictatorship of the proletariat' and campaigned for a worldwide Russia-led Communist front. A revolution in Germany broke out very soon afterwards: it was most successful in Bavaria. Communist movements in other European countries took likewise the offensive, most notably in Hungary where the local Communists ran the country for several months.

Piłsudski's foreign policy at that time was founded on the notion that Russia's Bolshevik Revolution presented for Poland a never-to-be-repeated chance to break the Russian empire apart. When, in February 1919, Russia's Red Army launched an anti-Polish offensive, it met unexpectedly strong Polish defence near Vilnius. The Polish army counter-attacked and gained considerable amounts of territory hitherto held by Russia. Then, they managed to impose on Russia an armistice, to last from November 1919 till April 1920. The next May, the Polish army captured Kiev.

Then, the Bolshevik government resolved it had to provide military support to the Communist movements of Western Europe. Poland, by its geographical position, formed a bridge that the Bolshevik Army had to cross if it were to provide direct physical support for Communist uprisings igniting further west. And so, in the summer of 1920, Russia attacked Poland.[152]

Early in July, the Red Army commanded by Marshal Mikhail Tukhachevsky launched a massive offensive in the north. Tukhachevsky's troops met with such success that within six weeks they reached Warsaw's outskirts. It seemed as if Tukhachevsky was to achieve what he set as a goal for his armies: *'The fate of world revolution is being decided in the west: the way leads over the corpse of Poland to a universal conflagration ... On to Vilnius, Minsk, and Warsaw — forward!*'[153]

Russian army was at that time still far superior to Poland's in terms of sheer military numbers. What Tukhachevsky had not predicted, however, was the gallantry and doggedness with which the Polish army defended its country. The Polish Army managed to crush the Bolshevik Red Army in the battle fought on the outskirts of Warsaw. The Polish triumph in this critical battle, against all odds which very much favoured Russia, has since been referred to as 'The Vistula Miracle.' After yet another major victory over the retreating Red Army as it attempted to cross the river Niemen[154], Poles emerged decisively victorious.

Not Poland alone, but all of Europe, was able to benefit from stalling the advance of communism.

Poland's post-Great-War boundaries were ultimately determined on March 18, 1921, when representatives of the Republic of Poland, of Soviet Russia (which included the Soviet-ruled Belarus [Byelorussia], as well as Russia proper), and of Soviet Ukraine signed the Treaty of Riga. The Treaty allocated all disputed territories to its parties. It also put an end to the Polish-Bolshevik war.[155]

According to this Treaty, Poland was to have all works of art taken between 1795 and 1914 from Poland by Russian troops returned to their rightful owners. It also provided for Russia to pay a reparation amounting to thirty million roubles[156], to compensate Poland for all the economic damage inflicted upon its citizenry. In the ninety-seven years since this Treaty was signed, no Russian government has ever indicated it was ready to honour Russia's Riga Treaty obligations.

PART II - HIS JOURNEY OF DUTY

*'He does much, who loves much.
He does much, who does a thing well.
He does well, who serves the common good,
rather than his own interests'*[157].

Thomas à Kempis,
The Imitation of Christ

A FEW WORDS ON PILECKI'S ANCESTRY

Pileckis can trace their roots to the early fifteenth century. Hailing from old Polish nobility, their most common coats of arms – Topór, or Leliwa[158], this family raised voivodes, castellans and starosts[159]. A part of this family which appears to take its surname from Pilcza castle, a medieval castle near River Pilica's[160] spring, moved north east after the Grand Duchy of Lithuania formed the Commonwealth with the Kingdom of Poland, and settled down in southern Lithuania, near the town of Lida. By the mid-nineteenth century, Pilecki family fortunes in Lithuania had somewhat declined.

As a punishment for his part in the 1863-1864 Polish uprising against the Russian occupant, Witold Pilecki's grandfather Józef was banished to exile in Siberia for an indefinite period, and his family's main estate (known as Starojelnia) was confiscated by the Russians. Ultimately, Józef benefited from sustained efforts of his mother Maria to gain clemency for him. After seven years in banishment,[161] Józef was finally permitted to return to Sukurcze (pronounced *Sookoortcheh*), the family's sole remaining estate. He rejoined his family in February 1871. The Sukurcze estate, however, had to be leased out. The Russian authorities had made it impossible for the Polish nobility to acquire new land, and the cost of maintaining existing land greatly increased.[162]

Józef's sons, Ludwik and Julian – the latter being Witold's father – were grown men at that time. They both decided to move to Russia, assuming they would have better career prospects there. Julian enrolled at the St Petersburg Forestry Institute,[163] where he came to know many other Polish expatriates, including Michał Osiecimski, his future brother-in-law. The Osiecimski family resembled the Pilecki family in also being nobility, and in having a similarly long record of fighting for Polish freedom against Russian occupation.

Once Julian had finished his studies, he accepted the position of forest ranger – the most prestigious job that he, as the son of a well-known Polish rebel, could hope to obtain from Russian government. This role required him to travel extensively. He would visit the Osiecimski home quite often, and in 1897 he married the family's very pretty daughter, Ludwika, eighteen years his junior.

CHILDHOOD IN KARELIA

Witold Pilecki, the third child of Julian and Ludwika, was born on May 13, 1901, in Olonets,[164] an obscure town in the northern Russian region of Karelia, with only around 1,500 residents. He had two older siblings: Maria, born in 1898, and Józef, born in 1900. Sadly, Józef died when only five years old. In addition, Witold also had two younger siblings: Wanda, born in 1907; and Jerzy (pronounced *Yezhy*), born in 1910.

Olonets was impoverished and dilapidated, with snowfalls that sometimes lasted almost half a year. The seemingly unending forests dominated the landscape with countless lakes, rivers and moorlands. From behind the river near his home, the young Witold would often hear wolves howl.[165]

But there were also enjoyable aspects to his childhood existence. Now and then, for example, the family would go on excursions out of the town in a horse-drawn carriage known as a *britzska* and would visit the local forests to pick mushrooms that grew there in abundance, including the highly-prized *porcini*. Theirs was a highly literate household too, with books and newspapers read there for several hours each day. There were six rooms in the house, not counting a kitchen, so living space was reasonably comfortable and spacious.

LUDWIKA PILECKA WITH HER DAUGHTER MARIA AND LITTLE WITOLD, OLONETS (1905)

(© Pilecki family, all rights reserved)

At that time, there was no Roman Catholic church in, or even near, Olonets. Exiled Polish priests would visit local Polish families' homes, and offer Holy Masses there. This helped generate an atmosphere resembling early Christian gatherings in the Roman catacombs, and it impressed upon all participants the notion of sacrifice. The childhood rites had a considerable formative influence on Witold's spirituality.[166]

Travel was likewise an important part of Witold's upbringing. For two months of each summer, Ludwika and her children would travel to, and stay in her parents' home at Havrilkov, about 1,000 kilometres to the south of Olonets. Journeying to Havrilkov was nothing if not elaborate. The first leg of the voyage would be undertaken by *britzska*. Then, when mother and offspring arrived at Lodieynoye Pole, they would need to board a ship to cross the vast Lake of Ladoga.

Upon reaching St Petersburg (at that time the capital of Russia), they would spend a few hours sight-seeing, marvelling at the grand city's palaces, river canals and streets. From there, they would go by train to the Bogushevskaya railway station. For the final twenty-odd kilometres of the trip, between Bogushevskaya and Havrilkov, they would travel in another *britzka*, along a road that mostly cut through birch forests, and that offered much spectacular scenery, including many beautiful glades.[167]

Havrilkov's climate was much milder than that of Olonets. In addition, the area was more suitable than Olonets for all sorts of physical activities involving the Pilecki youngsters. Witold thought up various games including in them not only his siblings, but local children, as well. His vivid imagination spurred him on to invent all sorts of military games, with narrow passages between highly stacked hay in the barn, these passages serving as paths leading to secret hideouts. Given what would befall Poland later, these activities must have prepared him well for some challenges of his adult life.

At Havrilkov, not everything was about fun. Ludwika had a niece there, Wanda Winnicka, a teacher from the nearby city of Oryol. Wanda helped with the Pilecki children's intellectual development. Whenever she detected a gap in the children's education, she would fill it.[168]

Havrilkov estate had a dairy farm within it: it was very modern and well equipped. Witold's uncle, Stanisław Osiecimski, was rightly proud of owning it. It came to serve as an inspiration for the young Witold, a vision of what modern rural life should be. It instilled in him the desire to convert, one day, the badly neglected Sukurcze estate into a similarly impressive and profitable enterprise.[169]

Julian's salary was generous enough to ensure that the Pilecki family never experienced financial need. They were even able to maintain domestic servants. Things improved further when Julian was promoted to the rank of forestry inspector.

JULIAN PILECKI IN HIS FOREST RANGER'S UNIFORM, OLONETS (1905)

(© Pilecki family, all rights reserved)

Of the Pilecki parents, it was Ludwika who had a much stronger influence than Julian, on the manner in which the children were raised. Here is how one of Witold's childhood friends describes that upbringing:

> *'Cavalry's dash, knights' courage, self-denial and sacrifice were what really thrilled and fascinated little Witold. His mother's stories about the January Uprising, about Muraviev 'the Hangman' in Vilnius, about how he maltreated and tortured Poles, about how their family's property was confiscated and the family forced into exile, all cut deeply into the boy's soul and left seeds there which produced his later deeds.'*[170]

Determined to acquaint her children with the Polish tradition and ethos, and to teach them the Polish language at its highest possible level, Ludwika would routinely read aloud many classics from the national literature. These included *Bajarz Polski,* a collection of Polish fables by an early-nineteenth-century writer called Antoni Józef Gliński. When the children were a bit older, their mother introduced them to *Trilogy*[171] by Henryk Sienkiewicz[172].

It should be stressed that while in Olonets, the Pileckis – despite their inculcation in Polish culture – maintained friendly relations with several local Russian families. Memories of ancestral persecution had no bearing on their dealings with ordinary Russians; they did not prejudge people. In turn, they were held in high regard by the local ethnic Russian and Karelian families. One Karelian acquaintance described interactions with Poles like the Pileckis as constituting *'a window through which to see the world far away from their own homes.'*[173]

Recollecting her childhood and her brother's part in it,[174] Maria characterised their father as someone focused on his work and on providing for the family to the best of his ability, but not showing otherwise much love in his daily interactions with its members. He would, she said, display tender feelings towards his wife and children only rarely. He was irritable and prone to outbursts. This made his children somewhat fearful of him.

Outsiders considered Witold, Maria, and their siblings to be somewhat deficient in confidence. Very modest in behaviour, they tended to underrate themselves. Maria went further and wrote that later in their lives, a result of this self-assurance deficiency, they found it very difficult to stand up for themselves and defend themselves against unfair accusations.[175]

There can be no doubt that his father's behaviour and outlook influenced young Witold significantly, and permanently. Throughout his life, Witold's predominant demeanour was gentle and suave. He exercised a great deal of self-control and showed forbearance towards others. This reluctance to push himself forward was compatible with the great strength of his moral conviction. He would come to demand much from himself and others.

In her memoirs, Maria remembered him as someone without the wish, or capacity to fight his way to, and secure, a career, promotions and distinctions. According to her, he never even had any real interest in those things.[176] Yet, not least because of his modesty, he won many a friend. He would frequently rely on the good will of people around him. Without that good will, his own financial situation and that of many another family member would have often been, as Maria pointed out, quite dire.[177]

RETURN HOME

In 1908, Witold turns seven. By this point, his parents had decided that if their children were to stay in Olonets even a few years longer, they would inevitably think and behave more and more like Russians. There was increasing pressure on them, from their peers and other local people, to adapt to the local expectations and conditions of life. Besides, there was then no secondary school in Olonets.[178]

That was why, first Maria (in 1908) and a year later her mother, along with Witold and the new baby Wanda, moved south well over one thousand kilometres to Vilnius, the former capital of what used to be, for two and a half centuries, the Commonwealth's vast province of Lithuania. Vilnius had at that time many secondary schools; the population of this city numbered about 200,000. Despite over one hundred years of Russian occupation, Vilnius still had a predominantly Polish populace, with several locally produced Polish-language periodicals which benefited from the relaxation in Tsarist censorship after the 1905 revolution. The Pileckis managed to find a comfortable four-bedroom flat, big enough for a piano, as Ludwika very much loved playing it.[179]

Maria moved to Vilnius directly from Havrilkov from her family's summer holidays. She was accompanied by her father, who left her with his mother, Flawia [*Flaviah*] Żórawska [*Zhuravska*], and her two sisters, Ewarysta [*Evaristah*] and Bronisława [*Bronislavah*] at their home at Zarzecze [*Zazhetche*]. The rest of the Pilecki family returned to Olonets.[180]

Maria would not tolerate her separation from her family very well, all the more that most of the time her only company were three elderly females. A friendly atmosphere at the state Vinogradov College in Vilnius could not compensate for the absence of her parents and sibilings. This had expedited Ludwika' decision for her and the remaining children to join Maria in Vilnius. She decided so while on her next summer holidays in Havrilkov. She advised her husband of this decision by sending him a letter.[181]

For his part, Julian had decided to remain in Olonets since he had a well-paying and secure forest inspector's job there. Until the outburst of Great War (World War I) in 1914 he would continue to live away from the rest of his family, a circumstance which will unfortunately prove detrimental to his psychological wellbeing.

At the time Ludwika and her children settled there, Vilnius had a predominantly Polish population. It had remained one of the foremost places in the Russian-occupied part of the country where Polish culture had been very actively nurtured, despite efforts by the Tsarist authorities after the January Uprising to suppress any such sentiments, and russify all ethnic Poles who lived in the Russian Empire.

For Witold, moving to Vilnius fulfilled his childhood dreams. He enrolled (1910) at a local commercial school where it was far less likely for him to suffer discrimination for being a Pole.

Discrimination against Poles was quite common at that time at schools in Russia. History lessons in Russian schools showed a significant bias against Poland and Poles. Students were told that the disappearance of the Commonwealth from the map of Europe was something natural, even a necessity. The achievements of three occupying powers' lessons were often exaggerated, and Poland's own heritage - belittled. Poles, so suggested the official history handbook of the time, should be grateful to Russia for 'taking care of them.'

At least Vilnius's Polish teachers would do their best to convey a less distorted picture. They would tell their students about the proudest moments in the Commonwealth's history.[182]

Once settled in Vilnius, the family more frequently than before travelled to its Sukurcze estate. At the time, the estate was being looked after by the trusted family servant, Józefa [Josephine] Mińska.[183] Two German maids were also employed there, from whom Maria and Witold both learned German. Swimming, rowing, croquet, picking mushrooms, visiting and receiving neighbours, and other diversions were all much-appreciated parts of the time they would spend in Sukurcze.

On March 3, 1913, Witold took a momentous step: he joined the then-clandestine Związek Harcerstwa Polskiego (ZHP)[184]. This organisation was in some ways akin to Lord Baden-Powell's Boy Scout movement which commenced its history at about the same time[185]. What made ZHP slightly different from the Boy Scout movement was that the former had an active political purpose which Baden-Powell's movement never had.

ZHP aimed to strengthen Polish youths' awareness of their true cultural roots, and their need to stay true to those roots. ZHP members would be secretly taught fencing, military tactics, and cartography. Their instructors were Polish officers, some of whom served in the Austro-Hungarian Army, some in the Russian one.[186] ZHP had a code which Witold, like all other members, swore to obey. The code involved: a faithful service to the Fatherland; always keep promises; show gallantry and courtesy; love and understand nature; be obedient to parents and superiors; be cheerful and ready for self-sacrifice; preserve chastity; avoid wastefulness; and, abstain from smoking and alcohol.[187]

IN WAR'S TURMOIL

Ludwika and her children were on holidays in Druskienniki (pronounced *Drooskyennyiky)*, a salt springs resort in southern Lithuania, when the news of Great War came on August 1, 1914. In the tension and commotion caused by it, when journeying by rail back to Havrilkow, Ludwika lost luggage which contained jewellery and family silver service items, the last valuable items of that kind remaining in her family's possession. This loss was only the first of the many that the family suffered over the next several years.[188]

From Havrilkov (Vilnius fell to the Kaiser's army in September 1915), the family moved further east, to the Russian city of Oryol, where lived their Winnicki cousins – including their teacher cousin Wanda. The Pilecki children soon found out that both the overall quality of education and the pupils' predominant intellectual calibre were significantly lower there than what had been their experience in Vilnius.[189] Luckily for Witold, he found enough Polish youth living nearby to warrant founding a local ZHP group.

In the summer months of 1917, the situation had grown from bad to worse. The spectre of revolution commenced to increasingly haunt Russia. Oryol's Polish community learned, with some relief, that a large Polish military unit was being formed – with permission from the Russian authorities – in the nearby city of Minsk. Led by General Józef Dowbór-Muśnicki (pronounced Dovboor-Moosnitski), the unit took the name 'First Polish Corps'. Witold joined it and persuaded some of his fellow ZHP members to do the same.[190]

Then came the shock of the Lenin-led October Revolution. With it, pro-Bolshevik troops started spreading waves of terror across the entire country. They particularly threatened owners of large estates, urging small local farmers to rob, attack, and kill their owners. For the Pileckis this was an increasingly dangerous period: it became clear that Russia's entire social and economic order would be overthrown, and the population's lives would be transformed, not necessarily to their advantage. The Havrilkov estate was confiscated in November.

With a great show of benignity, the Bolsheviks allowed each landlord to keep one-sixtieth of the land that he owned before, plus one horse and one cow. The remaining 59/60ths of the property went to Bolshevik loyalists. Fortunately, not all of them were devoid of compassion, some would indeed help the vanquished landlords when possible, so that they and their families did not actually starve.

During the autumn, Witold and his scouts carried out a few successful actions. They aimed to free political prisoners still held in that region. One of these prisoners was Józef Kazimierz Skwarnicki (pronounced *Skvarnitski*), who, even though only four years older than Witold, was already a veteran of the Pilsudski Legion. This new acquaintance, and the associated information about new Polish Army units, greatly influenced Witold's choices in his later life.

In the spring of 1918, Witold and his scouts broke into a Russian military depot, from which they took a quantity of uniforms and firearms. When preparing this action, Witold met someone who would exercise significant influence on the next few years of his life: Jerzy Dąmbrowski (pronounced *Dombrovskee*), who used the *nom-de-guerre* 'Łupaszka' (pronounced *Loopashkah*). Łupaszka was twelve years older than Witold, and was already an experienced soldier who enjoyed the fearsome reputation of a most courageous fighter.[191]

After that successful action, eight of the group's now fully equipped participants decided to join the First Polish Corps. As it happened, only Dąmbrowski managed to join the Corps, the presence of many Russian troops in the area preventing the others from doing the same.

The First Polish Corps engaged both Russian and German units, and at the same time it got outlawed by the Bolsheviks. No wonder, General Dowbór-Muśnicki soon disbanded it; he did so in order to save the precious lives of his soldiers. As it turned out, only two years later those soldiers would be much needed to fight against the Bolshevik threat.

In August 1918, at which stage the German-Russian front was only five kilometres from Havrilkov, the Osiecimski family was warned by a Bolshevik militia fighter (one known to the family for quite some time) that they needed to leave Havrilkov immediately, if they wanted to live.

The Bolshevik terror against all real and imagined enemies raged without cease. The Pileckis resolved to cross into the territory which remained occupied by the German army. Witold and Maria were the first to make the crossing. Feigning sickness, they succeeded in obtaining medical certificates from a German military doctor. With those documents they were able to return to their Vilnius home, where they arrived at the end of August.[192]

They found Vilnius to be very different from, and much less agreeable than the city that they had left nearly three years before. The population was so impoverished that many inhabitants were barely managing to survive. They depended upon soups made of pigweed, herbs, and nettles. Even those who were not thus suffering from hunger were almost always unemployed. This did not augur well for the Pileckis.

Luckily, on September 1, Maria was able to obtain a job in a local post-office. Without that, her relatives would have had great difficulty in making ends meet. Not long afterwards, Ludwika and the two younger siblings joined Witold and Maria in Vilnius.

POLAND EXISTS AGAIN!

The dramatic tidings came from Germany with astonishing speed: Kaiser Wilhelm abdicated on November 10. The very next day, all the German troops on the Western Front surrendered. On the Eastern Front, the Germans were still holding out, still occupying the territory of Lithuania and Byelorus (as Belarus was then called). Accordingly, ethnic Lithuanians and Byelorussians set about establishing new local authorities of their own. They openly resented the sizeable Polish population in those territories, and the Polish interests which this population innately represented.[193]

In many countries, November 11 has since been celebrated as Remembrance Day, sometimes called Armistice Day or Veterans' Day. To all Poles, this day acquired since a very special additional connotation. It marks Poland's Independence Day.

A few weeks before that date, on October 28, 1918, the Polish Liquidation Commission was established in Cracow. It seized power from Austria in two regions: Galicia and the easternmost part of Silesia. All Austrian military units in both territories were disarmed. During the night of November 6-7, a provisional Government of the People's Republic of Poland was formed in Lublin, under Ignacy Daszyński (pronounced *Dashinsky*), a socialist and a journalist long active in pro-independence groups. The Central Powers' forces near Lublin and Kielce laid down their weapons.[194]

On November 10, Piłsudski emerged in Warsaw from his Magdeburg imprisonment. He received so enthusiastic a welcome that he assumed supreme authority already on the 11th, formed a central government, and called parliamentary elections.

Around the same time, many Poles from the territories to the east of Vilnius, which were still controlled by Russia, arrived in Warsaw seeking refuge from Bolshevism. Many of them were young men from the landed gentry who had their own properties confiscated. They would often help form Polish self-defence units, providing horses, weapons, food, and money, if unable to fight themselves.

Witold's experiences, not least in the ZHP, ensured that only after basic military training he could join a ZHP section of the self-defence units in the Vilnius area. Soon he was training his younger colleagues, and disarming a number of demoralised German soldiers left in Vilnius itself.

Witold loved these activities. He had grown into an ardent Polish patriot who was proud to fulfil his utmost mission to serve his Fatherland. At that time, many Lithuanians would cooperate with the German occupying force. Witold was saddened at their resentment towards, and distrust of, the local Polish population. He could not comprehend, why they turned their backs on the centuries of common history when they helped each other successfully defend themselves against their joint enemies.

In December 1918, Poles who lived in and around Vilnius became aware of the preparations by Bolsheviks for their military units to fill in the void left by the retreating German Army which was in the process of surrendering the vast territory it had conquered in Eastern Europe in the course of World War I.

In face of this threat, the numerically dominant local Polish population, reinforced by the Polish fugitives from the Russian territories further to the east, started forming Polish military units whose duty it became to defend the territory of Lithuania and adjacent territories from the Bolshevik military units.

WARRIOR IN POLAND'S FIGHT FOR RESURRECTION

(© Pilecki family, all rights reserved)

Under the auspices of the Committee for Public Security [Komitet Bezpieczeństwa Publicznego], which the local Poles set up immediately after the Polish State had bedn restored, units of the National Self-Defence of Lithuania and Byelorus were formed. General Władysław Wejtko [*Veytkoh*] became the Commandant of this Polish military formation. His target was to form one cavalry, and two infantry regiments. By the end of December, he had one cavalry brigade and four infantry battalions under his command.

Junior Captain Mikołaj Zujewicz had the Second Infantry Battalion of the National Self-Defence of Lithuania and Byelorus under his command. Its Second Company had been formed from Vilnius scouts, most of whom were volunteers. Witold Pilecki was one of those scouts.[195]

On December 31, Vilnius scouts intercepted a wagon laden with weapons. The local Bolsheviks had attempted to smuggle it into the city, hoping to arm their supporters in Vilnius, as the Germans withdraw west. Obtaining such weapons considerably helped the Poles. General Władysław Wejtko, the Vilnius commanding officer for the Polish Self-Defence forces, had at the time approximately 1,200 volunteers at his disposal. He commenced to form one more cavalry regiment and two more infantry regiments. On the same day, he issued a general mobilisation order.[196]

The night bridging 1918 and 1919 had been a very memorable one for young Witold. Together with a few other scouts, he stood sentry at a place of great significance for Poles: Ostra Brama.[197] Being in this place, so heavy with the weight of Polish tradition and religious symbolism, made him very proud.[198]

On January 1, Witold took part in an evening attack on the Vilnius communists' headquarters in 5 Wronia Street. These local communists had sought to foil the plan for the Polish units to take control, in the German garrison's place, of the city. Fierce fighting occurred between communists and anti-communists. Only at two o'clock on the afternoon of January 2 did the communists surrender the building. They left behind many weapons, which Witold and his friends found: the communists had clearly planned to use them to support the approaching Red Army.[199]

OSTRA BRAMA, VILNIUS (AS AT 1912)

(a photo from public domain)

Following this victory, the mood among Vilnius's Polish population was nothing short of euphoric. The city blazed with lights; Polish flags and other Polish emblems were seen on display almost everywhere. Civilians delightedly embraced the Polish soldiers and offered them much needed warm food. But this joy was not to last long.

Already on January 3, on Vilnius's outskirts, the Poles had to fight Red Army units. It was one thing for them to vanquish local communists; it was quite another thing for them to deal with the Soviet invaders. However gallant and committed the Polish troops were, the Soviets surpassed them in numbers, in modern weaponry, and in combat experience. The whole Soviet attack had caught the defenders so much by surprise that they had not had the time to dig trenches or set up barbed-wire fences. During the night of January 5-6, Witold's company received the order to leave Vilnius. As its members marched out of the city, they saw that it was already burning; the Soviets had lit the fires.[200]

A few days later in Byala Waka, not far from Vilnius, those in command of the Polish Self-Defence units signed an agreement with the remaining German Army commanders still in the field. The agreement provided for the Poles to surrender their weapons to the Germans, in exchange for which they themselves would be transported by rail to the Polish state's provisional demarcation line at the town of Łapy. Altogether 154 Self-Defence officers and 1,035 soldiers accepted the German offer. Others refused to surrender to German forces. Witold was among those who refused.[201]

Then, he continued to serve under the Dąmbrowski brothers in the Vilnius Unit of the Polish Armed Forces (*Wileński Oddział Wojsk Polskich* was the unit's Polish-language name). This contingent carried out partisan warfare activities behind enemy lines. Witold got increasingly fascinated by – and respectful towards – the leadership of Second Lieutenant Jerzy 'Łupaszka' Dąmbrowski, who seemed fearless, would never leave his soldiers, would eat the same food as the humblest private did, and who would sleep on the same type of straw bed (often enough - insect-infested), as all of his subordinates. Witold noted that the ears and fingers of Łupaszka were as frost-bitten as those of his troops. Remarkably tough as he was, Łupaszka was no boor. On the contrary, he knew how to deal with all sorts of people, was extremely intelligent, and had astonishingly good manners.[202]

It was under this man's command that Witold, not even twenty years old yet, fought in the Polish-Bolshevik War of 1919-1920. This was a very significant formative experience for him, and required him to learn new military skills: how to refocus quickly under pressure, how to assess the situation in which he found himself, and how to overcome all sorts of difficulties. In combat, he would always show composure and courage.[203]

As for the unit in which Witold served, it grew very quickly until it numbered 700 soldiers. Still, it proved too small to delay (as the High Command had hoped it would) the crossing by the Red Army of the River Niemen. On its way towards Warsaw, it engaged German, Soviet, and Ukrainian contingents, winning almost every one of these encounters.

All Uhlans[204] from the unit were given sheepskin clothes to protect them from the frost and cold. To differentiate himself from other fighters, each Uhlan chose to apply a pink rim to his cap. Before long, the pink-rimmed cap was certain to inspire alarm in Poland's enemies. Shortly afterwards the unit had its named altered to the Vilnius Cavalry Division, and was formally incorporated, as a regular unit, into the Polish army.[205]

Poland's newly formed authorities were aware that from early 1919 the WWI enemies, Germany and Russia, once more had commenced to closely collaborate with each other. Germans started selling their surplus military equipment to the Red Army. Commander-in-Chief of Reichswehra[206], General Hans von Seekt, made it very clear that the emergence of a sovereign Republic of Poland was *'unbearable for Germans.'* Future German ambassador to Moscow, Gustaw Hilger, states that *'the shared hostile feelings towards Poland are the strongest bond between Berlin and Moscow, and a new partition of Poland is an objective that our governments share.'*[207]

Germans desired for a war between the communist Russia and Poland to start as soon as possible. They hoped for that war to seriously weaken the Polish Army which was barely in its early formation stages.

Witold remained in the unit until April 1919, at which date he went to Warsaw, hoping to resume and to finish his education. Around the same time, his father was released from a Bolshevik prison; but Witold was not yet aware of that good news. As well as enrolling in the Kulwieć (pronounced *Koolviets*) Secondary College for boys, Witold joined the 40th Boy Scout Squad.

On May 3,[208] students from Kulwieć formed a line in a street along which, they had been told, a convertible car would pass, transporting Piłsudski himself. When the car arrived, Witold and one of his fellows jumped onto the car's side-step. For a moment, Piłsudski's and Witold's eyes met. Piłsudski was heard to say: '*I also was a Vilnius student.*' That sentence Witold remembered and treasured for the rest of his days.[209]

On September 19, 1919, in Minsk-Litovsk – with Piłsudski himself present again – Witold's unit was formally given the new name of the 13th Uhlans Regiment. It acquitted itself splendidly over the ensuing months, in combat against the Bolsheviks. By then, though, Witold was no longer a part of the unit. He had left active military duty on October 1, and gone, not back to Warsaw, but to Vilnius. There, on the 11th, he was part of the frenetically enthusiastic crowd that witnessed Piłsudski solemnly reopening the city's university. Many wept with joy and pride at the spectacle.

Back in Vilnius, Witold renewed his associations with the local scouts, and became the Scout Leader of the Eighth Vilnius Scout Squad. Many of the scouts under his leadership were former soldiers who would come to meetings wearing their old military uniforms. They now had in civilian life the task of helping the official Vilnius police keep order in the city itself; sometimes they made arrests on their own initiative.

By this time, the mental state of his father Julian was giving Witold, and other family members, cause for increasing concern. Julian had fled Olonets soon after the Bolshevik Revolution, fearing, understandably, for his safety. He abandoned there all the family's furniture and other possessions. His life savings (40,000 roubles in gold), which he had kept in the government's savings bank, were gone.

Jobless, penniless, and unable to provide for his household, he was rendered still more depressed by discovering the pitiful condition into which the Sukurcze estate had fallen. Far from wanting to avenge himself, he was consumed by a profound apathy. Convinced that his loved ones had no future except extreme indigence, hunger and imminent death, he also developed an obsessive belief he would be incarcerated for money which he owed, and that he would die in prison. He withdrew from almost all activity.[210]

The more apathetic Julian became, the more obviously incumbent it was on Witold to provide for the Pileckis. He therefore went to Sukurcze, along with his mother and Maria. Full of youthful energy, he refused to waste time, and immediately set about improving the estate's condition. He regarded such labour as the debt which he had to pay to his family's and nation's heritage. Years later, he wrote:

> *'Yet, not only complaints did I hear in the rustle of leaves in alleys there. I also heard words, compelling and strong, I heard requests and the persuasion: 'You will make it good again, you will understand us'. And I felt an upsurge of energy. It was not just my own energy, it was one which was coming from the past centuries. And I fell in love with it all, the garden and the house.'*[211]

Not that Witold had much leisure in which to contemplate the nature of ancestral tradition. He was unable to join the 13th Uhlans Regiment (which left Vilnius on May 17, 1920), but volunteered instead for the First Vilnius Boy Scouts' Company of the 201st Infantry Regiment. This company had been ordered to defend, along with other Polish units, a crossing over the Niemen River near Grodno.

At the village of Pieski, for the first time in his life, Witold had the traumatic experience of watching soldiers die: hundreds of Polish soldiers at that. He felt the same sensation of overwhelming helplessness that any young man – especially a young man of Witold's natural sensitivity – is apt to feel in such circumstances.

For two days Witold's company held its position, but early on July 23, it received the order to retreat. In the confusion caused by the darkness (it was not yet sunrise), eight soldiers from Witold's platoon somehow became separated from the rest. An hour later, Witold noticed they were not with him, so he and another soldier went looking for them. Finally, the missing men were located, and, thanks to their rescue, saved from almost certain death.

Somewhere between Kuźnica and Sokółka, the retreating company fell into a Russian ambush. Soviet machine-gun fire blasted forth. Yet the company retained an exemplary calm, and regrouped. This spectacle of bravery attracted the notice of a higher officer, General Żeligowski, who rode up to Witold at a gallop and asked if the company could counter-attack. Witold blithely answered: 'What a question! Surely, we can!'. He then ordered his soldiers to launch a bayonet attack, one so ferocious that the Bolshevik cavalry hastily retreated.

At around the same time, the rest of the Pilecki family joined the wave of refugees fleeing the Red Army. This was a dramatic journey, especially after Ludwika and Wanda had lost track of Julian and Jerzy. With money running extremely short, Ludwika hoping against hope that they would be able to find safe shelter with Warsaw cousins, decided to return with Wanda to Sukurcze. For their safety, both took the precaution of dressing like village women. To their great relief, when they arrived at Sukurcze, Julian and Jerzy were there; and so, still, was the loyal Józefa Mińska.

Early in August, Witold's company reached Warsaw. A strange mood prevailed in the capital, one which might be called a solemn absorption in comparatively unimportant matters. Numerous Polish officers could be found out in the streets appearing, strangely, on the whole unconcerned. They made a great contrast with the French liaison officers, all of whom looked very worried, and in a great hurry.

Luckily for Witold, on or around August 4, he met Łupaszka again. Seeing Witold, Łupaszka exclaimed: 'What? My Uhlans in infantry? I will not allow this!'. Nor did he. The company reported on August 5 to Łupaszka's brother, Major Władysław Dąmbrowski. Nine days later, Witold was promoted to Senior Uhlan. On the next day, the Polish Army achieved its great victory (the aforementioned 'Vistula Miracle'). The Bolsheviks were completely routed.[212]

In that battle's aftermath, Witold's company chased Soviet units that were fleeing towards Białystok and Grodno. The 211th Nieman Uhlans Regiment (as Witold's forces were now called) had the unenviable task of fighting against Lithuanian units, because those were allied to the Red Army.

Not long afterwards, on October 9, General Żeligowski's forces – Witold by this time among them – liberated Vilnius. A grand street parade, in which Witold took part, took place in Vilnius on the 10th. The mood of the crowd, witnessing Polish soldiers marching under their regimental banners, was ecstatic.[213] But not till November 30 did the final day of the Lithuanian campaign occur. Witold, when he came to write his memoirs, expressed regret that Poland in 1920 had not assumed control of whole Lithuania: a control which not only would have revived proud Polish memories of the 1569-1795 Commonwealth, but could well have prevented the Soviet Union from seizing Lithuania two decades later.[214]

On January 31, 1921, Witold's active military service finished. In acknowledgement of his bravery, he received two medals: the Polish Cross of Valour, and the Central Lithuania Military Cross of Merit (the Polish name for which was *Krzyż Zasługi Wojsk Litwy Środkowej*)[215]. Thus honoured, he was discharged.

He could now complete his secondary school education. Like many other students in the war-torn Poland of 1921, Witold had to undergo final exams[216] before the Examining Commission for Former Soldiers. Despite many significant gaps in his academic knowledge – gaps which were hardly surprising, given the sheer length of time he had needed to spend in uniform – he managed to pass his last test on May 27. A few days later, he received his secondary education certificate document.

Witold's first priority had to be financial, for his relevant situation was quite alarming. No longer could he count at that time on any assistance from his parents. Sukurcze was little better than a ruin, and needed large investments of capital. What helped things somewhat was an agreement he had with his uncle Ludwik (who for the preceding thirty years had worked in Chelyabinsk, a city in the Urals). Under this agreement, the Sukurcze estate was divided into two halves of 240 hectares each. From now on, Ludwik would own one half; the other half would go to Julian, who had continued access to the family home and various other buildings, all of which were within his boundaries.

Not that this development eased Julian's black melancholy, which became worse than ever. Julian had no experience, or skills necessary for running a farm, let alone for improving one.

Julian had no awareness of the bigger economic picture, either. Without consulting Witold, he took the impulsive decision to lease out his property, at precisely the moment when the early 1920s' hyperinflation (notorious above all in Germany, but also to a lesser extent afflicting Poland) reached its absolute peak.[217]

The consequences were dire. What little money the lease brought to the family did not even suffice to feed the Pileckis for a month. This was quite aside from the estate-related taxes that the Pileckis were still obliged to pay. Things became so bad that the family, amid the depths of a Vilnius winter, had to rely on free meals provided by charities. A friend of Ludwika's helped with the cooking for both the Pilecki family, and her own.[218]

HIS PEACETIME SERVICE COMMENCES

Once Witold had passed his final secondary education exams, he reactivated his former scouting contacts, and looked to his colleagues for assistance with finding employment. He was at that time acutely short of money.

On February 11, 1921, Witold commenced his service with an organisation known as the Alliance for the Country's Security (the Polish name of it was *Związek Bezpieczeństwa Kraju*, known for short as ZBK). Regrettably, the income which he derived from his ZBK duties was so meagre he could not afford to rent an apartment on his own, and had to continue living with the rest of his family in the two-room flat at 7 Skopówka Street. This property was owned by two Żórawski (pronounced *Zhuravsky*) sisters.[219] Part of Witold's income went directly to keeping family members fed and clothed.

There were other compensations, though. Although Witold's ZBK work would bring him precious little money, it heightened – and accorded with – his sense of patriotic obligation. It involved defending the border population of central Lithuania from attacks by out-and-out Lithuanian nationalists from the west, and the east.[220] Another task of the ZBK was to launch various initiatives locally, with a view to foster a greater public awareness of Polish culture's riches and antiquity.

The circumstances in which Poland had assumed control of central Lithuania back in 1920 – with Vilnius as the largest Lithuanian city in the Polish orbit – increasingly fed the local population's enthusiasm for a League of Nations plebiscite, to determine who would ultimately gain sovereignty over the territory. It should be noted that although Poles formed the territory's largest single ethnic group, they did not form an absolute majority of the population. So, a sense of uncertainty about the political future lingered, and the need for the locals' physical safety to be assured was unmistakable. This is why there was such a dire need for a paramilitary organisation like the ZBK, for it to attend to all sorts of security-related tasks, and provide various forms of soldierly training.

In March 1921, Witold assumed the duties of ZBK Armourer. He attended a military instruction course, at the end of which he passed the exams needed for him to join the ranks of non-commissioned officers. Two months after becoming an armourer, he became an inspector, and in that role he assumed command of the ZBK branch located in Nowe Święciany (pronounced *Nove Sventsany*). It was a tense period, with numerous robberies committed, and with politically motivated murders by extreme Lithuanian nationalists, against whom the locals sought ZBK protection.

The educational and cultural aspects of ZBK work ensured a draining schedule for Witold, and they often seemed thankless. They involved adult literacy courses, distributing printed materials related to Polish history, evening classes for ZBK members, arranging visits by public speakers, organising discussion groups, theatrical events including ballet, ceremonies to mark national holidays, and sometimes even assisting Sejm election campaigning.[221] Witold's superiors held his ZBK performance in high regard, proclaiming that 'throughout his ZBK service he has been very diligent and accurate, and was also a very good soldier.'[222]

It was because of the nature of his ZBK duties that Witold had to cease his involvement with scouting. It was the ZHP's policy to forbid its members to take part in the ZBK. While Witold disagreed with this policy, he was compelled to accede to it, however bitter an after-taste his departure from scouting left in his mouth, after nine years' loyal scouting service. He continued to have many friends among Vilnius's scouts.[223]

Witold's financial situation remained quite austere. As a consequence, he had to abandon not one but two university courses – a fine arts course at the Vilnius University, and a distance-education agriculture course at Poznań University, six hundred kilometres away. He did not have the funds to continue with either field of study. The fact that at the Vilnius University he was already in his third (final) year made the decision to discontinue this course, in 1924, especially hard for him.

The ZBK work continued to keep him extremely busy. His responsibilities there brought him into direct contact with Demat, a company involved in selling surplus military property. This work required him to supervise the tendering process for military property, and make sure the process was carried out in a fair, legal and clear manner. His Demat work had the obvious advantage of bringing in extra income. He dealt there with a great many different types of goods: pumps, engines, hay presses, technological lines to produce dry ice, car parts, even complete small power stations.

Already at that stage, Witold Pilecki was showing his preference for jobs that required leadership and substantial obligations. His generous and selfless disposition was widely noticed. Perhaps less immediately obvious was the effort that he devoted to the task of strengthening his will, but this effort certainly made him stand out among his peers. His honesty was impeccable, and was acknowledged by Demat. It was certain that some other Demat employees accepted bribes; Witold invariably refused them. On one occasion, someone wanting to make an unethical deal with him, over the sale of scrap iron, offered him the services of prostitutes. To no avail: he rejected all such temptations.

WITOLD PILECKI IN GODZIENISZKI (1922)

(© Pilecki family, all rights reserved)

By this point, Witold had moved (July 1923) to the town of Łyńtupy (pronounced *Lyntoopy*). There he had a flat, the first of his own, which Demat had provided for him. The flat became a source of great pride for Witold, and to the limited extent that he had money to spend on the property's upkeep, he furnished it meticulously.

Sometimes the Demat work experience challenged Witold's innate idealism. He witnessed at first hand hypocrisy, corruption, and other low human instincts. These he abhorred. In one of his letters to his future fiancée Kazimiera Dacz, he rhetorically asked: *'Where is sincerity in this world? Are there still people left who live uprightly, and agreeably? At first, all appears fine, but once you get further into it, you find betrayal and lies everywhere.'*[224]

The job that Witold undertook in the early spring of 1924 certainly was not very happy for him. As a new secretary of the Farming Groups' Association (Polish name: *Związek Kółek Rolniczych*), he travelled a good deal. Encouraging farmers in need to assist one another, and to establish organisations to that end, he grew alarmed at the impact various leftist groups were having on local agriculture, and at the anti-intellectual attitudes which these groups were fomenting. Influenced by these groups, at its 1925 general assembly the association adopted conspicuously left-wing policies. Refusing to accept this outcome, Witold tended his resignation from the seceretary's job in October 1925. This time his departure was not the crushing blow to his financial prospects that it would have been a few years before.

Making his next career move, he defeated a sizeable field of candidates to a post that was to pay him very well indeed: that of secretary to the Investigating Magistrate (Second District) of the Vilnius District Court. For the first several weeks, however, he dutifully continued with his farm association job, since it took quite some time for his employer there to find a similarly trustworthy substitute worker.[225]

Employment in a magistracy involves much contact with human nature at its rawest and its least polished. This seems to have been part of Witold's motivation for first seeking, and then accepting, the District Court position in the first place. He wanted to find out more about the life of Vilnius's underclasses and criminal classes. The roots of evil in people, and the various manifestations of that evil: these things had become to Witold an abiding interest. Moreover, a few years before, he had lodged an application with the court system to have the disastrous Sukurcze lease agreement annulled. His new post enabled him to follow the course of that application more closely than would have been feasible for an outsider.

Meanwhile, there was more general legal exertion that had to be performed. As a court secretary, Witold needed to be present at a great many cross-examinations, usually concerning procurement, falsification of documents, theft, disturbing public peace, and other unglamorous crimes. The hours were long. His working day began at 9 a.m. and often did not finish until 8 p.m. In the evening, he at least had some balm for his soul, with his walks through the Bernardine Gardens, or along the banks of the Vilia River. By this time, the naturally romantic and idealistic Witold had fallen in love, with Kazimiera Dacz, who lived outside Vilnius.

There had been a personal bereavement in March 1925: the loss of his maternal grandmother, Wanda Osiecimska, who breathed her last in Vilnius. Witold was present at her death-bed. Later he reflected:

> *'And so passes the stormy and silly youth*
> *and you are left with your recollection of*
> *it, living now more quietly and peacefully*
> *... As there is always a sunset, a moment*
> *awaits each one of us when we will turn our*
> *last glance, as if a last sun's ray, towards*
> *our favourite objects and people. What*
> *a joy it must be to catch, with your dying*

glance, a glimpse of the face of the person you loved'.[226]

Being a court employee provided for a much more intensive social life than one Witold had previously had. The New Year's Carnival of 1926 was particularly memorable for him. He was now a regular guest at parties, dances, and even fancy-dress balls. He would receive frequent invitations to the homes of Vilnius's most respected and powerful families.[227]

By this time, he had also acquired considerable skill as a painter: this increased his popularity. He produced a good many pictures: mostly landscapes, portraits, and works with religious themes. Many of these he would present to someone he knew, as a gift. Among the numerous admirers of Witold's artistic achievements was Vilnius's Catholic Bishop, Władysław Bandurski.

He would also take a river cruise to Werki (*Verkee*), rest at the picturesque Wołokumpia (*Volokoompya*) river beach, or go to watch horse races at the Pospieszki (*Pospyeshkee*) Hippodrom.

All Witold's socialising made Kazimiera Dacz, who herself lived in the quiet little Nowe Święciany, a bit envious. Noticing this, Witold invited her to visit him in Vilnius. By this time, contacts between the two got less recurrent than they had been. In the days when he was living at Łyntupy, he would regularly take the short trip – via a narrow-gauge train – between that town and Nowe Święciany. Now, that he had settled down to his Vilnius employment, he was seeing Kazimiera less often.

Another impasse was complicating matters further: Witold had repeatedly proposed marriage to Kazimiera. Repeatedly, she had turned him down. A young woman of great beauty, she was so popular she was not ready yet to make the commitment which marriage implied. In Kazimiera's day-book, Witold wrote the following rather pointed observation: '*The happiest of all are those who do not look for friends, but are looked for to become friends.*

Remember this, Kazia, and do not ask too much of people lest you get disappointed in your life.'[228]

On another occasion Witold wrote this to her:

> *'People have become too clever now: they are guided by their intellect only. They want to be practical, yet are unable to foresee everything. They have forgotten about the most important thing: that love cannot come from the brain. What use they have of their brain, if they will never be happy. For happiness is love's own sister; it is born of heart, and not of intellect. They have forgotten that there is an order in the nature: all has its causes and consequences. Making use of his brain a man wins bread, love and happiness he attains using his heart. Things turn bad, if they do the other way and use their brain when looking for love - this can only cause them heartache'.*[229]

June 30, 1926 brought good news. On that day, Witold finally won his court case: the Sukurcze lease contract got annulled.

Witold is to move to Sukurcze on September 1. The prospect of finally being in charge of his estate makes him brim over with optimism. This shows in his letter to Kazimiera:

'Farming is the work that provides me with all I require: freedom, independence, fulfilment of my individual plans and prosperity ... [as a child] I listened to the rustle of old lime-trees in the [Sukurcze] alleys, and could feel how deeply wounded was the soul of this mansion: it was complaining about its abandonment ...'[230]

Some time later, when dining with her at the popular *U Żorża* restaurant he finds out they no longer are as close to each other as they once were. Soon after, they stop seeing each other.

BERNARDINE LANE IN VILNIUS, AS AT 2014

(© R.Maceikianec)

ŻÓRAWSKI SISTERS' RESIDENCE AT ZARZECZE 5, VILNIUS (AS AT 2014)

(© R.Maceikianec)

THE BERNARDINE GARDENS IN VILNIUS (AS AT 2014)

(© R.Maceikianec)

SAINT ANTHONY WITH CHILD JESUS, PAINTING BY WITOLD PILECKI

(© Pilecki family, all rights reserved)

HIS LIFE AT SUKURCZE

Only when Witold had established himself at Sukurcze, did he find out exactly how neglected the estate had become. Plenty of work had to be carried out; almost everything was in ruin or disrepair. Never a great spender of money on himself, Witold economised still further on luxuries once at Sukurcze. Most of his income went straight into the estate's improvement. He bought cows, pigs, horses, and new machinery. One of the horses he bought – a beautiful black mare called Bajka (*Byhkah*) – would be a part of his life for many years, and would do him supreme service in the turbulence of September 1939.

Ameliorating matters for Witold was the upturn in his family's fortunes. Finally, Julian Pilecki received a back-paid pension to cover the decades of work in Karelia. This agreeable development had a tonic effect on him. He shook off his melancholy, even exhibited a cheerfulness he had not shown for years, and resumed active life. At last, all the family debts had been paid off.

Altogether Witold was growing more confident, not only in his abilities as a farmer, but more generally in his character as a man. His will became stronger than ever before. It was probably no coincidence that around this time he acquired a habit which he retained for the rest of his life: he took to reading and re-reading Thomas à Kempis's fifteenth-century devotional classic

The Imitation of Christ. Always a regular Mass-goer, he more and more often attended daily Mass, and showed a new fervour joining in the pilgrimages to some of the most famous of Poland's shrines.

WITOLD PILECKI'S SUKURCZE HOME (ABOUT 1926)

(©) Pilecki family, all rights reserved

He needed such strength to cope with his duties. In 1927, a nearby farming co-operative was established: that made Witold's timetable even more crowded. On certain days, he had to oversee no fewer than two hundred workers. Conscientious to the point of pedantry, he showed a determination to impress upon all these workers an ethic of dedication, honesty, and reliability such as he himself demonstrated. Soon he was not merely esteemed, but actually popular.

Though a firm manager, he invariably proved a courteous one. His impressive results in farming production, combined as these were with his diligence and political neutrality, gave him an exalted standing among his neighbours. It helped that he paid the co-operative's suppliers prices higher than anything they could get from other customers, some of which had superior market influence and were prepared to abuse such influence, if they could.

Notwithstanding Witold's monetary generosity, the co-operative managed to make a good profit, because it was meticulously administered, and because Witold took advantage of economies of scale to make considerable savings with day-to-day expenses. Mindful that pockets of severe poverty existed nearby, Witold organised relief programs to aid those in need. He even established a volunteer fire brigade, and became its chief.

As if he had not burdened himself with enough commitments already, in the spring of 1927 Witold helped to set up a dairy co-operative along with a friend of his, Wacław Szukiewicz (pronounced *Vatslav Shukehvitch*), who came from the nearby town of Krupa.[231] Within six months, the new co-operative was recognised as being among the most significant companies in the entire Lida district. Unsurprisingly, it attracted painstaking and experienced workers. The cows benefited from much improved feedstuff, with carrots, beetroots and turnips of better quality than they had ever eaten before. It did not take long before the co-operative started exporting its excellent butter to Britain.

So completely by this stage did Witold devote his time and energies to farm management, and to the specific social interactions of this management, that his days as a party-goer were finished. Increasingly such amusements struck him as a waste of time. Seldom, now, did he go to Vilnius at all. Amid what little leisure he allowed himself, he wrote poetry, often replete with his loving impressions of all natural beauty of Sukurcze. Here is an excerpt from one of Witold's poems (translation by the author of this biography):

'...Three slopes of this little hill are covered in bush:
Spirea, lilac, and a shrub with odd berries,
Over long time they have grown there freely,
At nature's whim,
From Krupa only you can view it
Your eyes reaching far from here into the fields.
Under a little roof of intergrown branches,
A fine-wrought umbrella
Which offers protection from the summertime rain,
There is a little bench there for those
Who seek to hide from the world.
Here could young ones dream of shared happiness
Nestled into the lilac's fragrant blossom clusters
Looking towards the high summer night skies
From which countless stars would twinkle
And the moon would filter its silver glow through the leaves:
A fairy-tale world commemorated in mysterious penumbra...'[232]

HIS PHOTO FROM THE TWENTIES

(© Pilecki family, all rights reserved)

Farming kept Witold fit. To have even more exercise, he would ride Bajka across the local forests and marshlands. Now and then he still painted: to Krupa's parish church of the Holy Trinity, he presented two of his paintings. One of these depicted Our Lady of Perpetual Succour; the other depicted St Anthony with the Child Jesus.[233]

Nor did Witold forget the experiences of past war, or the need to prepare for future one. Promoted to the rank of Second Lieutenant

(Reserve) in 1926, he repeatedly underwent extra training as a cavalry officer, and offered training in cavalry manoeuvres to other locals.

On March 23, 1928, he was ordered to join the 26th Greater Poland Uhlans Regiment. For this, he needed to travel a great distance to the city of Baranowicze (pronounced *Baranovitcheh*). His six-week training session started there on May 14. Eight years away from the rough-and-tumble of active service ensured he achieved a disappointing result in his concluding exam there. His regret was short-lived. At the next test, on July 1, 1929, he performed much more satisfactorily; and he showed himself to be capable of greater endurance than most of his fellow trainees demonstrated.

PILECKI WITH A. ŻELIGOWSKI IN LIDA (1930)

(© Pilecki family, all rights reserved)

PART II – HIS JOURNEY OF DUTY   139

A SHOOTING RANGE EXERCISE (1931)

(© Pilecki family, all rights reserved)

Increasingly, Kazimiera Dacz belonged to Witold's past. Still, their relationship did not formally end till early 1930. About a year later, on April 7, 1931, Witold married Maria Ostrowska, a teacher from the Krupa school.

**A WEDDING PHOTO OF MARIA OSTROWSKA
AND WITOLD PILECKI**

(© Pilecki family, all rights registered)

Entering the married state and, in 1932, becoming a father – his first child, Andrzej, was born on January 16 of that year – did not significantly reduce Witold's military obligations. On the contrary. A few months after the wedding, Witold was required to go to the Cavalry Training Centre at Grudziądz (pronounced *Groodsiants*) for a one-month training course (July 6 to August 8, 1931) which specifically focused on instruction for platoon commanders. After that, the military authorities ordered him to the 78th Infantry Regiment, again in Baranowicze, for a one-week course aimed at reviewing his newly acquired skills. This course he passed with the result 'Good.'

For the time being, most of the little Andrzej related duties fell inevitably upon the shoulders of Maria. Having passed the Baranowicze exam, Witold commenced his own cavalry training program at Sukurcze. In February 1932, he formed a volunteer cavalry unit, the members of which he called *Krakusy*. Whatever extra time and extra finances Witold had, he usually devoted to horses, and to military equipment. In July 1932, he became the Commander of the Polish Army's First Lida Cavalry Squadron.

**WITOLD PILECKI WITH HIS WIFE MARIA
AND SON ANDRZEJ (1932)**

(© Pilecki family, all rights reserved)

Witold's family grows further. His daughter, Zofia Matylda, was born on March 14, 1933, and baptised on the following August 15 (being the Feast of the Assumption and, at the same time, the anniversary of the 'Vistula Miracle'). But there were losses as well as gains. The year 1932 saw not only Andrzej's birth, but also Julian Pilecki's death. Two years later, in 1934, Józefa Mińska, *'the good spirit of the ancient Sukurcze estate'*, also left this world.

Also in 1934, Witold's mother decided to divide the Sukurcze estate among her children. Both of Witold's sisters, Maria and Wanda, received thirty hectares each, with no buildings. Brother Jerzy received land with buildings, eighty hectares in his case. Witold himself received 100 hectares, together with the old mansion, the orchard, and the farm buildings. These were meant to compensate him for all the hard work and money he had put into the reconstruction and development of the enterprise; he was, after all, the only sibling who actually farmed at Sukurcze.[234]

WITOLD AND MARIA WITH THEIR YOUNG CHILDREN AT OSTRÓW MASOWETZKA (1934)

(© Pilecki family, all rights reserved)

Once Wanda had passed her final high-school exam in Vilnius, she returned to Sukurcze to aid in the running of the household. At the same time, Maria (Witold's sister, not his wife) worked as a teacher in nearby Lida, and Jerzy continued to study medicine – in Vilnius – full-time.

Witold would not abandon his military training exercises. At drills in Lida and Baranowicze, between August and September 1934, his performance earned him the highest praise from the cavalry's high command. A brief military report issued on that occasion contained the following laconic description of Witold's qualities:

> *'Very true to the values espoused.*
> *Dedication and work morale – very high.*
> *Very well trained. Extensive tactical*
> *capabilities. Perseverance in face of*
> *difficulties – good. Fit to be a platoon*
> *commander at war.'*[235]

His sister-in-law, Eleonora Ostrowska, offered this view of Witold in his Sukurcze days:

> *'He was a man of action, unremitting in*
> *the pursuit of his objectives, demanding*
> *much from himself and from others [...]. He*
> *could apply himself to a task very promptly.*
> *He would overcome difficulties with ease.*
> *He would assess any situation swiftly and*
> *then act resolutely, with great calm and*
> *courage.'*[236]

WITOLD PILECKI AT THE HEAD OF CAVALRY PARADE IN LIDA

(© Pilecki family, all rights reserved)

All spare time and spare money that Witold was not pouring into military activities went on many social initiatives, including charitable works, that he undertook for the benefit of the wider community. All this was accepted by his spouse.

Maria's own employment as a part-time teacher at the local school assisted the family's finances considerably.

Zofia remembers her father:

> 'He had to be always active. My mother did
> extra work at school so that she could buy

> *her children new clothes. My father would*
> *spend money to hold military training drills,*
> *or on his other social projects. Locals*
> *appreciated that a lot and after the Soviet*
> *invasion of September 17, 1939 they cared*
> *for us a great deal, returning all [favours]*
> *they received earlier from my father.'*[237]

Witold was very proud of his *Krakusy*. In his memoirs, he wrote: 'They ride their own horses and have their own uniforms; only lances, sabres, horse trappings and rifles they get from the army ...'[238]. He regularly conducted drills across trackless forest areas around Sukurcze. His *Krakusy* took part in several inter-regimental contests for the best cavalry squadron. For seven years in a row, they won the Fourth Uhlans Regiment Competition.

It might be thought that Witold's children would have cause to complain of being neglected. That was not the case. Far from it. They could see with their own eyes the strength of their father's commitments, and they took pride in him, although they were not invariably happy about all his methods. Quoting Zofia again:

> *'He made sure his children said their*
> *morning prayer, washed their teeth*
> *and reported to him their readiness for*
> *breakfast. Porridge was a perennial part*
> *of each breakfast of ours: you could take a*
> *smaller helping of it, but you had to finish*
> *it. That was one of his ways to teach us*
> *responsibility'.*

To overcome Zofia's dislike of porridge, Witold would say: *'Horses eat a lot of oats and just look at what beautiful coats they have. If you, Zosia, often eat oats, you will also have such stunning hair.'*[239] Zofia also recollected:

> *'He was warm, yet demanding of us.*
> *Maybe he had a premonition that he only*
> *had a short time in which to bring us up.*
> *[...] We had to obey him. [...] In Sukurcze,*
> *he would spend a lot of time with us. [...]*
> *Sometimes, our father asked us to dress in*
> *style to welcome [their mother's] returning*
> *from her work: my brother dressed as an*
> *Uhlan, myself – as a Lady. [...] He would sit*
> *me on his favourite mare, Bajka, and then*
> *say with the greatest pride: 'Here is my*
> *Lady General [Polish: Generałka]'.* [240]

A particular emphasis Witold would put on teaching his children to tell the truth, always, at whatever cost to themselves. On one occasion while they were playing, they scratched, by accident, his favourite large mirror. As soon as he spotted the scratches, he asked of them: *'Which one of you did this?'*. They both, accurately, owned up. Rather than punishing them, Witold praised them for admitting their culpability.[241]

Honourable and decorous behaviour were central to Witold's expectations of the children. He introduced them to the values of the scouting movement, instilled in them a seemly national pride, and taught them a proper reverence for nature. One day Zofia (so she wrote long afterwards) was out walking with her father. She was about to step on a ladybird. But before she could do so, her father lifted the ladybird onto his finger, and showed it to Zofia. Then he let it fly off, and told her that all living beings had been put on earth for a purpose, and that they should not be unnecessarily hurt. In addition, he urged his children to love the soil which they walked on, for one day it would receive their bodies.[242]

While Maria was away teaching, Witold would think up games for the children. Sometimes he would teach them words in foreign languages. A competent musician, he often played the piano and could perform respectably on other instruments too.

Sport was also important in Witold's instruction. Frequently, he would take Andrzej to horse races. To make horses seem still more attractive to his son, and at the same time to introduce him to the history of cavalry, he bought him a magnificent book that dealt with the history of Poland's own cavalry.

By this point, Witold's own social circles consisted primarily of soldiers, by no means all of whom had been involved in his own drill sessions. Some of them he had known from back in 1918-1920.[243] The single most important military acquaintance he had made was with one of Poland's most influential men: General, later Marshal, Edward Śmigły-Rydz.[244] This friendship, for such it duly was, dated from the late 1920s, when Śmigły-Rydz received the Borówka (pronounced *Boroovkah*) estate, as a gift from his troops grateful for the liberation of the Lida distinct in 1919.

Given that his estate adjoined Sukurcze, the commander and Witold had a fair amount to do with one another anyhow. Even when Śmigły-Rydz was not at Borówka himself (he usually went there only for his summer holidays), his mother-in-law and father-in-law were there permanently, anyway.

During Śmigły-Rydz's stays there, he tended a small orchard, and, like Witold, indulged himself in painting pictures. Since painting was a passion that he shared with Witold, it was especially easy for the two men to get on well. Many a time in conversation they would exchange their memories of the fight for Poland's independence.

Temperamentally, as well as in terms of shared interests, Śmigły-Rydz found Witold most agreeable. He grew increasingly tired of the period's bitter political disputes, and the more tired he grew of those, the more he appreciated the refreshing contrast of Witold's political neutrality.

Both men truly relished their dealings with one another. Sometimes, the General (whose own estate was very small and thus did not permit hunts) would accept Witold's invitations to join him for hunting in Witold's forest. To both men's joy, Witold was decorated in 1938 with the Silver Cross of Merit, in recognition of his outstanding and varied community work.[245]

HARBINGERS OF WORLD WAR II

The peaceful atmosphere of Sukurcze got at times disturbed by unsettling news from Germany which increasingly pointed to Hitler's belligerent intentions.

After its 1920 victory over Russia, the Republic of Poland[246] acquired in the eyes of other, smaller than her countries of Central and South-Eastern Europe, a status of a quasi-guarantor of their independence from Russia, and then from its successor, the Union of Soviet Socialist Republics. For their part, both Russia and Germany regarded the Republic of Poland as an ephemeral state.

Russia viewed the Republic of Poland as a transitional state established on some of the territories she had always aspired to control, one way or another. For Russia, the Republic of Poland was a barrier between Russia and the Western Europe, a barrier that needed to be pulled down.

As for Germany, it considered the terms of The Peace Treaty of Versailles[247] imposed on the country as unfair and unduly harsh. Germany was forced to accept its own and its allies' responsibility for causing all the losses and damage during WWI. The Treaty forced Germany to disarm, make substantial territorial concessions and pay reparations to the Entente countries. In 1921, the total value of these reparations was assessed at 132 billion Marks (then

US$31.4 billion or £6.6 billion, roughly equivalent to US$ 442 billion or £284 billion in 2014).[248]

Germany denounced this treaty, and referred to it as *'a dictate'*. Their first Prime Minister after the war, Philipp Scheidemann called it *'a murderous plan'* for the German economy, and considered it unacceptable.[249]

The Soviet Russia was not even a party to the Treaty of Versailles. It was not invited to be part of it because the Entente powers, France and Great Britain, had not by that time recognized the new Bolshevik government yet, the same government that in March 1918 signed its separate truce agreement with Germany at Brest-Litovsk. That truce violated the terms of the previous agreements between the allied powers. As a result, Russia was not recognized at Versailles as an allied victorious country.

Given the circumstances, it was not an unnatural development for Russia and Germany to sign, in 1922, the Treaty of Rapallo under which each party renounced all territorial and financial claims against the other. Russia and Germany agreed to normalize their diplomatic relations and to *'co-operate in a spirit of mutual goodwill in meeting the economic needs of both countries'*.[250]

It was at Rapallo that secret military cooperation commenced between Germany and Russia, a cooperation that led to the outburst of WWII.[251] To each of those two countries the *status quo* introduced by the Treaty of Versailles was unacceptable and so they both agreed to conceive and pursue a joint strategy to do away with it, and to provide to each other all required mutual support to this effect.

Once the Treaty of Locarno (1925) had been concluded, a treaty which guaranteed the post-Versailles borders of the countries to the west of Germany but did not deal at all with Germany's eastern borders[252], Poland realized that rather than count on France alone, its main Western ally, it should seek to establish a network of alliances with smaller countries of its region. In the end, it only managed to sign one such mutual assistance treaty – with Romania.

When Adolf Hitler, the leader of the Germany's National Socialist-Democratic Workers' Party, took over power as that country's Chancellor (January 30, 1933), things on the European scene started changing for Poland for the worse. In 1935, Hitler refused to conform to the requirements imposed on Germany by the Treaty of Versailles.[253]

In blatant violation of the Treaty of Versailles, on March 7, 1936 German troops marched into Rhineland, a province which was demilitarised by the Treaty of Versailles. Poland immediately suggested to France for both countries to undertake a joint military action against Germany. At that time, when the Polish army alone was still bigger than the German one, the chances to prevent the outburst of WWII were still very good. France nevertheless refused.[254]

On March 14, 1938, Germany annexed the neighbouring German speaking country of Austria, as other Western powers just looked on.

On September 30, 1938, a pact was signed in Munich between Germany, France, Great Britain and Italy. It allowed Hitler to annex Sudetenland, a relatively large and strategically very important strip of land along Czechoslovakia's northern and western borders where ethnic Germans made up at the time a majority. The Munich pact was negotiated without Czechoslovakia's knowledge or consent.

Czechoslovakia was told by Britain and France it had two options: to resist Nazi Germany on its own, or to accept the annexation by Germany of Sudetenland. In this hopeless situation, the Czechoslovak government capitulated and agreed to abide by the agreement.[255] The military alliance agreements Czechoslovakia previously signed with France and Great Britain proved useless. The pact itself would soon prove to be a failed attempt to appease Germany, signed without Czechoslovakia even being present at the table.[256]

In early November 1938, the first Vienna Award (urged by Germany and Italy) provided for Czechoslovakia (after its secession

- for Slovakia) to cede southern Slovakia (one third of the Slovakia territory) to Hungary. Shortly thereafter, Poland got awarded a few small disputed territories (totalling 1132 km^2), which included the town of Český Těšín with the surrounding area, and the regions of Spiš and Orava.[257]

On March 14, 1939, Slovakia seceded from Czechoslovakia, and became a separate pro-Nazi state.[258] On the following day, Carpathian Ruthenia proclaimed its independence as well. A mere three days later, however, Hungary laid its claim to Carpathian Ruthenia, and occupied it since.

Czechoslovak president Emil Hacha went to Berlin. There he was forced to order Czech troops to lay down their arms, or otherwise Germans would bomb the capital city of Prague. Hacha also accepted the German occupation of the remainder of Bohemia and Moravia, which was subsequently transformed into the Reich's Protectorate. In so doing, Germany acted in blatant violation of its Munich Pact obligations.

By seizing Bohemia and Moravia, the Third Reich gained access to all its skilled labour force, to its very well developed modern heavy industry, and to all the weapons of the Czechoslovakian army. When Hitler attacked France in May 1940, roughly 25% of all German weapons came from the Protectorate. The considerable industrial potential of the former Czechoslovakia presented a valuable addition to that of the Third Reich.[259]

On March 31, Great Britain unilaterally guaranteed Poland its independence (but not its territorial integrity). It promised Poland military help if it was endangered, or attacked by Germany.

Hitler proceeded regardless. On 28 April 1939, he demanded that Poland allowed construction of an ex-territorial motorway across its territory, to connect the main German territory with that of its East Prussia enclave. He also demanded for Poland to agree for the Free City of Danzig to be annexed by Germany. Believing it was sufficiently backed by its mutual military assistance treaty with France, and by the Great Britain's guarantees, the Polish government refused to yield to these outrageous German demands.

The war became imminent.

*

On June 13, 1939, Witold's mother dies. Witold's sister remarks later: *'The good God has spared her the sufferings this war and occupation have brought upon us, has spared her worries about each one of her children, has spared her worries about us all.'*[260]

*

The Polish high command continues to expect significant military help from Great Britain and, insofar as it could recriprocate, it provides such help to Britain, as well. On July 25, 1939, the Polish high command hands over to the French and British military intelligence working copies of the German coding machine Enigma. It also supplies documentation, prepared by Polish cryptologists, which will make it possible to decode future German military messages.[261]

Two days after the German-Soviet Commercial Agreement is signed on August 19, 1939, on August 21, Stalin receives from Hitler an assurance that Germany would approve secret protocols to the proposed non-aggression pact between the two powers.[262] In his August 22 address to the Wehrmacht's High Command, Hitler makes it clear that the objective of the imminent Fall Weiss (the German plan to invade Poland) is not to gain a territory, or move a border, but *'to destroy the enemy'*.[263]

On August 23, a 10-year non-aggresion pact, to be known as the Ribbentrop-Molotov Pact, is signed between Germany and Russia. Only very few know at that time that this pact has a secret protocol.[264] This secret protocol guaranteed that Finland, Estonia, and Latvia would all become part of the Soviet zone of influence, even before the USSR formally annexes them (which, in 1940, it did). Lithuania would become part of the German zone of influence, its northern border serving as the boundary between the two zones of influence.

After Poland's predicted military defeat (neither Hitler nor Stalin considered serious Polish resistance on simultaneous two fronts even as a hypothesis), the country would be – yet again! – partitioned. By this scheme, the areas east of the Pisa, Narev, Vistula, and San rivers would go to the Soviet Union, as would Bessarabia, at that time a part of Romania. Germany would obtain Poland's western territories.[265]

The Polish government at the time, as far as can be determined, knew little of this secret protocol. Still, it was quite alarmed enough. Hence the treaty of mutual military assistance that Britain and Poland signed on August 25. In fact, all this treaty could change was to delay Hitler's invasion by five days. Still, even that breathing space was something.

*

On August 26, a dispatch rider sent by Major Gawryłkiewicz (pronounced *Gavrilkevitch*) arrives at Sukurcze. There, he meets Witold. He reveals he had brought him a secret mobilisation order. As a cavalry scouts platoon commander, Witold is assigned to the Nineteenth Infantry Division. His military unit is a part of the Polish Army Group "Prusy".

SECOND LIEUTENANT WITOLD PILECKI (1939)

(© Pilecki family, all rights reserved)

Before Witold leaves Sukurcze to join his comrades, his sister Maria asks him: '*Will the war now really break out?*' He responds: '*Maybe we will scare the Germans off, and it will not come to that.*'[266]

On August 29, the *Krakusy* – with Witold among them – ride on horseback from Krupa to the Lida military headquarters. At Lida's railway station, there is a train of no fewer than sixty freight cars, to transport the soldiers east. The prevailing mood among the soldiers themselves is solemn and exalted. No more mere drilling; action is now inevitable.

*

We will never know if Witold Pilecki had a premonition on that day that he would never see Sukurcze again. Anyway, before he left home, he visited his parents' graves, and said there his prayers.

*

On August 30, full mobilisation of all Polish forces is announced by Marshal Śmigły-Rydz. It was just as well that he does so, since the Germans are wasting no time.

During the night of August 31-September 1, German units posing as Polish stage, in Upper Silesia, the so-called Gleiwitz Incident.[267] Gleiwitz itself – the Polish spelling is Gliwice – is at that time an industrial German city very close to the Polish border. It has a radio station the Nazis seize control of. They then transmit an anti-German message from the station, in a 'false flag' manoeuvre, which has been organised by the SS as part of the Nazis' propaganda aimed at putting the blame for the forthcoming invasion on "Polish aggressors".

POLAND ATTACKED BY HITLER'S GERMANY AND THE SOVIET UNION

No formal declaration of war troubled Hitler's conscience. Instead, starting on September 1, at 4.45 a.m. local time, the German invasion was unleashed. Many members of the German High Command, more realistic, or less optimistic, than their Führer, thought that subjugating Poland would take up to three months. Hitler demanded that the process be carried out in a mere six weeks.[268]

The German army invaded Poland from three directions. While the main force crossed Poland's western border, heading in the direction of Łódź (pronounced *Woodz*), Cracow and Warsaw, other German forces launched their attack from eastern Prussia southwards across the base of the Polish Corridor, at the same time as a third army group – which had the backing of loyal Slovak units – attacked Poland from the south.

In numerical terms, Germany had a substantial advantage. It could call on 1.8 million soldiers (not counting the Slovak auxiliaries) whereas Poland was being defended by only a million men. Moreover, almost half of those million men were, during the campaign's first days, still on their way to the areas of their envisaged deployment. This was the regrettable consequence of the delay in Poland's government calling for full mobilisation.[269] Nor was that all.

Whereas the Wehrmacht had approximately 2,400 tanks, the Polish army had only about 880. The Luftwaffe had 2,135 aircraft at its disposal, and it had also benefited from the experience of participating, unofficially, in theatres of the Spanish Civil War.[270] In 1939, it certainly was the most experienced and best-equipped air force in the entire world. By comparison with the Luftwaffe, the Polish Air Force was largely untested and possessed only about six hundred aircraft.[271]

Still, all was not lost yet. On September 1 itself, Witold Pilecki's Uhlans notched up their first significant success of the war when they shot down a three-engine Luftwaffe plane of an old type (presumably on a reconnaissance mission), as soon as the plane came within the reach of the Polish anti-aircraft weapons.

*

Two days later the French and British declare war on Germany. They do not provide any meaningful military support to Poland, despite the treaties they had signed. In the starkest imaginable contrast to the war fought in Poland, the German-French border sees at that time only a few minor skirmishes. No wonder, a term was of "phoney war" was soon coined for it.

As the Polish Army bleeds in its uneven struggle against the Wehrmacht and Luftwaffe, those fighting along the Siegfried line, the fortified German defence along the French border, only met occasional local skirmishes.[272]. A French offensive in the Rhine River Valley starts on September 7. Eleven French divisions advance 8 km towards Saarbrücken against weak German opposition. The halfhearted offensive is soon halted at Warndt Forest, anyway.

*

As Pilecki and his Uhlans continued their heroic fight they knew nothing of the French and the British Prime Ministers' secret meeting on September 12, 1939 on the French side of the Channel, in Abbeville. There, in full knowledge that the entire Polish plan of defence was based on the French and British guarantees, and despite the increasingly dramatic situation of the Polish Army of which they were well aware, they decided not to launch a full-scale relief offensive against Germany.[273]

On his trip to meet the French Prime Minister and Commandant-in-Chief of the French Army, Mr Edouard Daladier and General Maurice Gamelin respectively, the then British Prime Minister, Mr Neville Chamberlain was accompanied by Harold Adrian Russell "Kim" Philby. A high-ranking member of MI-6[274], it turned out much later he was at that time an agent for the Soviet NKVD.[275] Interestingly, two French ministers who accompanied Mr Daladier at that meeting were also, as was determined later, agents of the Soviet NKVD. One can therefore be sure, that Joseph Stalin did not have to wait very long to be apprised of the decision reached in Abbeville.

The Abbeville decision helped Stalin resolve his dilemma, as to whether he should, or should not invade Poland from the east at the time the Polish Army fights Wehrmacht advancing from the west, north and south.

Once France and Great Britain resolved they would not launch in September 1939 a full-scale relief offensive, Stalin's invasion of unsuspecting Poland became, all of a sudden, a strategically safe option for him. It became a safe option as Hitler would have to withdraw many and possibly most of his division from the Polish theatre before the campaign there had been completed. He would need to move these to the west so as to defend the Third Reich's fragile western border.

Now, if Hitler decided to transfer most of its divisions to the west before the Polish campaign was decided, Stalin would have to withdraw his invading armies from Poland in order to avoid the Soviet Union being seen for what it indeed was: a co-aggressor and Hitler's ally in his September 1939 attack on Poland.

On September 13, the Head of the French Military Mission to Poland, General Louis Faury, informed the Polish Chief of Staff, General Stachiewicz [*Stakhyewitch*] that the major offensive on the western front planned for September 17–20, had to be postponed.[276] French divisions had been ordered to withdraw to their barracks along the Maginot Line regardless of the nearly 5 to 1 numerical advantage France and Great Britain had at that time over the German divisions left to defend the country's western border, and the more than 2 to 1 advantage in air force over the part of Luftwaffe left to defend Germany at the time the September campaign in Poland commenced.

It should be emphasized here that the French land forces were at that time the third largest in the world (after the Soviet Union and German ones); further, the British and French navies were the largest and fourth largest navies, respectively, in the world.[277]

This French and British inaction whilst a vast majority of German forces were engaged (including practically all their armoured forces) in Poland was, and still is, very difficult to comprehend.

*

In stark contrast, the September campaign in Poland had nothing "phoney" about it.

On September 4, the Nineteenth Infantry Division, to which Pilecki's squadron belonged, finally reached its designated defence position: a forest north-west of Piotrków Trybunalski (pronounced *Pyotrkov Treeboonalsky*).[278] On the same day, the Division's units were heavily bombarded by Luftwaffe planes. Several of Pilecki's Uhlans were wounded in that bombardment, and some were killed.[279]

Subsequently, the Division was engaged in heavy fighting, as part of a vain effort to stop advancing German tanks. In effect, the Division was pushed back towards Tomaszów Mazowiecki, incurring very heavy casualties. During this retreat, Uhlans formed the Division's rear guard. At Wolbórz (pronounced *Volboosh*), on the night of September 4-5, the Uhlans' squadron for all practical purposes ceased to exist. Among the dead was Pilecki's horse, Bajka.[280] On September 5, the Division as a whole – or rather, what was left of it – suffered a crushing defeat. The Germans took prisoner the Division's commander, General Józef Kwaciszewski (pronounced *Kvatsishevsky*).[281]

Pilecki, with the energy born of desperation, gathered sixty-three surviving Uhlans and, via Tomaszów Mazowiecki, arrived at Warsaw on the night of September 6-7. For two days, he tried to organise a defence of the capital's bridges, but eventually abandoned this plan, and led his Uhlans towards Siedlce (pronounced *Syedltse*) and Łuków (pronounced *Wookoov*). Via Radzyń and Parczew (pronounced *Partshev*) they reached, on the 13th, Włodawa (pronounced *Vlodava*). There, the Forty-First Infantry Division recruited new soldiers as best it could, to compensate for the severe losses it had suffered during the previous days.

Overall, the news was bleak. True, some Polish units had managed to achieve limited success in some minor battles. But everywhere else, the technical, operational and numerical superiority of Hitler's troops was just overwhelming. Polish contingents were compelled to fall back towards Warsaw and Lwów.

The largest battle of this campaign – the Battle at Bzura River – lasted ten days, from September 9 till September 19. Two retreating Polish army groups, *Poznań* and *Pomorze*, attacked the flank of the advancing German Eighth Army. This attack provided a temporary distraction, but no more than that. It could not and did not inflict any profound damage upon the invaders. By this stage, the Polish armed forces no longer possessed the ability to seize the military initiative. Nor could they conduct large-scale counter-attacks. Against Germany's vastly superior air power they had no hope of victory.

*

Ignacy Mościcki – who had been Poland's president ever since 1926 – decided, along with his government (headed by Prime Minister F. S. Składkowski) and the military chiefs of staff, that Warsaw needed to be evacuated. All of them headed southeast. On September 13, they reached Zaleszczyki (pronounced *Zaleshchikee*), a town on the Polish-Romanian border.[282] Marshal Śmigły-Rydz still thought at that time of a last-ditch defence of the country's south-eastern region, the so-called bridgehead to Romania. To this end, he ordered the Polish Army to retreat behind the Vistula and San rivers.[283]

*

When in Włodawa, Pilecki met Major Mandzenko[284], who ordered him to recruit as many new soldiers as possible. Most cavalry units were at that time already terribly depleted. Pilecki soon had no fewer than 160 Uhlans under his command. On September 15, a long-standing acquaintance of his, Major Jan Włodarkiewicz (pronounced *Vlodarkevitch*), brought with him thirty more Uhlans. Pilecki surrended the overall command to Włodarkiewicz. He served since as the second-in-command. Pilecki and Włodarkiewicz were to continue their close contacts after they both have joined the Polish underground.

Pilecki and his troops would have still maintained the sanguine hope that Britain and France would undertake a major offensive on the Western front to give beleaguered Poland some relief, as per the signed treaties. If they really did hope this, that would explain why their mood was still far from despondent.

*

The Germany's Soviet ally did deliver as under the secret Ribbentrop-Molotov partition bargain.[285] Once the Nomonhan cease-fire with Japan in Russia's East came into effect on September 16, 1939, ending the conflict in Mongolia which had rumbled on since May and which had served the Japanese their first taste of military defeat in almost a decade, Stalin ordered his forces to invade Poland on the next day.[286]

By September 17 – scarcely more than a fortnight, it will be remembered, after the German invasion began – the Polish lines of first and second defence had already been broken through. The only remaining hope for the Polish army was if it could regroup and defend Poland's south-eastern region (the bridgehead to Romania, mentioned earlier), which, with its mountainous terrain, offered better chances of repelling the invaders than did the rest of the country. Yet this plan, too, came to naught when – in a blatant violation of the Riga Peace Treaty – a Soviet force of more than 800,000 men attacked Poland from the east.[287]

SEPTEMBER 17, 1939 – SOVIETS INVADE POLAND

(a photo from public domain)

The Polish troops along the eastern border were ordered to fall back, and not engage the Soviets.[288] All hopes of strong and protracted resistance on Poland's part, resistance which also presupposed an Allied onslaught against Germany from the west, had to be abandoned and could no longer be implemented.[289]

Still, the Polish government never even contemplated signing a surrender to Germany. Instead, through Marshal Śmigły-Rydz, it ordered all the Polish soldiers who had evaded capture to leave the country forthwith, and make their way to France, thence to continue their fight against Nazism.

Not all Polish soldiers obeyed this order. The Forty-First Infantry Division – Pilecki's Uhlans – suffered, on September 20, a crushing defeat at Khelm (*Chełm*). Initially, the members of the divisional cavalry followed the order to leave Poland for France. Very soon, they changed their minds. They decided not to leave their country, and turned their horses back.

Despite sustained and very heavy German attacks, Warsaw held out until September, 28. In a speech delivered shortly afterwards in Danzig, Hitler boasted: '*Poland never will rise again as was formed by the Versailles Treaty. That is guaranteed not only by Germany, but also ... Russia.*'[290]

By September 28, the Red Army had reached the line along the rivers Narew, Bug, Vistula, and San. There, it met the German units which were advancing from the opposite direction. On the Hel peninsula, some Polish defenders held out, but on October 2 even they had to concede defeat. Four days later, on October 6, the last operational unit of the entire Polish Army, General Franciszek Kleeberg's Independent Operational Group Polesie (its Polish name was *Samodzielna Grupa Operacyjna Polesie*, the group having only been formed on September 11) capitulated after the Battle of Kock (pronounced *Kotsk*), near Lublin, which had raged since October 2.[291]

*

On the day of Kleeberg's submission Hitler, in the Reichstag, offered peace to France and Britain, provided that both those countries recognised the Nazi-Soviet conquest of Poland and the subsequent partitioning of Polish territory. Neville Chamberlain, still British Prime Minister, in his October 12 House of Commons response rejected Hitler's offer.

This rejection meant that the conquest of Poland was not going to retain its proposed status of isolated conflict between Germany, supported by the Soviet Union, and Poland. So, Great Britain set about forming a broad anti-Germany coalition which would include the United States and the Soviet Union. Great Britain's preferred strategy was to defeat Germany by running a war of attrition against it.

*

Whether Witold Pilecki and his Uhlans knew of what Hitler and Chamberlain were saying in public at the time can be subject to doubt. One thing is certain: Pilecki's Uhlans intended to continue, for as long as possible, their defiant resistance to both German and Soviet aggressors. Carrying on the fight in a fashion that amounted to guerrilla warfare, they did enjoy some success.

Their anti-tank guns enabled them to destroy seven German tanks, and they also destroyed two Luftwaffe planes which had landed on a temporary airfield.[292] A number of uhlans from other decimated units join Pilecki's squadron as it moves north-west. They cross a large complex of forests near Lubartów (*Lubartov*). For a while, they are pursued by a motorized German unit, but manage to give them a slip. From a forest near the Wieprz (*Vyepsh*) River, they can on 6 October hear the dying sounds of the last battle of this campaign, the Battle of Kock.

But by October 17, they could no longer continue. That day, Pilecki finally dismissed his soldiers, and ordered his unit's officers to get through to Warsaw somehow. He had the intention of holding a meeting at the flat owned by Major Włodarkiewicz's mother. Before setting out, the officers changed into civilian clothes.

Pilecki, for his part, first thought of returning to Sukurcze.[293] But that would have meant having to cross the German-Soviet demarcation line. He sensibly concluded the associated risk was simply too great, so he jettisoned the idea. He left his horses in Treblinka, and continued afoot until he got to Ostrów Mazowiecka, where he spent nearly two weeks with his in-laws. However agreeable it was for him to see them again, it was frustrating for them all that there was no news from Sukurcze, or, for that matter, from Pilecki's wife.[294]

LET DOWN BY ITS ALLIES

Having suffered a heavy defeat at the hands of the two sworn Polish enemies in September 1939 Poland lost their independence after less than twenty-one years of enjoying it. This was a hard experience for the Poles. That this defeat was a result of Poland's two Western allies' failure to deliver on their military assistance obligations caused also a great deal of bitterness among Poles.

Over the ten years that he had known his Sukurcze neighbour Marshal Śmigły-Rydz, Witold Pilecki spent many hours with the Marshal, not only hunting, or painting (both of them were prolific, and talented, amateur painters), but also discussing Poland's strategic situation at that time. One can therefore safely assume that prior to September 1939 Pilecki had, among others, a good idea of the obligations and responsibilities France and Great Britain took upon themselves by signing their mutual military assistance pacts with Poland.

Prior to the commencement of the September campaign, Poles were led to believe that France and Great Britain will respect their obligations from the mutual assistance treaties according to which France has the obligation to commence an air war against Germany on the next day after Germany attacks Poland, launch a land offensive three days after that attack commenced and the full-scale land offensive - on the fifteenth day from the day Poland was attacked.[295]

Poland's two strategic allies never delivered on their obligations vis-à-vis Poland. The question is: had they ever intended to deliver on these?

THE GALLANT DEFENCE

In September 1939, one million Polish soldiers fought most valiantly in defence of their country. The Polish Army was able to inflict very heavy casualties on the aggressor.

By September 24, ten days before the end of that campaign, German internal sources mentioned 91,728 killed, 63,417 heavily wounded, and 34,938 German soldiers with lighter wounds[296]. In the entire campaign, the Luftwaffe lost at least 285 planes, not counting those damaged. The Wehrmacht lost nearly 1,000 tanks and armored transporters. Clearly, the German losses, despite their army's vast superiority in numbers of soldiers and in materiel, in particular – its air superiority, were very heavy.

Fighting the German Wehrmacht, about 64,000 Polish soldiers and 2,000 officers died (many times more Polish officers than that were killed by Stalin's order at Katyń in April 1940, whilst Soviet POW's). 134,000 Polish soldiers were wounded during that campaign and about 420,000 were placed into German camps as prisoners of war.[297]

Poland's defence plans relied on the relief from the allied forces. Had Poland obtained that relief timely, the Polish Army would certainly have avoided defeat in September 1939. On the other hand, from the German campaign communications of September 1939, since made public, one learns on the day the Polish campaign ended, the German tanks and airplanes had fuel reserves sufficient for just about one week of intense war activities.

Had it not been for the Soviet backstabbing of 17 September, the Polish Army would have certainly continued its defence for a longer period. It is likewise certain that with its airplanes grounded, and its tanks – immobilized, Germany would have been unable to secure a quick victory in this campaign.[298]

The Polish September campaign soldiers knew as early as in 1939 that the main reason they lost that campaign was that they have been let down by France and Great Britain. They refused to give up, though.

DEFEATED - YET UNYIELDING

Poland's government refused to surrender to either Hitler or Stalin and vowed to continue the struggle outside the country. Ignacy Mościcki resigned the presidential office near the end of September (he was to spend most of the war in Switzerland); a long-time senator, Władysław Raczkiewicz, became President-in-exile, of the Polish government-in-exile, the first Prime Minister of the Polish government-in-exile became General Władysław Sikorski who will later, on July 4, 1943, die in an air catastrophe at Gibraltar when returning from visiting Polish troops in the Middle East.[299]

At first, the Polish government-in-exile stayed in France. After May 1940, with France's defeat, it transferred itself to London. For the remainder of the conflict, thousands of Polish soldiers would serve in Britain, the Near East, Africa, Italy, and elsewhere.

All too many of the Polish troops became Soviet prisoners-of-war in September 1939. Those who were not killed at the outset – most notoriously through the massacres committed in and near Katyń Forest during April-May 1940 – were kept in labour camps, only to be freed in 1941 once Hitler had turned against his fellow dictator and unleashed Operation Barbarossa. Some of them, under the command of General Władysław Anders ('Anders Army', they were called), were permitted during early 1942 to escape to the west via Persia (where the pro-Nazi Shah had been deposed in favour of his pro-British son), Iraq, and British-controlled Palestine. Still other Polish troops remained under Soviet control and fought, perforce, alongside the Red Army.

From very early in the war, the government-in-exile had set up what became known as the Secret State: a permanent, highly structured resistance movement, at the apex of which was the *Delegatura Rządu Rzeczypospolitej Polskiej na Kraj* (Government Delegation for Poland). The head of this delegation was, for all practical purposes, Poland's Deputy Prime Minister.

At the very centre of the Secret State's rationale was the conviction that since the Nazi-Soviet occupation of Poland had violated every tenet of international law, loyal Polish patriots had a duty to perform all the functions which had been carried out by the pre-war Republic.[300] The largest of all Secret State's military formations was the Home Army: it would eventually have almost half a million members, and would become one of the very largest resistance movements anywhere in Europe.[301]

GOING UNDERGROUND

Having arrived at Warsaw in mid-October 1939, Major Włodarkiewicz since stayed with his mother at her villa in the capital's southern suburb of Mokotów. While there, he established contact with the following soldiers: Major Zygmunt Bohdanowski (a.k.a. "Bohdan", "Bończa"); Captain (Res.) Jerzy de Virion, an advocate; Lieutenant Eugeniusz Zaturski, from the Air Force; and Second Lieutenant Jerzy Maringe, likewise from the Air Force. Soon this group would be joined by Witold Pilecki, and by some of the cavalry officers from Pilecki's disbanded unit. Pilecki himself reached Warsaw on November 1, riding on his bicycle from Ostrów Mazowiecka. On his way to Warsaw he encountered an armed German, and had to shoot him.[302]

On November 9, Pilecki established, together with Major Włodarkiewicz, the Secret Polish Army (*Tajna Armia Polska*, or TAP for short): one of the first underground organisations in occupied Poland.[303] TAP provided much-needed military expertise and leadership to the Armed Confederation (*Konfederacja Zbrojna*, KZ), which was the military arm of the Confederation of the Nation (*Konfederacja Narodu*, KN). Importantly, TAP held aloof from all the various political parties' ideologies, although its national-Christian basis was unmistakable.

Pilecki himself assumed a false identity of Tomasz Serafiński, a reservist officer who, it was understood, had previously spent some time hiding in the flat of his acquaintance Helena Pawłowska, a physician. Pilecki chose to explain his lack of authentic identity and employment documents by him having left those documents at Ms Pawłowska's home. And so, pretending to be Serafiński, Pilecki submitted to the German authorities a photo purporting to be one of Serafiński. From the authorities he soon obtained other documents he needed, all these documents invariably bearing Serafiński's name, and not Pilecki's.

The foundation meeting of TAP was held on November 9 in Żolibórz, at al. Wojska Polskiego 40/7, in an apartment owned by Eleonora Ostrowska. Her husband, Lieutenant (Reserve) Edward Ostrowski, Pilecki's brother-in-law, had served in the Fifth Zaslav Uhlans Regiment.[304] At this time Ostrowski was absent from the family home: in fact, he was a German POW.

Those attending this meeting were Pilecki himself, Włodarkiewicz, Maringe, and three other men: Jerzy Skoczyński (pronounced *Skotchinsky*), Jan Dangel, and Stanisław Dangel.[305]

Jan Dangel, a Warsaw School of Economics student, was entrusted with the specific task of attracting young people to the organisation. TAP members without history of pre-war political activism included: Stefan Bielecki (pronounced *Byeletski*); Witold Maringe, who was an engineer by profession; Stanisław Maringe, Witold's nephew; and Captain (Res.) Dr. Władysław Dering, a renowned Warsaw gynaecologist. These four were to look for and encourage suitable candidates to become TAP members.

Dering, long afterwards, wrote memoirs which provide important information on the whole period. He wrote there:

> *'Major Włodarkiewicz was ordered to*
> *establish an underground military unit.*
> *He suggested I join the organisation, and*

> *appointed me its medical officer. I made my flat at 15 Mokotowska Stree, and all my funds, available to Włodarkiewicz, who, temporarily, moved in with me. Over the period of several months, my flat was the most convenient option for headquarters of our organisation, which was to be known as TAP [...]. Its Head became Major Włodarkiewicz; its Chief of Staff became Witold Pilecki. Since the Bolshevik war, I had been on friendly terms with both of them.*'[306]

On November 10, the TAP's founding members took a solemn oath in one of the chapels of the Warsaw Garrison Church, at 15 Długa Street. The oath was witnessed by a loyal priest, Father Jan Zieja. On the next day, the founders elected the members of the TAP's commanding body, and they also decided what the TAP's main activities should be. Jan Dangel was elected Włodarkiewicz's deputy. As mentioned before, Pilecki became the TAP's Chief of Staff.

By the end of 1939, the TAP had extended its reach until it covered not only Warsaw but other major cities of central Poland: including Siedlce, Radom, and Lublin. Shortly before Christmas, Pilecki sent a postcard to his sister Wanda – then residing in Vilnius – with a bland-seeming message that was really in code. Witold's words to Wanda were: '*Since I left you, I had to swap my horse four times, my saddle girth got tinged. Recently, we established a commercial partnership; your acquaintance W.S. got into it.*'[307] Wanda knew, 'W.S.' signified Lieutenant-Colonel Władysław Surmacki (pronounced *Soormatski*), husband of Zofia Szukiewicz, whose Krupa estate had a common border with the Sukurcze estate. When Witold wrote the postcard, Surmacki still lived in Warsaw, and he did so under his real name, which was risky.

Pilecki's initial focus in his TAP work was on the capital's western suburb of Wola (proncouned *Volah*). There, he rapidly formed three TAP platoons, which soon became a full company, one that managed to survive until the 1944 Warsaw Uprising. As well as that, Pilecki formed two further companies, this time not in Wola, but in the northern suburb of Żolibórz (pronounced *Zholiboozh*). Not content with that, yet, he then shifted his focus to other suburbs: Mokotów, Ochota, Śródmieście and Praga, the last of them being a suburb on the eastern bank of the Vistula River. In Praga, he set up the bases for two battalions.[308]

In May 1940 Pilecki's responsibilities changed. During that month, the aforementioned Władysław Surmacki took Pilecki's place as TAP Chief of Staff. Pilecki became the TAP's Chief Inspector, and as his assistants in this role he had Stefan Bielecki and Jan Dangel.

As Pilecki stressed in his memoirs, he always disregarded individuals' political views. What mattered to him was individuals' capacity and willingness to help Poland regain freedom.[309]

By this stage, Pilecki had acquired two more aliases: 'Witold' and 'A Chequered Fellow' (the Polish for which is *Pan w kratkę*).[310] He had to have a number of contact points. One of them was Eleonora Ostrowska's flat. During his visits there, he would often express without any hesitation his belief that the Germans would lose the war.

True to his principles, when in the underground movement, he never sought to acquire power in his own right over other people.[311] TAP's chief secretary at that time, Janina Dal Trozzo-Pieńkowska, wrote this about him later: *'Whatever he did, he did accurately, neatly; all was settled down to the smallest detail.'*[312]

Major Włodarkiewicz's pet occupation during 1940 was a political section within the TAP called *Znak*, which is the Polish word for 'sign'. He edited *Znak*'s regular bulletin. By June 1940, while very small in terms of formal membership numbers – no more than a few dozen people – *Znak* could count on several hundred outside sympathisers. At a food shop at Żelazna Street, which was owned by one Szczepan Rzeczkowski (pronounced *Shtshepan Zhechkovsky*), copies of the *Znak* bulletin were eagerly awaited and surreptitiously distributed from.[313]

So thoroughly absorbed did Pilecki become in his TAP duties, and so great was the potential for danger which these duties had, he could no longer afford the risk of living under the same roof with his wife and children. Maria Pilecka had to visit her sister in the latter's Żolibórz flat. Meetings between Maria and Witold would often take place there. Usually, she would bring the children with her to the flat; naturally, they missed their father very much.[314]

Not till those meetings did Witold find out the details about what his loved ones had undergone after the Soviet invasion. As it turned out, at first Maria and the children hid in a local farmer's hut. Whenever Soviet functionaries were seen approaching the hut to check on the whereabouts of its residents, Maria and the children would quickly hide themselves under a large pile of feather-and down-filled pillows and doonas which happened to be kept there. They had some hair-raising brushes with mortal peril. Once, a Russian soldier came up to the pile of pillows and doonas, and stabbed it several times with a bayonet. Luckily, he missed those who were hidden underneath.

To make matters worse, the winter of 1939-1940 was remarkably severe. So much snow fell, that Maria and her children had to walk along dug-out paths as if between white walls. Twice they tried to cross the Soviet-German demarcation line. At their first attempt, they discovered to their horror that the man who was to have smuggled them across the line was an unprincipled cheat. He took their money, and then abandoned them while they were still in the

Soviet zone. This forced them to go back, in the hope of acquiring a fresh sum of money which they would need to pay a new – and, they desperately hoped, more honest – smuggler.

First, they went to the home of Maria's sister, Wiktoria Rogowska, who lived in Volkovysk. She assisted them with the required finance. Unfortunately, they had no better luck at their second attempt to cross the line than they had had at their first, except that now, instead of being robbed, they were intercepted by Soviet troops.

As Maria was taken to a room in an army building for an interrogation, her children waited on the stairs inside that building. There, the Soviet soldiers proclaimed who was in charge. They kicked and manhandled the children so much that the panic-stricken Andrzej vomited. The whole family was compelled to stay with the Soviets for the entire night.

Next morning, the Soviets took from Maria all her valuables, all her money and rings, including her wedding ring. Luckily, the Soviets never discovered that Zofia had a sum of money sewn within her own clothes. She also kept on her person her baptismal picture, which depicted Our Lady of Ostra Brama. Perhaps some sort of divine intervention was involved, because when a female Soviet approached Zofia, wanting to body-search her, Zofia threw such a ferocious tantrum that the woman, astonished by such juvenile boldness, retreated.

Finally, mother and children were all released. At this stage Andrzej and Zofia, in particular, were ravenously hungry. Ever afterwards, they remembered the aroma of freshly baked bread which wafted towards them as they walked to the nearby railway station.[315]

Eventually, after negotiating tangles of barbed wire, the family managed to cross over to the German side of the line. After still more difficulties, they succeeded in reaching Maria's parents in Ostrów Mazowiecka.

This township was surrounded by a dense forest, where, it so happened, Polish guerrilla fighters were hiding. At night, they would launch attacks against Germans. Each time after they did so, the Germans would take revenge on the local Polish population, killing anyone whom they felt like killing, regardless of whether those victims had the slightest connection with the original attacks. The ever-present threat of Nazi aggression made walking to and from school a very scary experience for the children; the school was located well away from their home, on the opposite side of the township.[316]

*

By August 1940, the TAP had approximately 19,000 members. More than half of them were armed; their weapons included machine-guns and anti-tank rifles.[317] Later on, the organisation became incorporated into the *Związek Walki Zbrojnej* (a Polish phrase meaning 'Union of Armed Struggle'), which itself was subsequently renamed the Home Army.[318]

In a report prepared during early 1942 for the benefit of General Sikorski (still the exiled government's Prime Minister), the TAP's membership was assessed at that time to be approximately 12,000 thousand men. Within Warsaw alone, the TAP could count on over one hundred rifles and machine-guns, most of which had been provided by a friend of Włodarkiewicz from pre-war days. This friend was a guerrilla fighter from the Kielce (pronounced *Kyeltseh*) province, namely, Major Henryk Dobrzański (pronounced *Dobshansky*), who used the alias 'Hubal.'[319]

Not every member of the TAP had the relevant skill and aptitude for underground political and military work. And so some of the less experienced TAP members were arrested by the Germans in 1940. In May of that month, Jerzy de Virion – while attempting to reach France via Hungary – was apprehended by the Nazis in Slovakia (then a Nazi satellite state with the priest Joszef Tiso as its figurehead president). On August 30, de Virion was sent to the Auschwitz camp. It was to his family's benefit that the documents which he had on his person at the time of his arrest and imprisonment were in the false name of Jerzy Hlebowicz. Otherwise his loved ones would certainly have paid the penalty for their connection to him.

Somewhat earlier, on July 3 to be precise, Dr. Dering received an early-morning visit from Gestapo agents. The Gestapo now had its Warsaw headquarters at Aleja Szucha. After the questioning began, Dr. Dering realised that the Gestapo did not yet have any hard evidence of his clandestine activities, and that the Gestapo wrongly assumed membership on his part of another organisation: ZPN (short for *Związek Powstańców Narodowych* – the Association of National Insurgents), which he had never joined. By coincidence, another organisation in Poland had the very same initials: ZPN. This was a soccer association, *Związek Piłki Nożnej*, which Dr. Dering accurately and jokingly told the Gestapo interrogator he had likewise never joined. It was never a good idea to attempt humour with an angry Gestapo agent undeterred by qualms against physical violence. Dr. Dering's attempt at a joke cost him two of his front teeth.[320]

A month later, the Gestapo made another arrest: that of Surmacki. Both Surmacki and Dering, on August 15, were transferred to Auschwitz.[321]

In the meantime, Włodarkiewicz and Pilecki had come to differ in their views as to whether the TAP should be formally incorporated into the structures of the ZWZ (that is, the *Związek Walki Zbrojnej*[322], the Polish Underground State's main army). Włodarkiewicz believed that there were three reasons because of which TAP should keep itself independent from the ZWZ: first, because it was established before the ZWZ; second, because it was the larger of the two organisations; and third, because it had already established contacts on its own initative with the exiled Sikorski and his General Staff. Pilecki thought otherwise. He favoured a much closer relationship between the two armies than Włodarkiewicz thought desirable.

In the spring of 1940, Pilecki established formal contact with the ZWZ. Furthermore, he categorically opposed an idea which Włodarkiewicz advocated: that of the TAP issuing a formal ideological declaration of purpose. He was convinced that emphasising political divisions would have a totally detrimental influence on the entire Polish underground movement, and that any such emphases should be avoided. Possibly because of the differences between Pilecki and Włodarkiewicz on this issue, Włodarkiewicz ordered Pilecki to attend to TAP tasks that increasingly took him outside Warsaw.

A VOLUNTEER TO KL AUSCHWITZ

Following the arrests of Dering and Surmacki, a meeting of the TAP high command was called at the end of August 1940. At that meeting, Lieutenant-Colonel Tadeusz Kurcjusz (pronounced *Koortsyoosh*) was appointed the new TAP Chief of Staff. The suggestion was made during the meeting that Pilecki should enter the Auschwitz camp himself, to assess the chances of success for an attempt to liberate the captives; to establish a secret military organisation inside the camp; and to smuggle out descriptions of the crimes already being committed in the camp by the SS.[323]

When interrogated in 1947 in the lead-up to his trial, Pilecki had this to say about the matter:

> *'Let me explain: it was Major Jan Włodarkiewicz who suggested I do this. He revealed to me that when talking to the ZWZ Commanding Officer, General Rowecki (pronounced Rovetsky) (alias: 'Grot'), he mentioned my name as a person who would be prepared to get into any [German concentration] camp, and commence conspiratorial activities there.'*[324]

In early August 1940, Włodarkiewicz said this to Pilecki: *'Well, it is a great honour to you: you are known to Grot as the only officer who can pull it off.'*[325]

A big round-up occurred in the streets of Warsaw later in August 1940, and by this stage the TAP already knew from its own intelligence sources that those being rounded up by the SS on this occasion would be consigned to Auschwitz. Nevertheless, Pilecki did not let himself be captured at the time. Once the SS transport had left Warsaw, Włodarkiewicz made to Pilecki a notably acidic remark: *'Well, you have just wasted a very good opportunity to get into the camp in an "innocuous way." They would not have been able to make any case against you.'*[326]

We will probably never exactly learn how much Pilecki knew in August 1940 about conditions in Auschwitz. It should be noted, that at that stage KL Auschwitz (then called Auschwitz I) was a concentration camp of the sort all too familiar at that time in Nazi Germany itself. Still, it was not yet an extermination camp.

Auschwitz I had been set up in April 1940; in May of the same year the first mass intake of – mainly Polish – prisoners to KL Auschwitz took place (there had been a previous, far smaller, intake of non-Polish KL Sachsenhausen inmates).

The Wannsee Conference – which formally implemented the plan for the genocide in Nazi-occupied Europe – was not held till January 1942. Still, even as a concentration camp, Auschwitz I was already monstrous enough.

*

Seventy-eight years later, our knowledge about the Auschwitz camp is practically complete. Oświęcim, the Polish town next to which the camp was established was a town in the pre-war Poland's south-west, close to both the German border and the Czech border. This location was appealing to the Nazi bosses for three reasons.

First, Oświęcim had convenient railway network connections. Second, Oświęcim was a town in the part of Europe which had an exceptionally large proportion of Jews *vis-à-vis* the general populace. Third, there was a complex of pre-war Polish barracks available which made establishing a camp there a relatively fast exercise.

The existence of Nazi-controlled camps on Polish soil was also a critical terror measure in the Nazi devised plan. It was believed to be effective in bringing Poles into compliance with the occupant introduced laws.

Until early 1942, most of those who were brought to KL Auschwitz were Poles. Some of them had been involved in resistance activities. Others had broken – not always with intent – some capricious occupier-imposed law. Still others were individuals who had violated no written statute, but who just had the bad luck to be in the wrong place at the wrong time when a street round-up was being carried out by SS. Such round-ups, unpredictable in scale and timing, were among the Nazis' favourite methods of instilling fear into the general Polish population.

In October 1941, the construction of Auschwitz II, the Birkenau extermination camp commenced. As an Auschwitz I inmate, Pilecki witnessed some of the related activities, and also heard some inmate stories. The official reason for founding Birkenau was to ease the 'congestion' – the preferred Nazi euphemism – at Auschwitz I. Foundation of Birkenau increased the camp complex's total extermination capacity. The extended camp was able to house 200,000 inmates at any one time.[327]

Even before the construction of Auschwitz II commenced, large numbers of Auschwitz I inmates were already dying from starvation, overwork, and disease. Yet, as far as the SS was concerned, Auschwitz inmates were not dying fast enough. The Auschwitz SS and Gestapo were expected to meet a quota of dead inmates each month. So, whenever any such quota had not been achieved, they would carry out mass shootings, or would inject inmates with phenyl, or club them to death.

The increasing rates of extermination in Nazi camps after 1942 (not only at Auschwitz II) were a result of the war not going so well for the Nazis as they had previously assumed, it would. Even before their first Soviet front heavy defeats of late 1942/early 1943, Nazis realized they might have to countenance the defeat in this war. Hence, the dramatic increase in the speed of mass murder in Nazi extermination camps since that time.[328]

In March 1942, the first of the Auschwitz complex's crematoria (ultimately there would be five of them) became operational. Exactly a year later, a mortuary was turned into Crematorium II, having been fitted out with gas-tight doors, with vents that allowed for the cyanide-based pesticide Zyklon B to be dropped through the roof into the death-chamber, and a ventilation system which after such mass-killings removed the traces of gas from the inside.[329] Crematoria III, IV and V, all similar in design, were finished during the spring of 1943, and all were being used by June of that year. These crematoria accounted for most of the death toll of Auschwitz victims.[330]

It is believed that Auschwitz Jewish victims accounted for approximately one-sixth of the total Jewish population that perished in the Holocaust. Of every ten people who died at the Auschwitz camp complex, nine were Jews. The body count of Auschwitz would eventually reach no fewer than 1.1 million persons,[331] including around 150,000 non-Jewish Poles; 23,000 Romani and 15,000 Soviet prisoners-of-war.

The first 'trial' extermination of prisoners at Auschwitz took place in September 1941. It was witnessed, and reported, by Pilecki. His official report is provided later in this book.

A relatively small number of Auschwitz inmates were lucky enough to be released. Most of them were people employed by occupant's companies who were providing some supplies to the German army, and who were taken to Auschwitz only because of being in a wrong time and place, when a random street round-up was taking place. Their employers would normally need only a few weeks to get their employees released from the camp.

Not so many others, a total of 196, succeeded in escaping from this camp[332]. As it turned out, Pilecki was to be one of them.

*

It certainly was Pilecki's uncompromising concern for human dignity and freedom, his selflessness, fearlessness and compassion for the others that made him accept his superiors' request for him to volunteer to become an Auschwitz inmate.

In late August 1940, he decided he would let Germans arrest him in Warsaw's next street round-up[333]. To Stefan Bielecki, he previously had assigned all his TAP duties. TAP intelligence sources had briefed him about the occupying power's methods in its treatment of arrested and incarcerated Poles. What was left for him, was to wait.[334] Through Eleanora Ostrowska, he let his wife know of his decision to voluntarily go to Auschwitz.

To this day, Zofia believes her father did not know prior to his arrival at Auschwitz how brutal and horrible the place was. How, indeed, could he have known? She remains convinced he went there simply to help and unite all inmates in a common cause, regardless of their pre-war political affiliations. In Zofia's words: *'he lived to help others.'*[335]

AN AUSCHWITZ INMATE

In his plea for clemency he sent to the Polish President Bolesław Bierut eight years later, Pilecki described the circumstances in which he accepted his Auschwitz task, as follows:

> 'As soon as [ZWZ Commanding Officer] Colonel Rowecki had presented an authorisation by General Sikorski for [Rowecki] ... to merge [underground Polish military] units, I decided to try and persuade my commanding officer, Major Włodarkiewicz, to sacrifice his personal ambitions, and to subordinate himself to Grot [...]. Following the briefing by Grot, in which he presented arguments for the conspiratorial activities in the concentration camps to commence, considering also that Major Włodarkiewicz put me forward as a candidate [to go there], I decided to accept this task; I then received

> *an order, and got into the second Warsaw round-up on September 19, 1940. This was how I got to Auschwitz.'*[336]

Early on the morning of September 19, an SS planned and executed massive new round-up took place in Warsaw. The SS and other German military formations and police surrounded all residential buildings in various Warsaw suburbs, and apprehended all males who looked to be between the ages of eighteen and forty-five. They targeted areas of Warsaw known to them for their high numbers of the country's intelligentsia. Eleonora Ostrowska reported:

> *'...our janitor, Jan Kiliański, a loyal TAP soldier, came to me and let me know that we were surrounded by uniformed Germans who apprehend males and put them onto trucks [...] He offered Witold two ways of avoiding capture: one was to escape through the gardens at the rear of our block of flats since they were not cordoned off by Germans; the other was to hole up in the boiler room of our block's heating system, which was an often-used hide-out. To my amazement, Witold rejected both of his suggestions: he did not even try to hide himself anywhere in my flat.*
>
> *Soon, we heard an energetic knock on our door. I opened it. A German soldier asked*

> about people who lived there. I had not even
> had time to respond when Witold already
> exited his room. The soldier did not check
> his identity. Witold put his coat on and,
> bidding me farewell, whispered: 'Report,
> you know where, that I have carried out
> my orders.' He was then escorted out. Soon
> after, I heard trucks depart.[337]

All those apprehended in this round-up were taken to the military barracks of the First Józef Piłsudski Light Cavalry Regiment at Warsaw's Szwoleżerów Street. On the bare floor there, they spent two nights. After that, a registration began of all those who had been apprehended: 1,139 people in total. A further 566 people were taken from the Warsaw prison of Pawiak.[338] The building they were kept in was at all times surrounded by SS forces. From the roofs of the surrounding buildings one could see barrels of machine guns pointing down.

On September 21, all captives were taken to a railway station, where a train with goods carriages already awaited them. At the station, they were divided into three groups. Those in the first group were sent to East Prussia, to do forced labour there. Those in the second group were sent also to carry out forced labour, but in the western regions of Germany. Those in the third group, Pilecki among them, were bound for Auschwitz.

The ghastliness of the journey to Auschwitz was an indication of what they could expect once there. All the floors of the carriages were covered in lime. The carriages were permanently locked. There was, of course, no food or drink. Later, Pilecki provided his account of this railway trip: *'On the previous day, they gave us some bread. We refused to eat it for we had not learnt [yet] to value it. We were very thirsty. The carriages shook, causing the lime to* *break up into the dust which got suspended in the air; it irritated our noses and throats.'*³³⁹ During the night of September 21-22, the transport arrived at Auschwitz.

THE MAIN GATE OF THE AUSCHWITZ CAMP

(© The Auschwitz-Birkenau Memorial and Museum, all rights reserved)

On arrival, the prisoners were told to form columns. Then, they were ordered to march towards the camp's barracks. To humiliate them even more, they were beaten with all sorts of implements by SS men and by Auschwitz's own *Kapos*³⁴⁰, yelled and jeered at, and often frightened into obedience by having German shepherd dogs set upon them.

One of the prisoners was ordered, by an SS member, to run towards a pole that was away from the road. As he ran, the SS soldier fired on him with his machine-gun, and mowed him down. The SS pretended that the dead prisoner was 'attempting to escape.' Immediately ten other prisoners were shot by the SS, as 'accessories' to the 'escape attempt.'

This behaviour of Auschwitz guards and everything else he found out about Auschwitz in his first hours there seemed to Pilecki something unreal, not to mention grotesque. It was all a far cry from anything he had so far encountered in his life. He likened it to an insane asylum, but an insane asylum where anything went, and where those inside needed always to expect the very worst.[341]

AT AUSCHWITZ[342]

Pilecki got registered at Auschwitz under his false name of Tomasz Serafiński. He received the inmate number of 4859.[343] To the camp authorities, he gave his occupation as a tanner. It was necessary for him to do so (although he had never done any tanning whatever) because very often an inmate who incautiously gave his true occupation, especially if it was an occupation held in contempt by the Nazis – that of judge or priest, for instance – would be killed on the spot.

Very soon Pilecki learned how ruthless, swift and brutal was the punishment at Auschwitz of those who would not follow orders, even orders of the most minor type. Like all the other inmates, at the registration he was told to carry his number tag in his mouth. Instead, he kept it in his hand. When the guards discovered this disobedience, one of them struck Pilecki on the head with a rod. The impact knocked out two of his teeth.

THE AUSCHWITZ MUG PHOTOS OF WITOLD PILECKI (1940)

(© The Auschwitz-Birkenau Memorial and Museum, all rights reserved)

In their first hours at the camp, all inmates were told that they were Polish bandits brought to Auschwitz because they had assaulted Germans (which was a false claim), and that they would not leave the place alive (this one, it turned out, was more likely to be an accurate prediction). Other Poles known to Pilecki who arrived in the same transport as he were: Antoni Kocjan (pronounced *Kotsyan*)[344] and Władysław Bartoszewski (pronounced *Bartoshevsky*).[345] Years later, Bartoszewski would admit: *'They sought to break us down, to dehumanise us. They succeeded. We became fearful.'*[346] Readers of this book will soon find out that Bartoszewski could not have spoken for Pilecki.

Pilecki's first Auschwitz job was an indoor one, of a cleaner in Block 17a, then he did the same role in Block 25. The Head of the latter Block (his official German title was *Blockführer*) was a German inmate: Alois Staller, a communist, who took pride in his alias of 'Bloodthirsty Alojz.' Since Staller expected inmates to treat each other as cruelly as he treated them, and since Pilecki refused to conform to this expectation, Pilecki did not last long in the role.

Pilecki appreciated that at Auschwitz one needed to be vigilant always. In his own words:

> '... it was your muscles, your shrewdness, and your eyes that helped you survive. You had to have the strength to push your wheelbarrow, you needed to keep it on the board [as you push it], you needed to be able to see and choose the right moment to stop it, to let your tired lungs catch breath. [...] All those who could not work, or did not have any strength left to run with a wheelbarrow, were beaten. If they fell, they were finished off with a rod, and kicked to death.'[347]

Before Pilecki could start setting up what he had envisaged, namely - the secret *Związek Organizacji Wojskowej* or ZOW (the name meant Military Organisation Association), he needed to track down all his arrested TAP colleagues. The first one of them whom he encountered was Władysław Dering. Pilecki found him in the camp hospital for inmates (*Häftlingskrankenbau*), as he was recovering from a serious illness there.

Soon, Dr. Dering had improved sufficiently to be employed on nursing duties.[348] The camp's Head Medical Officer, Dr. Max Popiersch, assigned to Dr. Dering the role of establishing an outpatients' department.

Patients would often be sent to the hospital after a work accident, or when worn out by physical labour which was simply beyond their strength, or after they had been beaten, or when they were even more seriously undernourished than the rest. Very few medications were available in the hospital: seriously ill patients were frequently given instead lethal injections.

As Pilecki was setting up the ZOW, the tasks he would assign to the members of his secret organisation were: keeping up inmates' spirits, disseminating information obtained from sources outside the camp, procuring and distributing additional food and clothes from sources inside and outside the camp, delivering camp information through secret couriers to outside recipients, and building up the military capacity of their organization. The latter was done to make it possible for their organization to be able to control the camp for a few precious moments in the event of an assault on the camp undertaken by Polish underground army units. What Pilecki had in mind was for such assault to be synchronised with an operation involving distribution of weapons and dropping of allied forces paratroopers in the immediate vicinity of the camp.[349]

The organisational structure that Pilecki chose was designed in such a way as to minimise the chances for the Nazis to find out about the ZOW's existence or its scope. It was a decentralised structure, so that even if it got exposed, only a small number of its members would be affected by that outcome.

The typical ZOW basic unit was a cell made up of five – sometimes of six – members only. Such individuals would be referred to as Upper Five. They were aware that Pilecki (or, as they thought of him, Tomasz Serafiński) was the ZOW's head; but other than that, they did not know – and they were not meant to know – about any other ZOW member who was not in the same cell. Consequently, they had no idea of the ZOW's true extent, or the number of persons whom it involved. The less information they had, the less they were in danger of revealing it if captured.

The first Upper Five was made up of Dr. Dering, Lieutenant-Colonel Władysław Surmacki, Captain (Res.) Jerzy de Virion (known in the camp, it will be remembered, by his false name of Jerzy Hlebowicz), and two other men: Eugeniusz Obojski and

Roman Zagner. Surmacki was the cell's head. Before the war, he had been a surveying engineer by profession, At Auschwitz, he was employed by the camp's internal *Baubüro* (the SS's construction office) to help carry out land surveys both inside, and outside the camp.

Surmacki's role at Auschwitz was crucial for the ZOW, as surveyors had the precious privilege of being allowed to leave, sometimes, the camp proper (albeit under SS escort, to ensure that they would not attempt to flee). This privilege made it possible for the surveyors to establish direct contacts – as no other prisoners could hope to be able to – with local population and underground organisations. Thus, they could not merely receive messages from (and send messages to) individuals outside the camp, but could also obtain medications, food, and clothes. The names of two local women, whose related help was most valuable for the ZOW at that time, need to be mentioned here: Wincencja Stolarska and Helena Stupka.[350]

What, though, of Pilecki himself?

During his first weeks at Auschwitz, Pilecki worked under the authority of Captain Michał Romanowicz, as part of a group of twenty inmates who were made responsible for the demolition of local houses considered by camp authorities to be too close to the camp's perimeter. These houses had earlier been vacated by their Polish occupants.

Pilecki was carrying out his job well. While working with this group, he sent out the first of his secret messages about the appalling conditions of sickness, hunger, forced labour, and murderous punishment at Auschwitz.

Pilecki sent his early report through a fellow Polish captive, Aleksander Wielopolski, who was released from the camp in October 1940. Wielopolski made sure this report reached the ZWZ Commander-in-Chief, General Rowecki. For his part, Rowecki ordered the message to be sent on to 'Anna'[351] in Stockholm. From Stockholm, it reached London, and General Sikorski's cabinet-in-exile, on March 18, 1941.[352] The exiled Polish leaders made the message immediately available to governments all over the world: including not only those of Allied countries, but also that of neutral America.[353]

Exceptionally cold weather marked the autumn of 1940 in eastern Europe. The inmates at Auschwitz had to wear clogs, and were allowed neither caps nor socks. Because of the cold and the very primitive tools that they had been given, the inmates found the demolition work extremely hard to carry out.

For Pilecki it was essential that he remain in as good a state of health as the camp's hideous conditions would permit, if he was to retain his capacity to carry out his ZOW duties properly. Were he to collapse from simple exhaustion (as he could easily have done), the whole survival of the ZOW would have been imperilled. He therefore sought to obtain a job which would keep him indoors for most of the time and would involve less back-breakingly demanding physical activity.

Fortunately, he succeeded in obtaining such a post. Captain Ferdynand Trojnicki, a TAP member who had arrived in Auschwitz via the same transport which brought Pilecki there, was able to find for Pilecki a workplace in the camp's joinery. He started there on December 8. Although he had no experience in that line of work, another Polish captive – Corporal Czesław Wąsowski – helped him acquire the skills he needed to do his tasks to the satisfaction of his superiors.

Pilecki could not, alas, avoid all the diseases that raged through the camp. Shortly after beginning at the joinery he came down with a severe case of the flu, which gave him a dangerously high fever. He was moved to the hospital in Block 15, and there spent several days. The hospital was as poorly equipped as one might expect. Most of the patients there were already fatally ill, and often emaciated. The best they could hope for was the chance (which so many others at Auschwitz were denied) to die in bed, with a semblance of human dignity and decency.

Exacerbating the horror of Pilecki's situation was the hospital's infestation with lice. So many lice, indeed, that Pilecki - as soon as his temperature dropped a bit - sent a message to Dr. Dering, pleading with him to arrange a transfer elsewhere. He feared that if he stayed where he was for much longer, he would be further afflicted with typhoid fever, and would – as he graphically put it – *'soon leave the camp through the crematorium's chimney'*.[354]

Dr. Dering, shocked by this news, promptly arranged Pilecki's transfer to a somewhat better equipped, and less filthy hospital in Block 20. Pilecki spent ten days there, and at the end of the ten days made a remarkably comprehensive recovery.

His captors were not to be denied the exercise of their malice, though. On February 1, 1941, they sent him back to the previous hospital. This time he was there for more than a month. Even though he had no medical training he did have prodigious compassion, so he tried his best to help nurse the most desperately ill patients there.

Amid all this misery Pilecki wrote letters to his family as often as he could. Because he had to continue using his false identity, his letters followed a circuitous route: from Eleonora Ostrowska they went to their intended recipients.

His children were treated there with a great deal of tenderness. At times, he would include in his missives to them some drawings. Zofia has retained a particular fondness for a drawing which showed two little genies on a swing. Andrzej, for his part, received a drawing of a fret-saw, of the type that his father recommended there for him to use when working on his model ships and model planes. Pilecki paid a great deal of attention to teaching his children, both by his words and by his example, how one may live an upright and dignified life, even in the most appalling captivity.[355]

On February 11, 1941, Pilecki managed to pass on a secret message through another ZOW member: Tadeusz Burski, who on that very day was to be released from the camp.[356] Previously, Eleonora Ostrowska had received from Pilecki only one of the letters that he sent via the camp's post office. It was as well for her that the camp authorities had no clue about her familial relationship to Pilecki. To them, she was just an acquaintance of Pilecki's in Warsaw.

The personal file on Pilecki – which of course was in the name of Tomasz Serafiński – described him as a bachelor whose mother lived in (by this time Soviet-occupied) Vilnius. It contained nothing about a wife, child, or sister-in-law. Nonetheless, Pilecki had a justified concern that if he wrote anything which would give clues as to his identity, Eleonora would likely be arrested. For that reason, even though every Auschwitz inmate was permitted - indeed expected – to send at least one letter per fortnight, Pilecki chose to make his letters to Eleonora more intermittent.

After a while, Pilecki's very prudence on this subject attracted the camp authorities' hostile attention. On March 7, 1941, he was called to an interview. His interrogators demanded an explanation as to why his correspondence with Eleonora had not been more regular. Luckily for him, he had prepared himself for such a contingency. He could show his questioners several unsent letters of his, all of them addressed to Eleonora, all of them containing the recommended German phrase: *'Ich bin gesund, und es geht mir gut'* (the English for which is 'I am well and all is fine with me'). Each one of them had affixed to it a note from the camp's censors, prohibiting the despatch of the letter.

What the authorities did not discern was that the censor's note in each one of these cases had been forged. How could Pilecki have forged these censors' notes so truly? Well, he had obtained several envelopes from the camp post office. From those he was able to see for himself the manner in which censors would indicate that some letters were to be returned to their senders, rather than to be sent on to their intended recipients. So, all that he needed to do was forge the required censorship mark, using the same type of green pencil which the censors themselves had used.[357]

At the end of this interview, Pilecki was told to apply to the camp's commanding officer – in German, the *Lagerkommandant*

– who would grant him the requisite permission to write to his 'acquaintance', rather than to his mother. Naturally, he conformed with this demand.

On the very same day, Pilecki needed to move back to Block 3A where he was accommodated prior to his hospitalisation. Meanwhile, he found another suitable indoor job, this time in a large joinery shop in the so-called *Industriehof* 1 (Industrial Area 1 of the camp). Another Polish inmate, Corporal Czesław Wąsowski, recommended Pilecki to the man in charge of that shop, *Oberkapo* Artur Balke (inmate No. 3). Balke took Pilecki on.[358]

Balke was one of Auschwitz's original Sachsenhausen inmate intake. He arrived at Auschwitz on May 20, 1940. Like all others in his transport, Balke wore a green triangle, which signified he was a convicted criminal. Unlike most of the others in his transport, who thought nothing of torturing and otherwise tormenting the inmates in their power, Balke – along with a few of his fellow inmates in that transport - namely Otto Küsel (No.2), Fritz Biessgen (No.4, alias *Mateczka* [literally, 'Mummy']), Hans Bock (No.5), and Jonny Lechenich (No.19) – treated inmates relatively decently.

Balke's reputation had been common knowledge among the inmates. It was why a member of the ZOW would usually approach Balke whenever an indoor job was needed for anyone. Others received similar approaches. For example, if someone was especially weak in physical terms and no longer capable of the heaviest industry, members of the ZOW would sound out Otto Küsel in the hope that the prisoner in question could be assigned a lighter form of work. ZOW members would bring to the attention of Fritz Biessgen any particularly emaciated prisoner who would benefit from a bit more soup. Hans Bock had the specific task of facilitating extra care at the hospital. As for Jonny Lechenich – who oversaw the *Landwirtschaft*, the camp's farm – he could be relied upon to turn a blind eye whenever a ZOW member needed to contact a member of the local Polish underground organisation on the outside.

OBERKAPO ARTUR BALKE – INMATE NO. 3

(© The Auschwitz-Birkenau Memorial and Museum, all rights reserved)

There is no evidence these men had the slightest suspicion of how the ZOW was operating, or for that matter, one that the ZOW existed. It was their compassion towards fellow inmates that motivated them.

FRITZ BIESSGEN (*MATECZKA*), INMATE NO.4

(© The Auschwitz-Birkenau Memorial and Museum, all rights reserved)

Inmates who could count on tolerance from their *Oberkapo* had access to the most precious of Auschwitz commodities: hope.

The mortality rate among prisoners was so high, mainly because of hunger and slave labour, that even those who could withstand torture and physical disease were prone to the blackest despair. With remaining hope, and a sense of human dignity, they were more likely to endure, even if food was in dreadfully short supply and even if officials were dreadfully sadistic towards them. Pilecki understood this very well.

The task of defending human dignity at Auschwitz was a mammoth one. Yet, Witold Pilecki was indefatigable. Arguably, this task carried the highest priority for him when at Auschwitz. It would be impossible to tell how many victories in this struggle he had achieved. But there must have been very many of them. However implausible this may sound to some of those who read these words, Auschwitz without Witold Pilecki would have been a much tougher place to many of its inmates. Without him, it would have been a place where very few inmates would have retained their hope.

In his early twenties, as a Secretary to one of Vilnius Court's Investigating Magistrates, Pilecki had abundant opportunity to observe the extent of degeneration with people from the Vilnius demi-monde. Being present at their interrogations, he did not seem to be able to take it in how some of them were prepared to freely forsake their human dignity. How pale must have their vices looked like, compared to what he was able to later witness at Auschwitz. Yet, rather than overwhelm him, or make him despondent, what he experienced at Auschwitz urged him to match his efforts to do good with the needs of inmates there.

As we go through his Auschwitz confessions, most of which are contained in his *Report W*, we find that there were many moments in the camp when Pilecki thought Auschwitz was offering him, for all the unspeakable horror of that place, a heaven-like experience.

A confession like this must leave anyone dumbfounded for a while: how could an Auschwitz inmate possibly feel like that?

A key to this most startling confession is offered by one of his post-war writings. The following ones are words which help us answer the above question: *'There were so many, who only when facing their death were finally able to realise that they never gave anything [of real value] to anyone, (...) that only when leaving this earth they leave a vacuum behind themselves, that their heart which is about to turn into a lump of a matter has in fact always been a dead unfeeling lump.'*[359].

Well. Witold Pilecki's heaven on earth was simply giving to others in abundance, regardless of the person, place, or circumstances.

In the entire history of mankind, there probably were very few places where the opportunity to give to those in dire and extreme need would have been equal to that at the German Auschwitz extermination camp. Confronted with the immensity of suffering in Auschwitz, Pilecki wasted not a minute. And he gave in abundance. For his was a true compassion, a compassion with all human beings who suffered at that horrible place.

*

> *A man is raised up from the earth by two*
> *wings—simplicity and purity.*
> *There must be simplicity in his intention,*
> *and purity in his desires.*
> *Simplicity leads to God, purity embraces*
> *and enjoys Him.*[360]
>
> Thomas à Kempis, *The Imitation of Christ*

*

Pilecki understood he needed to retain what physical strength he still had, if he was to be able to continue helping others, as much as he desired, and much as they needed this help as Auschwitz inmates. He could keep up his strength only if his camp role was not beyond his muscular capacity to carry out; if he did his best to avoid disease; and if he consumed whatever food was available, even when he felt no appetite.

In March 1941, Pilecki founded the ZOW's second Upper Five cell. The members were: Platoon Leader Bolesław Kupiec (Inmate No. 792); two of his brothers, Platoon Leader Władysław Kupiec (Inmate No.793) and Jan Kupiec (Inmate No. 795); Witold Szymkowiak (No. 938); Officer Cadet Antoni Rosa (No. 923); Tadeusz Słowiaczek (No. 1069); pugilist Tadeusz Pietrzykowski (alias 'Teddy', No. 77); Second Lieutenant (Res.) Mikołaj Skornowicz (No. 940); and, most likely, also Sergeant Antoni Woźniak (No. 5512).

Upper Five cells were so crucial to the survival of the ZOW that only persons who had Pilecki's full trust were members of them. So, the relevant membership numbers were never great.

Moreover, between the formation of each cell and the next, a substantial period would elapse. In his *Report W*, Pilecki would so explain the related arrangements: '*None of those Fives knew about any other; indeed, each one of them assumed it was the pinnacle of our organisation, it would grow its numbers independently, branching out as far as energy and capacities of its members allowed.*'

Initially, Pilecki carried the restrictions on ZOW membership still further. He allowed nobody to join the ZOW who was a high-ranking officer, or whose authentic personal details were already known to the Auschwitz authorities. As early as April 1941, he learned about a very naïve escape plan which had been developed by two inmates (both of whom were senior Polish army officers), and which was thwarted. He decided not to involve its authors in any ZOW activities for quite some time.[361]

Also in April 1941, more transports arrived at Auschwitz. One of them, which reached the camp on April 6, contained 1021 inmates from Warsaw's Pawiak prison. Some of these people Pilecki already knew from his TAP activity. Another transport that reached Auschwitz the very same day brought 1249 inmates from the Lublin Castle prison.

CHILDREN ARRIVING AT AUSCHWITZ

(© The Auschwitz-Birkenau Memorial and Museum, all rights reserved)

MALE ARRIVALS AT AUSCHWITZ

(© The Auschwitz-Birkenau Memorial and Museum, all rights reserved)

AUSCHWITZ INMATES WORKING ON DEEP EXCAVATIONS

(© The Auschwitz-Birkenau Memorial and Museum, all rights reserved)

THE KRANKENMANN VEHICLE OF TORTURE

(© The Auschwitz-Birkenau Memorial and Museum, all rights reserved)

On May 29, yet another transport arrived: it brought 304 Pawiak prisoners. Among them was one of Pilecki's own nephews, Kazimierz Radwański (No. 16778). The unfortunate youth, a mere sixteen years of age, was arrested by the occupation forces in Ostrów Mazowiecka, where he lived. Along with several of his fellow school students (all of whom were, like him, also scouts), he was sent to Auschwitz for the "crime" of singing, in public, Polish patriotic songs.

Some of the other new arrivals were people well known to him, people whom he valued very highly. One was Stefan Bielecki, his TAP deputy from Warsaw. Another was Lieutenant Włodzimierz Makaliński, a commissioned officer from the 13th Uhlans Regiment. Owing to these new intakes, Pilecki could form a third Upper Five cell. This cell was made up of Makaliński; Stanisław Stawiszyński; Captain Eugeniusz Triebling (No. 6955)[362]; Lieutenant (Res.) Stanisław Gutkiewicz (No. 11003); and Wincenty Gawron (No. 11237). Gawron was so close to Pilecki he actually shared with him for a while the latter's straw mattress. Once the curfew had sounded, Gawron would tell Pilecki various tales of his ancestors, who had belonged to the Lithuanian nobility and who, like Pilecki's grandfather, had fought for Poland's independence.[363]

Also in May, Pilecki sent, through his clandestine channels, two letters to family members in Ostrów Mazowiecka. In them, he specifically asked that no attempt be made to seek his release from Auschwitz in exchange for money. He requested this because he knew that some inmates had indeed been released from Auschwitz through such an arrangement.

Determined to complete his Auschwitz underground mission, he wanted to stick it out, and to deliver whatever good results he could attain. Were he to be freed early from Auschwitz, continuation of his mission would simply be impossible.

Mindful that the censors would be reading every word he wrote, he concealed in missives everything he knew about the miseries of his surroundings. He blandly described in his letters the conditions in the camp as fine. Both of those letters were later on forwarded by his family to the ZWZ's High Command in Warsaw.[364]

In the following October, Pilecki formed his fourth Upper Five cell. This one comprised the following men: Second Lieutenant (Res.) Henryk Bartosiewicz (No. 9406); Captain Stanisław Kazuba (No. 1630); Second Lieutenant Konstanty Piekarski (No. 4618); Stefan Bielecki; and Lieutenant (Res.) Tadeusz Lech (No. 9235).[365]

During November 1941, Pilecki was given a new role. This time, it was in the camp's casting and sculpting shop. His new surroundings made it possible for him to form yet another Upper Five cell: the fifth, and as it turned out, the last. It was made up of: Second Lieutenant (Res.) Bernard Świerczyna (No. 1393); Officer Cadet (Res.) Zbigniew Ruszczyński (No. 1360); Officer Cadet (Res.) Mieczysław Wagner (No. 5831); Officer Cadet (Res.) Zbigniew Różak (No. 6609); and Platoon Leader Tadeusz Szydlik (No. 2198).

On November 11 – Poland's Independence Day – Pilecki's ongoing self-sacrifices in his service for his country, and the remarkable achievements of his underground activity to date, were formally recognised. The ZWZ Commander-in-Chief promoted Pilecki to the rank of Lieutenant.

Sadly, the very same day, November 11, 1941 would be memorable to Pilecki for another, very sad, reason: it was the day of Auschwitz's first mass execution. At the Wall of Death (Block 11), no fewer than 151 inmates were gunned down by *Rapportführer* Gerhardt Palitzsch.[366] Palitzsch later bragged of having personally killed 25,000 Auschwitz inmates by a shot to the back of head (German: *Genickschuss*). Combining his zeal for mass murders with extreme greed, he would eventually be expelled from the SS as a penalty for his thieving and – worse still in Nazis' eyes – for having sex with non-Aryans.

SS-RAPPORTFÜHRER GERHARDT PALITZSCH

(© The Auschwitz-Birkenau Memorial and Museum, all rights reserved)

THE AUSCHWITZ WALL OF DEATH

(© The Auschwitz-Birkenau Memorial and Museum, all rights reserved)

Almost all Palitzsch's victims on that day were Poles. One of them was Tadeusz Lech, a Jagiellonian University student, a member of the fourth Upper Five. Lech's unflinching composure on the day was astounding. Proud, he will perish on the Independence Day, he told Pilecki: '*I am so happy to meet my death today.*'[367]

Lech was not the only one: Pilecki greatly admired some others who died in Auschwitz during the second half of 1941. Dr. Jan Hrebenda (No. 3665), Officer Cadet (Res.) Remigiusz Niewiarowski (No. 13957), Captain (Res.) Jerzy de Virion, and Professor Teofil Witold Staniszkis (No. 18624). They all perished of either hunger, or illness.[368]

In October 1941, Pilecki was moved to Block 25. There, he came to know Henryk Bartosiewicz, a member of his fourth Upper Five, more closely than he had previously done. It was from Bartosiewicz that Pilecki learned about an initiative by Lieutenant-Colonel Kazimierz Rawicz – another Auschwitz prisoner – which very much resembled Pilecki's own.

Rawicz, whose true identity and military past remained uknown to the camp's bosses (they knew him under his alias of Jan Hilkner, No. 9,319, and wrongly thought that before his incarceration he had been a civilian), had been forming in Auschwitz yet another underground movement, one which had links to the ZWZ.

Pilecki thought this duplication undesirable and decided for it to be eliminated. Later in October, he handed over to Rawicz the formal command of his own network; Rawicz was, after all, of higher military rank than Pilecki himself.[369] Notwithstanding this change, Pilecki remained very actively involved in the movement he founded, and retained his responsibility for all ZOW's operational matters.

Because of the very way that the ZOW was set up, Pilecki personally knew only very few members of the Lower Five cells in Auschwitz's ZOW structures. Nevertheless, he was kept well apprised of what was being achieved by those who worked in the construction and surveying groups.

In November and December 1941, Pilecki passed on to Warsaw two further secret messages, one of them through Captain Trojnicki, and the other - through Lieutenant-Colonel Surmacki. Both of them were released from Auschwitz.[370]

Surmacki was probably unable to deliver his message to its intended recipients, as, after his arrival in Warsaw, he was arrested by Germans. Straight away, they took him to the Pawiak prison, and there they kept him until, in the summer of 1942, a mass execution was carried out. He was one of its victims.

At the very end of 1941, Pilecki learned that Colonel Jan Karcz (formerly in command of the Mazowiecka Cavalry Brigade) had arrived in Auschwitz. Very soon, he decided to involve Karcz in the activities of ZOW. A year ago, Karcz's high military rank would have made him ineligible to join ZOW. At this point in time, however, Pilecki no longer considered it essential to reject senior officers for ZOW membership. On the contrary, he was more and more convinced that a political body composed of senior officers and former party activists needed to be formed if the ZOW was to mature fully as an organisation.

Besides, some of Pilecki's Auschwitz acquaintances would assure him that involving senior officers in ZOW activities would help quash anti-Pilecki rumours that were being spread by some inmates. According to these rumours, Pilecki had avoided involving senior officers due to his inflated ambition, him wanting to retain full control of the entire movement.[371]

In fact, a spirit of unity and comradery was very much alive within the ZOW's ranks, and this delighted Pilecki. He would afterwards insist:

> *'Only when in Auschwitz did I achieve in*
> *my work what I could only dream in vain*
> *about when free. Only when faced by heaps*
> *of dead bodies, did our politicians stop*
> *wasting their energy on mutual bickering,*
> *which had always been so detestable to*
> *me. In our organisation's political cell,*
> *all worked together peaceably, and in an*
> *exemplary fashion.'*[372]

The organisation's new Political Committee had members from all major Polish pre-war parties. This Committee was formed during a very simple 1941 Christmas Eve celebration. Profesor Roman Rybarski, a pre-war activist of the *Stronnictwo Narodowe* (National Party, or SN), became the committee's chairman. Its deputy chairman was Stanisław Dubois, who before the war had been an eminent member of the *Polska Partia Socjalistyczna* (Polish Socialist Party), in brief - PPS. Others on the committee included Jan Mosdorf (No. 8230), co-founder of the *Obóz Narodowo-Radykalny* (National-Radical group, or ONR); Rawicz; and Pilecki himself.[373]

Early in 1942, Pilecki formed more ZOW cells. They included Colonel Aleksander Stawarz (No. 11513), Lieutenant-Colonel Karol Kumuniecki (No. 8361), and Captain Włodzimierz Koliński (No. 3135). In or around March 1942 – the precise date is not certain – the ZOW called into being Colonels' Council, whose prerogative it was to determine the date on which an uprising by inmates would commence, if one were to be called. Soon afterwards, Stawarz got executed, and this prerogative was transferred to the Political Committee instead.[374]

Of all his years at Auschwitz, 1942 was the one in which the ZOW achieved its greatest successes. An important part of these successes was owed to two ZOW members: Dr. Rudolf Diem (No. 10022), and to the seemingly indefatigable Dr. Dering. Both of them worked tirelessly at the outpatients' department of the hospital. They made a great many of the decisions as to whom the hospital would admit as patients. Apart from bringing their medical skills to the aid of sick inmates, they helped numerous prisoners who were in severe trouble with the camp authorities to survive as "patients" at the hospital. In so doing, they saved many lives; they also helped the ZOW remain undetected by the camp authorities and improved ZOW members' morale.

Owing to the ZOW's astuteness and persistent efforts, the anti-typhoid vaccine kept on being smuggled in. The vaccine was delivered to the camp's perimeter by various underground groups outside the camp. Some ZOW members managed to purloin medications which had been stored in the Birkenau warehouses after confiscating them from newly arrived inmates.[375]

Specific mention needs to be made here of two ZOW members, named Witold Kosztowny (No. 672) and Marian Toliński (No. 49). Both men produced several dozen litres of injection fluids, having used glucose and calcium chloride that had been secretly delivered to the camp's borders. Their efforts saved the lives of a great many prisoners who would otherwise have been killed by disease.[376]

Some inmates worked in the outpatients' department of the SS hospital. Superior-quality meals assigned to sick SS-men would often be intercepted by ZOW operatives at the SS kitchen, and requisitioned to inmates who were actually weak with hunger. The ZOW was even able to persuade the Chief Nurse at the outpatients' department of the SS hospital – an Austrian woman by the name Maria Stromberger – to help supply, to the benefit of sick inmates, some of the food and medicine that had been allocated for SS personnel.[377]

Early in 1943, those in charge of the camp finally gave permission for food parcels and other items to be supplied to Auschwitz inmates from outside. The ZOW promptly took advantage of this new ruling. Many a time, the name of a dead inmate would be provided to Polish resistance workers outside Auschwitz, so that they could send to the camp packets that were addressed to the dead prisoner. Usually the packets would contain medicines and bandages. They would be seized by ZOW members labouring in the parcel division of the camp's post office (the German word for this division was *Packetstelle*), and then the items would be delivered to the inmates' hospital.

Those who worked in the *Packetstelle* included, for a few months, Pilecki himself. Each time a food parcel came, bearing the address of a recently dead inmate, Pilecki would readdress the parcel to a living inmate. Before it was taken to where the inmate was kept,

Pilecki (or some other ZOW member) would advise the inmate of the parcel's imminent arrival, so that the planned beneficiary would not be tempted to greet its arrival with surprise, and thereby make the camp's bosses suspect that some conspiracy was involved.[378]

Those in the ZOW often had to exercise a macabre efficiency when it came to dealing with hospital patients' deaths. By such means, they could gain extra food for those inmates who most needed it. How was that possible? The bodies of the dead were taken to the crematorium the evening of the day that they had died. If ZOW members delayed by several hours the reporting of a patient's demise, it would often be possible for the living patients to get extra meals that had been originally intended for the dead patient.[379]

Some other stratagems were also relied on at the hospital. One particularly common one was to discharge a patient, and then (with great discretion) tell him to report again at the hospital the following day. In the meantime, his existing patient card would be destroyed, so that he would have to be admitted as if he were a new patient.

Now and then, a number of Auschwitz inmates were moved to another camp. Inmates sometimes feared that the other camp would be still worse than Auschwitz itself. In such cases, a member of the ZOW would inject a willing inmate with a protein solution, which would cause him to experience a high fever lasting several days, but which would do him no long-term damage. That delay could well suffice to keep the inmate out of the scheduled transport. Or else, sometimes, a patient would be told how to fake the symptoms of appendicitis. Once the transport had departed, of course, the alleged appendicitis sufferer would rapidly recover.[380]

Whenever ZOW members had been told that a sick inmate was about to be released from the camp, they would quickly get other members who were also in the hospital to conceal all abscesses and wounds on that person's body. They would do this by applying skin-coloured ointment to the person, plus, where necessary, applying small pieces of thin blotting-paper over the wounds, and finally masking such eruptions with cosmetic powder. Though these procedures did not always prevent an inspecting SS physician from blocking the release of an inmate, they usually did so. Thus, the inmate was freed, and returned to his family, where he had a far better chance of making a full recovery than he could possibly have done amidst Auschwitz's miseries.[381]

For Pilecki and his allies, there was a constant danger that certain inmates might inform on ZOW operatives to the camp's rulers. The existing arrangement was that if a prisoner wished to report something (or someone) to the authorities, he had to go to the camp's main gate, from which he would be taken to the Gestapo camp headquarters. From the authorities' point of view this arrangement had a serious disadvantage, in that the very public nature of this journey would often reveal the informer's identity to other prisoners, with potentially drastic consequences for the informer himself.

Bearing that problem in mind, the camp authorities eventually devised a new method of encouraging inmates to inform. They installed a box, painted in black, where inmates were meant to insert their denunciations at any time of the day or night. There was no need for the inmates who wrote the denunciations to reveal their own identities. Conveniently for ZOW, the box was installed in a place where, through the hospital's windows, the authorities could keep an eye on it. As a result, those working at the hospital who were involved with the ZOW acquired an additional duty: they had to monitor all the movements near the box.

Pilecki ordered one ZOW member to make, in secret, a new key which would fit the box's lock. Once the ZOW movement gained access to the box's contents in that way, three members – Lieutenant Tadeusz Biliński (No. 830), Captain Tadeusz Dziedzic (No. 16246) and Tadeusz Jakubowski (No. 2541) – regularly monitored the documents. Sometimes Pilecki would assist these three men. This was how he afterwards described this monitoring:

> *'We reviewed all letters that had been dropped, leaving those that were harmless to us. We would then find out who was the informer. Sometimes we would write anonymous letters ourselves to provide some leads to those who were engaged in gold procurement and other activities. These letters would take the camp authorities' attention away from us [i.e. the ZOW] and focus it, often with a very good result, on investigations that concerned informers.'*[382]

There were times when ZOW members dealt ruthlessly with informers, as well as with particularly murderous *Kapos* and *Blockführer*s, often Germans with long histories of criminal behaviour before the war. These individuals would be lured to an isolated place, and killed there, usually by a single blow to the head with a heavy bar or, alternatively, by a lethal injection at the prisoners' hospital. To prevent the SS from establishing the precise cause of death, the corpses would be hurried to the crematorium.[383]

ZOW members would sometimes obtain information from inmates employed at the camp's Gestapo offices. They used this information to influence the assignment of particular jobs to particular inmates, thereby increasing many inmates' chances for survival. ZOW members also worked in the camp's main office, in the carpenter's shop, in the tannery, and in the clothing store.

At that time, Colonel Karcz got denounced by an informer whose identity unfortunately could not have been determined. The informer advised camp bosses about Karcz's secret activities. Subsequently, Karcz was transferred to the Birkenau sub-camp.

Pilecki asked Karcz to build up the ZOW network in Birkenau. He agreed.[384]

In 1942, more and more non-Poles were transported to Auschwitz. Among the new non-Polish arrivals was a Czech solicitor by the name of Karel Stransky (No. 25625). He became the first non-Polish member of ZOW.[385]

The year 1942 was significant for another, and horrific, reason: it marked the beginning of the mass exterminations of Jews at Auschwitz II (the Birkenau subcamp). This development was closely watched by ZOW members who worked at, or near, Birkenau, for it was at Birkenau that all the trains with their Jewish captives would arrive. Most of the Jews were killed within a few hours of arriving. ZOW members had the grim task of collecting as much information as they could about how these slaughters were organised, about the gas chambers and crematoria being used to dispose of all bodies, and about the sheer numbers of Jews being murdered.

THE INSIDE OF AN AUSCHWITZ GAS CHAMBER

(© The Auschwitz-Birkenau Memorial and Museum, all rights reserved)

AN AUSCHWITZ CREMATORIUM

(© The Auschwitz-Birkenau Memorial and Museum, all rights reserved)

INCINERATORS IN AN AUSCHWITZ CREMATORIUM

(© The Auschwitz-Birkenau Memorial and Museum, all rights reserved)

THE MASS EXTERMINATION OF JEWS IN GERMAN OCCUPIED POLAND: REPUBLIC OF POLAND'S OFFICIAL REPORT DELIVERED TO THE LEAGUE OF NATIONS IN 1942

624.

REPUBLIC OF POLAND
Ministry of Foreign Affairs

THE MASS EXTERMINATION of JEWS in GERMAN OCCUPIED POLAND

NOTE
addressed to the Governments of the
United Nations on December 10th, 1942,
and other documents

*Published on behalf of the Polish
Ministry of Foreign Affairs by*

HUTCHINSON & CO. (Publishers) LTD.
LONDON : NEW YORK : MELBOURNE
Price: Threepence Net.

440

(© The Archive of the Republic of Poland's Department of Foreign Affairs, all rights reserved)

The respective secret reports based on this information were forwarded by Pilecki to the ZWZ high command. Later, they would be delivered to the Home Army's headquarters in Warsaw. One of these reports was taken on February 19, 1942, by Aleksander Paliński (No. 8253), who got released form the camp. When in Warsaw, Paliński sought out Eleonora Ostrowska, to whom he gave a separate message from Pilecki. He gave it to her in person, because it was too risky for Pilecki to write it down.

On March 4, another inmate – Antoni Woźniak – got likewise released from Auschwitz. The ZOW had entrusted him with a very delicate mission outside the camp, a mission on which Pilecki's life might well depend. It concerned the personal data of Pilecki's fictional alter-ago, Tomasz Serafiński. Some of this data, such as the given name and the maiden name of Serafiński's mother, Pilecki had to improvise instantaneously at the time he was being registered at the camp. Early in 1942, Pilecki made an alarming discovery: the camp bosses had begun to do some serious checking on all personal details supplied by the inmates. By such means, the camp bosses hoped, false identities assumed by inmates would be no longer tenable, and information about underground activists could no longer be concealed from the occupying power's notice.

Speedy remedy was therefore essential. Before Woźniak left Auschwitz, Pilecki asked him to go to the parish priest in Bochnia, and once there, have amended the details of the parish's births register entry for Tomasz Serafiński, so that they agreed with the details that Pilecki provided in 1940 to the Auschwitz authorities. Woźniak acquitted himself very well.[386] As a result, not a single official at the camp ever suspected the inmate 'Tomasz Serafiński' was, in reality, Witold Pilecki.

At approximately the same time, the camp authorities received a new directive from Berlin: to never again resort to group responsibility as a means to intimidate inmates, and discourage them from attempting escapes. Faced with this new situation, Pilecki decided to change the corresponding ZOW tactics accordingly.

He believed, in this new situation the ZOW could safely start to plan, and carry out, escapes, which it had held off before.

The first break was undertaken by two ZOW members already mentioned in this narrative: Stefan Bielecki and Wincenty Gawron. It took place on May 16. Both Bielecki and Gawron were, at the time, facing the extreme likelihood of swift execution. Both of them were labouring at Birkenau, their work involving the construction of irrigation mechanisms. Marvellously, both got out alive. They also took reports about how the mass exterminations at Auschwitz – of Soviet prisoners-of-war, as well as of Jews – had already started. Bielecki delivered the reports to Warsaw, handing them personally to General 'Grot' Rowecki, the Home Army's Commander-in-Chief.

Some other inmates were less lucky than Bielecki and Gawron. Two other ZOW members, Platoon Leader Stanisław Maringe and Lieutenant (Res.) Jerzy Poraziński, also tried to flee from Auschwitz; but were fatally shot when attempting to escape. More and more shootings took place at the Wall of Death. Victims included ZOW members Lieutenant Włodzimierz Makaliński and Captain Tadeusz Chróścicki. A more immediately harrowing bereavement for Pilecki himself occurred on April 12, when his brother-in-law Bronisław Ostrowski (No. 19893), who had been brought to Auschwitz after his arrest in Ostrów Mazowiecka, died.[387] Pilecki's grief at this loss was aggravated by him being unable to save his brother-in-law.

The toll among would-be escapees continued to be dreadfully heavy. On June 10, no fewer than fifty inmates attemped to escape from where they worked. Only nine prisoners made it to freedom, one of them having been Captain Chróścicki's son, Tadeusz Lucjan Chróścicki.[388] Of the others, twenty-eight were caught, and another thirteen were shot dead as they tried to flee. It was on the following day that Captain Chróścicki was shot, one of twenty prisoners killed in the same manner. A further 320 persons were gassed before nightfall.

Yet another escape attempt took place on June 20. This time, only four prisoners were involved. Perhaps because it entailed so few participants, it was successful. All four escapees were able to smuggle to Warsaw documents prepared by Pilecki. According to these documents, the inmates were ready and able to liberate themselves. Pilecki asked there for an official order to start an inmates uprising. Rawicz had prepared a plan whereby the uprising would begin once inmates involved in outdoor work would be returning for the evening roll-call.[389]

This call to arms the Home Army High Command never authorised, though. It deemed Pilecki's and Rawicz's ideas far too risky. To start with, there were several thousand extremely well armed SS men at, or near Auschwitz alone. For another thing, SS and other well-armed German formations were stationed in nearby cities, such as Katowice, Mysłowice, Bielsko, and Cracow. Within an hour of receiving a summons, these contingents would have been able to arrive at Auschwitz to suppress any trouble. Further, there were far too few local Polish guerrilla fighters in the area to be able to launch a successful attack on the occupiers from outside the camp, even if inmates were to instantenously gain access to Auschwitz SS armories, which was an optimistic assumption.

Pilecki had also advocated a large drop of weapons and Allied paratroopers near Auschwitz. This idea, too, the Home Army High Command ruled unfeasible.[390] The High Command remained convinced any attempt to liberate Auschwitz at that time was certain to fail, and besides would result in the deaths of several thousand inmates, to say nothing of Allied personnel.

Nevertheless, Pilecki's efforts at Auschwitz had certainly not been in vain. It is thanks to these efforts, probably more than to any other single factor, that many Auschwitz prisoners could *'live, act and die [there] believing they [are] still soldiers taking part in the fight against Germans.'*[391] Their human dignity had been upheld, against all the designs of the enemy to degrade and dehumanise its captives.

On July 7, 1942, Rawicz left Auschwitz accepting a transfer to Mauthausen, another German concentration camp. Before departing, he recommended to Pilecki that the next ZOW commanding officer be Lieutenant-Colonel Juliusz Gilewicz.[392] Pilecki accepted his advice. At the very same time two other senior officers, Lieutenant-Colonel Kumuniecki and Lieutenant-Colonel Kazimierz Stamirowski (No. 66786), joined ZOW. Its next field commander was Major Zygmunt Bohdanowski (No. 30959), whom the Auschwitz authorities knew only by his false surname of Bończa.

In accordance with the increasingly complex nature of this organisation, the ZOW was taking up some familiar military shapes. Each barracks with sufficient number of ZOW members became the location for a two-platoon company, one platoon being made up of those who lived on the ground floor, the other being made up of those who lived on the floor above. Each commander of a company lived in the same premises as the soldiers who answered to him. If barracks were adjacent, their occupants would be combined in a battalion. Once a signal was given for the uprising to start, ZOW members from each barrack were meant to take with them as many non-ZOW inmates as they could.

Altogether there were four ZOW battalions. The first one was commanded by Major Edward Gött-Getyński (No. 29693); the second one, by Captain Stanisław Kazuba (No. 1630); the third one, by Captain Tadeusz Paolone (No. 329); and the fourth one, by Captain Zygmunt Pawłowicz (known to the camp authorities under the alias 'Julian Trzęsimiech'; No. 9321). There were plans also for a fifth battalion, which was to be commanded, it is believed, by Bronisław Motyka (No. 3546).

Dr. Rudolf Diem was put in charge of the ZOW's medical division, while Dr. Dering became the hospital's chief executive officer. Father Zygmunt Ruszczak assumed the duties of the ZOW's military chaplain.[393] At this stage, religious services were not held at Auschwitz regularly, for Catholics, or for anyone else. Sometimes priests from outside the camp would provide communion wafers for consecration as sacred Hosts. For this purpose, they used members of local population who had already established contacts with some of Auschwitz inmates who regularly worked outside the camp. Whenever the Catholic Mass was celebrated, it was celebrated by either of two inmate priests: Father Zdzisław Piotr Uliasz (No. 12988) and Father Zygmunt Kuzak (No. 39884). Astonishingly, these Masses seemed to never have come to the attention of the camp authorities.

Astonishingly, the ZOW had somehow acquired a clandestine radio receiver. It should be emphasized, that the Third Reich's authorities were so acutely aware of foreign radio's subversive potential that in many occupied lands, Poland being one, they made it a capital crime to possess without permission a receiver capable of transmitting foreign broadcasts. All of the receiver's parts had been supplied by ZOW members who had been assigned to the camp's electrical workshop.

During the day, Dr. Dering would always keep the receiver hidden in the office of the chief SS doctor. The receiver remained concealed underneath a washbasin, the office itself was made of concrete. A piece of linoleum and a rug were neatly placed over the receiver, so that no prying eyes would suspect its presence. Only at night, when the SS medical personnel were far away, sound asleep, or both, did any ZOW members take the receiver out of its hiding-place, turn it on, and listen eagerly to all the available news reports: particularly those that dealt with the progress of the war. The ZOW members even constructed a makeshift antenna, from twenty-five metres of an established telephone cable which had connected the hospital with the neighbouring block.

All the information obtained through the illicit receiver's broadcasts – especially if it involved actual or rumoured military defeats for Hitler's forces – was passed on to inmates. The Austrian-born Chief Nurse Maria Stromberger proved to be of great assistance in this respect, as well. As a non-inmate, she could move about the various parts of the camp without attracting official attention. Having access to truthful news about the war's progress, as opposed to the invariably optimistic propaganda of official broadcasts, helped lift the morale of many prisoners a great deal.

Sometimes, Stromberger's camp responsibilities would compel her to leave Auschwitz, and travel to various cities in Upper Silesia on official business. Each time she was leaving to make one of these journeys, she would take with her various messages which ZOW activists in the camp had written down on tiny pieces of thin parchment. The messages contained, among other things, hard data about the strength of Auschwitz's SS contingent; the names of the cruellest and most homicidal among the *Kapos, Blockführers*, and SS members; and the approximate numbers of victims who had been either gassed, or shot.[394]

Conveniently, SS men who owned radio receivers would sometimes bring them in to the electrical shop, for repairs. This provided further opportunities for ZOW members to listen surreptitiously to short-wave broadcasts from Allied countries. Alas, they did not always do so without any consequences for them. Four inmates – one of them an engineer and former Polish Radio employee, Jan Pilecki, no relation to Witold – were uncovered to be listening to such broadcasts. The camp bosses punished them by sending them to the Auschwitz penal unit.

Early in 1942, Witold Pilecki secured for himself, for a limited time, a role with the camp's SS-controlled Radio and Telegraph Office. There, together with Mieczysław Januszewski, he drew maps at the SS's insistence. Owing to opportunities offered by this work, Pilecki was also able to pass on some much-needed radio parts to ZOW members. In addition, one of his fellow inmates in the office, Eugeniusz Dulin (No. 31007), passed on for the benefit of ZOW a number of German coded messages he came across there.

This was not Pilecki's only spectacular camp activity. During the summer of 1942, a particularly fierce epidemic of typhus broke out in the camp. It extracted a terrible toll on prisoners. Pilecki did what he could to save lives. One man whose life he saved was that of Tadeusz Stulgiński (No. 31315), previously a Pawiak inmate, who was brought to Auschwitz on April 17. When at Pawiak, Stulgiński met Lieutenant-Colonel Surmacki, who gave him this counsel: *'always ask Tomasz Serafiński for help there, whenever [the] situation is perilous.'*[395]

ZOW members smuggled into the camp large quantities of extra medications. They were supported in this regard by almost all of Auschwitz's regular non-ZOW outdoor labourers.

Yet, there were limits to what they could achieve. On August 29, the Auschwitz SS conducted a thorough survey of both those who were still desperately ill with typhus, and those who were convalescing from it. On the ostensible pretext of combatting the epidemic, the SS consigned that very day 746 typhus sufferers to the gas chambers of Birkenau.[396]

Had Pilecki been stricken with typhus then, he might well have been among the 746. As it happened, he did come down with the dreaded disease a few days later. Fortunately, thanks to a good deal of solicitous attention from Dering and Edward Ciesielski (the latter inmate brought Pilecki extra food), he survived. Kazimierz Radwański, his nephew, provided him with an extra blanket and a pillow. Yet, even this terrible illness could not prevent Pilecki from carrying out ZOW activism. While at the hospital, he recruited for the ZOW yet another member, Andrzej Rablin (No. 1410), who had likewise been suffering grievously from typhus, and whose bed was not far from Pilecki's own.

One thing that Pilecki did shortly before he fell ill was a throwback to earlier and happier times. At Block 24, he painted a few pictures. A few inmates from this Block who had artistic talents were briefly allowed to undertake works of art, including, in some cases, pictures which showed scenes from the inmates' lives. This situation ended abruptly, though, when SS-Rapportführer Gerhardt Palitzsch, with the spite so characteristic of him, ordered all these pictures to be destroyed.[397]

Once he had recovered sufficiently to leave the hospital, Pilecki was not reassigned to the carpentry shop. Instead, on the recommendation of Bartosiewicz, he went to the tannery. There he worked for four months.

The mass murders continued. News of Polish guerrilla activities in Lublin made the Auschwitz SS want to take revenge (October 28, 1942) on inmates. Many of the captives chosen for this reprisal – 280 altogether – were themselves from Lublin. Once the all-too-familiar executions had started, a few inmates frantically tried to start a revolt. They failed, and they were themselves shot before any of the other prisoners selected for the scheduled massacre.

In his *Report W* from Auschwitz, Pilecki expressed his view that the long-awaited Auschwitz inmates' uprising could, and should have begun right at that very moment. It would indeed have begun then, had only there been a clear signal from the captives who awaited their deaths. If only, so thought Pilecki, the condemned prisoners had wanted to sell their lives more dearly, the uprising would have spread, and would probably have been impossible for the Nazis to quell. Pilecki remarked: *'We waited. They decided otherwise. We saw how bravely they all met their deaths.'*[398]

From March till August 1942, female inmates occupied no fewer than ten barracks in the main Auschwitz camp. The ZOW established contacts with some of them, before they were moved elsewhere, to the BIa sector of Birkenau (KL Auschwitz II-Birkenau). Even after that move, some of the women prisoners, especially those sent to the Auschwitz hospital, were able to smuggle in food, medications, and news for the ZOW cells' benefit.[399] Especially worth citing here are the following names: Maria Maniakówna (No. 18229), Wiktoria Klimaszewska (No. 25993), Zofia Bratro (No. 27182), Stanisława Rachwał (No. 26281), Antonia Piątkowska (No. 6805) and Helena Hoffman (No. 8549). These five women would then form – during the summer of 1943 – Birkenau's first Upper Five cell. By that time, though, Pilecki was no longer in Auschwitz.

Female ZOW members from Birkenau had the specific tasks of: establishing contacts with Soviet POWs; establishing contacts with inmates from other countries; procuring extra medicines; obtaining intelligence regarding the numbers of gassings at Birkenau, as well as the numbers of bodies cremated there; organising escapes when possible; fighting against informers; and caring for newly arrived inmates, whom they would caution about the most dangerous individual *Kapos*, *Blockführers* and SS members. All these activities were supervised by Colonel Karcz, who at the time was undergoing at Birkenau his 6-month term with the penal unit.

Towards the end of 1942, two of the camp's most active and industrious informers were busier than ever reporting to the camp chiefs. One of them was Ernst Malorny (No. 60368), a German; the other was Władysław Smalski (No. 7638), a Pole. The camp command would often use both informers as stool-pigeons. They were also put into the Death Block cells, together with other inmates.

On Christmas Eve, 1942, Block 27 was the scene of a traditional Polish *Opłatek* Advent ceremony, involving sharing a wafer with, and exchanging best wishes with, others present. Alas for ZOW hopes, both Malorny and Smalski attended the ceremony. Pretending to be as anti-Nazi as anyone, they encouraged some of the other inmates to confide in them. Through this process, their targets revealed ZOW-related secrets. The consequences of this indiscretion came to surface less than a fortnight later.

On the following January 6, SS functionaries suddenly appeared and singled out some former army officers from the block: Colonel Kumuniecki and Major Gött-Getyński among these. All these men were promptly taken by SS to Death Block 11.[400] Similar confrontations took place in the *Effektenkammer* (store for personal effects), and in the *Erkennungsdienst* (personal files archive).

All the inmates who were seized in these raids were divided into four groups. Inmates who were either *Reichsdeutsch*, or *Volksdeutsch*[401] were returned to their work groups. Of the remaining captives, some were kept in the Death Block cells, some were sent to do some exceptionally hard physical work, such as digging up gravel with inadequate implements. The remainder was promptly murdered by the usual SS executioner, Gerhardt Palitzsch.

Among those confined to the Death Block was Colonel Karcz. On January 25, he was one of fifty-three prisoners shot dead. Other ZOW members who perished that day alongside Karcz included Colonel Kumuniecki and Major Gött-Getyński.[402]

Yet another blow to the ZOW's chances of survival fell on April 1, 1943, when over seven thousand Polish inmates at Auschwitz were transferred to various other camps. The camp bosses were deliberately dispersing Auschwitz long-time inmates to make it as hard as possible for them to continue their involvement in secret activities.[403]

Camp informers had also achieved successes in their work. By this time, the camp authorities had realized that, leaving aside a few exceptions, all those involved with the ZOW were Poles. The authorities had even begun to discern parts of the extensive underground network that the conspirators had set up, involving the Polish population outside Auschwitz. The camp authorities had good reasons to suspect that local guerrilla groups had become well apprised of what was going on behind the barbed wire. The question was: were such groups already hatching a plan to start an all-out attack on the camp, so as to liberate at least some of the captives? To the Nazi hierarchs' minds, the answer to this question seemed to be an all too likely 'yes.'

Hence the decision by those running the camp to relocate much of the Polish prison population deep into German territory. This relocation would serve two purposes for them. It would weaken, if not wholly destroy, the anti-Nazi underground network; and it would buy precious time for the Nazis themselves. However effective the Berlin censorship might have been, it could not have altogether prevented rumours circulating as to the scale of the February 1943 disaster at the Battle of Stalingrad, which had cost three quarters of a million Axis lives. Hitherto, the prospect of Hitler losing the war had seemed a mere conjecture; now it seemed eminently very likely.

Those whom the camp overseers would transfer from Auschwitz were mostly individuals who had been there for a long time and were still, by the criteria prevailing in the camp, endowed with reasonably good physical health. Among the ZOW members who left Auschwitz on April 1 were: Stanisław Barański, Leszek Cenzartowicz (No. 870), Wacław Kafarowski, Major Zygmunt Pawłowicz, Second Lieutenant Konstanty Piekarski, Officer Cadet (Res.) Tadeusz Pietrzykowski, Kazimierz Radwański, Second Lieutenant (Res.) Władysław Rapa (No. 30901), Wiktor Śniegucki, and Second Lieutenant (Res.) Jerzy Wiśniewski (No. 31361).

Well before the day of the intended transfer, word had reached the prisoners concerning it. Pilecki was among those to be transferred from Auschwitz on April 1. But Pilecki was having none of it. He did not want his underground efforts to be even more impeded than they already were. So, when appearing before the military medical commission he resourcefully decided to feign a serious injury. Marian Toliński, from the inmates' hospital, provided Pilecki with a truss. He had to wear it when before the medical commission if his ruse was to work.

On March 10, Pilecki was brought before the commission whose role it was to decide who would leave Auschwitz on April 1. He had donned his truss to give the impression that he had suffered an extremely bad internal rupture. Circumstances helped him: his turn to face the commissioners did not come until 2 a.m. on the next day, by which stage the commissioners were themselves extremely tired. As soon as they caught sight of Pilecki, wearing nothing except his truss, they yelled: 'Away! We do not need people like him!'. And they removed the name of 'Tomasz Serafiński' from the list of prisoners to be transferred.[404]

A week after his truss trick, Pilecki was once again called before medical examiners. This time, the examiners were assessing the physical suitability of inmates for yet another transport, one that was scheduled to leave over two days (April 12, and 13) for Mauthausen. This time, Pilecki developed a presentiment that those found medically unfit for the transfer would be sent, instead, to Birkenau's gas chambers. Accordingly, he eschewed further fakery with the truss. Instead, he asked Dr. Dering for help.

It was Dr. Dering's good fortune to have certain methods at his disposal for persuading Pilecki's immediate superior – an SS man in charge of the camp's packets office – to retain Pilecki's services. He convinced the SS man to plead to the authorities the necessity of keeping Pilecki and three other inmates, fellow ZOW operatives who worked in the same office, in Auschwitz. So utterly indispensable were the four captives, it was argued, to the office's appropriate functioning that it would be disastrous to let them go to Mauthausen. The gambit worked. All four inmates had their names deleted from the Mauthausen transfer list, and all four stayed at Auschwitz.[405]

Pilecki, nonetheless, was thinking more and more of getting to Warsaw. He still believed – and he wanted to convince the Home Army chiefs – that military action should promptly be undertaken to liberate the Auschwitz captives still alive, or, alternatively, that the essential extermination infrastructure of Birkenau (railways, gas chambers and crematoria) be bombed, so that a few months time could be bought, and thus several hundred thousand human lives at Auschwitz - saved.[406] He needed to start planning his own escape. So much depended upon his own survival that his planning required the utmost meticulousness.

*

Since December 1942, Pilecki had been discussing various escape ideas with fellow inmates. One such idea was presented to him by Second Lieutenant (Res.) Witold Wierusz, who worked with the surveying unit outside Auschwitz. Since Wierusz's plan involved the likelihood of SS men being killed, Pilecki disapproved of it. He feared that taking SS lives would simply unleash still worse reprisals by the rest of the SS against other prisoners.

There was another alternative escape option that Pilecki had also assessed, an escape through the camp network's sewer system. He throughly investigated this option: he descended into the system itself, and inspected it, while wearing appropriate protective clothing. From what he saw in the sewers, however, the option did not have good enough odds of success for it to be relied on.

Further inspiration came from an unusual, well-prepared, and effective plan of egress which took place on December 29, 1942. There were four inmates involved with it. Otto Küsel, the German whom this narrative has mentioned before, was one of them. The three others were Poles: Jan Komski (No. 564, known to camp's authorities under the fake surname of 'Baraś'); Bolesław Kuczbara (No. 4308); and Mieczysław Januszewski (Küsel's deputy). All four managed to escape in – of all old-fashioned conveyances – a horse-drawn cart.

Preparation for this achievement had been largely Küsel's doing. He was responsible for selecting the work areas where the captives labouring outside the camp's perimeter had to carry out their tasks. This responsibility gave him the very precious advantage of being able to move from work area to work area without arousing any suspicions. Even when he ordered a horse-drawn cart, the authorities suspected nothing. He then told the other three inmates to load four wardrobes onto the cart, and then he drove the cart through the main gate, the one with its notorious *Arbeit Macht Frei* sign.

An SS-man outside the camp, who had ordered two of the wardrobes, received the objects. With the remaining two wardrobes still on the cart, Küsel drove on, collecting on his way Januszewski, Komski and Kuczbara. The last-named, who had the function of an escort, wore an authentic SS uniform he had been able to surreptitiously procure for himself from the camp's SS storeroom.

All four escapees reached, without any incident, the nearby village of Broszkowice. There they met people who had been expecting their arrival. Having discarded their camp uniforms (and, in Kuczbara's case, the SS uniform), the four men changed into ordinary civilian clothes which had been kept for them in readiness. Soon, they were on their way.

Certain things Kuczbara had taken very good care *not* to discard when he donned his new attire: namely, various documents that contained details of inmates from the first Warsaw transports who had in the meantime been killed, either by shooting or by gassing. He passed on these papers to an underground courier from Warsaw who came to their temporary hiding-place at the town of Lubiąż, in pre-war Poland's south-west.[407]

Sad to relate, Januszewski and Komski did not enjoy freedom for very long. Having gone to Cracow, they were recaptured there and soon identified as Auschwitz escapees. Both were put on the next transport to Auschwitz; and it is believed that Januszewski, once back in the camp, committed suicide.

Kuczbara and Küsel made their way to Warsaw. There, Gestapo agents arrested them both. Kuczbara struggled to resist arrest, and a Gestapo bullet badly injured him. The agents then took him to the Pawiak prison; he gave them his assumed name of Janusz Kapur. Facing the prospect of horrific Gestapo tortures as soon as he would recover from his gunshot wound, and fearing he would disclose crucial secrets when subjected to such interrogations, he asked his wife to supply him with poison. She was unable to do so. Not long afterwards, Kuczbara was shot dead.[408]

Meanwhile Pilecki had received, through Dr. Dering, alarming information supplied by former Pawiak inmates now in Auschwitz. Through this means, Pilecki learned of Kuczbara being behind Pawiak's walls. During his time at Auschwitz, Kuczbara was known to often behave erratically, and irresponsibly. Examples of this behaviour were provided by Pilecki in his *Report W*.

Kuczbara was considered high risk for breaking down under Gestapo torture and revealing many ZOW secrets. Because of this, Pilecki decided he needed to leave Auschwitz as promptly as possible.[409] He contacted Major Bohdanowski, who agreed to take over all Pilecki's ZOW duties.[410]

HIS ESCAPE FROM THE CAMP

Finally, Pilecki formed the view that the escape method with the best prospect of success was one which would require him to secure a night shift at a bakery that produced bread for Auschwitz inmates. The bakery was situated outside the perimeter of the main camp complex, so that an escape attempt from there was likelier to succeed than one from within the camp itself.

In this scheme, Pilecki involved two other inmates, Jan Redzej (No. 5430, known to the Auschwitz authorities as 'Jan Retko') and Edward Ciesielski. The plan was that they would all try to escape together. At that time, Pilecki was still carrying out his role within the packet section of the camp's post office, while Ciesielski worked at the hospital, and Redzej worked at the storeroom of the inmates' kitchen.

First, though, came the task of seeking a night shift on the bakery's premises. Redzej set about preparing for this move. He went to the bakery to acquaint himself with the building, with the area surrounding the building, and with the possible difficulties that any escape attempt would entail.

At the bakery, several persons from outside the camp, as well as several Auschwitz inmates, were on duty for each shift, day or night. During the night, two SS men kept guard. A massive iron door was at the back of the bakery. Somehow, the aspiring escapees would have to open this door without alerting the guards: no mean feat, since the door had across it an iron bar, connected to the floor by several nuts. Without anyone noticing, Redzej made an impression of one of the nuts, and he passed on this impression to a trusted inmate – a fitter by profession – for him to make a wrench of the corresponding shape and size.[411] Once the wrench was ready, Redzej – having by this time obtained a night shift for himself – took the wrench along with him and hid it there for further use.

Now came the job of trying to acquire permits from the camp authorities for Ciesielski and Pilecki (or, rather Tomasz Serafiński) to work as bakers. Without such a permit, no inmate was allowed to attend to any duties outside the camp's perimeter. Marian Toliński persuaded the *Arbeitsdienstführer* Franz Hössler[412] to sign these permits for two other inmates. Once these permits were in Ciesielski's hands, he carefully and skilfully removed the other inmates' names, substituting his own name and Tomasz Serafiński's.[413]

The three men decided that their escape would be best attempted during the Easter period, when the number of SS guards was reduced (many guards went away on holidays then). Even so, they willingly conceded the likelihood of the remaining guards mounting a dogged pursuit within an hour or so of the escape. But if the escapees cut, beforehand, through the telephone cable connecting the bakery to the main administration, they would give themselves extra time.

Fear of arousing official suspicion, and a reluctance to trigger reprisals against his post office colleagues, prompted Pielecki this time to refrain from actively seeking a transfer to the bakery. Instead, he persuaded Dr. Diem to admit him to the inmates' hospital, on the grounds he was suspected to be suffering from typhus again. Ciesielski spoke to another physician at the hospital – Dr. Władysław Fejkiel – and requested that Pilecki be discharged on Easter Monday. He also asked Colonel Gilewicz to seek from Dr. Fejkiel a discharge note vouching for Pilecki's being well enough to work.[414]

And so, on Easter Monday, Ciesielski and Pilecki were moved to Block 15, which was where all inmates who worked in the bakery were accommodated.[415] They decided that they would try to escape during the April 26-27 night shift.

Soon, yet another difficulty confronted them: the Kapo responsible for the bakery's workforce had already allocated to Ciesielski a day shift, not a night shift. It was fortunate that Redzej had considerable powers of verbal persuasion, which he used on the Kapo. It was even more fortunate he was able to produce, for the Kapo's benefit, home-made jams, some sugar, and a packet of apples. This combination of eloquence and food made the Kapo change his mind.

At about 6.30 p.m., with the rest of the inmates carrying out their night shift work at the two outside bakeries, Pilecki, Ciesielski and Redzej all walked towards the *Arbeit Macht Frei* gate. Underneath their striped Auschwitz uniforms, Pilecki and Ciesielski wore civilian clothes. By contrast, Redzej had painted red stripes over his own civilian clothes. They could hear an SS guard call out from the gate the word: '*Bäckerei!* [Bakery!]' As Pilecki went through the dreaded Auschwitz gate, he experienced an overwhelming wave of hope that he would never again need to see it.[416]

Soon, two groups formed. One group consisted of two inmates and two SS escorts, who walked to the small SS bakery, while the other group consisted of six inmates – with two SS escorts of their own – who walked to the much larger bakery that produced bread for the captives. Pilecki and his two colleagues were in the latter group. They had about two kilometres' walking ahead of them.

On their arrival at the large bakery, the SS guards locked the members of the latter group inside, and the inmates immediately began their work. After several hours, when Pilecki and Ciesielski were among those busy baking the bread, Redzej stole out to the wood-shed where he had previously hidden the wrench. He found it, and - unnoticed by the SS guards- began to work on the nut of the back door. While he was at it, he cut through the telephone cable.

By this time, the guards were showing less than rigorous vigilance. One SS man was busy writing a letter; the other was eating. They failed to notice that Pilecki, Ciesielski and Redzej were leaning against the door, trying to open it by their combined pressure. After a while that seemed like an eternity to them, they finally managed to force the door open. Whereupon they crept out, closed the door behind them (barricading it from behind), and then ran as fast as they could.

Soon they needed to cross two rivers, the Sola and the Vistula. To cross the Sola, they used a railway bridge left temporarily unguarded. But to cross the Vistula, they needed to use a boat. Fortunately, they found one moored at a jetty. For the second time on this night, the wrench that they had brought provided invaluable help to them: they employed it to remove the chain which bound the boat to the landing-place. As they crossed the Vistula, the sun started to rise.[417] After their crossing, they hid in the forest, where they spent the rest of the day.

Only when the sun had set again did they continue their escape. They traversed the border between the Reich and the *Generalgouvernement*.[418] On meeting a priest, Father Legowicz from the Alwernia parish, they obtained from him all help they required. After that, they continued their trek eastwards, through the Niepołomicka Forest, where they glimpsed a frightening sight: some armed Germans. Happily, they eluded their pursuers, but not before a bullet had grazed Pilecki's arm.

Shortly they reached Bochnia, where they found shelter in the Obora family house, the Oboras being friends of the Zabawski family, one of whom was himself an Auschwitz captive. Concerned that if they stayed with the Zabawskis it could well bring trouble upon that family, they decided to instead stay with the Oboras.

No sooner had they arrived at Bochnia than Pilecki requested a contact with the local Home Army commander. He met the local deputy commander in nearby Nowy Wiśnicz on May 3, 1943. When introduced to that person, Pilecki was for a while left speechless with amazement: the deputy commander's name was ... Tomasz Serafiński. Pilecki's surprise was equalled only by that of the other person.[419]

THREE ESCAPEES FROM KL AUSCHWITZ: JAN REDZEJ, WITOLD PILECKI AND EDWARD CIESIELSKI IN NOWY WIŚNICZ, IN FRONT OF THE SERAFIŃSKI FAMILY HOUSE

(© The Auschwitz-Birkenau Memorial and Museum, all right reserved)

Serafiński – the true Serafiński, that is – invited Pilecki to live with him in his family home. There, Pilecki stayed for three and a half months.[420] There, as well, he worked on his original Auschwitz report, which would come to be known as *Report W*.[421]. He almost, but not quite, finished it there. Fragments of it, during June 1943, were forwarded to Warsaw for translation into the major European languages, so that they could be used to alert the Allies to the crimes against humanity being committed at Auschwitz itself.

Alas, not everyone was convinced of Pilecki's bona fides. Zygmunt Szydek, the Home Army commander in the city of Wiśnicz, Julian Więcek, the commander of Home Army's Bochnia district, and the regional Home Army command in Cracow: they all suspected the same thing – namely that Pilecki and his two fellow escapees were Gestapo agents. Even after all three men revealed to the Home Army officials an abundance of authentic data about Auschwitz's horrors, the suspicion remained. The result of that meeting was that Serafiński received orders to end his personal contacts with the three escapees.[422]

Pilecki, at this juncture, thought it best to sound out the Warsaw headquarters of the Home Army. From Warsaw, an emissary was sent to Pilecki: none other than Stefan Bielecki, fellow Auschwitz survivor. Bielecki brought some new forged documents for Pilecki, and a sum of money. He tried to convince Pilecki to return with him to Warsaw. Pilecki declined, insisting that he had a commitment, which he needed to honour, and namely - to organise local action for the liberation of Auschwitz captives.

Then, Pilecki spoke with the Bochnia District Home Army's Head of Diversion and Armament, whose name was Andrzej Możdżeń. To Możdżeń, he recommended that a unit made up of local volunteers be formed, with the specific purpose of attacking Auschwitz's SS forces and freeing the inmates. Once again, the local Home Army command was unprepared to support this idea. They argued that, first, the number of guerrilla fighters in the area was too small for Pilecki's scheme to succeed and, second, that a safe evacuation of inmates from the camp complex would be impossible, even if the attack managed to surprise and initially overwhelm the SS guards.[423]

WITOLD PILECKI IN FRONT OF KORYZNÓWKA, THE SERAFIŃSKI FAMILY RESIDENCE

(© Pilecki family, all rights reserved)

Meanwhile, some Auschwitz prisoners sent Pilecki a secret message, urging him to abandon the concept of liberating the camp. As he read this message, he found there a piece of welcome news: there had been no reprisals against any inmates in revenge for their escape.

While at Nowy Wiśnicz, Pilecki took part in some local guerrilla diversion actions. He had new identity cards Bielecki had supplied for him. They bore the names of Leon Bryjak and Jan Uznański. Equipped with those, he arrived in Warsaw on August 23 (Redzej and Ciesielski followed him there a few days later).

Four months afterwards, the Tomasz Serafiński affair took another unexpected twist. On Christmas Day 1943, the occupiers arrested the real Serafiński at his Nowy Wiśnicz home. They believed he was one of the Auschwitz escapees.[424] At first, they kept him in Bochnia's prison, from which on December 28 they transferred him to Cracow's Gestapo headquarters. There, he was cruelly interrogated before being taken to the city's gaol in Montelupi Street.[425] His wife approached the German authorities, pointing out that her husband could not have been at Auschwitz, because he had no tattooed number on his forearm. After a few weeks, he got released from the prison; unsurprisingly, however, three months passed before he had fully recovered from his ordeal.[426]

PILECKI'S *REPORT W*
FROM KL AUSCHWITZ[427]

FROM THE TRANSLATOR OF *REPORT W*

As Captain Pilecki wrote his three consecutive versions of his Auschwitz report, he did not mean for any of them to get published. Their sole purpose was to present to his superiors and through them – to all Western allies of Poland, how Auschwitz inmates' life looked like in all its significant aspects. They were all written in a hurry.

The first version of his Auschwitz document, called *Report 'W'*, was to a very considerable extent based on notes made by Witold Pilecki, when still at the camp. He naturally had to be particularly careful about their contents, for he was aware of the risk for inmates and their families, if any of his notes fell into hands of occupant's authorities, and names of inmates were identified. It is also for this reason, that he had to keep some of his comments and reflections there rather cryptic.

All this had combined to produce a challenge to both the translator and the reader. The report's text is coarse at times, its syntax is sometimes broken. On the other hand, it is exactly these characteristics that underscore the character of this document.

Out of respect for its author, and to preserve the authentic character of his report, the translator's interventions had been kept to a minimum. The translator resorted to them only when it was, in his view, required to reduce, if not eliminate altogether, possible significant reader's confusion as to the meaning of some comments made by Pilecki. All such interventions took the form of square brackets insertions. In the translated text of this report, readers will also find a few explanatory notes by one of the most eminent Polish Auschwitz experts, Dr. Adam Cyra, which have been inserted by him into the version of the report prior to it being presented to this translator. All such notes are marked in the text with the A.C. initials.

As already mentioned, Captain Pilecki had an overriding concern for the safety of all the people he referred to in his report. The original text of this report had only numbers in place of most people's names and surnames. The key to this report was kept by Pilecki separately from his other notes. Many years of painstaking research, and comparisons with other documents from the World War II period, have made it possible, though, to positively identify most of the people he directly refers to in his report.

Second, Pilecki wrote his report for Poland's underground military organisations in the German occupied Poland. He wrote it as an officer who reports to his superiors. This, naturally, greatly affected the style of his report.

Third, Witold Pilecki used in his report many slang terms used by Auschwitz inmates, a few obscure expressions, and the German camp-related terminology. All of them are explained by this translator, if deemed necessary. In some instances, an outside assistance was required. Again, most of it was very competently provided by Dr. Adam Cyra. His assistance is therefore acknowledged here, once again, with the greatest gratitude.

Fourth, when *Report W* was being typed in 1943 additional spacing between letters was applied whenever Witold Pilecki thought it desirable to emphasise the particular significance of some of his observations, or reflections. In this translation, additional spacing used by Witold Pilecki had been replaced with bold lettering, for additional spacing inside words would have presented a hindrance to readers.

Fifth, all obvious errors in the original text of this report (of which this translator found a few, mostly concerning dates), have been corrected.

Sixth, longer associated notes, including those provided by Dr. Adam Cyra, are provided at the end of this report. This again was done in order to retain, as much as possible and desirable, the original appearance, and thus the integrity of this Pilecki's report.

Last, Captain Pilecki's reflections on the attitudes of some of his compatriots he observed both during the war, and outside the wartime, show a considerable restraint on his part. He keeps his reflections very short. He often uses references which are deeply grounded in the Polish culture and history, or vaguely refers to his experiences which extend far beyond the situations he describes in his report. A full explication of these reflections would be a task very few translators could carry out successfully, even if one felt authorised to do so.

*

In 2012, a translation of Pilecki's later, 1945 version, of Auschwitz Report, by Jarek Garliński (*The Auschwitz Volunteer: Beyond Bravery by Aquila Polonica*, Los Angeles, 2012) was published in the United States by Aquila Polonica. The author of this translation had fortunately been able to acquaint himself with that translation prior to completing his translation of *Report W*. This has helped him in his work in two different ways.

First, it provided him with some more comprehensive descriptions of events included by Pilecki into his 1945 Auschwitz report: this often helped this translator avoid possible inaccuracies, or misconceptions, when translating the far more compact 1943 version of his Auschwitz report. Second, it provided to him a glossary of camp related terms and acronyms which helped keep both translations consistent in this respect.

All German proper nouns in the English text commence, in accordance with the rules of the German orthography, from capital cases.

The first of the three versions of the Pilecki's Auschwitz report had been prepared in the least conducive conditions imaginable: notes had to be made surreptitiously and then smuggled out from the camp. Similar to Jarek Garliński, this translator believed that preserving this report's character was essential, even if it meant leaving some style, syntax, and punctuation imperfections uncorrected.

Adam Jan Koch

REPORT W

by Witold Pilecki

INTRODUCTION TO REPORT W

After thirty-one months, when things came to the point that a further extension of my stay at the camp would not only have meant a continued burden of torment but also would have produced – in my view – no further gain [for the cause - addition by this translator], I decided to leave the *Vernichtungslager* 1 [Extermination Camp 1].

From my colleagues who at that time were still with me in the camp I handpicked two very determined ones: 'J' and 'E'. Even though I received a light gunshot wound during our escape, with God's help I succeeded.

Each one of us described their own experience, what they saw and went through at Auschwitz. In so doing, we divided our respective duties, with 'J' and 'E' in such a way that they were to provide their general camp's description, whilst my aim was to preserve for eternity various particular events [that took place there]. My separate report on our 'S' activity I kept strictly coded since it turned out, once we have escaped, that the enemy's intelligence penetrated almost everywhere. Whilst our descriptions may have some shortcomings, be they of style, or due to our failure to include certain pictures from this hell because of our inability to squeeze them all into less than twenty pages, there is no misrepresentation in these recollections. We did not write a lot: there is not one superfluous word in our accounts.

(-) Witold

On September 14, 15 and 16, 1939, on General Piekarski's order and assisted by Major Mandzenko, I formed in Włodawa a cavalry detachment – 185 horses as well as an infantry detachment over 160 men strong. On September 16, an officer from the same brigade as I and a friend of mine, Major Jan Włodarkiewicz, came to Włodawa; due to his seniority in rank I handed over to him the command of these detachments.

The above-mentioned cavalry and infantry detachments fought on until October 17, 1939. This campaign has been recorded by my younger colleagues-in-arms.

The same detachments became a nucleus of an organisation we named *Tajna Armia Polska* (TAP) [Secret Polish Army] which was set up in early November 1939 in Warsaw.

In Warsaw, I served as TAP's Chief of Staff (my *nom-de-guerre* was "Witold"). I sought to merge TAP with ZWZ [Związek Walki Zbrojnej – Union for Armed Fight]. I had difficulties with it. There were differences of opinion [on it] (witnesses still alive: Janina Pieńkowska, Stefan Bielecki and Major Zygmunt Bończa-Bohdanowski). The [respective] decision was taken on September 19, 1940 (witness: Eleonora Ostrowska).

At the third anniversary of the establishment of the Auschwitz camp I present this report concerning the fate of those countless who having completed their tormented way through this hell left it through the barrel of the crematorium's chimney becoming, as we would call it, 'puffs of smoke', "little clouds', or 'tiny wisps of fog'.[428]

Below, I mention the fate of members of the *Organizacja Wojskowa* [Military Organisation] in Auschwitz, as known to me at the moment of my escape from the camp.

Murdered during an interrogation
Platoon Leader Bolesław Kupiec (No. 792).

Executed by shooting
Eugeniusz Obojski (No. 194), Col. Aleksander Stawarz (No. 11513), Lieut.Col. Karol Kumuniecki (No. 8361), First Lieutenant Tadeusz Biliński (No. 830), First Lieutenant Włodzimierz Makaliński (TAP, No. 12710), Second Lieutenant (Res.) Stanisław Gutkiewicz (No. 11003), Stanisław Stawiszyński (TAP, No. 13689), Second Lieutenant (Res.) Tadeusz Lech (No. 9235), Col. Jan Karcz (No. 23569), Off. Cad. (Res.) Zbigniew Ruszczyński (No. 1360), First Lieutenant St. Dobrowolski (No. ..), Leon Kukiełka (No. 16465), Stanisław Dubois (No. 3904), Maj. Edward Gött-Getyński

(No. 29693), First Lieutenant (Res.) Eugeniusz Zaturski
(TAP, No. 1387), Cav.Capt. Włodzimierz Koliński
(No. 3135), First Lieutenant Mieczyslaw Koliński
(No. 68844), Capt. Tadeusz Dziedzic (No. 16246),
Capt. Dr Henryk Suchnicki (No. 19456), Off. Cad.
(Res.) Aleksander Jaskierski No. 2450), Corp.. ...nicki,
TAP, No. ... (the surname in the names code partly
illegible), Capt. Tadeusz Chróścicki – father (TAP,
No. 13484), Tadeusz Lucjan Chróścicki – son (TAP,
No. 16655), Antoni Suchecki (No. 595), Second Lieutenant
(Res.) Stanisław Wierzbicki (TAP, No. 3558),
Stefan Niebudek (No. 18531), Stanisław Arct (No. 12654),
Roman Radoliński (No. 13471), Sen. Uhlan Stefan Stępień
(No. 12970), Platoon Leader Edward Berlin (No. 19490).

Murdered by lethal injections

Sailor Lolek Kupiec (Karol Kupiec No. 794), Zygmunt
Masewicz (No. 1394), Alfred Stössel (No. 435).

Died (killed in the camp's public area or died as a result of the prevalent conditions or epidemies in the camp)

Cav.Capt. (Res.) Jerzy de Virion (in the camp
known as Jan Hlebowicz, TAP, No. 3507), Roman
Zagner (No. ...), Capt. Michał Romanowicz (No. ...),
Capt. Eugeniusz Triebling (No. 6995), Eugeniusz Dulin
(No. 31007), Teofil Banasiuk (No. 1698), Jan Hrebenda
(No. 3665), Jan Mielcarek (No. 3569), Off.Cad. (Res.)
Remigiusz Niewiarowski (TAP, No. 13957), Maj.
Wacław Chmielewski (TAP, No. 37995), Tadeusz
Dobrowolski (No. ...), Jerzy Wierusz-Kowalski,
father (TAP, No. 31356), Platoon Leader Stanisław
Kotarski (No. ...), Plat.Lead. Józef Chramiec (No. 101),

Stefan Gaik (No. ...), Serg. Maj. Zygmunt Jaworski
(TAP, No. 18435), Prof. Roman Rybarski (No. 18599),
Kazimierz Rogalewicz (No. 3473), Bolesław Leśniewicz
(No. 21991), or Stanisław Leśniewicz (No. 14449), Czesław
Sikora (No. 76159), Stanisław Polkowski (No. 6398),
Teofil Staniszkis (No. 18624), Off. Cad. (Res.) Jan Wysocki
(TAP, No. 13436), Alojzy Fusek (No. ...), Józef Gałka
(No. 10611), Cav. Cpt. (Res.) Tadeusz Czechowski
(No. 18369), Witold Myszkowskl (No. 2606), Andrzej
Marduła (No. 18855).

Released by the camp's authorities

Aleksander Wielopolski (No. ...), Corp. Czesław
Wąsowski (No. 5298), Second Lieutenant (Res.) Tadeusz
Burski (No. ...), Off.Cad. Krzysztof Hoffman (No. 2738),
Dr. Marian Dipont (No. 2186).

Released by the authorities and took report for the Organisation

Col. Władysław Surmacki (TAP, No. 2795), Cpt.
Ferdynand Trojnicki (No. 5145), Serg. Antoni Woźniak
(No. 5512), First Lieutenant (Res.) Karol Świętorzecki
(No. 5360), Aleksander Paliński (No. 8253).

Transferred to Dachau when ill (arranged)

Jan Dangel (TAP, No. 13486).

Transferred to other camps

Second Lieutenant (Res.) Mikolaj Skornowicz (No. ...), Tadeusz Słowiaczek (No. 1069), Platoon Leader Władyslaw Kupiec (No. 793), Col. Tadeusz Reklewski (No. 6471), Second Lieutenant Konstanty Piekarski (No. 4618), Col. Jerzy Zalewski (No. 21514), Off.Cad. (Res.) Zbigniew Różak (No. 6609), Off.Cad. (Res.) Zygmunt Wanicki (No. 2199), Wiktor Śniegucki (No. 6274), Tadeusz Pietrzykowski 'Teddy' (No. 77), Cpt. Julian Trzęsimiech (No. ...), Stanisław Ozimek (TAP, No. ...), Henryk Kowalczyk (No. 64276), Leszek Cenzartowicz (No. 870), Second Lieutenant (Res.) Jerzy Wiśniewski (No. 31361), Second Lieutenant (Res.) Lech (No. ..), Father Zygmunt Ruszczak (No. 9842), Wacław Kafarowski (No. 12079), Czesław Darkowski (TAP, No. 8121), Lolek Słowiaczek (No. 1054), Cav.Serg. Jan Miksa (No. ...), Edward Nowak (No. 447), Second Lieutenant (Res.) Władysław Rapa (No. 30901), Aleksander Bugajski (No. 74503), Kazimierz Radwański (No. 16788), Dr. Zygmunt Zakrzewski (TAP, No. 39249), Tadeusz Kowalski (No. ...), Józef Putek (No. 267), Michał Szarzyński (No. 82795), Olek – room supervisor at Block 6 (No. ...), Wawrzyński, (TAP, No. ...).

Requested transfer to attempt an escape while in transit

Col. Kazimierz Rawicz (known in the camp as Jan Hilkner, No. 9319), Off. Cad. Witold Szymkowiak (No. 938), through whom I send this report.

Shot dead during an escape

Platoon Leader Stanisław Maringe (TAP, No. 12691), First Lieutenant (Res.) Jerzy Poraziński (TAP, No. ...).

PART II – HIS JOURNEY OF DUTY   249

Left the camp in an arranged escape to deliver a report to the Organisation

Wincenty Gawron (No. 11237), Stefan Bielecki (TAP
No. 12692), Off.Cad. Mieczysław Januszewski (No. 711),
Stanisław Jaster (No. 6438), Second Lieutenant (Res.)
Jan Redzej (known in the camp as Jan Retko, No. 5430),
Edward Ciesielski (No. 12969), and myself – Witold Pilecki
(TAP, No. 4859).

Still at the camp

Cpt. Dr. Władysław Dering (TAP, No. 1723), Off.Cad.
(Res.) Antoni Rosa (No. 923), Off.Cad. Michał Ziółkowski
(No. 1055), Platoon Leader Tadeusz Szydlik (No. 2198),
Col.Teofil Dziama (No. 13578), Second Lieutenant (Res.)
Jan Olszowski (No. 6157), Second Lieutenant (Res.)
Jan Pilecki (No. 808), Henryk Bartosiewicz (No. 9406),
Cpt. Stanisław Kazuba (No. 1630), Second Lieutenant
(Res.) Bernard Świerczyna (No. 1393), Off. Cad.
(Res.) Mieczysław Wagner (No. 5831), Maj. Zygmunt
Bończa-Bohdanowski (TAP, No. 30959), Off.Cad.
(Res.) Zygmunt Bujanowski (No. ...), Zygmunt Kotecki
(No. ..), Jan Ziębma (No. 66), Zygmunt Sobolewski
(No. 88), Antoni Trzaskowski (No. 13321), Col. Juliusz
Gilewicz (No. 31033), Cpt. Tadeusz Lisowski (No. 329),
Motyka (No. ..), Alfred Włodarczyk (No. 1349), Witold
Kosztowny (No. 672), Dr. Rudolf Diem (No. 10022),
First Lieutenant (Res.) Marian Moniczewski (No. 18859),
Second Lieutenant (Res.) Leon Murzyn (No. 820), Second
Lieutenant Witold Wierusz (No. 9479), Second Lieutenant
(Res.) Edmund Zabawski (No. 19547), Jan Machnowski
(No. 724), Off. Cad. (Res.) Zbigniew Goszczyński
(No. 1728), Zdzisław Uliasz (No. 12988), 'Alojz' from
the uniform store (Bekleidungskammer) (No. ..),

Andrzej Gąsienica (No. 5654), Roman Frankiewicz (No. 9430), Tadeusz Jakubowski (No. 2541), Cavalry Sergeant-Major Stefan Gąsiorowski (No. 9201), Wacław Weszke (No. 9530), Stanisław Kożuch (No. 325), Sergeant-Major Szczepan Rzeczkowski (TAP, No. 13600), Jerzy Wierusz-Kowalski – son (TAP, No. 31357), Platoon Leader Antoni Koszczyński (No. 4075), Cpt. Michał Więcki (No. 1036), First Lieutenant 'Włodek Owczarz' (No. ...), Serg. Władysław Kielczyk (No. 4266), Sailor Aleksander Kasper (No. 3894), Cpt. Janusz Goślinowski (No. 8252), Konstanty Jagiełło (No. 4507), Cpt. Stanisław Machowski (No. 78056), 'Czesiek' (presumably: Czesław Sowul, No. 167), 'Tadek' (No. ...), Tadeusz Stulgiński (TAP, No. 31315), Henryk Szklarz (No. 1132), Edward Sikorski (No. 25419), Józef Gralla (No. 25249), Dr. Władysław Tondos (No. 18871), Jan Mosdorf (No. 8230), Marian Toliński (No. 49), Władysław Fejkiel (No. 5647), Stanisław Głowa (No. 20017), Off.Cad. (Res.) Tadek, *sekretarz bloku* 22a (No. ...), 'Mały Zygmunt' from the laboratory (No. ...), Ignacy Wołkowicz (No. 7143), Ryszard Wiśniewski (No. 9580), Zdzisław Ryndak (No. 10746), Andrzej Rablin (No. 1410), Off.Cad. Leon Mackiewicz (No. 3618), Col. Kazimierz Stamirowski (No. 86786), Karol Karp (No. 626), Ficek and Tadek .... – grave-diggers (Nos ...), Dr. Bolesław Świderski (No. 952), Edward Kowalski (No. 1701), Witold Kupczyński (No. 3829), Roman Kostrzewski (No. 4612), Stanisław Kocjan (No. 11544), Jerzy Żarnowiecki (No. 616), Tadeusz Myszkowski (No. 593), Stanisław Wolak (No. 1058), Maksymilian Piłat (No. 5131), Off.Cad. (Res.) Witold Wysocki – from Vilnius (No. ...), Off.Cad. Jurek ..... – electrician (No. ...), Stefan Dziurkacz (No. ...), Stefan – a colleague of Heniek B. (No. ...).

June 1943

The following [report] records facts and names of Auschwitz inmates who worked there for the *Organizacja Wojskowa* [It was written – addition by this translator] after the successful individually arranged escape from the camp during the night from 26 into 27 April 1943, that is after 31 months I had spent in the camp. From the beginnings of the camp until March 1943 some 11,200 inmates had been shot there, some 34,000 gassed in the chambers, about 41,000 died from various causes, killed otherwise in public, died of diseases or due to various other circumstances; some 6,000 had by March 1943 been transferred to other camps, and 1115 inmates had been released.

In March 1943, there were about 25,000 inmates in the camp. Numbers being allocated to new arrivals at that time were just over 121,000. Those numbers applied to inmates [*Häftlings*]. Upon their arrival, they were all duly registered and had their successive inmate numbers tattooed.

Numbers, however, were not given to huge masses of other people who were brought here for them to be instantly killed. The latter [mass killing] activity took place a few kilometres away from the Auschwitz camp, in Rajsko, where an associated Birkenau [Brzezinka] camp was established. There, whole transports of people were delivered by trains or trucks – often a few thousand people per day, amounting to a total which was by August 1942 more than 800,000, and by March 1943 over 1.5 million. Most of those people were Jews, but there also were Czechs, Germans and other nationalities among them. It caused us a particularly great pain when in enormous piles of clothes and things left by the gassed people we coul find children's little shoes and prams, also rosaries and Polish prayer books. Among others killed in this horrific slaughter there also were people from a few villages from the Lublin province. Moreover, during that period some 11,400 war inmates [Bolsheviks] were killed in various ways in our camp and all its sub-camps.

After my arrival at the Auschwitz camp (the night of September 21-22, 1940), I suddenly found myself, as all new arrivals at Auschwitz do, in a situation that defied all my former experience. During the first few days I felt bewildered, as if dropped off onto another planet.

With SS-men urging us with rifle butts into a floodlit, barbed-wire-surrounded area, we ran past some loudly laughing Kapos decorated with green and red patches in places where one would display one's orders. Making most of their cudgels the Kapos lined us up, and, jeering wildly and exchanging jokes, they killed most of sick and weak people [from this transport], as well as anyone who imprudently confessed to being a judge, or a priest. All this made me feel as if we were being locked up in an asylum.

During my first few days there I witnessed some very gruesome incidents, such that the Dante's description of hell would pale beside them. I will not describe these here, nor any of those I witnessed during the years I spent in the camp. This will be done by my colleagues: 'J' and 'E'. I keep these to myself. [The Polish phrase Pilecki uses here is: '*wejrzałem w siebie...*', this phrase must leave one guessing as to what exactly he meant here – translator's note]

Out of necessity, I will digress here. When describing my experiences to a few acquaintances after my return from the camp I touched upon [the matter of extreme cruelty]. Their view was that 'normal people' would find it difficult to comprehend. Courtesy would require not to call these people by any other name here (I will do it later in this report, though) since for a number of years I had referred to a certain kind of these 'normal people' using very different expressions.

We live in a time and age that some people define as a threshold of two epochs. Some people say: 'we are right now taking a turn ...' Others seek to provide to the mankind a new political system, and they write about it. All those wiser than most agree on one thing: that we have got bogged down very badly, as the Scholastics did before.

Apart from that, we (by which I mean here the 'normal ones') are paralysed by a fear psychosis. This does not allow us to do or say anything that goes beyond the framework deemed appropriate for 'the average people', lest they flare up. God forbid that they should be ridiculed by others. For instance, I met some people, most of them males, supposedly believers, who feel ashamed to make a clear sign of cross and only make something vaguely resembling this sign. This is an excellent example of the shame-and-fear psychosis: not to make this sign lest some idiot from a crowd ridicule them. Better to idle away, surrounded by a pack of idiots, than to have someone point finger at them and regard them as someone unintelligible to an average person. I certainly do not write about it, so as to lord it over anyone.

On the contrary, I only would like to shake everyone up so that, instead of them remaining at a certain mob-normalised level, new shoots emerge here and there of thoughts and deeds conceived by individuals unconcerned about a chance that some jealous blockhead next to them will hit them on the head to make sure that none of those near them towers over the crowd, that none grows above the rest. And yet it is only those who do grow above the average that are able to create new ideas and introduce these to other people to open new horizons before them.

My digression explains that in no way would I expect to be counted amongst those you could call 'some normal people from a crowd.' I would not like to have to force myself to fit the tight frames of their notions. Having explained this, I hope it should become easier to comprehend what I found in myself and what I chose to write about, the very things I initially intended to remain silent about after I have heard from my acquaintances that 'those things are very difficult to grasp.' To leave anything [essential] out could well render the successive parts of my story unintelligible.

[At Auschwitz] I once found inner joy at a moment one would think was least likely to produce that kind of feeling.

It was when I stood in the ranks made up of the 'Bloodthirsty Alojz' block inmates – and when I saw Krankenmann [elsewhere: Krankemann] 'thin out' the ranks of the penal company right in front of us, with a knife that he would plunge into the abdomen of any person who would move a few centimetres too far forward – that, with some surprise and at first unprepared to believe [the genuiness of] that feeling, I did realise that I had just found a joy in myself: I became aware that I again wanted to fight: my initial few days crisis had luckily been over. That at last (it has been my yearning since 1939, a yearning which a soldier can understand better than other people), I stood in a line as straight as a tightened string, a line of furious men standing arm to arm, united by the same purpose and the same thought, a line of Poles prepared to fight. These were ideal people with which to start an organisation.

This was the source of the force that told me to believe and create. So, I commenced this work. After a few weeks, I had the first cell of *Organizacja Wojskowa* established at Auschwitz. It comprised some people from Warsaw.

In October 1940, I sent my first message to Warsaw. I handed it in to Captain Michał Romanowicz, who had contact with Aleksander Wielopolski, an intelligence operative working under Tęczyński. Wielopolski was about to be released from the camp.

I made Colonel Władysław Surmacki in charge of the first 'Upper Five' (Col. Władysław Surmacki, Cpt. Dr. Władysław Dering, Cavalry Cpt. (Res.) Jerzy de Virion, Eugeniusz Obojski and Roman Zagner). I had known him for a long time and had involved him in May 1940 in Warsaw in TAP work as its Chief of Staff. In March 1941, I put together the second 'Upper Five' (Officer Cadet Witold Szymkowiak, Officer Cadet Antoni Rosa, Tadeusz Słowiaczek, Second Lieutenant Mikołaj Skornowicz, Władysław Kupiec, Bolesław Kupiec, Tadeusz Pietrzykowski) from among inmates with the lowest numbers. In May 1941, from among those who came in the fourth and fifth Warsaw transports, I formed the third 'Upper Five' (Cpt. Eugeniusz Triebling, First Lieutenant Włodzimierz Makaliński, First Lieutenant (Res.) Stanisław Gutkiewicz, Wincenty Gawron, Stanisław Stawiszyński). In October 1941, I formed the fourth 'Five' (Henryk Bartosiewicz, Cpt. Stanisław Kazuba, Second Lieutenant Konstanty Piekarski, Stefan Bielecki, First Lieutenant (Res.). Tadeusz Lech). [By the way], I never blindly stuck to the number of five.

None of those 'Fives' knew anything about the other 'Fives'. Believing that their own cell formed the peak of our organisation, they would develop it independently from the others, extending its branches for them to reach as far as the collective energy and capacity of its members made it possible. Each cell was further augmented by the capacities of members at the lower rungs of this organisation, whose numbers have been steadily growing, due to the efforts from all Upper Fives. Our work consisted in saving lives of our colleagues through providing supplementary food, recommending them to those in charge of individual blocks, ensuring [proper] care when at the *Krankenbau* [the camp's hospital for inmates was named *Häftlingskrankenbau* – A.C.], providing fresh linen and underwear, finding better jobs/positions, providing moral support, distributing the information from outside the camp, maintaining contacts with the local population, delivering camp messages to the outside world, putting together all active individuals **into one system, to prepare for a co-ordinated action to take over the camp once an outside order has been given, or** [to coincide with] **a raid** [from outside] **on the camp**.

To increase our security, I have decided that the first Five should know nothing about the next one. For the same reason, I **initially** did not approach senior officers who were registered under their own names. Some of them, colonels whose ranks were hardly a secret, were at that time already developing plans to take over the camp. In April 1941, my colleagues reported with increasing frequency that Colonel Aleksander Stawarz and Lieutenant-Colonel Karol Kumuniecki were of the view that inmates should liberate the camp. Approximate dates for it were circulated. Lieutenant-Colonel Kumuniecki was to take all healthy inmates towards Katowice, and Colonel Stawarz was to stay put with all sick ones. Bearing in mind the openness and naïveté of this planning, I kept myself for a while away from it all. On May 15, 1941, I sent a corresponding message to Warsaw through Lieutenent (Res.) Karol Świętorzecki as he was released from the camp.

Meanwhile, our organisation (we never referred to [its true name] in the open, and used [this word] only in a different meaning) had been growing quite fast.

The huge milling stones of this camp incessantly churned out new corpses. Many colleagues died and they had to be replaced with others. And so, we had to repeatedly reconstruct [our organisation], again and again.

We have kept on sending messages to the outside world. They were broadcast by foreign radio stations. The camp's command went mad about it. They would strip the floors in the lofts looking for something there. Once they have branched out far enough, individual 'Upper Fives' would report to me a 'tangible' existence of another organisation (i.e. another 'Five'). In November 1941, I sent a message to Warsaw through Captain Ferdynand Trojnicki as he got released from the camp. At the very same time, in my letters to my family which went by a roundabout way, I asked that no attempt be made to buy me out from the camp. This would have been feasible since they had no case against me. I was thrilled by this game and its expected finale.

In December 1941, I sent a message to Warsaw through Colonel Władysław Surmacki who got released. Next day after his arrival at Warsaw he once again got arrested and [later] shot at Pawiak. Nonetheless, in March 1942 he still managed to pass on through Sergeant Antoni Woźniak a few words about our work to his wife.

In Autumn 1941, Colonel Jan Karcz and First Lieutenant-Colonel Jerzy Zalewski were brought to the camp. I invited Colonel Jan Karcz to join our organisation. He agreed. A few months later he was taken to the bunker and tormented there. Since he did not divulge anything he was released from the bunker and transferred to Brzezinka, an Auschwitz sub-camp. He did some work for our organisation there.

As already mentioned, out of prudence I had so far tried to avoid involving in our organisation's work higher ranked officers which had been known here under their true names. However, lest it be wrongly attributed to my 'exaggerated ambition', I decided to subordinate myself to Colonel Kazimierz Rawicz. He was approached by my friend Henryk Bartosiewicz. Colonel Rawicz came here under an assumed name and was positively and widely believed to be a civilian person. Colonel Rawicz joined our organisation. His work plan had been agreed with him and we since continued to work together.

Then I put together the fifth 'Upper Five' (Second Lieutenant (Res.) Bernard Świerczyna, Officer Cadet (Res.) Zbigniew Ruszczański, Officer Cadet (Res.) Mieczysław Wagner, Officer Cadet (Res.) Zbigniew Różak, Platoon Leader Tadeusz Szydlik).

In March 1942, Major Zygmunt Bończa-Bohdanowski arrived at the camp. I had known him for many years. I enlisted him in the TAP as its commanding officer for the Warsaw area. At the camp, I made him Operation Commander of all organised units.

In January 1942, I sent to Warsaw some brief messages through our colleague Aleksander Paliński.

In 1941, we had in the camp the ten-times-responsibility rule, which meant that ten prisoners were executed for each escaped prisoner. Because of that **we did not at first organise any escapes**. Early in 1942 Berlin banned this, so we started planning escapes. In May 1942, our colleagues Stefan Bielecki and Wincenty Gawron were successful, and I was able to send my message to Warsaw through them. Following their escape, there were no repressions at the camp.

In June, First Lieutenant Włodzimierz Makaliński from the 13th Uhlans Regiment got executed by shooting. He had worked very closely with me and had fought very bravely in the 1939 war. I grieved over his death.

At the same time, more than eighty inmates from Silesia, among them a member of our organisation First Lieutenant (Res.) Stanisław Gutkiewicz, were shot. The November 11, 1941 execution, which claimed the life of [among others] our very brave First Lieutenant (Res.) Tadeusz Lech, was the first one on such a large scale.

Owing to Henryk Bartosiewicz's exertions, we managed to reach an understanding with Colonel Aleksander Stawarz for him to join our organisation's planning cell.

In June 1942, the camp authorities ostentatiously put on display a body of a German soldier who allegedly had been killed by some Polish inmates, [ostensibly] seeking to provoke some reaction and unrest within the camp. The authorities hoped the [resulting] tension among the Polish inmates would reveal what our actual reading of all this was. [Nothing eventuated, so] they undertook no further action and the whole business got eventually burked.

At that time and for many following months, until March 7, 1943, we were perfectly capable of taking over the camp at any moment and only because we would consider the general situation on the outside, absence of an order [to commence an inmates' uprising], **or of a** [scheduled] **air strike** [on the camp], **either of which would have untied our hands (as a vis maior),** [taking also into account] **a possibility of a conflict with the best understood overall interest and similar concerns, we had not initiated such a spontaneous action.**

Our tragedy was not that, as [some] **people in Warsaw thought, we were only 'walking bags of bones.'**

On the contrary, our tragedy was that despite being strong and having influence on our local situation, due to our concern for the general consequences [of our action]**, our hands were tied and we faked helplessness.**

We needed an order, a permission, an assent from our authorities in Warsaw lest we were told later: Mr W., J. or H., your ambition had cost our nation a number of victims. [We needed it] **lest we were pointed out as an example of our centuries-old national vices: lack of discipline and insubordination.**

Due to [the members of] our commanding bodies being at that time in various blocks, we divided our forces into four main large detachments according to their respective tasks when taking over the camp. Two scenarios regarding such an event were considered: (1) there would be a call to action when the camp was at work, or (2) there would be a call to action when all [inmates] were in their blocks (night-time, lights on).

Around that time, I sent out a message through Stanisław Jaster who, in a joint effort with his three colleagues, arranged a brilliant escape in the camp's commandant car. When already en route they encountered [outside the camp] the *Lagerführer* [Camp Head] and, very cheekily, made him salute back inmates dressed in [German] military uniforms.

Only when at Auschwitz and doing our [daily] work did I experience a moment one would dream about in vain when free. Only when faced with heaps of corpses, did our politicians[429] abandon their party-versus-party bickering – a waste of energy I have always found so loathsome. The political cell of our organisation included Prof. Roman Rybarski, former MP Stanisław Dubois, our colleagues Konstanty Jagiełło, Piotr Kownacki, and Kiliański. All of them worked together, very accommodatingly, and in an exemplary manner.

In July 1942, Colonel Kazimierz Rawicz and Officer Cadet Witold Szymkowiak from the 10th Uhlans Regiment applied for a transport to another camp and left [Auschwitz]. [They both] intended to escape whilst in transit. I sent a message through Szymkowiak. Neither Colonel Kazimierz Rawicz, nor Officer Cadet Witold Szymkowiak managed to escape during their transport. They are now at another camp and I corresponded with them via their families. Before his departure, Colonel Kazimierz Rawicz suggested for me to turn to Colonel Juliusz Gilewicz to involve him in our work in place of the departing Colonel Kazimierz Rawicz. I spoke to Colonel Juliusz Gilewicz: he agreed and then joined our organisation. We continued our work in a new make-up. Thanks to Henryk Bartosiewicz's efforts we were [also] joined by Lieutenant-Colonel Karol Kumuniecki. And so there hardly were any officers left [in the camp] who would not work for our organisation.

Soon thereafter, Colonel Aleksander Stawarz and our colleague Stanisław Dubois were executed by shooting.

During the typhus fever epidemic in August 1942, the authorities killed in gas chambers many inmates who had already recovered, but were still in the typhus block (No 20) as convalescents. This was done under the guise of a 'delousing measure.' They went to the gas chamber with full awareness that their death was a result of them happening to be still inside this block on the day they [the guards] took all people from it to kill them in the chamber. The block was cordoned off and all [who were inside], except for physicians and nurses, were driven away in cars to be gassed. Captain Dr. Władysław Dering was very helpful: he saved lives of over twenty Poles by providing nurses' uniforms to them.

I fell ill with typhus six days after this mass gassing, but luckily managed to recover from it. Almost all 'old numbers' contracted typhus.

After the general delousing of the camp, the authorities relocated inmates in such a way that all members of all detachments found themselves in the same block. Unbeknownst to them, they made our tasks simpler in case a [liberation] action was to be undertaken. Now that the two scenarios (1. Detachments at work, or 2. Inmates at block) were no longer necessary, I divided all our forces, ignoring the frameworks of individual 'Fives', into battalions, companies and platoons, and assigned areas of operation for all of them combining individual blocks into battalions. As their commanding officers, I appointed:

Operation Commander – Major Zygmunt Bończa-Bohdanowski, Battalion 1 – Major Edward Gött-Getyński, Battalion 2 – Captain Stanisław Kazuba, Battalion 3 – Captain Tadeusz Lisowski and Battalion 4 – Captain Julian 'Trzęsimiech'.

At a roll-call on October 28, 1942, under the pretence of a need for some inmates to call at the *Erkennungsdienst* [the camp's records office] regarding their photos many of our colleagues, mostly from the province of Lublin (even though there were among them also people from other regions of Poland, such as our brave Stanisław Stawiszyński), had to step forward from the line. When all camp was at work, all 265 of them were executed in Block 11 by shooting. For the first time ever, five of the condemned inmates, among them Captain Dr. Henryk Suchnicki and Leon Kukiełka, encouraged others to resist. Except for these five, however, everyone else decided that it was their duty to die, due to the likelihood of reprisals against their families. They had a few hours to think it over. The above-mentioned five inmates had already barricaded the entry into Block 11. Tipped off by a man from Silesia, their informer, the camp authorities arrived there, disposed of the five first, and then proceeded to kill each one of them with a single shot to the back of head from a small-calibre rifle, or an air gun.

October 28, 1942 was a day of huge tension for us. At first, we did not know why some of us were called out. Later, we were unable to communicate with each other. At the top of our organisation we were nearly biting our finger nails: if only we obtained a word from our kinfolk from outside [the camp].

What we awaited from these 265 was their decision. Their mutiny would have untied our hands. Our scruples would have been pushed aside by this change in the situation, regardless of whether we had liked it or not. We would have taken over our camp. So, we waited. They decided otherwise. We saw how bravely they met their deaths.

From the very moment, they were arranged near Block 3 in fives by Palitsch who carried a small calibre rifle, they knew they were going to die. From Block 3, they took a bend between Blocks 14 and 15, the kitchen and [Blocks] 16, 17, 18, then proceeded between [Blocks] 25, 26, 27 and 19, 20, 21. At the timber canteen building, the column hesitated a second, then promptly made up its mind and - turning at the right angle - aimed right at the death gates of Block 11. The day was sunny. The column of 265 inmates marched briskly in well dressed-up fives, [all of them] strong, young, select. Quite a few of them cracked jokes: most mouths were smiling for most of them were camp veterans. Many times before, they saw larger or smaller groups of their colleagues march to meet their death. They would later have made comments on who was facing death and how they behaved. Never before, though, had there been that many victims: 265 of them, a whole column without any escort, all alone, followed by the select pair talking to each other: 'Bruno' and Palitzsch with a rifle on a belt [looking] as if they were having just a walk. One must concede this: Palitzsch was not a coward. It would have sufficed for the last five to do a sudden turn-about, and both Palitsch and 'Bruno' would have breathed their last within half a minute. They were, however, sure of themselves: they knew that the people who marched to meet their death would have learned from recent arrivals that the enemy does not spare families of those who engage in a mutiny. To save their lives they would not condemn their mothers, wives and children to death or tortures. Their experience of hell had already elevated their souls: they simultaneously experienced here heaven and hell. Apart from those who had already died, how many of them had more than once risked their lives to save a friend?

Exchanging comments on this with a few of my friends later in the evening we asked ourselves: **will people outside this camp ever come to appreciate and understand this?** Maybe those five did not have any relatives, or maybe they had reached their breaking-point? Still, they were unable to take the remaining ones with them. Maybe they made up their minds too late - when they were all already locked up in Block 11. They only expedited their own deaths. The rest had to wait for theirs a few hours longer, until noon.

This [execution] was a pay-back for what occurred earlier in the province of Lublin. In Autumn 1942, there arrived at the camp a few people I knew from my work in Warsaw: Second Lieutenant (Res.) Stanisław Wierzbicki, Czesław Sikora, Kiliański, and Captain Stanisław Machowski who, according to Second First Lieutenant

(Res.) Stanisław Wierzbicki, was a staff officer at the Warsaw High Command. Even though they had all, until the last moments before their arrest, worked in Warsaw, these four people knew very little about Auschwitz. Second Lieutenant (Res.) Stanisław Wierzbicki only knew he needed to find 'Witold', yet he knew nothing about mass killings by gas, about 'Kanada', about phenol injections, 'pyramids', the Block 10 secret, or about the Block's 11 'Death Wall'. Second Lieutenant (Res.) Stanisław Wierzbicki brought me some good news: Stefan Bielecki we sent [with reports] had luckily got through to Warsaw and had now a job. He himself gave him once a lift by car to Mińsk Litewski. This cheered us up as up to that moment we had had no news about our **emissaries**. All of them would, as it were, melt into thin air.

When asked what people on the outside think about escapes from Auschwitz Second Lieutenant (Res,) Stanisław Wierzbicki answered: there are two opinions on that. Most people condemn it, as they believe that ten people are still executed for each escapee. The Warsaw High Command, in turn, decorates escapees from Auschwitz with Virtuti Militari. Now that I got out myself I can only laugh about it. Poor thing: he told us this story to talk us into an escape from Auschwitz, possibly together with him. He did not survive even two months.

All of them: Sec.Lieut (Res.) Stanisław Wierzbicki, Czesław Sikora and Kiliański told us they were surprised at our physical condition (in Warsaw they had a picture of the Polish inmates here as "bags of bones'). They brought us also some less pleasing news: in general, **very few** people think about Auschwitz, and **there is no intention to save Auschwitz inmates, as this would not pay off**. After all, they are all **'good-for-nothing'**: just bags of bones. Thinking about it was both bitter, and funny. We saw our Polish mates standing before us: all of them pictures of health. We were **not asking** anyone for any help: all we were waiting for was an order, **an authorisation** for us to commence an action of our own, or an order **banning** it.

At the end of their briefing, the newly arrived asked us for help. Captain Stanisław Machowski was taken care of by his former acquaintance and subordinate Motyka, who worked for us, and the rest were taken care of by others. We found some light jobs for all of them.

History repeats itself: both those who die in the camps and those who **live on** in the camps are **misunderstood**. I think, it will take many years for their remains to be given due tribute.

Over the years that I had spent in the camp, now and then some inmates would seek to persuade me that one should not get involved in any conspiracy when at the camp, as this would be against 'the wishes of society.' I could not accept this, since following this line of thinking, it would be necessary for each Pole brought to the camp to die as quickly as possible, in order to fulfil 'the wish of the **rest of the society**'. He should not struggle for better conditions, or take care of his colleagues, or provide moral support to anyone. [All that] so that he, when the moment [of liberation] arrives, if he is still alive by then, could melt into a pack of torpid blockheads who naturally would no longer be any threat to the enemy, or to other Poles who consciously or otherwise appear to view their brothers, imprisoned in the camps, as their future competitors for laurels.

Those in the camp had, however, other things than laurels on their mind. In our daily work, we sought to strengthen our Polish brethren in their fight so that as few as possible Polish beings would leave through the crematorium's chimney. Sometimes, one day appeared to us as long, as a year.

Further, some people insisted that it was only they themselves who had the authority to do any underground work. This happened even in the camp, Inside their minds, others apparently had ceased to be Poland's sons. Let's take 'Czesiek' and 'Tadek' as an example: they had good contacts with the local population, and thus their communication lines reached further [than those of the others]. Their 'Upper Five' had also branched out the widest of any unit, and had gone so far from its basis that its members suggested to me, through Second Lieutenant Konstanty Piekarski, that they alone were [truly] authorised by Warsaw to do the work in the camp's area (reports, photos). In "Warsaw's view" all others, so claimed 'Czesiek' and 'Tadek', should discontinue their [resistance] activities. That amounted to almost the same as if to tell the others to cease to exist. Earlier in Warsaw, I had got used to that kind of exaggerated self-opinion which is quite widespread among Poles: the idea that one person and he alone can do a certain thing, and thus [only] he is **authorised** to do it. Because of that, I did not take this too much to my heart, all the more so that this was their usual way to defeat competition in order to secure future spoils **for themselves**.

Concerning our wireless [communication]: apart from our portable radio transmitter which we had to dismantle in Autumn 1942, because of some careless tongues, and our receiver, I also managed to get access, together with Second Lieutenant Konstanty Piekarski, to the local German camp radio station. There, we replaced our former Commander Sokołowski who had acted a bit clumsily. Our task there was to prepare maps for the camp authority. With the help from Officer Cadet (Res.) Zbigniew Ruszczyński, we managed to set up our cell there. From that cell, I obtained a complete set of slips as well as coded abbreviations used by the *Funkstelle* [the radio and telegraphic communications centre at the Oświęcim SS garrison headquarters – Translator's note]. They were referred to [by Germans] as *Verkehrabkürzungen* [communication abbreviations – Translator's note].

I passed on these slips through my colleague Eugeniusz Dulin using the contacts some inmates had established with the civilian workers in Brzeszcze, who were themselves the organisation's civilian members on the outside. They maintained that a 'recapture' of the Auschwitz camp and avenging the death of so many martyrs was in their plans. Inmates of weaker morale were quick to pick this up and would later contend we should ourselves do nothing of the kind, but only wait for us to be 'freed by someone.' It turned out, we were to wait in vain.

In 1942, without any difficulty, I reassigned our organisation's members to appropriate Kommandos [camp work details – Translator's note], so as to prepare the ground there for the commencement of the work for our organisation. This became possible because of a member of our organisation, Officer Cadet Mieczysław Januszewski, who managed to secure an Arbeitsdienst [work assignment officer] job. As a result, many members of our organisation were able to secure convenient jobs, i.e. jobs with a good Kommando [a camp work detail], where they stood a better chance of staying alive or, taking our organisation's perspective, with a Kommando in which it was easier to organise an escape as was the case with Wincenty Gawron and Stefan Bielecki who took a message to Warsaw; [thanks to which] we were able to save the lives of these two colleagues who already had death sentences for possessing weapons.

1942 ended with a prank that four inmates from the camp's elite, all of them *Arbeitdiensts* (ie. those whose responsibility was to allocate jobs to other inmates –

translator's note) – these inmates being Mieczysław
Januszewski, German Otto Küsel, Bolesław Kuczbara
and Jan Baraś-Komski [1] – played on the *Lagerältester*[430]
Bronisław Brodniewicz, alias Inmate No. 1, a Pole
who spied for the Germans. Brodniewicz was dubbed
'Bruno – Black Death' (*Bruno – czarna śmierć*). The
first two pranksters, Mietek (Officer Cadet Mieczysław
Januszewski) and Otto (Inmate No. 2), both brave, of
amiable appearance and popular with inmates, taking
advantage of their freedom of movement within the camp
and around the outer chain of sentries, escaped in a horse-
drawn cart, taking two of their colleagues with them. At
the same time, they did a great favour to us inmates by
sending a letter to one of the camp's [foremost] torturers,
namely Brodniewicz. The letter was written in a friendly
tone (even though Inmate No. 1 and Inmate No. 2 hated
each other's guts, and made this hatred rather well known).
It contained apologies that everything had occurred in such
a way, that they had to hurry away and could not, despite
a [previous] agreement, take the *Lagerältester* with them.
Even though [for us inmates] no agreement with Bruno was
ever possible, let alone one regarding an escape, the camp's
authorities deprived that butcher of his freedom, and
confined him to a bunker. There, for three months, he had
to explain this matter. The escape took place on December
30. Locking Bruno up on the New Year's Eve caused
all festive season, until January 6, to abound in parties,
masquerades, boxing matches, concerts and dancing
events, all unheard of before. To the oldest inmates, all that
business looked like a folly before the storm.

**From the camp's very beginnings, the discipline
in the camp had slowly but steadily been weakening.**
[The experience of] someone who arrived at the camp
a month later than somebody else did not differ all that
much, in that the former had merely spent 30 days fewer

than a longer-term inmate, but rather it lay in the fact that [the former] had experienced fewer methods of tormenting inmates, for some of these methods could simply have been discontinued since the previous month. Many methods [of tormenting inmates] were available to those in all sorts of positions of authority and to their tout pack. Some would apply them because of their inner urge to destroy the lives of those they hated, while others would apply them to endear themselves to those in positions of authority. SS-men would often openly say, as if to justify their behaviour: '*Das ist ein Vernichtungslager*' ['This is an extermination camp']. No wonder, those who had stayed at Auschwitz the longest reacted to the above-mentioned festive riotousness with these words: 'There once was a camp called Auschwitz. But now, thanks to God, it is no more. Barely, its last syllable had remained: "*wic*".' [The German word *der Witz* means 'joke'; the colloquial Polish uses a word of similar derivation, *wic*, which has the same informal meaning – Translator's note].

When returning in the evening to our blocks behind the barbed wire after all-day work, we would see a scene that could appear ghastly to people from outside this camp, a scene which did not trouble us, however, at all: the camp orchestra – made up of our colleagues who were musicians (doing a very good job), very much admired by all the commissions arriving from Berlin, and an orchestra in which our Camp Commandant would take pride (whenever it had a vacant position, a replacement was easily found on the outside, and brought to the camp) – played with much zest a march tune, usually a very lively one. At times, Kommandos marched to the tune of a *polka* or an *oberek* [two popular Polish folk dances – Translator's note]. However, not all of these could march as briskly as 'the old numbers', most of whom were employed at workshops. Some Kommandos could merely shuffle along:

these were 'the new numbers'. They carried [comrades] who had fainted, or hauled those who were too weak to walk by themselves. Some blood-covered heads which had been beaten by the hands of some moron from Silesia or Germany drooped inertly, or rested on the shoulders of their colleagues who carried them, their distressed faces next to [these blood-covered heads]. One could not help asking oneself a question: which of these heads were still alive? Here, they hauled a man more dead than alive, his abdomen touching the ground. Those who carried the man could barely walk themselves. They nevertheless needed to match the rhythm of this lively march, if they did not want to get blows on their own heads.

Our detachment is five hundred men strong, all of whom work at workshops. We are healthy, strong, even cheerful whenever we can muster. You see different faces here: most of us are camp veterans. Our step is firm. We now walk past a group representing camp authorities and we can still see on their faces, and in their eyes, their amusement brought about by the sight of the previous, pitiable column. The strong step of our colleagues, most of whom belong to our 'Fives', wipes away that smirk from our tyrants' faces. Even though they take pride in their workshops, in our work, even in ourselves, and often present us as model inmates to all sorts of commissions [visiting Auschwitz], they are now unwilling to look straight into our eyes, and turn theirs away. Our thought is: when will we finally be able to spring at you? Next to them, as an emergency, there are two detachments of heavily armed soldiers. Yet, this means nothing to us: we would not even give them time to breathe. **Yet we must not! Colleagues: we must not! The outside society would have paid dearly for that**, so it is being suggested to us from afar. **Is this not a calamity, a misjudgment?**

We walk past the crematorium. Next to its entry, we can see a group of men and women. [They are] Poles. We feel as if we were just a few steps from a slaughterhouse. My God, once we have got into the camp, these Polish women will be taken alive into the crematorium, issued a small piece of soap and a towel: all these males and females will think that they will have a bath. Sometimes, [the authorities] do not consider it necessary to play this comedy. When they are already inside the crematorium, a window in the ceiling will be opened and a container with gas thrown in through it. It will break open on impact. The metal container will contain diatomite crystals saturated with prussic acid, so-called cyclone-B. And such will be their lives' end. A small group will even be grudged the gas: they will simply stun them with a head hit and carry them while still alive right to the [crematorium's] grate. We walk past them, we can almost touch them. Us – healthy, strong men. We hope we will not see contempt in their eyes. Maybe, they still have some hope. Still, they do know that people come here to die. We have passed them. In many eyes we saw death, but not contempt. In many eyes, we saw even pride: that they would die at Auschwitz. One of them was a young boy, maybe ten years of age. He stood on his tiptoes, so that he could see us better. He smiled at us, maybe looking for someone he would know. We all have our beloved women. Some of us have small tots at home. We have seen here many infernal scenes, yet the eyes of these people keep us later awake at night. At the gate further down, there is another group of women and men that are turned away from us. They will remain there until this ghastly procession entering the camp has all walked past them. Later, they will be taken to Block 11 for examinations and then to the end of their peregrination: to the Death Wall. Afterwards, their bodies will be brought out in bloodied coffins to the same place to which the bodies from the first group would go and their ashes, together with the *Häftlings*' ashes, will be blown about by wind along the fields. Looking at these women, how many of my colleagues would think: it could be my Mother, my sister, my daughter. Yet, the camp resident's heart is hardened. Only a half an hour later, his thoughts are exclusively occupied with where to find some extra food. He strikes with a colleague some 'margarine deal', paying no attention to the fact that an enormous heap of naked corpses, killed on order by phenyl injections, is just a step away from him. Today, there are 'only' a hundred-odd of those. They are thrown down one on top of one another as they are brought from the hospital, their limbs spread, their dead pupils watching the business deal being struck, waiting for a cart to take them in a few hours to the crematorium. No-one would shudder if they happen to inadvertently touch, or even step on one of these naked ones. Yesterday, he may have been his colleague, today he lies here quietly, tomorrow maybe my body will lie here – big deal!

Following the festive season the year 1943 brought, apart from the replacement of the Lagerältester and a further softening of discipline, a continued supply of the usual camp scenes. In January 1943, they executed Colonel Jan Karcz as well as First Lieutenant (Res.) Eugeniusz Zaturski, once a TAP worker in Warsaw, by shooting. On February 16, they shot First Lieutenant (Res.) Stanisław Wierzbicki, also a former TAP worker. Later, they also shot the men whom they had kept for a long time in the bunker: Lieutenant-Colonel Karol Kumuniecki, Major Edward Gött-Getyński, First Lieutenant Tadeusz Biliński, Cav. First Lieutenant Włodzimierz Koliński and First Lieutenant Mieczysław Koliński – the two last-named were brothers – and many more, all with a single shot from an air gun to the back of their heads, a slight variation from the Katyń way.[431]

Similar to the Katyń massacre, the bodies of those killed by gas were at first buried in Brzezinka in huge trenches. For that they used a special Kommando of Jews only. They would be given two weeks to live, and then would be killed by gas themselves. Later, they found out that [burying corpses there] was not a good idea, because the local groundwater had acquired a nasty smell and 'the clues' had been left behind. So, they dug up the corpses, piled them up and burned them. At first, it was manual labour, but later they would use a crane. It was out of question to burn the bodies in the [existing] crematoria, as all of them were lagging behind [in their job]. As a new project, they designed two new crematoria with eight-body burning grates each. Burning a body by electrical current was to take only three minutes there. Calculations were made that when working two shifts, and burning two corpses on each grate at a time, the two crematoria could burn down about five million corpses yearly. The project was given a priority approval in Berlin, and the construction of these [machines] commenced. They were to be ready by February 1, 1943. Out of necessity, this deadline had to be later extended. By April 1943, they were all ready.

Witnessing killing healthy people by gas makes a strong impact only when you see it for the first time. A few months after the war with the Bolsheviks commenced [Hitler's Operation Barbarossa, beginning in June 1941], the camp authorities received its first transport of the prisoners of war: about seven hundred of them. In front of a commission of sorts they were crammed into one room at Block 11 (gas chambers were not ready for use yet) so that they could hardly stand by themselves. The whole room got then sealed up, and in the presence of onlookers protected by gas masks, [all of them were] killed by gas. Those who were able to peep in as the room was being aired later spoke of some most gruesome scenes there. Judging by the uniforms in which they have been gassed, they were all high-ranking Bolsheviks from various units. It looked as it was a try-out for killings with gas.

In November 1941 I witnessed, shortly after leaving my block in the morning, a march of several columns of completely naked people towards the crematorium. There were several hundred of them. Icy snow was falling at that time, and I shuddered at the thought how cold they must have been. They were all Bolsheviks. As this was the first instance of people being taken alive to the crematorium, I at first wondered what the purpose of this might be, given that there was no time there for anything else but burning corpses. The inmates who worked there in two shifts could hardly cope with the heaps of our colleagues' bodies. It turned out that they were made to undress and [then] brought straight to [be burnt in] the crematorium, so as to save time.

From the very beginnings of the camp's operation, although quite rarely, individual inmates – particularly those who were just randomly rounded up on the streets of Warsaw – would be released. However, as soon as the killing by gas started, all releases stopped until late in 1942, when many inmates, particularly those from Silesia, were allowed to leave the camp after they had signed the so-called *Volksdeutsch* list. They were then promptly drafted into the [German] military units, so that they had had little time left in which to put the information about the camp into circulation.

From the very beginning, the camp authorities sought to deprive us of our private time after work, however little of it was already left to us, for we also worked on Sundays. This was done by arranging various uniform reviews (*Sachenappell*), keeping us locked up inside the blocks

(*Blocksperre*) and – from the moment a typhus epidemic started – by looking for lice and checking of our linen by the nurses (*Läuseappell*). Under the guise of concern for hygiene, the idea was to leave to inmates as little time as possible during which they could talk to each other.

Once the authorities realised that Poles were doing well (thanks to their solidarity, their control of better jobs, support of ill inmates, the high percentage of recoveries made by ill persons, as well as 'accidental' deaths of stool-pigeons planted on us), an inkling [of the Organisation's existence] started forming in the minds of the authorities. In Autumn 1941, they deprived us of two hours of our private time on Sunday between 1 p.m. and 3 p.m., forcing us to sleep during that time. This was strictly enforced by the camp authorities. A prisoner who did not sleep after the Sunday lunch was regarded as a saboteur who was wasting his energy.

Seeing, nevertheless, that the efficacy of this new order was not as great as desired, the authorities adopted in 1942 another approach. Outside Block 15, they set up a mailbox into which they ordered (as announced in all blocks) informers to drop anonymous or signed details regarding various overheard conversations, and the like, for the authorities' attention.

We decided to fight it

The matter was taken care of by: First Lieutenant Tadeusz Biliński, our colleague Tadeusz Jakubowski and Capt. Tadeusz Dziedzic. A few hours before Palitzsch or someone else representing the camp authorities were to open it [the mailbox], our colleagues would open it using a self-made key. They would peruse all letters dropped in there and would leave only those we considered harmless to us. We would then find out who were the informers. Sometimes, we would write anonymous letters ourselves, so as to provide some food for thinking to the authorities about 'the gold procurement', or some other activities we were uninterested in, but the authorities were greatly absorbed by. Sometimes, we achieved good results instigating investigations against the informers.

'Gold procurement' was a reference to all that concerned gold, notes, or precious stones hidden in briefcases, suitcases, tubes with cream, toothpaste, shoe soles, soap, any place where one would least expect them. All these had been left behind by, mostly, but not necessarily, Jews, who came here expecting they would be taken to Germany to work there and got instead gassed. They came here from France, the Protectorate of Bohemia and Moravia, Greece, the Netherlands, Norway, or elsewhere. They had been allowed to take one item of hand luggage with them. It contained all their wealth: gold, dollars and brilliant jewels which they wanted to smuggle through. After a cursory, incompetent examination by SS-men or Kapos, inmates involved in this work could find, so clever they were at those things, all such objects and, if unburdened by scruples, would often appropriate themselves (I myself witnessed this many a time) very fine jewels, gold and notes as well as all sorts of things a woman and a man would need when away from home.

I then worked at the tannery where they would bring suitcases, children's prams, ladies' handbags and many other even luxurious items for them all to be either immediately burned down in a large industrial furnace, or sorted out and made pairs from virtual [small] pyramids of men's, women's and children's shoes of all forms, colours and sizes. If we add to it a huge quantity of some very fine underwear, then we will get a rough idea what this particular 'Kanada' was like.

Another type of 'Kanada' were food reserves brought by the people who thought they were going to get some work in Germany, and **were** [in fact] **leaving - only through the Auschwitz crematorium's chimney**. All sorts of canned meat and fish, sardines, oranges, lemons, sugar, chocolate, cocoa, sweets, cakes, dates, figs and the like. This was just a part of what made up the other 'Kanada'. All those articles were subject to exchange between inmates, and this gave SS-men and Kapos an excuse to do daily searches, which often resulted in a rich booty for them, and resulted in many inmates ending their lives in the bunker, or in SK [*Strafkompanie* = penal company/unit – Translator's note].

Gold procurement' was the reference used for appropriation of objects which belonged to people who were killed by gas, and the business of exchanging these. [Even] an accidental one-time exchange between inmates who had not met each other [before] was mutually binding; it required discretion from both parties involved. An investigation followed each detection of gold [in the possession of an inmate]. After the prisoner had been thrashed within the bunker, there would sometimes be arrests of a number of other inmates, to whom the respective clues were leading. The greed for gold among the SS-men often also saw investigations inside that group.

Auschwitz soon became a centre from which small streamlets of gold and jewels would flow in various directions. The camp authorities had themselves their hands in it. The camp commandant who had good relations with the greatest thug at our tannery, *Oberkapo* Erik, officially gave permission, having probably his cut in the spoils, for suitcases containing selected watches, perfumes from Paris, scissors and the like to be delivered to Erik by car. Many such objects were later sent to Germany.

Along all roads from Auschwitz there were sentries stopping even military cars, doing personal searches of SS-men and anyone else, who would drive or walk from our camp's direction.

It was because of this 'gold fever' (gold procurement) that duping the SS-men by providing to them some related leads could serve as an effective 'lightning-rod' for our organisation's work. **[2]**

People react to gold in various ways. Personally, I never thought brilliants or gold with blood on them could bring me happiness. To be frank, I never expected I would be able to go past these with almost perfect indifference. I knew some people who worked in the [camp's] slaughterhouse, and who sold smallgoods for gold. Later, when preparing to leave the camp, I turned to one of my colleagues who had some money, and who proposed a joint escape with me. [Naturally] we could need some of this money on our way. When I asked him how much he had already gathered, it turned out he had more than one kilogram of gold. A few weeks later, he had over one kilogram and a half. As it happened, we did not escape from the camp together. I instead took others with me who had not a penny to bless themselves with.

It was not gold alone, but the camp conditions and experiences in general, which would set characters apart. People have various values. Some people would slide down becoming ever worse cads with no scruples; others, as if to compensate [for the rest], would continuously rise, sculpting and polishing their moral characters till they resembled crystal. Surprises would still take place: some who looked very strong would break down, and some weak persons would suddenly experience their moral revival.

Apart from 'Kanada', we would also experience other surprises, courtesy of new arrivals who would come from

Pawiak, Montelupi and other prisons as well as from the street round-ups. Our "Fives' would screen them for their kinfolk, acquaintances and the organisation's [outside] members. We would take good care of them [providing them with] linen, [extra] food, a better job. We always scrutinised them with caution, as you never knew how a [former] colleague [of yours], fresh from outside, would behave. One of them, Major Wacław Chmielewski who worked with us at TAP in Warsaw (his *nom-de-guerre* was 'Sęp'), and who I thought I could rely on, spotted me during my walk along the camp's assembly square. In front of a dozen or so colleagues who stood close by, he embraced me with great joy, exclaiming: 'And you are here under your own name! Think of it, the Warsaw Gestapo cut up my bottom into squares trying to get out of me where Witold was'. Luckily, there was no informer close by at that moment. To [completely] defuse the situation, we later had to work on it. First Lieutenant (Res.) Karol Świętorzecki, currently out of the camp, witnessed this [incident].

Sometimes, even old inmates would also surprise us. Take a typical schizophrenic: Janusz Kuczbara, rumoured to be of Jewish faith, devoid of principles, ethics and scruples. To take advantage of the opportunity to get rich through the 'Kanada', he managed to attain sway over 'Czesiek', 'Tadek' and Second Lieutenant Konstanty Piekarski. The last-named maintained, Janusz Kuczbara **was an extraordinary person**, the only person who had Warsaw's approval to carry out [underground] work here. Apprised by Second Lieutenant Konstanty Piekarski about who led our organisation, [Kuczbara] resorted to an unusual ruse to hamper our work. When his efforts to frighten us off failed, Kuczbara, though he spared my person because of Second Lieutenant Konstanty Piekarski's intervention, sought to ridicule a few persons from our top. To achieve his aim, with assistance from another prisoner, he painted on Bristol board sheets 'Diplomas of Honour' that vested the 'Order of the Garter' on our colleagues Henryk Bartosiewicz and Colonel Juliusz Gilewicz (with their names, caricatures, and stamps on them) for *'their work for the cause of independence inside the camp.'*

With these sheets made into rolls and with garters obtained from 'Kanada', in plain daylight during a lunch break, making no attempt to disguise anything, Kuczbara went to the hospital, [hoping] to get credit there for this strange exploit in front of his acquaintances. This was a mindless act. Any SS-man, or someone else from the camp's leadership, could have asked him what he was carrying under his arm. His motives aside, his conduct was more than just inappropriate: he was recklessly imperilling two of his colleagues, who could well have ended up facing an interrogation leading to their deaths. [Moreover], this could well have led to a further investigation in the camp. Our colleagues, Cpt Dr. Władysław Dering and Dr. Rudolf Diem, managed to wrest these diplomas from Kuczbara, and then destroyed them. Apart from that, [Kuczbara] was a smart person: one evening I saw him in the camp before Block 23 wearing an SS uniform. It suited him well on December 30, 1943 [an error – should be 1942 – Translator's note], when it made possible his escape as earlier mentioned.

In February 1943, they brought to Block 2a four hundred fifty men and women. They were tortured in various ways, and forced to make confessions. For weeks, they were made to lie face down. They were Poles. In Block 11 Palitzsch, a particularly dedicated torturer, would "hunt' children. He told girls to run around a closed yard and would shoot at them, killing them like rabbits. He would snatch a child from its mother's embrace and would smash its little head against a wall or a stone. A true degenerate, he was followed everywhere by tears and death. Having committed a most heinous crime he would come out smiling, handsome and polite, calmly smoking a cigarette.

From Spring 1942 till Autumn 1942, our camp was divided by a wall. Behind it, there was the women's camp. Later, all women were transferred to the camp in Brzezinka, where they would die in conditions worse than us, in filth, since water and other conveniences were lacking there. Initially, our camp consisted of twenty blocks, all of them separated [from the outside] by a fence. Six of them were double storey, and fourteen of them were single storey. During my stay at the camp, they built eight new blocks on the former parade square. All blocks got a first floor and had sewage installations. Open air toilets and pumps were moved to the blocks. All these construction projects [must have] cost thousands of human lives. Bricks and roof tiles were carried by hand for several kilometres.

In March 1943, they brought to Brzezinka various Gypsy families for whom a separate camp was established. Later, some Gypsy males were brought over to us. Together with Dutch, Norwegians, French, Jews, Germans, Yugoslavs, Greeks, Russians, Ukrainians, Belgians, Bulgarians and Rumanians, we had made a virtual Babel Tower.

Rumors were in circulation at that time about all Poles going to be taken out of the camp. At the beginning, we thought camp authorities would not decide to take all Poles elsewhere, as they were the best workers of all inmates.

Yet they did, after all, decide to take Poles out of there. The reason for it was that keeping such a large group of Polish inmates on Poland's territory with Polish population close by all around the camp was [potentially] very dangerous [to the Germans], due to the ease of communication within that group, [particularly] if there was to come to an air ride, or a weapons drop-off. **What had not [earlier] been taken into consideration by our friends, our enemy had after all recognised.**

During the night from 7 into 8 March 1943, numbers of all Poles were called in whom the local political department [Gestapo] had no intention to interrogate, or execute. After that night, further numbers were called in over the next two nights. They did it at night so as not to leave time to anyone to try and stay in the camp. It was a common knowledge that Polish camp inmates who had stayed there the longest would always find an excuse to stay on in the camp, such as a violent onset of an "illness'. Had it been done during the day, SS-men responsible for various work areas and those in charge of individual Kommandos would have very gladly helped Poles out, as they always preferred Poles as workers. During the night, however, one could do nothing of that sort. From a locked-up block, an inmate would walk to another block which was assigned for this purpose. All doors were locked up there, as well.

[Visibly] agitated, inmates responded to their numbers being called. A load was off many a heart when their number was called: 'it means, they have given up on tormenting me here.' 'well, so I am leaving', 'they will not shoot me here.' One would also hear, here and there, some of our colleagues say: 'God, why they have not called my number yet?'

Inmates with jobs providing good food and contacts with the local population did not welcome, in the least, the prospect of their transfer. At the new place, they would be again 'new arrivals' (Zugangs). They would need to start anew, once again try to come up close to the top. And yet, not all would succeed. A ruthless selection, once again. The prevailing opinion, however, was that it would be a good thing to leave.

For quite some time, it had been known (based on opinions from the inmates who came from other camps) that there was no hell like this anywhere else. Apart from that, attachment to colleagues [whose names had already been called – Translator's note] encouraged [many] to also transfer. It was impossible to know earlier, whose number would be called in. Our '[top] fives' members who would always provide to us detailed briefings, including those from the political department, could not help at all with this. Two camp gods, Grabner and Palitzsch, kept the inmates transfer lists close to their chests.

From 'our' SS-men (and there was in the camp a dozen or so SS-men who had contacts with Volksdeutschs, some of whom once served in the Polish Army as NCO's) we would usually receive early warnings about all types of actions, and would also receive other news which always proved to be true. They assured us that if it came to [a confrontation], they would be on our side and would hand us in keys to armories. To tell the truth, we would have hardly needed those keys. Whilst repulsive and two-faced, they were very useful to us in this hell, and could be even more so. We already knew that the camps [Auschwitz] inmates were being transferred to were the best ones in Germany. It would not have made sense to try and wriggle out of these, because the next transports were likely to be to the camps worse than the first ones.

My number was called already on the first night. I was to go to the Neuengamme camp. They kept us locked up for the rest of the night in Blocks 12a and 19. On the next day, we stood all day in files along "the Birch Avenue", and were then examined by a medical commission. The examination continued on, and on over the next night. I stood next to my friend Tadzio (Colonel Tadeusz Reklewski) and Kazio (Kazimierz Radwański) [both of whom were] destined to go to Buchenwald.

My mind worked frantically. A transfer meant for me to drop all my work here. I had to make up my mind. A very good team of my friends and colleagues was due for a transfer.

A camp friendship is a feeling which is founded on a level far higher than what free people call a friendship. Many a time, when rescuing their [camp] friend's life people were putting their own one in danger. Oftentimes, in retribution [for it] they would later be sent to the penal company where they would soon die.

In my mind, I quickly went through all their profiles classifying all of them and adding current information, such as: shot, died other death, alive, leaves or stays. It was a massive review.

I want to emphasize here that the names of those fellow inmates whose work for our organisation at Auschwitz deserves a special mention (there is however so many of them that it is impossible to mention all their names here). So, I will mention some since **I believe that this should, after all, be of interest to someone in the future**. On the top of those already mentioned, **all those listed on the separate sheet** with their numbers from eight to two hundred eight **have worked for us**. [3]

Over the last six months (I write about it separately), an outstanding contribution was made by Cpt. Dr. Władysław Dering and Dr. Rudolf Diem. In his area of work – by Second Lieutenant Bernard Świerczyna. Isolated from others, yet mentally very strong [were]: Henryk Szklarz, Sergeant Major Stefan Gąsiorowski who got transferred to Brzezinka with a special authority and Cpt. Dr. Henryk Suchnicki, who bravely faced his death. Officer Cadet (Res.) Zbigniew Ruszczynski, Officer Cadet Antoni Rosa and the unforgettable "Wernyhora' – Jan Mielcarek take the credit for shutting off the power supply to the fence, and for taking care of the camp's radio station.

From amongst the early pioneers who gathered in Warsaw at the memorable tea at number 40 building I met here, among others, Cpt. (Cavalry) (Res.) Jerzy de Virion whom for all our efforts we regrettably were unable to save due to his breakdown. He was eaten up by "kreca' [a polonised German word: die Krätze = scabies – Translator's note]. Stanisław Ozimek, who had a stopover here on his way to a quarry, and Jan Dangel whom we provided with an ill person's documents, and then secured his transfer to Dachau. Apart from that, when planning [anything] I would regularly contact a member of our organisation, Col.Teofil Dziama and my friend Tadzio (Col. Tadeusz Reklewski), a very brave person who did not die despite his emaciation, owing this presumably to his strength of will alone. He was always such a wonderful example to others. It was him I stood next to immediately before we were examined by the medical commission.

Tadzio was happy to go to Buchenwald since it was one of the best camps. Rumors circulated that from there they were to send us on to do some voluntary work somewhere in Germany and so on. Tadzio and Kazio were at the time of the view that it was better to get transferred. I also sincerely wished them that, since that camp was, similar to Neuengamme, one of the best camps. Soon, they were to examine us.

Having considered everything, and after some quandary, I decided (Tadzio agreed with that after giving it some thought of his own) that due to my duty to the Organisation I for the time being need to stay in this hell. That meant, we unfortunately had to bid farewell of each other.

One had to act swiftly. The decisive moment was approaching: either-or. I was healthy, and weighed 75 kilograms. In a hurry, I put on a truss provided to me by a friend of mine 'Staszek', who was not to be transferred. I have never suffered rupture in my life, and yet I stand here [wearing the truss] before the [medical] commission.

It was two o'clock at night, and the commission was tired. Tadzio, a weakling compared to me, more than ten years older at that, was accepted for the transfer. As for me, as soon as they spotted me without uttering a word they pointed towards the exit. So, my hoax was successful. Through the transfer block, I returned to my own and on the next day – to my regular work.

During the examination, doctors shook their heads with admiration as they looked at the robust, muscular and well fed bodies of the Polish inmates. That obviously was owing to the work they did. "Kanada' had likewise made its contribution. Since they started to kill larger transports by gas, we no longer suffered hunger, not by camp standards anyway. Half of the Poles (all those who were "organised') had enough food. Besides, since November 1942 we could receive food parcels.

On March 10, a total of 5,000 Poles were transferred: one thousand to Neuengamme, one thousand to Buchenwald, one thousand to Sachsenhausen, one thousand to Gross-Rosen and one thousand to Flossenbürg. Since all most significant operatives from *Organizacja Wojskowa* had avoided the transfer, we could continue our work.

One week later, we again had a commission for all remaining Poles. Its task was to reduce the amount of work when qualifing for the next transports. Next to our numbers, they would note down: 'A', or 'U'. (Possibly these were abbreviations: A – arbeitsfähig (capable to work) and U – arbeitsunfähig (not capable to work). To me, it was a surprise for to get category A meant to be in the next transport, and to get U meant to be recognised as not capable to work. On the other hand, they were supposed to take us [all] to Dachau. Who could guarantee that if they need to kill people by phenyl injections or by gas, they would not take them from the 'U' reserve? So, I decided to have category 'A', and I did receive it. After that, I decided to shirk transports by acquiring the status of "indispensible' worker. Whilst in principle they did keep skilled workers, it was difficult for me to pretend I was one in my own Kommando since my last job there was to handle parcels in the post office. Still, as one of only five out of the forty inmates who worked in the post office in two shifts, I managed to avoid two next transports. On April 10 and 11 **two thousand and five hundred healthy Poles** were sent to Mauthausen.

The second medical commission, the one which was entrusted with the task of dividing the Poles into categories A and U, loudly expressed their admiration of our supreme physical fitness. They said: 'What a regiment you could form from these guys, how they had been able to retain a physical condition like that?'

At mass executions by shooting or gas, the Krankenbau would receive victims lists with an order to proceed fifty numbers daily to the main Schreibstube [camp's office – in the original Pilecki uses a spelling "Szrajbsztube' – Translator's note] giving as a cause of the death heart [disease], typhus, or another "natural' illness. The family was advised only once a special order had been issued by the political department. Often even six months later, the family would still believe that their relative was still alive, just not writing letters, and would thus [continue to] send him parcels.

Most recently, I worked at the parcels' reception. Each day, we would select a great number of food parcels which were addressed to colleagues who had already died. SS-men who supervised this would eagerly put aside better parcels. These were next taken in baskets to the SS mess room. "Worse" parcels were destined to the inmates' kitchen. Since the parcel section was headed by a fairly decent SS-man, an Austrian, after a few parcels had arrived addressed to the same deceased person he would try to stop that family from sending next ones by sending the last one back with a stamp on it: "Neue Anschrift abwarten" (wait for the new address). In so doing, he would stop these from continuing to arrive. Despite the original weight limit of 250 gram on these, parcels were often quite big, sometimes as big as a suitcase. All of them were delivered, and never confiscated. Naturally, it depended on the boss. The SS-men particularly liked parcels from the Czech Republic as they, apart from cakes and sugar, would always contain wine, oranges and lemons. Wines were always confiscated through the authorities. As most Czechs and French Jews who would receive such attractive parcels had already been dead, whole parcels [addressed to them] went to the SS-men.

From time to time, SS-men would make evening calls at a block, gather some Jews, and tell them to write letters to their homes with the standard phrase: 'I am well, and doing nicely'. Those letters were bringing new transports of Jews: having learned how well their co-religionists were doing, they would more readily present themselves 'for the work in Germany'. They were also bringing in new parcels for SS-men, since the authors of these letters would in the meantime have got killed.

Transferring Poles out [of Auschwitz] was, as Kapos and some SS-men explained, a consequence of escapes organised by the Polish inmates, and of their contacts with the local population.

Among the SS-men, there also were chiefs of Kommandos, some of them Austrians, who had for quite some time been on good footing with the Polish inmates. They would happily accept food organised by the Poles, and assure us that they have never hit a Pole. They hinted they would gladly escape with one or a few inmates, provided only that the latter would find a [safe] place for them in Poland to stay in until the war is over. In February 1943, there were two such SS-men who maintained it was 'high time' (an incident with our colleagues, Officer Cadet (Res.) Zbigniew Goszczyński and First Lieutenant (Res.) Marian Moniczewski).

One should also emphasise here, at least in a few words, how bravely priests conducted themselves [at the camp]. To tell the truth, however, not all of them. In the early beginnings [of the camp], priests would not survive here longer than a few days. At the assembly square, they would [often] be killed with clubs. Jews, on the other hand, were [often] killed as they pulled a roller they were harnessed to **[4]**, or as they did another form of 'work' that would be invented just to torture them. In early 1941, following an intervention from Rome, priests got transferred to Dachau, where conditions were more bearable to inmates - apparently. The next transport of priests to Dachau took place in summer 1942. It was between these two transports, that I got to know a few brave priests, among them Father Zygmunt Ruszczak (No. 9842) who was our (Military Organisation's) chaplain. In spite of seemingly insurmountable difficulties apart from confessions, we would also (secretly) celebrate Masses. Wine and Hosts we would obtain from outside [the camp].

Escapes

Ever since the camp had been established, and during my stay there, many escapes were attempted. About half of them were successful. How they resonated in inmates' hearts depended on how the camp authorities responded to each one of these. We would sometimes witness fundamental changes in those responses.

First escapes were of unsophisticated kind: across, or over the fence which at that time was a single barbed wire one with no electricity connection. They were attempted either during the night or the day, [sometimes] from a workplace outside the fence. [Inmates] would hide for the night in sheds, barracks, or behind other screening objects. Those escapes all resulted in orders for all inmates to stand at attention at the parade square for many hours [so-called *stójka* = punishment parade], assaults on individuals, beating inmates by raving mad SS-men, annoyances in the blocks and searches. Sometimes, they would find run-offs hidden somewhere where they worked ("Industriehof I' or "Industriehof II'). They were either **killed** immediately on detection, or sent **to the bunker**.

The name of the first prisoner to make off in the first few months of this camp's existence was, as if out of spite to the camp authorities, Tadeusz Wiejowski (No. 220) [the surname has affinity with the Polish verb "zwiać' = to make off – Translator's note]. His colleagues paid **an inordinate price** for it. All inmates stood at attention lined up at the square without any food or a chance to go to toilet for eighteen hours. During the day, they fainted from heat. During the night, they shivered from cold. At the end of this very long *stójka*, they were all very miserable: half of them had dropped to the ground.

In time, the punishment routines became shorter, and the inmates would remain standing only until the escapee was found. If he was not, we would stand only until the evening roll-call. Yet, even a few hours' *stójka* **would often be hard on us**. For instance, on October 28, 1940 we had rain mixed with snow. We had neither coats, nor caps. A large majority of inmates, of which I was one, did not have socks either. A cap I only got on December 8, 1940. Before the **escapee was** found and **killed** and the standing drill was called off, about one hundred forty of the **weakest inmates died** of fatigue, food deprivation and cold combined.

Later, standing drills as retribution for an escape got even shorter, their duration was calculated in such a way as to leave enough time for the dinner before the night rest's gong. That did not mean we were not kept, on occasions at sub-zero temperatures or when it was raining, for hours gathered for the roll-call at the assembly square.

[Sometimes], even when **nobody had escaped**, they pretended inmates were missing. So, they would go indoors to "do their computations'. This was done to finish us off.

At the end of November 1941, while the camp's commandant was away and his deputy in charge, we had Seidler's Week ("Tydzień Seidlerowski').

After our return to the camp from work, **even though no-one was missing, we stood each day at the evening roll-call** almost until the night rest gong, and only then were we allowed to quickly gulp down our soup which by then was cold like ice. The gusts of wind were penetrating, frost would creep down our heads, backs and limbs. With the whole resistance our bodies could muster, we fought not to catch a cold.

From Spring 1941, escapes became more common. It was then, that the camp authorities came upon the idea to apply **the rule of collective responsibility** to the entire block. For one escaped inmate, they would select **ten from the same block to be killed**. They would be sent to the bunker, and then **killed** by shooting, or in any other way practiced. The moment the commandant was selecting ten inmates to die was **very difficult** for the entire block. Yet, we also experienced some **very lofty** moments such as when an elderly man, a priest, offered his life for a younger man who had been selected to die. The priest's sacrifice was accepted, and the latter person was allowed to live. **[5]**

It was during that period that our organisation developed its negative view of escapes. During 1941, we organised no escapes and would denounce all independent attempts.

Following the day on which a letter arrived from Berlin which forbade any escape related reprisals in the Auschwitz camp (the message was passed on by our 'top Fives' who worked in the political section), we never had ten inmates killed for one escapee. The ban on these was, so they said, first introduced in the camps for Germans. Once again, escapes were on, and we started planning them.

From Spring 1942 until the end of that year we had organised a number of escapes. I have already mentioned these.

In early 1943 (on February 27), seven colleagues escaped who worked in the SS-kitchen. These were: Kazimierz Albin – No. 118, Tadeusz Klus – No. 416, Adam Klus – No. 419, Bronisław Staszkiewicz – No. 1225, Franciszek Roman – No. 5770, Włodzimierz Turczyniak – No. 5829 and Roman Lechner – No. 3505. **[6]**

Inmates were now no more responsible for the escapes of their colleagues. Not only the death penalty, but also the punishment with bunker was banned and, from early 1943, the *stójka* as well (in 1943, following an escape, we had never been punished with *stójka* at the roll-call anymore). Aside from that, all inmates who worked inside the camp's fenced-off area were issued civil clothes from 'Kanada' with red stripes painted on them. All this **was encouraging inmates to attempt an escape**. That is why the camp authorities found a new way [to discourage us from attempting escapes].

At all blocks, an announcement was made that in retribution for an escape all escapee's family would be brought to the camp. One day, they even arranged a 'demonstration'. Returning from their work, my colleagues noticed a sight which made them very uncomfortable. Two women accompanied by an SS-men stood next to a post with a board affixed to it saying: 'Seeking to salvage himself, a prisoner very unwisely chose to escape; by this, he put the lives of his mother and his fiancée in danger; it was his thoughtlessness that brought them to the camp.'

At first, this made our hearts ache. What a scumbag [we thought] – to deliberately expose one's mother, or a fiancée, to such a danger. Or, any woman. A few years of separation from the opposite sex had its significance. We certainly had our tender feelings for women. On the first evening, the entire camp reviled the monster who would expose an elderly woman and such a nice fiancée to all those dangers. Yet, it turned out that the numbers these two women had on their uniforms were much lower than the current day numbers [given] in the women's camp. We were too clever for this trick. On the next day, we found out what was the current number in the women's camp: they played this trick to make an impact on us. This, after all, made us more relaxed: in effect, this episode encouraged, rather than otherwise, inmates to attempt an escape.

Two of our colleagues escaped soon after. Yet, we were not absolutely sure, if [by escaping] we would not put endanger our families. For that reason, most of our colleagues would shudder at a mere thought of an escape.

Later, we once again saw a young and nice-looking woman at that post with an announcement on the board [next to her]. This could impress only some new arrivals amongst us.

After mid 1942, all escapees who were caught were hanged publicly and with great fanfare. They were hanged by inmates who were to be hanged themselves two weeks later. This was done to increase the latter inmates' torment.

From early 1943, I had contact with a Montelupi [prison] hero – Aleksander Bugajski alias Szczęściarz ['The Lucky One'], who had a death sentence. He had no doubt they would finish him off here. He got closer with me to help him escape. I suggested a route I had in mind for myself – just in case. That was why I worked the night shift at the post office. At the same time, in December 1943 [an error – should be 1942 – Translator's note], Second Lieutenant (Res.) Witold Wierusz, who worked in the land-surveying Kommando often a few kilometres away from the camp, presented to me an escape idea. His project had a particular side to it though: if not feasible, and if calling off this escape was no longer possible, we would have to resort to violence. It is for this reason that I took a negative view of his idea. I explain it below.

To start with, escaping from the camp was not easy. It was made even more difficult by the need to escape in such a way as not to cause revenge killing of inmates. This was the hard part.

With some Kommandos working a few kilometres away from the camp, one would be very tempted to organise escapes. The obstacle to it [often] was – oh, what an irony – the life of one, or a few SS-men. While opening one's road to freedom, their death could well cost many lives of our Polish colleagues [at the camp]. This being so, an escape involving killing SS-men would have been an act of such ruthless selfishness that no decent Pole would do it.

An escape plan had to be therefore conceived in such a way as to consider not only its success prospect, but also its consequences for those remaining in the camp.

Once we had introduced a few corrections to the plan which was developed by Second Lieutenant (Res.) Witold Wierusz, I acquainted the latter with Aleksander Bugajski. Since 'The Lucky One' Aleksander Bugajski considered the Witold Wierusz plan to be less risky than my own, he transferred to the Kommando where Second Lieutenant (Res.) Witold Wierusz worked, and started preparations for this escape. A few days later, Szczęściarz proposed to prepare an escape plan for me, as well.

As I have already mentioned, on 10 and 11 April 1943 two thousand and five hundred Poles were sent in two separate transports to Mauthausen. **This had finally forced me to take my decision.** Staying on in Auschwitz [because of my tasks here] had ceased, in my view, to be a necessity. What I could have done, I already did. The "better' half of my colleagues had already left. Awaiting for "something' to happen had proved to be in vain. Besides, threats were being made for the remainder of Polish inmates to be transferred to other camps. Once I had formed a view I would be of more use on the outside than when remaining inside the camp, I chose to leave it.

The news which had since early March been circulating in the camp about Janusz Kuczbara having been captured in Warsaw, and put into the Pawiak prison, made me want to leave the camp as soon as possible. I regarded him as someone with no scruples, as someone who to save his own life might well spill the beans about the top of our organisation, all the more likely that he had already attempted to do this when at the camp, and in no need, in relation to Colonel Juliusz Gilewicz and our colleague Henryk Bartosiewicz. So, on April 11, 1943, I discussed this issue with my colleague, Second Lieutenant (Res.) Leon Murzyn.

Bearing in mind my [imminent] 'departure' from the camp, I had a few talks with Major Zygmunt Bończa-Bohdanowski and my colleague Henryk Bartosiewicz advising them about this all, and entrusting to them all further work.

On April 13, I spoke to my colleague Cpt. Stanisław Machowski. I told him that after the two-and-a-half years long wait I no more wished, or **needed,** to stay here. Maybe, once on the outside I would be able to help my colleagues in the camp sooner. Cpt. Machowski put a question to me: 'Well, is it however all right to come here when one so wills, and leave when one so wills, as well?' I answered: 'I believe, it is.' And indeed, for the last few months it had been possible for me to escape from the camp on any night even though, admittedly, [the idea of that escape] was rather uncomfortable, and a bit risky. Szczęściarz prepared an alternative escape route.

As it happened, I used an entirely different route leaving the first one to the colleagues that I let into my secret: Henryk Bartosiewicz, Maj. Zygmunt Bończa-Bohdanowski, Zdzisław Uliasz and Andrzej Gąsienica.

Prior to my escape, I had also spoken to my colleague 'Tadek' regarding his communication with Warsaw and the lack of any instructions. Referring to his communications he said: *'now Warsaw thinks about Auschwitz differently'*. I do not know what he meant, and I did not change my decision.

The date of our escape from the camp, as set by Aleksander Bugajski, unfortunately for him coincided with a jocose night-time escape of a few colleagues from the Brzezinka camp through what we dubbed 'the Diogenes barrel'. All [Auschwitz] soldiers were later involved in the search for these escapees. As there were no Posts [=guards] [left inside], the camp remained shut. For three days, we had not been let out for work. The authorities used this time to de-louse the camp. During these few days, the boss and Kapo from the Kommando where Aleksander Bugajski previously worked (post office/parcels) found out Szczęściarz transferred to a new Kommando illicitly. This was regarded as **'an attempt to escape'**. Consequently, for his wilful change of Kommando Aleksander Bugajski was sent to the penal unit[432]. The date for our own escape attempt was set on the next day after the 'Diogenes barrel' night.

So, in this instance, 'The Lucky One' was out of luck. As for me, I had to try something else.

One of my colleagues, Jan Redzej, was with a Kommando which transported bread to the camp from a bakery in the town. At the bakery, he noticed large iron gates. At first glance, they looked a formidable obstacle, yet a possible gate to freedom all the same. To have a closer look [around the bakery], he managed to get his Kapo's permission to stay there for a few days. The work in the bakery was very hard: one had to bake thousands of loaves daily as per the order. For any underperformance at work you were sent on the next day to the bunker. A few civilian bakers and a few inmates worked [in that bakery]. Over the few days that he needed to have 'a closer look' at the door our colleague Jan Redzej, a ninety-five-kilogram tall strapping fellow, lost six kilos. In the end, he came to the view that even when some tricks were used, the door would not yield and open, so he returned to his Kommando.

After a further consideration of this matter, we **jointly developed a plan we later implemented**.

Through my colleague Wacław Weszke, I had Redzej perfectly legally placed at the bakery by an *Arbeitsdienst*. We used the Easter mood in the camp and the reduced level of alertness from the celebrating authorities. To save my block and work colleagues from possible repercussions, I misled both my block's and my Kommando's authorities on the Easter Saturday by faking illness. I got transferred to Krankenbau: to play even safer, to Block 20 (the one for typhus victims), which the authorities would visit only very reluctantly. On the first day (Easter Sunday) I was 'ill', since the bakery had the time off. On the next day (Easter Monday) I had to [however] leave the hospital, since the bakery was resuming its work. Worker substitutions [arranged] immediately after a festive break were less likely to attract anyone's attention.

The success all depended on me being sent back not to my own block – as they would normally have to do, according to the camp regulations – but to another one, Block 15, where all bakers resided, further, on me being kicked out from the typhus block after two days, i.e. against hospital rules (one was not allowed to leave prior to completing one's quarantine) and [finally] on no-one from my Kommando, or the block authorities, seeing me 'recovered'. After all, at the very time after my transfer to a new block and as I was to start my baker's 'work', [authorities and colleagues] needed to be convinced that I was ill [at the hospital].

The hospital check-in, as well as check-out formalities when leaving to another block, were taken care of by my colleague Edward Ciesielski (Marian Toliński helped me with the check-in, and Władysław Fejkiel with the check-out). Since Ciesielski's assistance with my escape was likely to be discovered [by the authorities], on Sunday night I offered to let him escape with me. My decision to offer him a joint escape necessitated some changes to the plan. It was influenced by his conviction for the possession of a weapon. He kept on saying he only waited for his number to be called for him to be shot. During the two years, whenever we would meet he would always finish our conversation with the same words: 'Tomek, I can only count on you'. I did not want to disappoint him, so I contacted Jan Redzej. Edward Ciesielski promptly decided to quit his very good job at the hospital block. On Monday morning, the second day of the holidays, together with me, he reported at Block 15 where bakers resided.

We misled both the Block authorities and the bakers' Kapo. We let the bakers' Kapo believe that the block leader had received the required transfer forms from the *Arbeitsdienst* (even though I did not want to take those forms, lest I implicate him in assisting us with our escape). The block leader saw that we were coming to his block as new bakers to be employed at the newly established mechanical bakery. We still had to overcome the resistance from the two inmate bakers. This proved most difficult.

We had to somehow convince those two bakers to give up their work spots for this night. We thought that the disorientation of the camp authorities which we have brought about could not last very long. Likely, it was going to be only a matter of hours. We had to hurry, yet our talk with the bakers proved tough. They could not understand why we were so keen on the night shift. And, naturally, we tried very hard to ensure that they did not. Besides, they were fearful that we wanted their bread-baking jobs. Finally, we overcame that obstacle, as well.

I went all the way. Jan Redzej and Edward Ciesielski could both return safely to the camp if the night attempt at escape failed. For the former, such return would be no different from any other day since he had held a permanent baker's job. As for the latter, he had settled all necessary formalities with the authorities from his previous block, and [all formalities] regarding the job he abandoned as well (he would only need to change his job again as he would not be able to last long [in the baker's job]). In contrast, my return to the camp after a failed night escape attempt would see me [immediately] transferred to the penal unit, as I would not have a chance to justify my appearance on a wrong block, or my leaving for the night shift at the bakery. After all, I belonged to another Kommando and neither the Kapo, nor the head of my Kommando, had any knowledge of my release from that Kommando. Moreover, we dealt here with the same parcels section whose management knew how to deal with Szczęściarz (Aleksander Bugajski) in identical circumstances. A formal transfer from the parcels' section was impossible too, because only about two weeks earlier I had sought a status of **indispensible** worker there, the status I had been granted.

We therefore decided to not return [be what it may]. **First, however, we needed to be able to leave** [the camp]. The Kapo, a Czech, had long stuck to his guns insisting that today only one of us (apart from Redzej who had a permanent position) would go to the bakery and the other – only tomorrow. **Whilst we felt as if we were at the boiling point inside, on the outside we all tried to appear indifferent.**

Redzej took care of the Kapo, explaining to him that his two colleagues were fools who were taken in [by someone], and who thought that the bakery work was easy. The best way would be to take them for this night [shift] and he, Redzej, would put them through such a mill that they would not last in this Kommando long. Maybe they would be no longer attracted to this job after this [first] night. The most difficult task of them all was to overcome the resistance from the two bakers. Finally, Redzej's glib persuasion, preserves, sugar and apples from parcels provided by myself, and the merry mood of the second day of Easter, all combined to bring enough influence on them.

It's 6.30 p.m. The SS-man calls out from the gate: '*Bäckerei* ...' [bakery...]. We run towards the gate. As we do, I pass many inmates having a walk there, and catch sight of three familiar faces (Second Lieutenant (Res.) Jerzy Olszowski, Zdzisław Uliasz, Mieczysław ... rowiec) all surprised at seeing me there. They all are my good friends. We are being counted. The number is exactly as it should be: eight. It means that the other two gave up this night's shift. Had there been one too many, one of us being the new ones would have had to stay. We walk on escorted by four SS-men. We pass through the gate. How many times have I passed through it and thought: 'When will be the time that I will not have to walk back through it?' Today, I am leaving with the thought: '**Under no circumstances must I walk back through it ever again**'.

My mood is difficult to describe. At any rate, our definite resolve lends us wings. When already in the town, we split into two groups. Two inmates and two SS-men walk to the small bakery, and us – six inmates and two SS-men – walk to the large one. This has been agreed on with Kapo. We are to be 'severely tested' there, a task entrusted to our colleague Jan Redzej.

During the night, five batches of bread need to be made. We work hard – except for Ciesielski who already at the outset 'stages' an incident with a bag which 'causes' him 'a sprain'. He then complains of pain in the small of the back. Not all of us are able to malinger like that.

We were to try our luck at the first, or the second, batch. Meanwhile, we have already finished the first, the second, the third and the fourth one, and we still can not move. Things are made more difficult by it being Monday – on Mondays they always change guards. Towards the end of the week, they already get used to the workers, and do their slumbers. And by then, they are almost always tired-out. On Monday, the new ones are the proverbial 'new broom'. As we were leaving the camp at the gate they loudly cautioned our guards: 'Be alert'. I wondered: 'Do they have any inkling about what is to happen?' At the bakery, one guard takes an interest in 'our' door, examines it thoroughly and shakes his head in disapproval deeming the door to be unreliable. Jan Redzej has to use his persuasive powers to convince him to the contrary.

When Monday passes and, at midnight, Tuesday commences, our situation starts improving (only one guard is awake, the other one snores). Nonetheless, it continues to be fairly difficult.

We work half-naked. The heat from the ovens makes us sweat profusely. We drink immense quantities of water. It would have been impossible to make sense of all moves we make to meet our different objectives, each of whom **is in a direct conflict with another**: hurrying with work to meet the requirements of master bakers, preparing to open the door and moving to collect our clothes. All this needs to be masked before the guard who remains alert and often follows us closely. Besides, as long as the door remains closed we can not be 100% sure that it will open once all obstacles are removed, for one of the hooks is fastened **outside**.

The accompanying feeling is as if I played a game of solitaire, only it is stronger for it is my life that is here at stake. As with the game of solitaire, where all depends on some lucky cards sequels, and on how they have been shuffled, also here we need some lucky coincidences so that with people walking in various directions, bakers running here and there and the guard crisscrossing from one grainer into another, we in the end have a moment when no [guard's] eye watches the door. It has to coincide with all three of us being near that door, and being able to diverge slightly in order to collect our clothes, as we are about to open the door. That we must escape [on that night] hangs above everything, like the proverbial Damocles' sword. Particularly, after we have cut out a few centimetres of a cable from a place right over our guards' heads. Our chances of escape are increasing, or decreasing, from one minute to another. And so does the tension.

Once Ciesielski, with confidence and quite cleverly has completed his 'surgery' on the phone's cable and Redzej has drawn aside the bolt and unscrewed a nut pushing out the outside catch which holds together the two leaves of the double door, the latter gives us signs for us all to lean with our arms against the door, in order to force it open. It is then, that the guard **comes to the door to check it**. I see it from a few steps' distance and expect him to shout for alarm. Why he does not notice the bolts that have already been drawn aside, or the cable that has been cut through, or Redzej who is already fully dressed and pretends he was only using the toilet, I will never be able to explain. I think that he must have pondered this himself on the next day, when in the bunker.

Finally, the moment is suitable. I run up to Redzej, and at the same moment Ciesielski starts closing another door to provide a screen so that the guard who is just six steps away from us cannot see what we are doing. Together with Redzej we hurry and strongly push the door. We apply even more strength and, suddenly and quietly, the door opens in front of us.

We can see stars, and feel a pleasant whiffle of wind. We leap out, and run as quickly as we can with our clothes under our arms. And thus, in the company of Jan Redzej and Edward Ciesielski, I leave the Auschwitz camp, farewelled with shots by the guard, who realises what has happened rather too late for him.

I leave at night. And I came at night. I have spent in this hell 947 days and as many nights. It is already past two o'clock, the highest time we escaped. The night is from 26 into 27 April 1943.

Leaving [the camp] I have a few teeth less than I had when arriving here. And a broken breast-bone. Quite a bargain given the length of my stay in this 'sanatorium'.

Running into **this night I have a clean conscience,** for no more are ten inmates shot for each one escapee, and I have used an assumed surname. I thus leave no traces leading to my family.

It would be hard to describe in just a few words how great we feel during our first night's march and during the next few days. We must have set speed records running up steep walls of gullies, and then down headlong. We also have a few remarkably lucky happenstances: [one] when passing a railway bridge, [the other] when our key fits the lock of a moored boat. Before the sunrise, from a few hundred metres a strong forest's aroma and birds' songs hit us. Once there we finally feel at home. The lush moss muffles our steps.

At night, we set our direction by stars, and at day – by sun. The town where I am to meet the people recommended to me is several dozen kilometres away. Since we need to take roundabout ways to avoid populated areas, we do, at least, one hundred thirty kilometres. After a rather incommodious crossing of the

Generalgouvernement's border, a task at which we are greatly helped by the hospitable parish priest at Alwernia, and our rest at Tyniec, at the house of our friendly Piotr Mazurkiewicz, we enter the Niepołomicka Forest. On May 1, we have an incident at a forester's lodge. I receive there a light wound in my right arm, shot by a German Vorschutz who shot nine times but was not very good at it. In the evening, we reach our destination.

After a few days spent in the warm Polish atmosphere of the Obora family home where we also met Edward Zabawski's wife, Helena, with Leon Wandasiewicz as my guide I go to where I was meant to. My friend Tomasz Serafiński sends his reports further on. The next level is Wiatr – 'Teodor'. A few days later, overcome with fear he comes to my friend and says, he has a detailed plan of Auschwitz, but there is no bakery there. And, since only three people have so far managed to escape from Auschwitz, so [to him]:

1. All this looks suspicious.
2. One needs to cover up one's tracks; [Pilecki's comments follow:] my friend cannot cover up his tracks to him since they know each other well, neither can I cover up my tracks to my friend since I have stayed at the camp for over two and a half years using papers issued in his name.
3. It would be best for the three of us to move on [Pilecki's comment follows:] and break our necks, presumably.

I seem to have come across one of those 'organisation giants' who, as we used to say at the camp, are very 'busy' (in their thoughts, only) with things to do with their brothers at Auschwitz – until they get there themselves. Still, we also meet some very sincere people here: apart from the Tomasz Serafiński's family we also avail ourselves of the hospitality of another brave and selfless Pole – Józef Roman.

When in the camp, I wrote letters about my work there and about my plan to leave the camp. Those written in plain Polish went along a circuitous way, while the "official' ones went straight to Eleonora Ostrowska. Only when already on the outside, did I find out that the latter ones were sent on by Eleonora Ostrowska to the 'Top' ['Góra'] through 'Skiba' (Edward Baird) – 'Zamek', currently 'Klucz'. The response from there was: *'your letters are of great interest to us'* and *'if possible, we are requesting further news.'* It appears that they thought such an official response should signify that they had settled the matter.

In October 1943, when already in Warsaw, I received a letter from Edward Ciesielski who in Bochnia met Antoni Gargul (No. 5665), a musician released from the camp in Autumn 1943. During that meeting [Gargul] told him there were no retributions in the camp after the escape of three inmates via the bakery.

What I found among the [free] people, after my return to a normal life, I would simply call a return to the twilight of spiritual life. I will touch upon this in the next chapter (No IX). Here, I will only say this: I thought, I suddenly found myself in a children's room, where everyone was very busy playing with their own toys.

And yet! On May 10, 1944, in Warsaw, on Marszałkowska Street I had the good fortune to spot, just a few metres away from me, Szczęściarz (Aleksander Bugajski). With a big smile on his face, he approached me and said that he could not believe they released me from the camp. I expressed identical doubts about him. He said he had escaped from Ravensbrück.

Throughout my stay at the camp – and throughout my life as well, I dealt with many 'coincidences', as they are called by the people whose faith can be questioned.

One of the so many of these coincidences was with *Krwawy Alojz*[433] ' [Bloodthirsty Alojz]. He never spoke to me before [that encounter]. I remember very well how, looking somehow embarrassed to me, he met me in the corridor of a block, in February 1942. Recognising me, even though he had bloody encounters with many thousands of inmates, he stopped me, exclaiming in surprise: *'Du lebst noch!'* ['So, you are still alive!']. These were the first and [at the same time] the last words we ever exchanged. He soon died. [Next one] – 'Otto', a skilled tile-stove setter who salvaged me from a slow death when I received a 'gymnastics' treatment. [Further] a cad by the name of Wilhelm Westrych, who mistakenly assumed that I was some big fish in hiding who stayed [in Auschwitz] under a false name. Seeking to secure future favours with such a celebrity and to erase [the memory of] his current meanness as a *Volksdeutsch*, he saved me from death when I was very weak, by offering a job in his workshop. He was shot dead near Warsaw in 1943. And later, during the second phase, my success in developing the organisation, getting the overall camp situation under control, and the good recovery which I made after pneumonia and typhus. The way I was treated by some physicians, Artur Balke, Konrad Lange, and a few block supervisors. Thrown out on February 21, 1943, from my good work at the tannery because of my white-collar appearance, I immediately recognised it as a lucky coincidence, and commenced preparations for my escape. And I did not err in this regard.

Another coincidence was with Stefan Bielecki, when, after his release from the camp with a message from us (he was also to collect some information for us), he was unable to get access to the top, or send us the information we were waiting for. One day, he was driven to his work in Mińsk Litewski by Res. Second Lieutenant Stanisław Wierzbicki, to whom he confided [his mission] and who told me about it at the camp as soon as he got there.

Of them all, the most peculiar coincidence was when, at the end of 1941, copies of birth certificates from the parishes in localities named by our colleagues started flowing in [to the camp's authorities] commencing from the lowest numbers (they were presumably looking for rogues like myself). Had I not escaped [in the end], they would have found out about me as there were only a few of us [old inmates] left. At every payout of money, we had to queue in the order of our numbers, regardless of whether one was receiving money or not. One could easily see from there, how many inmates from each hundred were still alive. You saw three, four, six, rarely eight colleagues who remained alive from each hundred. It was then, that I sent through Sergeant Woźniak a message to Eleonora Ostrowska in which I asked her to contact the Bochnia parish and explain my situation there. This was because the registry data for Tomasz Serafiński **[7]** had to be slightly changed, to allow for a possibility that the real Tomasz Serafiński would one day be brought to the camp.

It was necessary to ask the Bochnia parish to be prepared to provide my registry data identical with those that I had already provided to the camp's political department. Eleonora Ostrowska entrusted this task to Warzyński. As soon as he had received a letter of recommendation from Palutyni, Warzyński, large-hearted as he was and a good friend of mine, took a trip to Bochnia and arranged the things as required. With a stroke of the pencil, the good people there corrected the relevant data in the book of births, next to Tomasz Serafiński's name. Warzyński could tell me the story in person, as he was brought back to the camp soon thereafter. As soon as I had escaped from the camp, I went straight to Bochnia since this was the closest place where I could receive help. My colleague Res. Second Lieutenant Edmund Zabawski's family lived there, and I had an introductory letter from him addressed to his family. As I was already there, I asked for contact with the commandant of the local [resistance] unit. Understandably, I was quite surprised and astonished when I learned that the name of that commandant is – can you imagine – Tomasz Serafiński, a person whom I had never seen in my life before, a person who had no knowledge someone who had assumed his name had spent more than two and a half years in Auschwitz. He opened his eyes very wide indeed when I came to his home and told him all about it. His warm attitude made us friends at first sight. I then contacted the Bochnia parish to let them know that they needed to rub out the pencilled note.

This is why I believe that [lucky] coincidences do not occur in novels only. When one reads about them, one should not suggest that all of them are only a figment of author's imagination.

*

[On the original copy of Report "W', there appear the following statements written by hand, which regard messages and work reports that concern *Organizacja Wojskowa* [Military Organisation] in Auschwitz.]

By Aleksander Wielopolski

Res. Second Lieutenant Karol Świętorzecki called on me in Warsaw in May 1941, in the second half of the month, whereupon I connected him with 226, to whom he described his work in Auschwitz. I brought the first news about Auschwitz. I officially presented it to Tęczyński, 226 and Dr. Zakrzewski (of Wawelska Street). It has been passed on [to its] overseas [recipients] by the official route. Privately, I had a detailed discussion with 225. That news has been sent to Italy using a private route.

Signed: No. 6, as per the key.

Warsaw, June 28, 1944

By Stefan Bielecki

Having been ordered by Witold (Witold Pilecki), I left Auschwitz on May 16, 1942 and arrived at Warsaw on June 30, 1942 where I immediately lodged my written report with 227. I personally described to him the state of our organisation's work in the camp. According to the statement [that I could see, the report having been submitted to Commandant 'Grot' (Gen. Stefan Rowecki), the Commander-in-Chief of ZWZ AK who got arrested by Germans on June 30, 1943, and executed by shooting in the concentration camp at Sachsenhausen after the outbreak of the Warsaw Uprising [this last mention would have to have been added after this note's date – Translator's note]. Since until early 1943 I had never been called on to present the details of our work, all of which could only be provided orally, I approached 'Skiba' to request a clarification from the Headquarters as to the cause of that delay. I received an answer that my report had arrived, and that I would be asked to come if, and when needed.

I sign with No. 41, as per the key.

Warsaw, June 30, 1944

By Sergeant Antoni Woźniak

Information entrusted to me by Witold regarding his work in Auschwitz I passed on orally to Eleonora Ostrowska.

I sign with No. 25, as per the key.

Warsaw, July 2, 1944

By Aleksander Paliński (died in the Warsaw Uprising)

Information entrusted to me by Witold regarding the state, and the activities in Auschwitz, I have passed on orally to Eleonora Ostrowska.

I sign with No. 53, as per the key.

Warsaw, July 2, 1944

By Captain Ferdynand Trojnicki

On arriving at Warsaw, I came in December 1942 to 228 and, in his presence, I orally reported to 229 who got introduced to me as someone representing the Headquarters on the organisation's work at Auschwitz. When asked, if I could submit this as an official report in writing, I made it clear that due to the need to keep it under strictest secrecy, I could talk about it, if required by the Commander-in-Chief, but only talk. No more was I called in later regarding this matter.

I sign with No. 24, as per the key.

Warsaw, July 10, 1944

By Eleonora Ostrowska

All official and secret correspondence from Witold about the organisation's work at Auschwitz, and the oral reports by arriving colleagues, I handed in to 'Skiba'. All this information went by the official route to 'Zamek' (now – 'Klucz'). Official replies ascertain interest in, and usefulness of, the information sent to them.

I sign with No. 5, as per the key.

Warsaw, July 13, 1944

By 'Skiba'

All information I have received regarding the organisation's work at Auschwitz I passed on to 230.

I sign with No. 218, as per the key.

Warsaw, July 15, 1944

By 'Jeż'
(Stefan Miłkowski)

Report W and the entire case of Auschwitz are known to me. At all times, I sought to help Witold by submitting these to the appropriate authorities so as to receive from them a resolute and formal reply – a decision. As far as I am aware, despite all these efforts Witold has not received any such reply, yet. If required, I am ready to provide all information and my commentaries that relate to this matter.

(-) "Jeż"

Warsaw, July 18, 1944

By Witold

After leaving Auschwitz, I did not visit my family but stayed near Cracow, to carry out an armed action to liberate Auschwitz. To this aim I started forming a detachment near Bochnia, assisted by Tomasz Serafiński and '232' **[8]**. *At the same time, I sought to contact the Headquarters in Warsaw to obtain its assent to this action, either through correspondence or orally. I brought there Stefan Bielecki from Warsaw. The way this idea was viewed by our authorities in Cracow, and the light in which the matter was presented by 'Wiatr' – 'Teodor' caused me to decide to go to Warsaw in person, after a three-and-a-half-month-long wait near Bochnia for the decision to come from Warsaw.*

In Warsaw, on October 23, 1943, through 'Jeż' I was able to contact the Deputy of '233' (presumably it was First Lieutenant Col. Jerzy Uszycki, since July 1942 Head of Signals with the Department V at the Armia Krajowa [AK] Headquarters, Chief of AK Corps of Signals and Deputy Chief of Department V at the AK Headquarters.), who I reported the Auschwitz issues to. Later, on October 29, 1943, as ordered by the Deputy of '233', I comprehensively presented all Auschwitz issues, including planning a military intervention there, to an operations officer '233' – nom-de-guerre 'Zygmunt', 'Wilk'. The response from him was as follows: 'After the war, I will show you how thick are the Auschwitz files in our archives.' When I suggested that the thickness of these files would bring no relief to the Auschwitz inmates, 'Zygmunt' – 'Wilk' responded: 'I can assure you that we will contact you as soon as this matter becomes current.'

Witold

Warsaw, July 20, 1944

On July 21, 1944, I spoke to the Chief of '233' (presumably Col. Kazimierz Pluta-Czachowski, Chief of Department V /Command and Signals/ at the AK Headquarters), to pass my report through him to the Commander-in-Chief of AK. The Chief of '233' told me this was not necessary, since the Commander-in-Chief knows the Auschwitz situation very well and has already sought to get KWP [Kierownictwo Walki Podziemnej – Underground Warfare Headship] to accept the necessity of this action. Still, all efforts to obtain an order to launch this action have been in vain, since it was difficult to contest [effectively] in a discussion certain sensible arguments, or answer some reasonable questions, such as how to find near Oświęcim a sufficient number of people [to attack the camp], or to transport them there, or what to do with the thousands of liberated people (including women, sick people, and people unable to walk longer distances).

Witold

Warsaw, July 20, 1944

I confirm that all copies provided above are identical with the original copies of statements by their authors' own hands.

Maria Szelągowska[434]

Warszawa, July 23, 1944

END NOTES TO REPORT W[435]

[1] this incident is described in more detail in: K. Garliński, 'Oświęcim walczący', pages 268-269, 277.

[2] It would certainly be worth the while to compare this opinion by Pilecki with the following observation made by the Auschwitz Gestapo operative, Pery Broad (A.C.):

> *'In the face of overwhelming quantities of suitcases containing amounts which were not counted yet, it was not possible to ascertain how many suitcases had been stolen by thieves, let alone what amounts had been stolen. At the same time, the Polish Resistance Movement had untiringly worked to uncover the Auschwitz secrets and inform the world about war crimes committed there. A great quantity of relevant information had been passed on by former inmates and escapees. Some letters had been smuggled from the camp by civilian workers employed in the camp's area. A report titled 'The death camp' was made public. Even though outsiders might have viewed that report as an exaggerated account of atrocities [which had been put together] for propaganda purposes, in fact it only contained a fraction of what actually took place there ... In Berlin,*

> *they were furious [about it]. They wanted to know how it was possible for that much [information] to get out. Poles knew even about the Block 11 murders.'*
>
> *(See: Oświęcim w oczach SS: Rudolf Höss, Pery Broad, Johann Paul Kremer, e-Oświęcim 2001, p.172)*

[3] This is the 'key' to *Report W*; it was found in Spring 1991 in the Population Registry Archives [Archiwum Ewidencji Ludności] of the State Security Office [Urząd Ochrony Państwa] in Warsaw; see: Adam Cyra, 'Raport 'Witolda'', published in the *Biuletyn Towarzystwa Opieki nad Oświęcimiem*, 1991, no.12.

[4] This was the so-called Krankemann roller with which they would smooth out the surface of that square – see: Antoni Siciński, 'Z psychopatologii więźniów: Ernst Krankemann', *Przegląd Lekarski*, 1974 No 1, p. 127.

[5] Most likely, this is a reference to the well-known sacrifice by Father Maksymilian Kolbe (No. 16670). Saved by the now Saint Maksymilian Kolbe, Sergeant Marian Gajowniczek (No. 5659) survived the camp. He died in 1995, at the age of ninety-five, a father and grandfather to a large family; he was buried in Niepokalanów, Poland.

[6] See: Archiwum Państwowego Muzeum Auschwitz-Birkenau w Oświęcimiu (APMA-B), Zespół 'Oświadczenia', t. 27, k. 22-29, as provided by former Auschwitz inmate Włodzimierz Turczyniak; also: D. Czech, 'Kalendarium der Ereignisse im Konzentrationslager Auschwitz-Birkenau' (APMA-B), Hamburg 1989, pp. 424-425.

[7] It is based on the final, far more detailed version of his Auschwitz report Captain Pilecki wrote during the summer 1945 when with the Polish Second Corps in Ancona, Italy. Pilecki gave to the authorities there a fictitious maiden name of Tomasz Serafiński's mother (at that time he did not know the actual one); this could have easily been uncovered by the camp authorities. Also, Pilecki needed to be prepared for the eventuality the real Tomasz Serafiński is brought by Germans to Auschwitz.

[8] The latter person was, most likely, Andrzej Możdżeń, alias 'Sybirak', head of diversion and arms at the Bochnia Home Army District; in 1958, he stated:

> *'In July 1943, at Tomasz Serafiński's home in Nowym Wiśnicz I spoke without witnesses with 'Witold', an escapee from Auschwitz. The above-mentioned 'Witold' asked me, if he could count on help in forming a detachment of volunteers, one hundred fifty men strong, to attempt to liberate Auschwitz. This detachment was to be complemented by another detachment being formed in the Kielce province. I promised him that I would form such a detachment, and I prepared a route along which to reach the Auschwitz camp. In late Autumn 1943, I received an advice that this plan would not be implemented.'*

(See: APMO Zespół 'Wspomnienia', t. 130, k. 1, statement by Andrzej Możdżeń).

HIS KEDYW SERVICE

Once back in Warsaw, Pilecki first lived with Palińskis, the family of one of his Auschwitz fellow inmates. By this time, he had already received security clearance and got recommended for work with the Home Army Headquarters' Prisons Cell which reported to Desk 998 of the Home Army's Information and Intelligence Department. His co-escapee Redzej worked at the same department. After only three days, Pilecki left that job. He requested a transfer to the Department II Information [codename: Chameleon] of the Diversion Command [*Kedyw*] of the Home Army's High Command.

The head of this bureau was Lieutenant Stefan Wysocki (*nom-de-guerre*: 'Jeż'). Pilecki (his *nom-de-guerre* at that time: 'Witold' and 'TIV') became Wysocki's deputy.[436]

On October 23, Pilecki met Lieutenant-Colonel Jan Mazurkiewicz (*nom-de-guerre*: 'Sęp'), who held the position of the Deputy Commandant of Kedyw. He briefed Mazurkiewicz on the situation at Auschwitz. Mazurkiewicz ordered him to sound out Major Karol Jabłoński (*nom-de-guerre*: 'Zygmunt'), an officer in charge of Kedyw's Department III (Operations), also known under its codename of 'Cyrkiel'. Jabłoński asked Pilecki to present to that department his Auschwitz liberation plan.

As noted previously, Jabłoński showed little willingness to support Pilecki's idea. He said: '*After the war, I will show you how thick our Auschwitz files are.*' This greatly upset Pilecki, who pointed out to Jabłoński that the comprehensiveness of that archive would not of itself relieve the suffering of Auschwitz inmates. Jabłoński concluded this briefing with the following words: *'I can assure you, we will get in touch with you when this matter becomes current.*'[437]

Pilecki did not wait idly for Jabłoński to call him to further discuss this matter. Instead, he completed his *Report W,* and handed in its copy to the Home Army's High Command. This detailed report was then sent to London, where the scale of reported Nazi atrocities at Auschwitz was at that time widely believed to be grossly exaggerated.

The British military leaders were not prepared to provide air support to the Home Army for the operation to save the Auschwitz inmates. Subsequently, Pilecki wrote a coded letter to his Auschwitz colleagues, in which he advised them of his inability to get his camp liberation plan approved and implemented by the Home Army High Command.[438]

In September 1943, the latest round of mass arrests at Auschwitz ensured no fewer than seventy-four ZOW members were put into the Death Block cells. After long and brutal interrogations by the Auschwitz Gestapo, twenty of the seventy-four were released. But the rest – including Lieutenant-Colonel Juliusz Gilewicz, Major Zygmunt Bohdanowski, Lieutenant Lieutenant-Colonel Teofil Dziama, Jan Mosdorf, Captain Tadeusz Paolone, and Lieutenant Lieutenant-Colonel Kazimierz Stamirowski, altogether a very large part of the ZOW leadership at the time – were, on October 11, shot at the Wall of Death.[439] ZOW members believed that two Auschwitz Gestapo informers, Jerzy Krzyżanowski (No. 57125) and Stefan Ołpiński (No. 67214) were responsible for these arrests.[440]

After that execution, it was only because of the commendable dedication of some of the longest-serving members that the ZOW was able to continue its activities in the camp. Bernard Świerczyna, Captain Stanisław Kazuba and Henryk Bartosiewicz were among the remaining ZOW members whose courage and strength of will were particularly notable.[441]

At Kedyw, Pilecki was responsible for the preparation of the lists of Polish citizens who were identified as *Volksdeutsch*, as well as of other traitors whom the underground Polish authorities planned to do away with. He also prepared all the correspondence in relation to these areas.[442] Apart from his Home Army activities, he involved himself in providing financial assistance, wherever he could, to the families of Auschwitz captives.

Formally, Pilecki worked with Kedyw until the outbreak of the Warsaw Uprising on August 1, 1944 (his *noms-de-guerre* from that time were 'Witold Smoliński' and 'Roman Jezierski'). In fact, he was very busy from the spring of 1944 onwards, attending to the top-secret task entrusted to him by Colonel August Emil Fieldorf (*nom-de-guerre*: 'Nil'). Fieldorf believed – and his belief was soon proven correct – that the Polish nation would face subordination to, if not indeed actual inclusion in, the Soviet Union once the Nazis had been defeated. Pilecki was among those who were helping Fieldorf form a new organisation, one called *Niepodległość* [English: Independence], whose task was to come up with appropriate response to this situation. The code-name for this new group was NIE.[443]

A further honour had already come Pilecki's way. On February 23, 1944, he had been promoted to the rank of captain. This promotion was back-dated to November 11, 1943.[444]

In March 1944, 'Nil' handed over his position with Kedyw to his deputy, Colonel Jan Mazurkiewicz (*nom-de-guerre* 'Radosław'). 'Nil' himself had to focuss on forming a top-secret civilian-military entity inside the Home Army structures which would, after the Nazis' occupation had finished, seek to *'uphold the nation's soul as well as fight for, and secure an independent and free Poland on all Polish territories occupied by the Red Army.'*[445]

NIE had three departments. Its Department I was made up of three sections: Organisation, Communication, and Procurement. Likewise, Department II also had three sections: Intelligence, Security and Planning of Combat Operations, and Combat Units. But Department III had only two sections: Socio-Political and Propaganda, and Sitting Courts[446]

Department II was headed by Stefan Miłkowski. Pilecki became one of Miłkowski's three deputies, and was made responsible for the planning of combat operations. As his own deputies, Pilecki hired three familiar figures: Jan Redzej, Czesław Czernicki and Stefan Bielecki.[447]

For all his new pressing duties, Pilecki had not forgotten about the Auschwitz inmates. In late July 1944, a few days before the Warsaw Uprising started, he spoke to Colonel Mazurkiewicz, reminding him of the unresolved Auschwitz problem. Mazurkiewicz assured him that the Home Army's High Command was still involved in consultations with its regional commands regarding a possible liberation action. The High Command's position was that such an all-out assault on the Auschwitz SS contingent could only be undertaken if inmates themselves started a rebellion, or the SS decided to exterminate all inmates prior to leaving the camp.

Also in July 1944, Second Lieutenant Stefan Jasieński (*nom-de-guerre*: 'Urban') reported to the Command of the Home Army's Silesian Region. He brought with him a letter from the Home Army's Commander-in-Chief, General Tadeusz Komorowski (*nom-de-guerre*: 'Bór'). In this letter, Komorowski ordered the regional Home Army commandant, Major Zygmunt Walter-Janke, to put the Auschwitz camp under a close and ongoing surveillance.[448]

In the period between his return from Auschwitz and the commencement of the Warsaw Uprising, Pilecki would meet his family regularly. He had to take extreme care on all such occasions, for fear that his involvement in clandestine resistance operations might come to wider notice.

He treated his daughter Zofia, then eleven years old, as if she were already an adult. Zofia hoped to impress her father with her physical fitness: she could swim, run fast, and even do splits and bridges. At all times, she was mindful of the fact that it was her father's fitness which helped him survive Auschwitz's hell.

When walking with Zofia on the streets of Warsaw, Pilecki would sometimes play a game of sorts with her. In this game, she would walk some distance ahead of him, and he would make her responsible for giving him secret signals whenever she spotted approaching German soldiers or police. It was a game with very serious intent.[449]

After his return from Auschwitz (so Zofia recalled much later), his behaviour was a bit different when he saw his loved ones. For instance, during a visit to Ostrów Mazowiecka late in 1943, he so far forgot himself that once had he finished his meal, he put the remaining bread crusts into his pockets. The habit of hoarding food, a habit nigh-essential in Auschwitz, could not easily be broken.[450]

THE 1944 WARSAW UPRISING

By late 1943, it had become clear to all Poles that they were going to be freed from the German occupation not by their Western allies, as they had hoped not long time before, but by the Soviet Union.[451] The USSR had already obtained control of Estonia, Latvia, and Lithuania; it would soon bear down upon Finland, and after the war Hungary, Czechoslovakia, Romania, Bulgaria, Yugoslavia and Albania would become Soviet satellites.[452]

All that Stalin needed in each of those eventual satellites was a solid core of local politicians who would represent Soviet interests, if necessary through the threat of military blackmail. Hence the decision which the Home Army took in March 1944. From that time on, the High Command of Home Army worked very hard to prepare Poland for an effective resistance against *de facto* Moscow rule.

It was obvious that the Soviets would want to introduce to Poland the same ruthless and inefficient Soviet communist system as conceived and introduced by Lenin, and sustained by Stalin: a system which had terrorised its citizens and made their lives entirely dependent on the whims of murderous clique, a system similar to one which had killed, or starved, dozens of millions of Soviet citizens, deprived them of many basic freedoms and had ruined the Soviet economy, except for its armaments industry, a system which had failed to secure sufficient supply of about every consumer good to its citizens.

In July 1944, Poles had every reason to distrust the Soviet Union, and be fearful of it. The prospect of losing their independence to the Soviet Union, a country which had already proven its extreme hostility towards the idea of independent Poland, and towards patriotic Poles, the already mentioned NKWD 1937-1938 Polish operation, and the 1940 Katyn massacre of Polish POWs by Soviets being just two examples of that extreme hostility.

The vast majority of Poles would at that time counter any effort from Soviets to impose the radically different Russian mentality and customs upon the Polish nation, and to replace Poland's former political and economic systems with a Soviet-styled brutal political control system, and the Soviets devised very inefficient economic model. Such prospect was abhorrent and totally unacceptable to them.

The establishment on July 22, 1944, under close Soviet supervision and with Soviets' support, of the Polish Committee of National Liberation, known also as the Lublin Committee, sent a strong signal that that process already commenced. Poles realised that once the Soviet Red Army takes control of all Poland's territory, their country would lose its independence, and with it many of its civil liberties, so treasured by Poles, would be a matter of the past.

*

We need to make now a step back. The official Polish-Soviet relationships since April 25, 1943, the day the Soviet Union broke all diplomatic relationships with the Polish government-in-exile, had been non-existent. It came to that soon after Katyń Forest's mass graves had been uncovered by the retreating German Army. Stalin made no admission of his own responsibility for this massacre. Instead, he put the blame on the Germans.

On October 26, 1943, the Polish government-in-exile (led at that time by Stanisław Mikołajczyk, who became Prime Minister in July, after Władysław Sikorski's death in air catastrophy at Gibraltar) instructed the Home Army to remain underground after the Soviet entry into Poland, unless diplomatic relations with the Soviet Union are reinstated beforehand.

In response to this instruction, the Home Army commander General Tadeusz Bór-Komorowski presented on November 20, 1943 to the Mikołajczyk government his counter-proposal, called Operation Tempest (Polish: *Burza*). This plan provided for Home Army units to harass the retreating Wehrmacht forces from behind, as the Wehrmacht is pushed back by the advancing Red Army.[453]

Even though Wehrmacht had at that time several divisions in Warsaw's vicinity, and could also rely on other allied forces stationed both inside and outside Warsaw, General Bór-Komorowski obtained on July 25, 1944 an authorisation from the Polish government-in-exile in London to proclaim a general uprising in German-occupied Poland, whenever he and his advisers saw it fit.[454]

On the very same day, the deliberately misleadingly named Union of Polish Patriots (which, in reality, was under Stalin's complete control) in a radio forecast from Moscow called on all Poles on occupied territories of their country to fling themselves into an all-out fight against Hitler.[455]

As it happened, Soviet armoured units reached, on July 29, Warsaw's eastern outskirts. There, they met with a fierce counter-attack from two German *Panzer Korps*: the 39th and Fourth SS. Believing that the appropriate moment for Polish action had come, General Tadeusz Komorowski and Colonel Antoni Chruściel ordered, on July 31, the full mobilisation of the Home Army for 5 p.m. of the following day.[456]

Due to his very responsible role in the super-secret NIE operation, Pilecki was ordered by his superiors not to involve himself in the uprising.[457] These instructions he however ignored. The idea of waiting somewhere safely hidden, while his countrymen fought and died in what was a deeply uneven combat against Wehrmacht forces incomparably superior in numerical terms and armament, was insufferable to him. So, for the first time in his life, he disobeyed an explicit military order.

On the first day of the uprising, Pilecki took part in an attack on the German positions in the suburb of Wola. He then helped break the German defence of bunkers at the corner of Żelazna and Chłodna Streets. On August 2, he reported to Major Leon Nowakowski (*nom-de-guerre*: 'Lig') at the latter's headquarters: 40 Twarda Street. With him, he took Jan Redzej.[458]

Neither Pilecki nor Redzej admitted to being officers. Both men introduced themselves to Nowakowski as simply 'escapees from Auschwitz'. At that moment, Major Nowakowski was in the process of forming a significant fighting group which was to receive the name of Chrobry II. He very gladly accepted both of them into the group. He ordered them to set up their own combat unit, attack German positions in the area near the smaller of Warsaw's two ghettos, and eliminate German sharpshooters who, very well hidden in their vantage-points on the roofs of high buildings along Ceglana Street, were inflicting very heavy casualties on the Polish fighters in the area.[459].

Pilecki and Redzej formed a unit of seventeen fighters which was a part of the 1st company "Warszawianka". Their unit they called "Mazur Platoon". Their platoon acquitted itself very well. Once the platoon had successfully carried out its first combat tasks, Pilecki asked one of the unit's members, Kazimierz Sawicki (*nom-de-guerre*: 'Sawa'), to take over the command. Together with Redzej, Sawicki soon reported again to Major Nowakowski, and requested new orders. This time, soldiers were to assume control of a crossing which was strategically very significant: the point where Jerozolimskie Avenue intersected Żelazna Street, and which included Starynkiewicz Square. Their job was to prevent the Germans from moving along the adjacent sections of these arterial roads.

Also with this order they acquitted themselves splendidly.[460] On August 3, they fought for control of the Post Office building, next to the capital's chief railway station. They succeeded. From there, they launched an attack on a large building which housed the Military Geographic Institute (Polish: *Wojskowy Instytut Geograficzny* – WIG). Once that building was under their control, they obtained from Pilecki permission to fly the Polish national white and red flag on the building's roof. This drew very heavy German fire.

POLISH FLAG ON THE ROOF OF A BUILDING NEAR STARYNKIEWICZ SQUARE COPPED ALL THE FEROCITY OF GERMAN FIRE

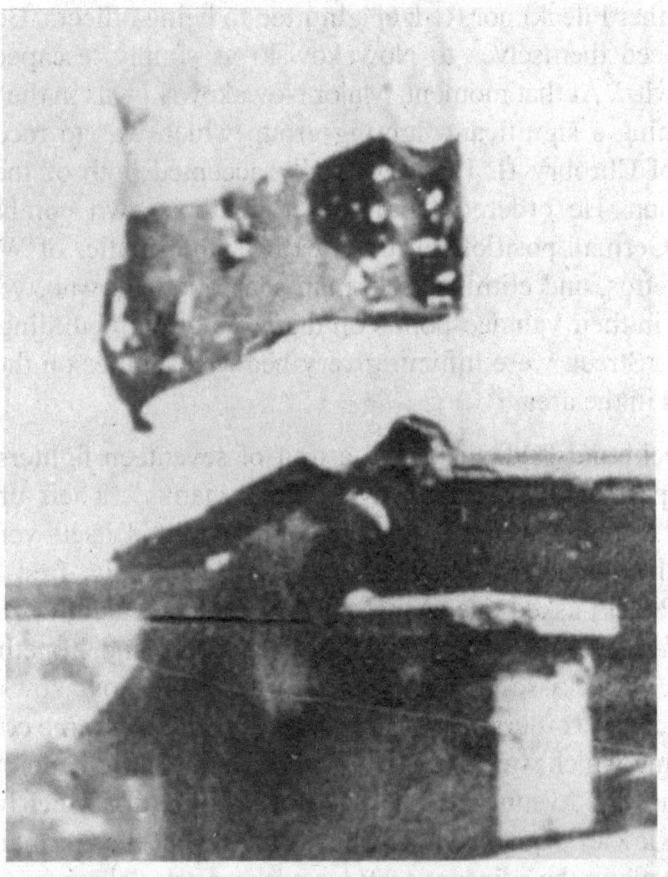

(©The Museum of the 1944 Warsaw Uprising, photo by an unknown, all rights reserved)

Afterwards, Pilecki and seventeen of his soldiers were able to stop three attacking German tanks, and destroy one of them.

On the next day, they were able to repulse yet another attack by several tanks and armed vehicles, accompanied by a German grenadiers' unit which was vastly superior to the Poles in numerical terms. The Wehrmacht attack all of a sudden stopped. The reason for it were several very conspicuous tin cans Pilecki ordered his soldiers on the previous day, to put on the road in front of them. The tin cans greatly resembled anti-tank mines, and the grenadiers mistook them for such. Having halted so as to first neutralise the 'mines,' they cautiously approached the barricade. As they did so, Pilecki's unit suddenly launched an attack which left several grenadiers dead. The survivors hurriedly withdrew, leaving several burning tanks behind them. Likely, they thought the Polish unit was a great deal bigger, and stronger than it actually was. This Wehrmacht attempt to open the militarily crucial thoroughfare along Jerozolimskie Avenue, which lead to the Poniatowski Bridge over the Vistula, ended in spectacular German defeat.[461]

The following day, August 5, brought grievous tidings for Pilecki. Redzej, as he led yet another assault on German-controlled buildings in the vicinity, received a terrible wound, from which, an hour later, he died. His last words were: 'For Poland!' It was by far not the only Polish fatality in his unit on that day. A further six soldiers were also killed, as were several nurses assisting the unit. The soldiers had been attacking the occupiers who defended the city's main water-works building.[462]

On August 6, Major Zygmunt Brejnak replaced Major Nowakowski as the commander of "Chrobry II". Nowakowski became Brejnak's deputy. The German destruction of the group's original defence at 40 Twarda Street forced a move to new quarters, this time at 45 Sienna Street.[463]

Three redoubts which "Chrobry II" was defending – WIG, the Treasury Building (*Izba Skarbowa*), and the Starost Office buildings – were subjected on August 8 to repeated German bombings. Meanwhile, Wehrmacht ground troops continued their assault. By this point, Polish insurgents were beginning to run short on munitions, grenades, and the self-made incendiary bottles they had so effectively used against Wehrmacht tanks on the previous days.

This is how an eyewitness to the Treasury Building's defence described the troops under Pilecki's command:

> 'They all were very young lads, inadequately dressed, with very poorly prepared firing positions, and very poorly armed even compared to other Warsaw insurgents who are, on the whole, poorly armed.
>
> They would only ask for weapons. Through a large gap in the wall, a result of tank shelling, I could see the firing positions of SS-men in trenches which were dug out at the other end of the square. They were also very young people [except that] they were well nourished, very well armed, and had proper uniforms.'[464]

POLISH FIGHTERS IN THE CITY, NEAR CORNER SIENKIEWICZA AND MARSZAŁKOWSKA STREETS

(© The Museum of the 1944 Warsaw Uprising, photo by Eugeniusz Lokajski, all rights reserved)

On August 13, the valiant defenders of all three redoubts were ordered by Captain Jan Jaroszek to abandon them, and to withdraw to the area where "Chrobry II" was to regroup. The last to withdraw was Pilecki himself, who wrote: *'The WIG-Treasury unit has for ten days controlled the Starynkiewicz Square, making it impossible for the enemy to move its vehicles through it.'*[465]

Once it had re-grouped, the "Warszawianka" company was responsible for the control of movements along the Starynkiewicz Square railway bridge, and along the railway line towards the Warsaw Main Railway Station. Its commander at that time was

Captain Mieczysław Zacharewicz, alias 'Zawadzki'. Pilecki was his deputy: after revealing to Zacharewicz his officer's rank, he obtained command over a platoon.

It was at that time that Pilecki met again his other Auschwitz co-escapee, Edward Ciesielski. Edward was apprehended by the Wehrmacht as he carried a message for an insurgency commander. He managed to escape, but was shot and badly wounded. At first, he thought he would die from loss of blood, but he did not. Once at a field hospital, he asked for Pilecki to visit him there. From Pilecki he learned about Redzej's death. Pilecki made sure that Ciesielski was immediately transferred to a better-equipped hospital, and operated by a suitably experienced surgeon.[466]

Beyond this, very scant information is available on Pilecki's further whereabouts during the Warsaw Uprising. We only know that around August 20, he seized from the enemy – in a night sortie – a considerable number of mines, detonators, and other materiel for sappers. These he later shared with other units. On other occasions, he seized a large quantity of guns. The common opinion of him during that time was that he was *'an excellent and gallant officer, who is respected by all.'*[467] That he remained alive, and without serious physical injury, was very fortunate indeed. During August, he had lost seventeen of his soldiers; a further eight were wounded.[468]

Towards the end of September, the remainders of the 2nd Company from the "Chrobry II" 1st Batallion, at that time under the command of Second Lieutenant Mikołaj Kobyliński, were transferred to the Group's 2nd Battalion. Within two days, Pilecki formed three platoons, and became the company's new commanding officer. Altogether, the company had eighty combat soldiers, not to mention twelve staffers responsible for liaison and nursing. Most of them were very young.[469]

In his Warsaw Uprising recollections, Lieutenant Zbigniew Brym, who was in command of the company which flanked Pilecki's company, emphasized Pilecki's outstanding characteristic as a commander: his strong protective instinct towards all his soldiers. No wonder that the youngest among them called him *Tata,* the Polish equivalent of 'Dad.' Pilecki not only accepted this nickname, but seemed to be actually proud of it.[470]

**RYBAKI STREET IN THE CITY:
A VIEW AFTER THE 1944 WARSAW UPRISING**

(© The Museum of the 1944 Warsaw Uprising, photo by Karol Pcherski, all rights reserved)

SZPITALNA STREET IN THE CITY: A VIEW AFTER THE 1944 WARSAW UPRISING

(© The Museum of the 1944 Warsaw Uprising, photo by Tadeusz Boncler, all rights reserved)

MARSZAŁKOWSKA STREET NEAR THE REDEEMER'S SQUARE; A VIEW AFTER THE 1944 WARSAW UPRISING

(© The Museum of the 1944 Warsaw Uprising, photo by Marian Grabski, all rights reserved)

After Pilecki had received the news of the Uprising's capitulation, on October 3 and 4 he hid all his company documents, and some of its weapons, in a secret place. This place was behind the oven in the flat owned by the mother of Second Lieutenant Bolesław Niewiarowski.

A GERMAN WAR PRISONER

As per the terms of capitulation signed by the Command of Warsaw's insurgents on October 2, 1944 in Ożarów, all "Chrobry II" units met three days later on Żelazna Street. At the Kerceli Square, they left their weapons. Then they began their march, four abreast, their commanding officers in front of them. They were flanked by their Wehrmacht escort.

1944 WARSAW UPRISING SOLDIERS ON THEIR WAY TO THE OŻARÓW CONCENTRATION POINT FOR POWS

(© The Museum of the 1944 Warsaw Uprising, photo by an unidentified German, all rights reserved)

As they were arriving in Ożarów, Eleonora Ostrowska, who at that time was staying with her local friends, spotted Pilecki. The two exchanged a few words.[471]

All prisoners of war were provisionally accommodated in empty production shops of the Ożarów cable factory.[472] On the next day, they had to cross over to the local railway station, where they had carriages awaiting them. They were then put onto the train, eighty soldiers into each carriage.

On October 8, the train with POWs left for the camp in Lamsdorf (the German name for the town known in Polish as Łambinowice). After a further ten days, all officers were transferred on to Germany. Their destination was the Murnau POW camp for officers.[473] This camp was situated in southern Bavaria near the Swiss border, about one hour journey by train from Munich. From there Pilecki sent, on October 23, a postcard to Nowy Wiśnicz. In this postcard, he advised Ludmiła Serafińska of Redzej's death, and of the wounds which Ciesielski had received during the Uprising.

At the Murnau camp, the Warsaw insurgents met – and were cordially received by – Polish POWs from the September 1939 campaign. The 1939 veterans had clothes, underwear, and shoes for the new arrivals. Not only did the new POWs look very different from the 1939 ones (in that the former wore, by and large, dirty and torn civilian clothes), but their demeanour was different from that of the 1939 captives. They behaved towards their German captors in a proud manner that bordered on arrogance. Often, the Warsaw insurgents found it difficult to adapt to the camp's conditions.[474]

Already when at Łambinowice, Pilecki had started planning an escape with one of his fellow POWs, Jan Mierzanowski. Neither man, however, wanted to risk such a venture in winter: the temperature so close to the Alps was simply too low, and they would have to leave behind in the snow traces of their departure. They therefore postponed notions of escaping until April, but by then the war seemed so close to its end that they gave up on the idea altogether.[475] Sure enough, on April 29, 1945, US Third

Army units under General George Patton liberated the POWs of Oflag VII A, Murnau. Pilecki, POW No. 101,892, was among them.

A few hours before the American troops' arrival, a Swiss representative from the International Red Cross arrived at the camp. He briefly spoke with some senior POWs, and with the camp's commanding officers. Then, he left.

Not long after he had departed, various POWs spotted, in the distance, a column of SS trucks heading in the camp's direction. A moment later, a column of American tanks appeared near that road, opening sustained fire on the SS vehicles until each one of them was destroyed. When the Americans searched the corpse of the SS general who was in command of the column, they found on his person an order to kill every single Murnau POW. Had the Swiss representative from the Red Cross not visited earlier in the day, the killings might well have been carried out.[476]

Following the camp's liberation, Pilecki kept on living there for several weeks. The fates of his fellow Auschwitz inmates, however, continued to prey on his mind. On May 26, he finished compiling a list which contained the names of more than seven hundred of them. Most of them had been murdered, died of starvation, or died of disease. In a short introduction to that list,[477] Pilecki pointed out that while much had already been written and spoken about the Ravensbrück, Dachau, Sachsenhausen and Mauthausen camps, very little information had yet entered public knowledge concerning Auschwitz, where the death toll was many times higher.

For a while, Pilecki was unsure as to what to do next. He had sworn, back in March 1944 (before he started developing the NIE structures for securing national independence), an oath to return to Poland. On the other hand, it was already obvious to him, and to his compatriots, that even if the Soviets had not started occupying Poland *de iure*, they already had it under their control.

Pilecki was aware of the vital role that the NIE structures were supposed to play in the future Polish people struggle against the USSR. What he did not know at that timer, was that the Soviets had arrested the NIE's General Fieldorf on March 7, 1945. Fortunately for the General, his captors did not know precisely who their captive was: he had false documents on him, which had been issued in the name of Walenty Gdanicki. Nonetheless, the Soviets took him back to the USSR and consigned him to a forced labour camp.[478]

Likewise, when in Murnau Pilecki remained unaware of the capture by Soviets – on March 28, 1945 – of the NIE Commander-in-Chief, General Leopold Okulicki. The following June, Okulicki went through a show trial in Moscow; shortly afterwards he was condemned to death there, and killed.[479] By that time, the entire Polish underground had already been deprived of all its leadership, and could thus be regarded as having effectively dissolved itself.[480] At first unaware of that, Pilecki believed that his 1944 oath was still binding upon him.

On May 9, three leading Polish soldiers visited Murnau: General Tadeusz Komorowski, General Tadeusz Pełczyński, and Colonel Kazimierz Iranek-Osmecki. Pilecki sought advice and instructions from these officers. After all, they represented the government-in-exile. On May 11, he spoke with Colonel Iranek-Osmecki, who gave him a clear answer to his question: yes, he should return to Poland.[481]

Another official visit took place in mid-June. This time it was the Commander-in-Chief of the Second Polish Corps, General Władysław Anders, who came. Anders encouraged Pilecki and the others to join the Second Polish Corps in Ancona, Italy. Two weeks later, Anders sent Captain Bornholz to Murnau, to prepare a list of those willing to join the Corps. Pilecki discussed with Bornholz the subject of his NIE oath and allied issues. He made it clear to Bornholz he wanted to go back to Poland if he could, to resume the struggle.[482] On July 9, he left Murnau for Italy.[483]

THE ITALIAN EPISODE

In a group of Polish officers from Murnau, Pilecki arrived in Porto San Giorgio, in Italy, on July 11, 1945. There, he immediately joined the Second Corps. At this point in time, Anders still believed – and shared this belief with many others – that Poland's Western allies would soon declare war on the Soviet Union. He thus ensured an extensive network enabling independent communication with Poland was set up, so as to make the Polish social and political situation better known to the world.

In August, Pilecki joined the II Department, dealing with military intelligence. In this role, he directly reported to Lieutenant-Colonel Stanisław Kijak. With Kijak, Pilecki discussed various options for the scope of intelligence operations in Poland. The relevant network was to have the task of collecting primarily political and economic information. Kijak reckoned that for such purposes, Pilecki would be able to rely on the NIE structures that had already been clandestinely established. Accordingly, he suggested Pilecki went back to Poland.

While in Porto San Giorgio, Pilecki lived in Kijak's villa near the seashore. Soon another Pole arrived: Maria Szelągowska, who had known Pilecki from Warsaw days, and who also managed to visit him in Murnau after the camp's liberation. He had requested that she typed up his Auschwitz reports and his reports covering the German occupation of Poland in more general terms. That was why she had arrived at Porto San Giorgio.

Another source of local support for him was Jan Mierzanowski, whom Pilecki would often take for pedal-boat trips. When the two men were far away from the shore, Pilecki read aloud to his companion freshly completed passages of his reports, inviting Mierzanowski's comments, suggestions, and corrections.[484]

Pilecki simultaneously worked on his Auschwitz exposé, and on his memoirs. The latter began with his childhood years; they ended on September 1940, when he was taken to Auschwitz.[485]

An extraordinary (and perhaps prophetic) incident occurred on a sight-seeing journey that Pilecki, Mierzanowski, and Szelągowska took to Rome. As they walked through the city's zoological gardens, they stopped before a cage with eagles, and discussed some matters there. While they were talking, Pilecki – with lack of caution so uncharacteristic of him – grabbed a rail of the cage. No sooner had he done this than a huge eagle flew down and pierced Pilecki's finger with its talon. Pilecki maintained his customary stoicism, conveying no hint to his companions that they should be overly concerned. His eyes suggested a fundamental calm. And indeed, just a few seconds later, the eagle released its grip on Pilecki's finger, and flew away.

Mierzanowski was convinced that if Pilecki had yelled, or tried to free himself by force from the eagle's grip, he would probably have lost his finger. Only after persistent persuasion from Mierzanowski and Szelągowska Pilecki went to a dressing-station, and let his wound be bandaged there.[486]

This incident is both symbolic, and emblematic of Pilecki. It is symbolic, since Pilecki is attacked by a black eagle. It is emblematic of Pilecki, because it shows his unflappable composure, and his exercise of good judgment.

Early in September 1945, Pilecki had two more meetings with General Anders.[487] At the conclusion of the second meeting, the General resolutely advised: 'Indeed, your presence in Poland is necessary.'[488] Subsequently, Pilecki had also two meetings with General Pełczyński.

SECOND LIEUTENANT MARIAN SZYSZKO-BOHUSZ, MARIA SZELĄGOWSKA AND CAPTAIN WITOLD PILECKI IN ROME (1945)

(©The Auschwitz-Birkenau Memorial and Museum, all rights reserved)

Just before his departure from Italy, Pilecki had a third meeting with General Anders (Rome, October 23). Anders bade him an official farewell, and gave him his 'fatherly blessings' for the work that Pilecki was to do in Poland.[489]

As with Auschwitz, so now, Pilecki employed a false name. This time his alias was Roman Jezierski (pronounced *Yezyersky*). He did not go alone: Maria Szelągowska accompanied him, and she too travelled under an assumed name, in her case – of Krystyna Kwiecińska. The third person present was Bolesław Niewiarowski, well known to Pilecki from the Warsaw Uprising and from Murnau. Niewiarowski's own alias was Jan Słubicki. He was to return to Italy, and brief on the outcome of the operation.

They journeyed via Bologna to Bremen in Germany. On October 28, they reached Regensburg, Germany. There, Niewiarowski obtained from Major Mikołaj Kozłowski, an officer from the Świętokrzyska Brigade, a car that they would need. Niewiarowski stayed in Regensburg. Pilecki and Szelągowska, for their part, traversed the American-Soviet demarcation line, and then continued to Plzeň in Czechoslovakia. From Plzeň, they took a train to Prague, where they spent a few days. Pilecki visited there a place that offered help to Poles who had been in German camps. In charge of the administration at this office was Dr. Karel Stransky, the very same Stransky who three years earlier had helped the ZOW in its Auschwitz work.

At the end of November, Pilecki and Szelągowska finally crossed the Czech-Polish border at Czechowice-Dziedzice. There, Pilecki was issued with identity documents issued in the name of Roman Jezierski. Szelągowska chose to abjure pseudonyms, and had her own identity document issued in her authentic name.

IN THE BEAR'S DEN

Their first destination in Poland was Zakopane, a mountain resort in the country's south, where they spent two days with Szelągowska's local acquaintances. From there, they went to Cracow, and spent four days in that city. In Cracow, Pilecki met again a fellow Auschwitz captive: Andrzej Rablin. He also re-encountered the Serafińskis, who had recently moved to Cracow from Nowy Wiśnicz.

He and Szelągowska stayed in Cracow with the mother of another former Auschwitz captive, whose name was Józef Cyrankiewicz, and who soon would become Poland's Prime Minister. Ludmiła Serafińska's father had been a schoolmate of Cyrankiewicz's father. This familial connection made it possible for the Serafiński couple to move in with Cyrankiewicz's mother, with whom they lived until 1960.

Pilecki also went to Bochnia. There, he met Edmund Zabawski and Edmund's father-in-law, Józef Obora, who after Pilecki's escape from Auschwitz had for nearly four months provided shelter for him.

From Cracow, Pilecki and Szelągowska travelled to Katowice; and from Katowice, they travelled to Częstochowa. They arrived in Warsaw on December 8.[490]

Once in Warsaw, Pilecki tracked down Makary Sieradzki, a former TAP member who now worked as a school superintendent. Makary and his wife Helena owned a flat, into which Pilecki moved. He stayed there until February 1946. Szelągowska, for her part, found accommodation with an acquaintance of hers, and later changed her address several times.[491]

Another task which Pilecki had set himself was to locate his NIE superior, Stefan Miłkowski, alias 'Jeż'. Here, alas, he had no luck there. He came to a reluctant conclusion that Miłkowski had either died, or else left Poland. Of the three persons who had reported to Pilecki in the NIE, Redzej and Czesław Czernicki had lost their lives during the Warsaw Uprising. So had Stefan Bielecki, who had been wounded, taken to a Warsaw hospital, and killed when the hospital was bombed by the Wehrmacht. In short, there remained nobody from the old NIE network on whom Pilecki could rely; and if he were to achieve anything useful, he would need to set up a new network from scratch. The prospects for his information gathering tasks were not looking as good as before.[492]

Undaunted by this, Pilecki established a new intelligence network, which comprised former Auschwitz inmates, former TAP and Home Army members, and some other individuals whom he had come to know during the Uprising. This new network had no name, and involved a relatively small number of people. Unlike the preceding networks, it required no membership oath. Some of those who took part in it might not even have been aware that they were involved in its operations. There were no drop-boxes, no liaison officers, no sabotage capabilities, no bulletins illegally published.

As meticulously as he could, Pilecki collected information about how former Home Army soldiers, members of other Polish underground military groups, and recent Polish arrivals from the West were being treated by the communists. He also gathered data about the state of the Polish economy after the war, in particular - about the trade agreements concluded by the Polish government. Apart from that, Pilecki assembled evidence of how communists were more and more indoctrinating Polish society at large. Of course, he regarded such indoctrination as pernicious and thought much about possible ways of neutralising it.[493]

One possible method of opposition against the Soviet control of Poland Pilecki certainly rejected: any form of armed opposition to the pro-Soviet forces. He believed such opposition would be ineffective, given the political situation of Poland at the time. For him, the purpose of his intelligence activities was, first, fostering and supporting ongoing opposition to the introduction of communist ideas and practices to Poland and, second, maintaining a strong influence on younger Poles by sustaining the traditional values of Polish culture.

He regarded the command of the Second Corps in Italy as a crucial co-ordination and support centre for all activities which aimed to restore Poland's independence. He did not view himself as a spy, but rather as a soldier who had received orders to collect necessary information. In his later plea for clemency to Bolesław Bierut (Poland's President 1947-1952), he emphasised that he had never worked for a foreign power and that he was merely sending information to his Polish military unit in the hope that, one day, the Polish [communist] government and the exile centres representing Poles would somehow reach an accord.[494]

Early in 1946, somewhere in Warsaw, Pilecki ran into his acquaintance from TAP days, Tadeusz Płużański, who had spent nearly five years as an inmate at the German concentration camp at Stutthof. Pilecki managed to get Płużański to accept the duties of a secret courier between Warsaw and Ancona. One month later, Płużański went to Ancona to report that Pilecki and Szelągowska had arrived safely at their destination, and that they had since started setting up their secret intelligence gathering network. When in Ancona, Płużański joined the Second Corps, was promoted to the rank of Second Lieutenant, and worked at the Corps' Intelligence Department for over two months.[495]

In February 1946, Pilecki met Bronisława Jarzyńska, whom he had come to know during the German occupation. He told her he had nowhere to live. She offered him a room in her Warsaw flat at Skrzetuskiego Street. He showed her an employment certificate issued in the name of Roman Jezierski, and told her that he had a job with a construction company.

Early in the morning, he would leave her flat, ostensibly to attend to his construction work duties. He would return to her flat late in the evening. By and large, he would spend days in the Sieradzkis' own apartment. There he had a room of his own, where he worked on the section of his memoirs which dealt with Auschwitz and the 1944 uprising.[496] Probably it was there, too, that he finished his reports for the Second Corps in Italy.[497] He received visits from his wife, who continued to live with the children at her parents' Ostrów Mazowiecka home. Husband and wife would meet in the Jarzyńska flat.[498]

During late February, Pilecki and Szelągowska welcomed the arrival of Bolesław Niewiarowski, whom they had not seen since Regensburg days. By chance, Niewiarowski met Szelągowska in a Warsaw street. She immediately contacted him with 'Witold'.[499] Pilecki handed in to Niewiarowski his three reports presenting the progress of his intelligence work. Also, he advised Niewiarowski about the contacts which he had established with some active Polish guerrilla units; and he asked Niewiarowski for money that he needed for further such activities.[500]

Before Niewiarowski had left for Italy, Pilecki told him that all the weapons which he himself had stored after the Warsaw Uprising (in a secret safe at the Śliska Street apartment of Niewiarowski's mother) would shortly be transferred to Pilecki's own room at the Sieradzkis' residence. He asked another former TAP member, Stanisław Furmańczyk, to construct a secret safe in that room; and there, with some help from Sieradzki and Szelągowska, he hid all these weapons.[501]

During the spring of 1946, in a Warsaw tram, Pilecki ran into another Auschwitz survivor: Witold Różycki, who had been released from the camp in December 1941. Różycki had obtained a post in the new Polish government, as Head of the Press and Information Section with the Department of Shipping and Foreign Trade. He surreptitiously provided to Pilecki a copy of the commercial treaty signed in April 1946 by Poland and the Soviet Union. As this document was about to be published by the Department, Różycki did not consider it being a secret one. Later, he furnished for Pilecki a copy of a similar treaty between Poland and Bulgaria, and supplied statistics concerning Poland's current foreign trade in general. He also made bulletins of the Polish Press Agency (*Polska Agencja Prasowa – PAP*) available to Pilecki [502]

In June 1946, Płużański returned from Italy. This time, he brought with him Captain Jadwiga Mierzejewska ('Danuta'), a Second Corps intelligence operative, who brought with her an order for Pilecki to make his way back to Italy. His superiors had reasons to believe that his cover had been blown. Pilecki knew of this order. Yet he not only refrained from returning to Italy; he shunned Mierzejewska for two months.

Apart from being the bearer of that order, Mierzejewska had also been supplied with a document issued by General Anders, which accorded her a plenipotentiary status that the London government-in-exile had accepted. The document gave her authority to establish contacts with underground organisations.[503] When she finally met Pilecki, she presented to him two instructions. First, that he should disband Polish guerrilla units, renounce sabotage plans, and dissolve the existing secret groups; second, that he should take further advice regarding the collection of information about Poland's post-war political and economic climate.

At that point in time, Pilecki's clandestine work becoming more and more challenging also from a moral standpoint. The Soviet-controlled terror apparatus was making life ever harder, not only for him personally, but for nearly all Poles. Most of his countrymen lived in a mood of growing fear. Many of them had already yielded, in one way or another, to Soviet threats. Often, they had families and other loved ones to think of. They had also jobs to think of. Thus, little by little, Poles got increasingly inclined to collaborate with communist-controlled government offices, which Pilecki could not bring himself to.

For Pilecki the champion of human dignity – Pilecki, whose indomitable spirit even Auschwitz and the Warsaw Uprising had not broken – it became more and more doubtful he could be of further significant assistance to his compatriots in his Second Corps role. Might he not be able now (with local Stalinists augmenting their power), to achieve more by fulfilling his life's mission outside Poland itself, than he could manage by staying on Polish soil? The question troubled him. He therefore mentioned to his wife the possibility of leaving Poland, and asked her outright if she was willing to come with him and to bring the children with her. Maria said, she was not.[504]

Only then did Pilecki decide to meet 'Danuta'. He managed to convince her that for the time being, at least, he had to stay in Poland because he could not find anyone else suitable to carry on his work.[505] Not for the first time in his life, his sense of duty had prevailed over cool self-interested judgement.

Just before Niewiarowski left Poland (taking his mother with him), Pilecki gave him a copy of his *Report No. 5* to be handed on to the Second Corps. In this document, he confirmed he had received the instructions which 'Danuta' had given him, and he defended his decision to remain in Poland. Subsequently, Płużański took with him to the Second Corps yet another report by Pilecki, this one concerning underground activities in Poland.

Pilecki kept encountering people whom he had known in wartime. In the autumn of 1946, he met again Fr Antoni Czajkowski, who had been the "Chrobry II" group's chaplain during the Uprising,[506] and who retained some contacts with various guerrilla units. When the two men met for a second time, Pilecki asked the priest to take to 'Huzar' – one of the Polish guerrilla leaders at that time – a copy of General Anders's order. For his part, Fr Czajkowski supplied Pilecki with copies of underground periodicals. One of them was called *Walka* ('Struggle'); the other was called *Z podziemia* ('From the underground'). The following December, Pilecki furnished to another guerrilla leader, this time Stefan Guz ('Dan'), who operated in the Tukholski Forest (Polish: Bory Tucholskie), a copy of the same General Anders instruction.

In the meantime, Makary Sieradzki routinely provided Pilecki with various pieces of information pertaining to the country's educational policies. One such item was a list of books that the communists had succeeded in banning. Again, this was not a secret document, but it was an instructive one for indicating the course for the future of Poland. To minimise the risk of being caught, Pilecki would since send his materials to the Second Corp's Intelligence Section in photographic, rather than written, form. Luckily, Wacława Wolańska, who owned a photographic studio and who had been recommended to Pilecki by a TAP member, helped out with the technical side[507]

In September 1946, Tadeusz Płużański met a former schoolfriend of his: a former TAP member, Leszek Kuchciński, who collected intelligence for a regional WIN (*Wolność i Niepodległość* [English: Freedom and Independence]) Command. It was through Kuchciński that Pilecki received what turned out to be a fateful report. This report contained information from Captain Wacław Alchimowicz ('Andrzej'), the Head of Section II, Division V of the Department of Public Security (*Ministerstwo Bezpieczeństwa Publicznego – MBP*).

The report was political dynamite. Its author had recommended that several high functionaries within the Department, including Colonel Józef Różański (pronounced *Roozhanski*), Julia Brystygierowa (pronounced *Breesteegyerova*) and Colonel Józef Czaplicki (pronounced *Chaplitski*), be assassinated. In addition, the report contained other data concerning the MBP's increasingly felonious activities, perpetrated at its highest level.[508]

Pilecki had not the slightest desire to commit murders, and even if he had wished to do so, he lacked the means to do so. Historians are now convinced that the report in question did not in fact originate with a genuine anti-communist, but was a hoax devised by the MBP itself.[509]

Not all Pilecki's activity was political. He also had the pleasure of spending Christmas 1946 with his family. His children had been living in Ostrów Mazowiecka with Maria's parents, where they attended school. By this time, Maria had found a Warsaw job.

For this special occasion, Pilecki managed to obtain a Christmas tree. He decorated it in white and red, with candles and ribbons. The glass in all the flat's windows had been shattered. To provide a limited amount of protection from the bitter cold outside, the family placed parchment over the windows. Zofia recalled: *'As the air was being warmed up by the candles, the parchment on the windows vibrated.'* She also recollected a piece of wise advice which her father gave to her that Christmas: *'Be grateful for the smallest blessings, and you will receive greater ones.'*[510]

Whenever possible, Pilecki visited his children in Ostrów Mazowiecka. He could not, however, afford to take any risk of his travel routine being noticed by communists. Accordingly, rather than alighting from the train at Ostrów itself, he would always leave the train at the last station before Ostrów, and then walked to the home across the fields.

Further reports and materials provided by Pilecki were taken, during January of the new year, to Ancona by a Polish courier called Maria Wolfówna (pronounced *Volfoovna*). These documents concerned, among others, Poland's foreign trade, education, the scouting movement (increasingly getting under the communists' influence) and the MBP.[511]

Once she had set up new courier routes connecting Poland with the West, Captain Mierzejewska, still known as "Danuta", left Poland in April 1947.

In the same month, General Kazimierz Wiśniewski (pronounced *Veeshnevski*) from the Second Corps issued a new instruction to Pilecki. He assigned to Pilecki the tasks of: collecting information about the persecution of former Second Corps soldiers after their return to Poland; setting up further secret transfer routes from Poland to western Europe, and arranging for the publication in Poland of articles in Dr. Dering's defence. At that time, Dr. Dering – whose activities at Auschwitz have already been widely presented in this book – was being falsely accused by the communists of having conducted unethical 'medical experiments' on his fellow inmates at the Auschwitz hospital.

Pilecki had a lot of material evidence to gather. He started his work in April 1947. Many members of the Home Army, and of the Second Corps had in fact been imprisoned in Soviet gulags; many had been killed.[512]

The national election in January 1947 was marked by blatant deception. More than 400,000 voters thought likely to oppose communism had been purged from the electoral rolls well beforehand. Official statistics credited the communist-dominated 'Democratic Bloc' with having obtained over 80 per cent of the popular vote. This was (as afterwards became obvious) nonsense. If the counting had been honestly done, the Democratic Bloc would have obtained no more than 28 per cent of the vote across the country, and the anti-communist Polish Peasant Party (PSL) – led by former Prime Minister Mikołajczyk – would have obtained 63 per cent.[513] Cheated out of electoral victory, Mikołajczyk left Poland just in time to escape arrest. He spent most of his remaining nineteen years in America.

Pilecki's own situation grew ever more precarious. He knew that at any hour of the day or night, he too could be arrested. Still, he refused to leave Poland. As he himself observed: '*I will stay. All of us cannot leave: someone must remain here regardless of consequences.*'[514]

HIS LAST PHOTO BEFORE HIS ARREST IN MAY 1947

(© Pilecki family, all rights reserved)

HIS ARREST AND TRIAL

With the growing resolve of the hard-line Stalinists within Warsaw's government after the fraudulently conducted January election, Pilecki's situation was getting more and more precarious.

Finally, on May 8, 1947, he did get arrested when entering the Sieradzkis' apartment: he was awaited there by security police officers who, on the previous day arrested the Sieradzkis. The officers subjected Pilecki to a thorough search of his person. He continued to give his name as Roman Jezierski, as per the identification documents he had on him.

This subterfuge no longer worked. The policemen already knew his real name. Moreover, they had already carried out a thorough search of Bronisława Jarzyńska's home, at 20/1 Skrzetuskiego Street. There, they found a great deal of evidence pointing to Pilecki's secret activities, just as they had found it in the Sieradzkis' flat.

Pilecki's family knew something had gone wrong when he did not appear that evening at Ostrów Mazowiecka. It was the name-day of Zofia's uncle, and Pilecki had confirmed he intended to come by train. That he should have failed to arrive was very much unlike him. Nor did he arrive four days later, which was the name-day of Zofia's mother. In Zofia's own words:

*'I remember we were waiting for him [...]
to come to my mother's name-day, which
was on May 12. Yet, he did not. Late in
the evening, after the celebrations were
over, I fell asleep. Suddenly I thought I
heard a knock on the window. I yelled out
to my mother that our father did come,
after all. We opened both windows in that
room. It turned out, there was nobody
there. I immediately sensed that something
must have happened to him. [At that time]
He would have already been through
some very brutal interrogations. Soon
thereafter we received, through my mother's
acquaintance, a message from my aunt
Eleonora Ostrowska, in which she advised
us of his arrest.'*[515]

Pilecki was not the only one to be arrested as part of this MBP operation. Two days earlier, on May 6, Tadeusz Płużański had also been captured; on May 7, as already noted, it was the Sieradzkis' turn; on May 9, it was Maria Szelągowska who was seized.[516] Other persons somehow connected, however slightly, with Pilecki's intelligence network ended up in cells during May and June. In the chronological order of their arrests, these persons were: Maksymilian Kaucki, Stanisława Skłodowska-Płużańska, Witold Różycki, Ryszard Jamontt-Krzywicki, Stanisław Furmańczyk, Jerzy Nowakowski, Władysław Kielim, Leon Knyrewicz, Stanisław Jaworski, Stanisław Kuczyński, Maria Kolarczyk, and finally (on June 7) the photography studio owner Wacława Wolańska.[517]

RAKOWIECKA STREET PRISON MUG PHOTOS OF PILECKI (1947)

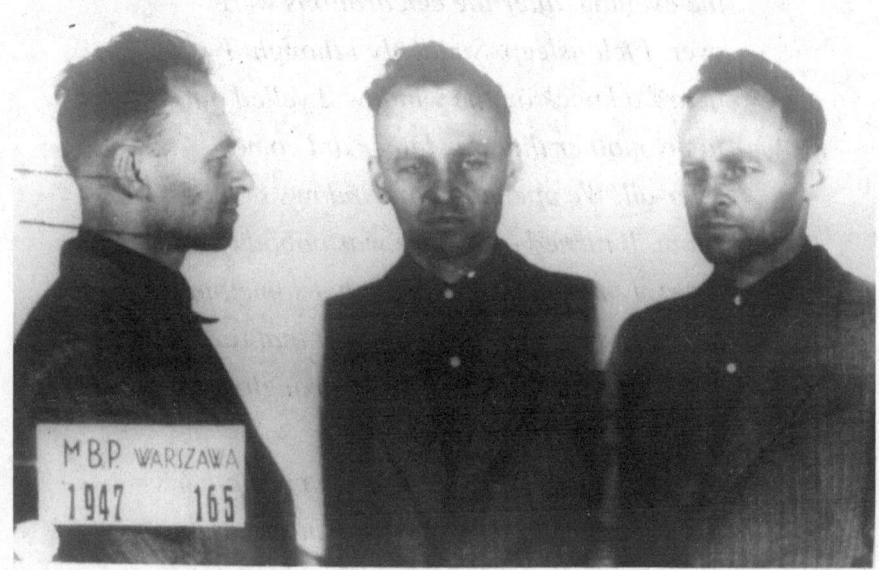

(©The Auschwitz-Birkenau Memorial and Museum, all rights reserved)

They were all detained in the same place: the Mokotów Prison on Rakowiecka Street.

All this indicated, to Pilecki's horror, that the MBP had known a lot about his activities. Sure enough, an MBP informer had infiltrated the group: a recent review of archive acts underscores the significance of Leszek Kuchciński sharing with Płużański a flat in Piastów (a township near Warsaw), where both of them were tenants.

Płużański supplied the following testimony: '*In early July 1946, in the Sieradzkis' flat at 85/9 Pańska Street, I met "Witold".*' He did not give Pilecki's real surname; he did, nevertheless, mention Witold's Auschwitz incarceration as '*Tomasz Serafiński.*' Then he said that on May 6 (the day of his own arrest), he had met Witold at the same flat, and that all his contacts with Witold had been via the Sieradzkis, who had known the latter for several years, and who described him to Płużański as a decent and honest man.[518]

It was probably soon after Płużański and the Sieradzkis had been arrested that the MBP found out about Szelągowska, who, after all, had initially stayed with the Sieradzkis for some time till she found other accommodation.[519] She had been administering, along with Pilecki, a company which served as a cover for their clandestine political doings. This company was a producer of *eau de toilette*. Now the MBP knew the score.

This left Pilecki with no choice but to tell the truth about the nature of the secret works which he had been carrying out alongside Szelągowska. On May 12, he sent her a postcard in which he advised her to be similarly candid. Characteristically, he did not seek to exculpate himself. From the first interrogation onwards, he shouldered the burden of responsibility for the entire network.[520]

During the preliminary interrogations, the arrested victims were harangued, insulted, and subjected to physical tortures, including beatings. Pilecki admitted his TAP activities; admitted volunteering to go to Auschwitz; admitted his setting up of the underground activity there; admitted his Auschwitz reports, his subsequent Kedyw service, his participation in the Warsaw Uprising, his contacts with the Second Corps, and the intelligence-gathering that he had been doing over the previous eighteen months. On one point, though, he was obstinate. Neither he nor his fellow victims considered their activities to be any type of espionage, such as the MBP accused them of having performed. They continued to maintain that, far from being traitors, they had always acted in Poland's interests.

On May 13, the government decided to launch an official investigation into Pilecki's intelligence network activities. It invoked, in doing so, Article Seven of a decree issued on June 13, 1946, which warned against crimes that were 'particularly dangerous' during the period of the country's reconstruction. To quote the article itself: *'Whoever harms the interests of the Polish*

State by collecting or passing on information, documents or other items that are protected as state or military secrets, is liable to terms of imprisonment of not less than five years, life imprisonment, or the death penalty.'

By this point, the MBP had found not only the incriminating documentation but also firearms from Warsaw Uprising days. It now had, in addition, access to Pilecki's Auschwitz reports. Wherever Pilecki had indicated a particular Auschwitz captive by a number, the MBP had found and written down the given name, surname, and (in the case of military personnel) army rank. In other words, the MBP now knew the identity of every individual to whom Pilecki had explicitly referred in his report.

Nevertheless, the reports themselves did not feature as evidence based on which Pilecki would be convicted. Had they been used, they would have helped his cause; and it goes without saying that the communists did not want that. Colonel Józef Różański, the Director of the MBP's Investigations Office (who ran the interrogations), dreaded the thought of Pilecki the 'spy' being known to the world as an Auschwitz hero. The reports, therefore, were suppressed. So, they duly went to the MBP archives, where they gathered dust for four decades.

Różański and his subordinates aimed to prove that Pilecki was indeed a spy; that he had run an espionage network answerable to the Second Polish Corps (which the communists regarded as a foreign entity); and that he with his colleagues had planned to murder several senior MBP functionaries. Pilecki had no difficulty in denying, indeed refuting, the last-named charge. On June 4, he wrote to Różański, a letter containing these poignant words: '... *after what I have gone through at Auschwitz I could not possibly murder anyone.*'[521]

As for the physical conditions in the Mokotów cells, let this paragraph suffice to convey them:

> *'In each cell there is one bed only; during the day-time all mattresses on which inmates sleep at night are stacked up on that bed. Other furnishings in the cell include a lavatory pan with running water, a cabinet and a little table. Apart from its normal purpose, the pan serves also as a source of drinking water, a place where to wash oneself as well as dishes and clothes. Inmates have only one change of clothes and underwear for the entire duration of the investigation which may last over one year. To wash one's clothes in the lavatory pan is quite an accomplishment. [...] Interrogations are conducted in sequences, with minimal breaks between them, for about a fortnight, and then get interrupted for several weeks. The investigation's long duration helps soften up hardened inmates, make them own up and point the finger at others, as well. It has worked... some could not take it, and signed whatever was presented for them to sign.'*[522]

Another quirk in the proceedings concerned the NIE. Pilecki was questioned a good deal about his involvement in setting up the NIE in the first place. Nevertheless, no charges were laid against him in relation to it.

But mere trifles like lack of charges on specific issues did not alter the inexorable machine of communist 'justice.' The Military District Court had passed its own verdicts even before the official investigation against Pilecki and his seven co-defendants had finished. On October 30, 1947, Stanisław Jaworski, Władysław Kielim, Leon Knyrewicz and Stanisław Kuczyński were all condemned to death. Clearly, the prosecution was determined to make a special example of Knyrewicz, who had been a bodyguard to President Bierut. He was executed on December 10. The three other men had their sentences changed to life in gaol.

Already in the autumn of 1947, some captives involved with Pilecki had been sentenced. Stanisław Furmańczyk was given six years; Maria Kolarczyk, six years; Helena Sieradzka, seven years; Stanisława Skłodowska-Płużańska, eight years; and Wacława Wolańska, six years.

The chief defendant had a harsher fate in store. These were the charges officially laid against Pilecki:

> ' ... having, since July 1945, as a foreign intelligence operative reporting to the Command of General Anders' Second Corps, conducted an activity harmful to the interests of the Polish State, consisting in setting up an intelligence network and including into it, as informers, Tadeusz Szturm de Sztrem, Makary Sieradzki, Witold Różycki, Stanisława Skłodowska, [Father] Czajkowski and others; retaining an ongoing organisational contact with the above-mentioned persons, directing their activities by issuing instructions and orders,

and storing in three safe flats in Warsaw, flat 6, 85 Pańska Street, flat 1, 20 Skrzetuski Street, and flat 8, 16 Woronicz Street, information and documents which constitute state, or military, secrets, [...]they concern information about the organisation and activities of the Department of Public Security and the Citizens' Militia [Polish: Milicja Obywatelska] and about holders of high positions within these organisations; further, information and documents which describe the balance of political powers within the State, the development of the democratic bloc, the workers' parties and youth organisations and the strength of their influences; the country's economic structures and achievements of its economy, the development of foreign trade and the contents of the trade agreements concluded with allied countries of USSR, Bulgaria, Sweden, and others. Once prepared, summarised and photo-copied, the above-mentioned materials were then passed on to the command of General Anders' Second Corps [...] In three places in Warsaw, he illegally stored firearms, munition, and explosives, namely: at 50 Śliska Street – two machine guns, 26 grenades and 260 pieces of munition of various types, at flat 6,

*85 Pańska Street – four automatic pistols
(Mas and Sten), one Parabellum pistol,
26 magazines for this pistol and 890 pieces
of munition of various types, at flat 1,
20 Skrzetuski Street – one Vis pistol, three
magazines, 203 pieces of munition for this
pistol, and explosives.'*[523]

Dated December 11, this indictment was formally ratified on January 23, 1948 by Major Adam Humer, the Head of Section II of the Investigations Office. It then went for approval (which it was given on February 5) by the Deputy Military Attorney, Major Mieczysław Dytra, and (two days later) by Dytra's superior, Military Attorney Lieutenant-Colonel Henryk Podlaski. It will be noted that Pilecki's network is referred to explicitly as an espionage group.

By the time the trial of Pilecki and his co-defendants began on March 3, 1948, two of Pilecki's allies had already been put to death. They were Wacław Alchimowicz and Tadeusz Bejt, both slain on February 11.[524] Their executions received no publicity. In contrast, the Pilecki group's trial was given a good deal of media coverage, both within Poland and to a certain extent elsewhere. The country's tame communist organs repeatedly referred to Pilecki and the other accused as 'traitors,' 'spies', and 'agents of imperialism.' Of course, there was not a syllable in such reports to indicate Pilecki had survived Auschwitz.

From the very day on which Pilecki was arrested, the already grievous situation of his wife and children became even worse. The children got bullied and stigmatised at school. A fellow student asked Zofia, if Witold Pilecki was her father, and then, on being told that he was, asked what Zofia thought about her father's '*collaboration with the enemy*'. Zofia responded calmly: *'Would you think badly about your father? Ask your parents, and they will tell you more about my father.'*[525]

The way in which the trial was run had a great deal in common with the show trials that were taking place in other pro-Soviet countries after 1945. Here is how Andrzej Werblan, a cadre communist, and a former chief ideologist of the Polish United Workers' Party, described these trials with a hindsight of forty years:

> *'Whatever form that terror took, as a rule it relied on very severe repression and a liberal use of the death penalty. Those trials dispensed with appropriate judicial processes, such as should be followed to establish the material truth, and often became merely a travesty of justice. The purpose of all this terror and repression was not so much the punishment of crime, as the persecution, intimidation, and extermination of all real, potential, or imagined adversaries. Hence the mass scale of such repressions and their, in truth, extra-judicial character. Many of their victims were innocent, some were even accidental.'*[526]

With the ever-intensifying Cold War between the Soviet and the Western blocs, the Polish regime increased its crackdowns against all underground military organisations and, in particular, against former Home Army soldiers. As the regime's bosses knew all too well, they could not rely on many more Poles to support communism by sincere choice. The 1947 election had demonstrated that. All Polish non-communists who could not be won over by bribes would have to be controlled by fear. So, wholesale arrests of genuine or suspected dissidents commenced. Death penalties in political trials became a matter of routine.

Alongside official terror, there came general impoverishment. Most of the privately-owned land in Poland was taken over by the state, without compensation. Scarcely surprising, then, that Polish society, as a whole, grew more and more apathetic, even if some Poles harboured obscure hopes of being able to live to see better days.

The timing of Pilecki's trial could not have been less auspicious for him. Him having set his face firmly against lies, injustice, lawlessness and crimes committed by the Soviets (as by the Nazis), made Pilecki an intrinsic enemy in the communists' eyes.

The judges involved with his case had received clear instructions from the MBP as to what verdicts they were expected to reach. Perhaps they had no fundamental objection to such instructions. High-sounding talk of judicial independence was understandably less appealing to them than securing their own careers in a country run more and more on Stalinist lines.[527]

*

On March 3, 1948, the trial of the Pilecki group commenced. As well as Pilecki himself, the defendants were Maria Szelągowska, Tadeusz Płużański, Makary Sieradzki, Ryszard Jamontt-Krzywicki, Maksymilian Kaucki, Jerzy Nowakowski and Witold Różycki. Most, though not all of the court proceedings were open to the public.[528]

When the hearings went into temporary recess, the families and friends of the accused were given permission to see their loved ones briefly. Not surprisingly, all such seeings were supervised by prison warders. Members of Pilecki's own family offered to plead with the regime on his behalf. These offers he rejected. For Eleonora Ostrowska, particularly upsetting was Pilecki's fatalistic comment during one such visit: *'I feel very tired indeed, and I want a quick end.'*[529]

THE BENCH OF THE ACCUSED IN THE PILECKI TRIAL (MARCH 1948)

(©The Auschwitz-Birkenau Memorial and Museum, all right reserved)

The judges assigned to this trial were: Lieutenant-Colonel Jan Hryckowian (Presiding Judge), Captain Józef Badecki (Military Judge), Captain Stefan Nowacki (Associate Judge) and Lieutenant Ryszard Czarkowski (Clerk of the Court). Major Czesław Łapiński was Chief Prosecutor. On the trial's last day, Łapiński demanded the death penalty for four of the accused: Pilecki, Szelągowska, Płużański and Sieradzki. He described them as criminals deserving to be condemned in the strongest terms, and despised by society.[530]

Pilecki delivered his testimony to the court on two consecutive days, March 3 and 4. He pleaded not guilty to the first charge, that of collecting intelligence for a foreign power. In the strongest terms he could think of, he denied any involvement in plans for violent action against MBP functionaries. He likewise rejected the third charge which had been levelled at him: that of having received from Colonel Kijak and Captain Mierzejewska $1,030 in American currency for services rendered to the Second Corps. Even though he did plead guilty to the charge of possessing undeclared weapons – he could hardly have denied that – he stressed that those weapons had been hidden by him immediately after the 1944 uprising, and before he was taken to the German POW camps. Neither he nor anyone else had used the weapons after the war. He admitted he had failed to register as an officer when returning to Poland in late 1945, and he also admitted to using forged documents in the name of Roman Jezierski.[531]

WITOLD PILECKI IN THE COURTROOM

(©The Auschwitz-Birkenau Memorial and Museum, all right reserved)

In some detail, Pilecki revealed to the court his activities between the liberation of the Murnau camp and his departure from Italy. He explained, he was asked to collect intelligence in Poland and forward it through couriers to the Second Corps, simply because he had contacts in Poland from the period when he was a NIE member. When involved with the Second Corps, he said he did not undergo any intelligence training. Instead, he relied on the skills and bitter experience that he had acquired in Auschwitz. He considered the Second Corps to have been an entirely legitimate Polish army unit in Italy, which had a very natural concern with what was occurring in Poland itself. In addition, he confessed to having signed all his interrogation protocols without reading them, because he was too tired to do otherwise.[532] His captors had accused him of wanting a Polish-Ukrainian alliance; this too he denied.

Some of his testimony was more personal than the above. He admitted to the court that his commitment to information-gathering and information-transmitting had begun to weaken, since he was harbouring doubts as to whether the Second Corps really needed the data that he provided. Also, he said that he had no evidence of the Second Corps having shared his intelligence with any foreign service. He denied the accusation of having been appointed an intelligence officer for Polish territory, and emphasised that in his intelligence-gathering he had not had any supervisor, nor was there any plan to make him a permanent residential head of intelligence anywhere.

Pilecki attributed his actions to the fact that throughout the time under discussion, he considered himself to have been in military service, just as much as if he were on a recognisable battlefield. It was not, he argued, a sensible option for him to report at an Office of Security on his arrival from Italy. Still less would it have been a sensible option for him to admit that General Anders had sent him.[533]

The trial ended on March 11. Four days later, the judges announced their verdicts. Nowakowski was condemned to five years' imprisonment; Jamont-Krzywicki, to ten years' imprisonment; Różycki and Kaucki, to fifteen years' imprisonment each; Sieradzki, to imprisonment for life. For Pilecki, Szelągowska and Płużański, the penalty was death, combined with the removal in perpetuity of their rights as citizens, and confiscation of whatever personal property they still had.[534]

Seeking to justify the death penalty verdicts, the court provided the following explanation. It constitutes a notable example of the convoluted Stalinist language so apt to be used with show trials in this era, and thus warrants quoting it at length:

> *'... apart from them committing the heaviest*
> *felony of betraying the state and the Nation,*
> *the Court took also into consideration*
> *that: in their felonious activities they have*
> *demonstrated extremely bad intentions,*
> *their hatred of the People's Republic of*
> *Poland and of the social reforms it has*
> *introduced, have sold themselves to a*
> *foreign intelligence service which receives*
> *direction from foreign imperialism [sic!]*
> *that seeks to inflict a significant harm upon*
> *the interests of the Democractic Polish*
> *State, and so have caused a tremendous*
> *harm to the State during the period of*
> *hardship accompanying its reconstruction.*
> *In discharging their duties as spies, they*
> *demonstrated a great deal of dedication*
> *by following the instructions they have*
> *been receiving from foreign commanding*

> *centres. Taking this into account, the Court came to the conclusion that [...] the laudable [a word partly blackened in the original] past of accused Pilecki [...] cannot lessen the enormity of his felonies which inflicted harm on the most vital interests of the State. For these reasons, it is only the severest punishment that can be a fitting retribution for the crimes he is charged with.'*[535]

At the last prison seeing, Pilecki uttered to his wife words which did not sound as if they could have come from his mouth: *'They killed me.'* One must wonder what could have possibly made him, a survivor of the Auschwitz hell and of the Warsaw Uprising, a person of such deep faith, so down-hearted?

Well, Witold Pilecki's main life's purpose was to serve and help all people around him. As long as he could make any positive difference to the lives of some of them, he seemed to be able to take any adversity in stride. Once he realized his service to those in need was almost certainly over this must have put an unbearable weight on him, and made him sound so dejected.

He must have realised that the communist rule would make it very difficult for him, even if his plea for clemency was granted, to be of any further service to those around him. That is probably also why he told his wife at the same meeting that the investigation and the trial were for him a far worse experience than that of KL Auschwitz. That Auschwitz was just a mere trifle compared to his Rakowiecka Street interrogations. At Auschwitz not only did he retain to the end his capacity to help those around him, but also did provide his help in abundance. That had also sustained his optimism there.

The ancient Greek myth about Antaeus and Hercules may serve here as a suitable simile. Antaeus, the son of two powerful deities: Poseidon, God of the Sea and Gaia, Greek Mother Goddess, the creator and giver of birth to the Earth and to all the Universe, would challenge all passers-by to wrestling matches, defeat them all, and kill thereafter. He was very strong and indefatigable, for as long as he remained in contact with the ground (ie. his Mother Gaia).

One day, Antaeus challenged Heracles, also famous for his super strength. Heracles very soon found out he could not beat Antaeus by throwing him to the ground, since that allowed him to immediately reheal. So, he changed his tactics: holding Antaeus aloft for a while, he crushed his opponent in a bearhug.[536]

Witold Pilecki had presented a very serious challenge to the enemies of his people for as long as he could maintain close contact with those around him, and retained his capacity to help them according to their needs. They were the ground he drew his tremendous strength from. Once his enemies could deny him this capacity, his tremendous tenacity was gone.

*

Destroying Pilecki was not enough for the Soviets and the Polish communist government: they unashamedly used his trial as a part of their campaign, the aim of which was to besmirch the reputation of the Polish Army's Second Corps, whose heroism at taking the Monte Cassino stronghold from Germans in May 1944 had already become a world-wide legend.

In September 1946, the Polish cabinet had stripped General Anders of his Polish citizenship. This was a calculated blow at a time when most Poles still identified General Anders with the cause of national independence, and when many of them still expected that the General would soon 'enter Poland on his white horse' to free the country – with some Western help – from Soviet despotism.

Once the news of verdicts of the Pilecki trial reached London (where Anders himself was based), energetic efforts were immediately undertaken to have all its death sentences commuted. These efforts involved – among other officials – General Anders; Edward Raczyński, Polish Government-in-exile former ambassador to London; and Józef Lipski, former Polish ambassador to Berlin. The efforts proved unavailing: most Western mass media ignored this subject.[537]

There were also some people in Poland, who struggled on Pilecki's behalf for mercy. One such person was Ludmiła Serafińska, at that time still living with her husband in the apartment owned by the mother of the then Prime Minister Cyrankiewicz. Hoping that this personal link to so powerful a politician would help, Ludmila Serafińska went to Cyrankiewicz and begged him to save Pilecki's life. Although the Prime Minister received her with unfailing politeness, he refused to grant her request. He explained to her that the matter was not in his hands, but in the hands of President Bierut alone.[538] Yet another woman who attempted to save Pilecki's life was one whom Pilecki had given much needed help during the days of the Nazi occupation: Barbara Abramow-Newerly.[539]

On March 23, Pilecki's defence lawyer, Lech Buszkowski – yes, there had been a defence lawyer in that travesty of a trial – submitted an appeal to the High Military Court in Warsaw, arguing against the capital sentence, and urging that it be commuted to a gaol term. He wrote, among other things: *'From the beginning of his involvement in the conspiracy against the [German] occupant, the accused took an important part in it. He took upon himself duties exceeding those of an average underground soldier. He went to Auschwitz to organise underground work there.*'540

This appeal for clemency was denied. On May 3, the High Military Court (specifically, Colonel Kazimierz Drohomirecki [Presiding Judge], Lieutenant-Colonel Roman Kryże, [Reporting Judge], Major Leo Hochberg [Judge], and Lieutenant Jerzy Kwiatkowski [Clerk of the Court], along with Major Rubin Szwajg [Deputy Attorney]) decided to turn down Buszkowski's appeal.[541] Undeterred, Buszkowski wrote – the following day – a letter, pleading for clemency, to President Bierut.

Pilecki himself sent a similar letter to the President on May 7, pointing out that once arrested he had revealed without any hesitation where his archive was located, and that throughout the investigation he had uttered nothing except the truth. Maria Pilecki wrote to Bierut her own desperate letter, citing the many years which her husband had spent fighting for Poland's freedom; his dedication in going to Auschwitz to save lives; and the fact that his children had hardly seen him for nine long years of struggle.[542]

Meanwhile, attempts had been made to prevent Płużański and Szelągowska from being executed. In an announcement on May 20,[543] President Bierut commuted both Płużański's and Szelągowska's sentences to life imprisonment.[544] Yet when it came to Pilecki, the regime was implacable. For him there could be no hope of presidential mercy. In a way, his wish – voiced to the investigators and to the court – that he would be assigned all the blame for his actions had been granted.

And thus, it was that Pilecki became one of the victims (approximately 2,450) of judicial murders which the communists committed in Poland between 1944 and 1956. About 15,000 Poles during that period were killed in various ways without any trial. Another 150,000 or so were gaoled. Approximately 100,000 former Home Army members – most of them from the Vilnius area, Eastern Galicia, Volyn, Podlachia, Pomoria, Upper Silesia and Greater Poland – were consigned by the Soviets to Siberia's gulags.

Only in 1956 did the Soviets begin releasing Polish survivors of those camps. At that time, Stalin had been three years in the grave.[545] In total, at least a quarter of a million Poles suffered the immediate impact of the communist terror between 1944 and 1956. The number of family members and friends who suffered in a less direct fashion through such terror is too large to count.

*

When Pilecki was arrested, his daughter was just fifteen years old, completing her first year at the local secondary college [*Gymnasium*]. Initially, people around Zofia were simply unaware she was the daughter of a man described in the papers as a traitor. One day, however, a teacher suspected the connection. He asked Zofia: 'That Pilecki, is he perchance your father?' Her resolute response was: 'Yes, he is, and I am very proud of him.'[546]

At the final harrowing meeting between Maria and her husband, he told her not to forget to read daily a randomly selected passage from Thomas à Kempis's *The Imitation of Christ*. This was his last wish for her.

At the same meeting, Maria heard her spouse utter words so unlike of him: '*I cannot live any longer. They have killed me. Auschwitz, compared with them, was just a trifle.*' It would be hard to think of any words which could more effectively convey the skill that Poland's communist bosses demonstrated in breaking the spirit of a man who, in the past, had so often shown superhuman courage.

There is still one thing which needs to be mentioned here. On the day of Pilecki's last meeting with his wife, notwithstanding the seemingly endless investigations, the subsequent tortures inflicted on him, the contempt which the communists had shown towards him throughout, the invectives hurled at him in the courtroom, the hideous privations of prison-cell life; notwithstanding all these things, he actually – and almost unbelievably – looked very much *healthier* on that day than he did when making a brief appearance as a witness at Fr Czajkowski's trial, or than he would look a couple of days later on, when he was led out on his last walk, a walk so redolent of Calvary.

After Maria's last visit, the surviving evidence suggests, the prison's communist thugs thrashed Pilecki with particular savagery. Maybe this was because of his refusal to tell them what he knew about Fr Czajkowski's underground role. He had assured the court that he was unacquainted with the priest in the dock. Perhaps this was the very last time he was able to help a fellow human being. His captors, for whom the very concept of altruism meant nothing, took after that their vengeance on him.

From Fr Czajkowski's own eyewitness account – and it should be remembered that the priest was being incarcerated in the same gaol as Pilecki – we know what physical state Pilecki was in during his final moments on earth. When being led out to his execution, he was unable to raise his head. His collar-bones had been broken; his arms dangled inertly by his sides[547] and his fingernails had been ripped out.[548]

*

Witold Pilecki is a martyr. He is a martyr for the truth he loved more than anything: the truth about God, Poland, and about his fellow man. Yet, it was not his execution at the Mokotów Prison that made him a martyr. He became one much earlier when he faithfully walked the path of heroic self-denial in the service of all people around him. It is to the people like him that the words '*Beata quae sine morte meruit martyrii palmam*' [Blessed is he, who merited martyr's palm without dying][549] apply to.

For all the sacrifice of his life, Captain Pilecki did not wish to be a martyr. All he did, he did because he wished to remain true to his calling of a servant to all those in need, regardless of the circumstances of his life. Being able to serve them, being able to meet their needs, in particular – their need for them to live as free people, and their need for their human dignity to be respected – meant far more to him than all wealth, fame, positions, and power he could probably have, had he only followed an alternative path in his life.

*

A human soul can be likened to a vessel that can hold a mixture of love, hatred, and indifference in any proportions. It is only when it holds love alone, without any hatred or indifference in it, that it can achieve things that appear to be beyond human capacity. Witold Pilecki's soul was such.

He loved God, he loved people around him, and yes – he also loved himself as a God's creation, for without loving himself he would not have been able to love others with the strength that he did. He was grateful to God for all His gifts, for they were making it possible to serve people to his heart's content. As for wealth, power, or significance in this world, he thought very little of them.

As a proper tribute to the extraordinary strength and abundance of the love Captain Pilecki had for others, let us invoke an excerpt from the famous St. Paul's eulogy of love our hero would have read many a time:

> *'Love is patient and kind; love does not*
> *envy or boast; it is not arrogant, or rude.*
> *It does not insist on its own way; it is not*
> *irritable or resentful; it does not rejoice at*
> *wrongdoing, but rejoices with the truth.*
> *Love bears all things, believes all things,*
> *hopes all things, endures all things.*
> *Love never ends (..).'*[550]

EPILOGUE

A loyal and loving wife of her martyred husband, Maria Pilecka endured in her life much suffering and hardship. Communists forbade to employ her as a teacher. She held whatever odd jobs she could, and for how long as she could, including casual positions at youth camps and holiday centres, just to keep her family alive and fed.

Zofia, not long after her father's execution, left Ostrów Mazowiecka and went to be closer to her mother in Warsaw. At one point in time, Maria found work at a training centre in Miedzeszyn, near Warsaw. This gave her the privilege, if privilege it was, of living in a very plain, small, weatherboard holiday house: a house stiflingly hot in summer, and so cold in winter that Zofia had to wear an overcoat and gloves as she prepared for her 1951 final-year school exams.[551]

Andrzej Pilecki had harboured, ever since he was a small boy, a dream of becoming a pilot. But the communists would not allow him to become one. Nor did they permit Zofia to complete her planned study at Warsaw's Technical University: she was compelled to abandon her course. Her uncle, Witold's brother Jerzy, lived in such terror of the regime that he went into hiding and stayed there for years. Only in 1950 was he finally able to finish his medical studies. The mere fact of belonging to Pilecki's family was, in the Polish communist leaders' view, an odious crime.

Seeking to comfort herself during the bleak years of the 1950s and 1960s, Zofia would often recall her father's words to her from her girlhood. He had observed: '[When nothing more is left from your inheritance] *fresh air will still be yours*.'[552] Very little indeed was left of her inheritance by this stage.

The Pilecki family home at Sukurcze, like so many good things, failed in its original form to survive communist terror. Warfare had left it unscathed, but in 1956 the authorities decided to demolish it. All the beautiful old trees around the house – the lime-trees and pines that Pilecki himself had mentioned in his poem named after the estate – were felled. The entire estate became government property.

In 1992, after the Berlin Wall had collapsed, Andrzej Pilecki was finally able to visit Sukurcze. It was a peculiar experience for him. He compared the estate's landscape to '*a steppe*.'[553] Luckily for him, there still remained a few old people in the area who happily share their direct memories of Witold Pilecki and his family. Theirs were all grateful, and happy, memories.

Very fortuitously, Pilecki's two paintings (one of St Anthony and the Child Jesus, the other - of Our Lady of Perpetual Succour) survived undamaged both WWII and the subsequent forty-five years of the Soviet rule. To this day, both paintings hang on the walls of the parish church in Krupa, or, as it is now called, Krupowo. Painted in 1930, they bear Pilecki's autograph.

On May 7, 2008, the Senate of the Republic of Poland recommended that Witold Pilecki be duly recognised in Poland as a most worthy example of a Polish patriot, someone whose dedication to his homeland knew no limits.[554]

Disappointingly, when the European Parliament voted in 2009 on a draft resolution concerning 'European Awareness and Totalitarism', majority of that parliament's members rejected two proposed alterations to that draft. The alterations sought, first, that

Pilecki be identified by name in the resolution; and second, that May 25 – the very day on which he was executed – be formally proclaimed an International Day of the Heroes of the Struggle Against Totalitarianism.

Sadly, among those who rejected the proposed alterations were also several deputies from Poland.[555]

*

Pilecki's daughter Zofia (her married name: Optułowicz) and his son Andrzej are still with us. They both have inherited their father's staunch optimism. For nearly three decades now, they have been very actively involved in telling the story about their father's heroic life and death to younger generations of Poles, many of whom were not even born when the Polish People's Republic collapsed in 1989. Zofia enthusiastically asserts today: 'The inter-generational relay does indeed continue.'[556]

*

Witold Pilecki would have rejoiced at his daughter's enthusiasm. And, he could possibly have recommended for Poles to follow today the advice given to them by a great Polish poet, Adam Asnyk (1838-1897):

HAVE HOPE!
BY ADAM ASNYK
(translated by: Adam J. Koch)

Have hope! Not one that is weak and shoddy,
One that a rotten core adorns with a sickly flower,
But a steadfast one, a seed of future sacrifice
Which rests in a hero's soul.

Have courage! Not for one day,
Not one which dies out in an act of despair,
But one that keeps its head high
And would not be driven away from its post.

Have courage... not the folly
That tears along mindlessly without a weapon,
But one that conquers adversities with constancy,
Its impregnable rampart.

We need to cease relishing our sorrows,
We must desist from our wails:
For lamentations are a female thing,
What befits a man - is to arm himself in silence.

We must continue to revere our sanctities
And preserve the purity of our ideals;
It is for us to vest in those dreams that might
and armor
That they need to become a reality.

In May 2014, a small crowd gathered in Warsaw's neighbourhood of Żoliborz at the very spot from which Witold Pilecki was taken from the street round-up on the morning of 19 September 1940.

Speaking for the Catholic Church of Poland, Father Józef Maj announced it was already abundantly clear to the Church that Witold Pilecki's good works greatly exceeded those of ordinary good people: his virtues had been deemed heroic.[557]

INDEX OF PERSONS

PLEASE NOTE:

This Index of Persons does not include names of persons which appear exclusively in the chapter 'Pilecki's Report W from Auschwitz', which is a translation of the document prepared originally in Polish by Witold Pilecki. That report has its own index of those Auschwitz inmates who were members of ZOW, the secret organisation Witold Pilecki set up in the camp.

Throughout this book, original Polish names, surnames, and some other proper names are offered. Whenever they are expected to present pronunciation challenges to English readers, guidance is offered.

Some persons in this index, most notably those foreign princes and kings who became kings of Poland by the way of election (the only exception to this rule was Louis I the Great), may have alternative versions of their names (one non-Polish, and one Polish) offered in this book.

All Polish, and foreign, monarchs who had been elected, and/or were not part of any ruling dynasty, Polish, or foreign, are entered into this Index according to the alphabetical order of monarchs' names; all other Polish, and foreign, monarchs have been entered, first, according to the name of the dynasty they belonged to, and then according to the alphabetical order of their respective names.

Words in inverted commas are noms de-guerre, or conspiracy aliases, by which the persons were widely known.

For all military officers, only their highest rank of relevance to this book is provided in this Index.

Positions held by persons included into this Index are provided only, when they directly relate to the reason that their name appears in this book for.

A

Abramow-Newerly, Barbara: 371
à Kempis, Thomas: 199
Alchimowicz, Wacław "Andrzej", Captain: 350, 362
Anders, Władysław, General: 339, 341, 343, 348, 371
Anjou, Capetian House of, Jadwiga, Queen of Poland: 45, 49
Anjou, Capetian House of, Louis [Ludwik] I the Great, King of Hungary and
    King of Poland: 48, 49, 69
Árpád, House of, Andrew II the Jerosolimitan, King of Hungary: 52
Asnyk, Adam: 379

B

Badecki, Józef, Captain: 365
Balke, Artur, Auschwitz Oberkapo:: 197
Bandurski, Władysław, Bishop of Vilnius: 125
Barański, Stanisław: 227
Bartosiewicz, Henryk, Second Lieutenant (Res.): 204, 207, 224
Bartoszewski, Władysław: 189
Bejt, Tadeusz: 362
Bem Józef, General: 84
Bielecki, Stefan: 171, 183, 203, 218, 345
Bierut, Bolesław, President of the People's Republic of Poland: 184, 372

Biessgen, Fritz, Auschwitz Oberkapo: 197
Biliński, Tadeusz, First Lieutenant: 212
Bock, Hans, Auschwitz Oberkapo: 196
Bohdanowski, Zygmunt ("Bohdan", "Bończa"), Major: 170, 231, 320
Bornholz, (..), Captain: 339
Bourbon, House of, Louis XIV, King of France: 71
Bourbon, House of, Louis XVI, King of France: 83
Bourbon, House of, Louis XV, King of France: 78
Bratro, Zofia: 224
Brejnak, Zygmunt, Major: 329
Bryjak, Leon (one of Witold Pilecki's aliases): 238
Brym, Zbigniew "Zdunin", First Lieutenant: 332
Brystygierowa, Julia: 350
Burski, Tadeusz: 194
Buszkowski, Lech: 371, 372

C

Caesar, Julius, Dictator of Roman Empire: 75
Catherine the Great, Tsaritsa of Russia: 30, 78, 79
Cenzartowicz, Leszek: 227
Chamberlain, Neville, British Prime Minister: 165
Chodkiewicz, Jan Karol, Grand Hetman of Lithuania: 68
Chróścicki, Tadeusz, Captain: 218
Chruściel, Antoni, Colonel: 326
Ciesielski, Edward: 223, 231, 232, 332
Cypryszewski, Stanisław, Major: 23
Cyra, Adam: 240
Cyrankiewicz, Józef, People's Republic of Poland's Prime Minister: 344, 371
Czajkowski, Father Antoni: 349, 350, 374
Czaplicki, Józef, Colonel: 350
Czarkowski, Ryszard, First Lieutenant: 365
Czernicki, Czesław: 322, 345

D

Dacz, Kazimiera: 124, 125, 126, 140
Daladier, Edouard, French Prime Minister: 159
Dal Trozzo-Pieńkowska, Janina: 173
Dangel, Jan: 171, 172
Dangel, Stanisław: 171
Daszyński, Ignacy, Poland's Prime Minister: 107
Dąmbrowski, Jerzy "Łupaszka", Lieutenant Colonel: 105, 106, 112, 117

Dering, Władysław, M.D.: 171, 177, 179, 190, 209, 220, 221, 228, 230, 352
de Virion, Jerzy, Captain (Res.): 170, 176, 191, 206
Diem, Rudolf, M.D.: 209, 232
Dmitry I, Tsar of Russia: 67
Dobrawa, Czech Princess: 40
Dobrzański, Henryk "Hubal", Major: 176
Dowbór-Muśnicki, Józef, General: 104, 106
Drohomirecki, Kazimierz, Colonel: 372
Dubois, Stanisław, Polish M.P.: 209
Dunin Karwicki, Stanisław: 73
Dytra, Mieczysław, Major: 362
Dziama, Teofil, Lieutenant Colonel: 320
Dziedzic, Tadeusz, Captain: 212

F

Faury, Louis, French General: 160
Fejkiel, Władysław, M.D.: 232
Feodor, Tsar of Russia: 61, 62
Fieldorf, August Emil "Nil", General: 321, 339
Franz II, Emperor of Austria: 30
Friedrich II, Holy Roman Emperor: 52
Friedrich Wilhelm, Elector of Brandenburg and Duke of Prussia: 73
Friedrich Wilhelm II, King of Prussia: 30
Furmańczyk, Stanisław: 355, 360

G

Gamelin, Maurice, French General: 159
Garliński, Jarek: 241
Gawron, Wincenty: 203, 204, 218
Gawryłkiewicz, Mieczysław, Major: 154
Gilewicz, Juliusz, Lieutenant Colonel: 220, 232, 320
Gliński, Antoni Józef: 99
Gött-Getyński, Edward, Major: 220, 225, 226
Gutkiewicz, Stanisław, Second Lieutenant (Res.): 203
Guz Stefan ("Dan"): 350

H

Habsburg, House of, Albrecht I, King of Germany: 53
Habsburg, House of, Anna, Archduchess of Austria: 63
Habsburg, House of, Constance, Archduchess of Austria: 63
Habsburg, House of, Leopold I, Emperor of Austria: 74

Habsburg, House of, Maximilian II, Emperor of Austria: 60
Habsburg, House of, Maximilian III, Archduke of Austria: 63
Habsburg, House of, Rudolf II, Emperor of Austria: 63
Hácha, Emil, President of Czechoslovakia:: 152
Haemerkken, Thomas (or similar). *See* à Kempis, Thomas
Haller, Józef, General: 87
Hitler, Adolf, Chancellor of the German Third Reich: 22, 149, 151, 152, 153, 154, 157, 159, 160, 161, 164, 165, 168, 169
Hochberg, Leo, Major: 372
Hoffman, Helena: 224
Hohenstaufen, House of, Heinrich [Henry] VI, Holy Roman Emperor: 52
Hohenzollern, House of, Albrecht, the last Grandmaster of the Teutonic Knights Order, and the first Duke of Ducal Prussia: 54, 73
Hohenzollern, House of, Georg Friedrich, Duke of Ducal Prussia: 60
Hössler, Franz: 232
Hrebenda, Jan, M.D.: 206
Hryckowian, Jan, Lieutenant Colonel: 365
Humer, Adam, Major: 362

I

Iranek-Osmecki, Kazimierz, Colonel: 339
Isserles, Moises ben Israel: 44

J

Jabłoński, Karol "Zygmunt", Major: 319
Jagiellon, House of, Anna, Queen of Poland: 59
Jagiellon, House of, Władysław III Warneńczyk, King of Poland and King of Hungary: 69
Jagiellon, House of, Władysław Jagiełło, King of Poland: 45, 49, 51, 53
Jagiellon, House of, Zygmunt I the Old, King of Poland: 55
Jakubowski, Tadeusz: 212
Jamontt-Krzywicki, Ryszard: 355, 364, 368
Jan III Sobieski, King of Poland: xi, 74, 75, 76
Januszewski, Mieczysław: 222, 229, 230
Jaroszek, Jan, Captain: 331
Jarzyńska, Bronisława: 347, 354
Jasieński, Stefan "Urban", Second Lieutenant: 322
Jaworski, Stanisław: 355, 360
Jezierski, Kazimierz, First Lieutenant, M.D.: 23
Jezierski, Roman (one of Witold Pilecki's aliases): 343

K

Kafarowski, Wacław: 227
Karcz, Jan, Colonel: 208, 213, 225
Kaucki, Maksymilian: 355, 364, 368
Kazuba, Stanisław, Captain: 204, 220, 320
Khmelnytsky, Bohdan Zinoviy Mykhailovych, Hetman in the Polish-Lithuanian Commonwealth: 44, 45
Kielim, Władysław: 355, 360
Kijak, Stanisław, Lieutenant Colonel: 340
Kiliański, Jan: 185
King András II. *See* Árpád, House of, Andrew II the Jerosolimitan, King of Hungary
King Louis. *See* Anjou, Capetian House of, Louis [Ludwik] I the Great, King of Hungary and King of Poland
Kleeberg, Franciszek, General: 164
Klimaszewska, Wiktoria: 224
Knyrewicz, Leon: 355, 360
Kober, Marcin: 37
Kobyliński, Mikołaj, Second Lieutenant: 332
Koch, Adam Jan: ix
Kocjan, Antoni: 189
Kolarczyk, Maria: 355, 360
Koliński, Włodzimierz, Captain: 209
Komorowski, Tadeusz "Bór", General: 322, 326, 339
Komski, Jan: 229, 230
Konarski, Stanisław: 73
Kossak, Wolciech: 38
Kossuth, Lajos: 84
Kosztowny, Witold: 210
Kościuszko, Andrzej Tadeusz Bonawentura, Major-General: 80
Kozłowski, Mikołaj, Major: 343
Kryże, Roman, Lieutenant Colonel: 372
Krzyżanowski, Jerzy: 320
Kuchciński, Leszek: 350, 356
Kuczbara, Bolesław: 229, 230, 231
Kuczyński, Stanisław: 355, 360
Kumuniecki, Karol, Lieutenant Colonel: 209, 220, 225, 226
Kupiec, Bolesław, Platoon Leader: 200
Kupiec, Jan: 200
Kupiec, Władysław, Platoon Leader: 200
Kurcjusz, Tadeusz, Lieutenant Colonel: 179
Küsel, Otto, Auschwitz Oberkapo: 196, 229, 230

Kuzak, Father Zygmunt: 221
Kwaciszewski, Józef, General: 161
Kwiatkowski, Jerzy, First Lieutenant: 372

L

Lechenich, Jonny, Auschwitz Oberkapo: 196
Lech, Tadeusz, Second Lieutenant (Res.): 204
Legowicz, Father (..): 234
Lenin, Vladimir Ilyich (surname at birth: Ulyanov), the first dictator of the Soviet Union: 33
Leszczyński, Stanisław, King of Poland: 77, 78
Lipski Józef, Poland's Ambassador to Berlin: 371
Luxembourg, House of, Sigismund, Prince-elector of Brandenburg, King of Hungary and Croatia, King of Bohemia, King of Germany, King of Italy, Holy Roman Emperor: 53

Ł

Łapiński, Czesław, Major: 365

M

MacIntyre, Alasdair: xii
Maj, Father Józef: 380
Makaliński, Włodzimierz, First Lieutenant: 203, 218
Malorny, Ernst: 225
Mandzenko, (..), Major: 162
Maniakówna, Maria: 224
Manuel, Count of Ourém: 77
Maringe, Jerzy, Second Lieutenant: 170
Maringe, Stanisław, Platoon Leader: 171, 218
Maringe, Witold: 171
Martusiewicz, Father Wincenty, Captain, Military Catholic Chaplain: 23
Matejko, Jan: 36
Mazurkiewicz, Jan "Sęp", "Radosław", Lieutenant Colonel: 319, 321, 322
Mierzanowski, Jan M.: 337, 341
Mierzejewska, Jadwiga "Danuta", Captain: 348, 351
Mikołajczyk, Stanisław, Poland's Prime Minister: 352
Miłkowski, Stefan "Jeż": 322, 345
Mińska, Józefa: 103, 116, 142
Molotov, Viacheslav, Foreign Affairs Minister of Soviet Union: 153
Mońko, Ryszard, Lieutenant: 23
Mościcki, Ignacy, President of the Republic of Poland: 162

Mosdorf, Jan, Polish M.P.: 209, 320
Motyka, Bronisław: 220
Możdżeń, Andrzej: 236

N

Napoleon Bonaparte, Emperor of France: 31
Niewiarowski, Bolesław, Second Lieutenant: 335, 343, 347, 349
Niewiarowski, Remigiusz, Officer Cadet (Res.): 206
Nowacki, Stefan, Captain: 365
Nowakowski, Jerzy: 355, 364
Nowakowski, Leon "Lig", Major: 327

O

Obojski, Eugeniusz: 191
Obora, Józef: 344
Okulicki, Leopold, General: 339
Ołpiński, Stefan: 320
Optułowicz, Zofia Matylda, (neé Pilecka - daughter of Witold Pilecki): ix, 16, 378
Osiecimska, Ludwika: 97
Osiecimska, Wanda (Witold Pilecki's maternal grandmother): 124
Osiecimski Stanisław (Witold Pilecki's uncle): 97
Ostrowska, Eleonora (Witold Pilecki's sister-in-law): 143, 185, 217, 337, 365
Ostrowska, Maria (the maiden name of Witold Pilecki's wife): 140
Ostrowski, Bronisław, (Witold Pilecki's brother-in-law): 218
Ostrowski, Edward, Lieutenant (Res.) (Witold Pilecki's brother-in-law): 171

P

Paliński, Aleksander: 217, 319
Palitzsch, Gerhardt, SS Rapportführer: 206, 223, 226
Pan w kratkę. *See* Pilecki, Witold, (aliases: "Witold", "TIV", "Pan w kratkę"), Captain (posthumously, in 2013, promoted to the rank of Colonel)
Paolone, Tadeusz, Captain: 220, 320
Patton, George, US General: 338
Pawłowicz, Zygmunt, Captain: 220, 227
Pawłowska, Helena, M.D.: 171
Pełczyński, Tadeusz, General: 339, 341
Philby, Harold Adrian Russell "Kim", Brigadier: 159
Piast, House of, Kazimierz III the Great, King of Poland: 44, 48, 69
Piast, House of, Konrad I, Prince of Masovia: 51, 52
Piast, House of, Mieszko I, Prince of Poland: 39, 40, 41, 43

Piast, House of, Siemowit IV, Polish Prince: 49
Piast, House of, Władysław Łokietek, King of Poland: 47, 48
Piątkowska, Antonia: 224
Piekarski, Konstanty, Second Lieutenant: 204, 227
Pietrzykowski, Tadeusz, Officer Cadet (Res.): 200, 227
Pilecka, Ludwika (mother of Józef Pilecki, neé Osiecimska): 96, 99, 102, 104
Pilecka, Maria (sister of Witold Pilecki): 142, 143
Pilecka, Maria (Witold Pilecki's wife, neé Ostrowska): 25, 140, 144, 147, 174, 374
Pilecka, Wanda (sister of Witold Pilecki): 95, 101, 104, 116, 142
Pilecka Zofia (daughter of Witold Pilecki): 142, 144, 145, 175, 183, 194, 323, 362, 373, 376
Pilecki, Andrzej (son of Witold Pilecki): ix, 16, 141, 147, 175, 194, 376, 378
Pilecki, Jerzy (brother of Witold Pilecki): 95, 116
Pilecki, Józef (brother of Witold Pilecki, deceased in childhood): 95
Pilecki, Józef (grandfather of Witold Pilecki): 32, 93
Pilecki, Julian (father of Witold Pilecki): 94, 97, 115, 116, 142
Pilecki, Ludwik (uncle of Witold Pilecki): 94
Pilecki, Witold, (aliases: "Witold", "TIV", "Pan w kratkę"), Captain (posthumously, in 2013, promoted to the rank of Colonel): ix, x, xi, 16, 17, 18, 19, 20, 22, 24, 25, 28, 29, 33, 95, 101, 102, 103, 105, 106, 108, 110, 112, 113, 114, 115, 117, 118, 119, 120, 121, 123, 124, 126, 133, 134, 135, 137, 140, 141, 142, 143, 144, 145, 146, 147, 148, 154, 156, 158, 161, 162, 164, 165, 166, 167, 170, 172, 174, 177, 178, 179, 180, 184, 185, 186, 188, 189, 190, 191, 194, 195, 198, 199, 200, 204, 205, 206, 207, 208, 209, 210, 212, 217, 219, 224, 227, 232, 233, 238, 240, 319, 321, 323, 327, 329, 330, 333, 335, 337, 338, 339, 340, 341, 343, 344, 345, 346, 347, 348, 349, 350, 351, 352, 354, 355, 356, 357, 358, 359, 362, 364, 366, 367, 368, 372, 374, 375
Piłsudski, Józef Klemens, First Marshal of Poland, Second Republic of Poland's Chief of State: 86, 87, 108, 114
Płużański, Tadeusz, Second Lieutenant: 346, 355, 364, 365, 368, 372
Podlaski, Henryk, Lieutenant-Colonel: 362
Popiersch, Max: 190
Poraziński, Jerzy, First Lieutenant (Res.): 218

R

Rablin, Andrzej: 223, 344
Rachwał, Stanisława: 224
Raczkiewicz, Władysław, President (in-exile) of the Republic of Poland: 168
Raczyński, Edward Bernard, Count, President (in-exile) of the Republic of Poland: 371

Radwański, Kazimierz: 203, 223, 227
Rapa, Władysław, Second Lieutenant (Res.): 227
Rawicz, Kazimierz, Lieutenant Colonel: 207, 209, 219, 220
Redzej, Jan "Ostrowski": 231, 233, 322, 327, 329, 345
Ribbentrop, Joachim von, Third Reich's Foreign Affairs Minister: 153
Rogowska, Wiktoria: 175
Romanov, House of, Alexander II, Tsar of Russia: 32
Romanov, House of, Alexander I, Tsar of Russia: 31
Romanov, House of, Mikhail I, Tsar of Russia: 68
Romanov, House of, Nicholas I, Tsar of Russia: 84
Romanov, House of, Paul I, Tsar of Russia: 81
Romanowicz, Michał, Captain: 192
Rosa Antoni, Officer Cadet: 200
Rowecki, Stefan "Grot", General: 192, 218
Rowland, Tracey: iii, xii
Różak, Zbigniew, Officer Cadet (Res.): 204
Różański, Józef, Colonel: 350, 358
Różycki, Witold: 348, 355, 364, 368
Rurikovich, House of, Ivan IV the Terrible, Tsar of Russia: 61
Ruszczak, Father Zygmunt: 220
Ruszczyński, Zbigniew, Officer Cadet (Res.): 204
Rybarski, Roman: 209
Rzeczkowski, Szczepan: 174

S

Saint Wojciech (Adalbert): 41, 42
Saladin, Sultan of Egypt: 51
Sawicki, Kazimierz "Sawa", Platoon Leader: 327
Scheidemann, Philipp, Prime Minister of Germany: 150
Schudrich, Michael, Chief Rabbi of Poland: 19
Serafińska, Ludmiła: 337
Serafiński, Tomasz: 171, 235, 236, 238
Shuysky, Vasily IV, Tsar of Russia: 67
Sienkiewicz, Henryk: 99
Sieradzka, Helena: 360
Sieradzki, Makary: 347, 350, 364, 365
Sikorski, Władysław, General, also Polish wartime (WWII) Prime Minister: xi, 169, 176, 192, 326
Skłodowska-Płużańska, Stanisława: 355, 360
Skoczyński, Jerzy: 171
Skornowicz, Mikołaj, Sec. Lieutenant (Res.): 200
Skwarnicki, Józef Kazimierz, Captain: 105

Słowiaczek, Tadeusz: 200
Smalski, Władysław: 225
Sobieski, Jakub (son of Jan III Sobieski): 76
Stachiewicz, Julian, General: 160
Stalin, Yosif Vissaryonovich (surname at birth: Dshugashvili), the absolute ruler of the Soviet Union in the period from 1924 till 1953): 159, 160, 163, 168, 373
Staller, Alois: 189
Stamirowski, Kazimierz (Colonel): 220
Stanisław II August Poniatowski, King of Poland: 78, 79, 80, 81
Stanisław I Leszczyński, twice King of Poland: 77
Staniszkis, Teofil Witold: 206
Starhemberg, Ernst Rüdiger, Count von: 74
Stawarz, Aleksander, Colonel: 209
Stawiszyński, Stanisław: 203
Stefan Batory, King of Poland: 58, 59, 60, 61, 62, 71, 72
Stephen Báthory. *See* Stefan Batory, King of Poland
Stolarska, Wincencja: 192
Stransky, Karel: 214, 343
Stromberger, Maria: 210, 221, 222
Stulgiński, Tadeusz: 223
Stupka, Helena: 192
Surmacki, Władysław, Colonel: 172, 173, 177, 179, 191, 207, 223
Szelągowska, Maria: 340, 343, 344, 346, 347, 364, 365, 368, 372
Szukiewicz, Wacław: 135
Szukiewicz, Zofia: 172
Szwajg, Rubin, Major: 372
Szydek, Zygmunt: 236
Szydlik, Tadeusz, Platoon Leader: 204

Ś

Śmietański, Piotr, Company Sergeant: 24
Śmigły-Rydz, Edward, Marshal: 147, 148, 162, 164, 166
Śniegucki, Wiktor: 227
Świerczyna, Bernard, Second Lieutenant (Res.): 204, 320

T

Thököly, Imre: 74
TIV. *See* Pilecki, Witold, (aliases: "Witold", "TIV", "Pan w kratkę"), Captain (posthumously, in 2013, promoted to the rank of Colonel)
Toliński, Marian: 210

Triebling, Eugeniusz, Captain: 203
Trojnicki, Ferdynand, Captain: 193, 207
Tukhachevsky, Mikhail, Marshal of Soviet Union: 88, 89

U

Uliasz, Father Zdzisław Piotr: 221
Uznański, Jan (one of Witold Pilecki's aliases): 238

V

Valois, Henri [Henryk Walezy], King of Poland, later – King of France: 70
Vasa, House of, Jan II Kazimierz, King of Poland: 42, 64
Vasa, House of, Johan, Crown Prince of Sweden, Prince of Finland, then Johan III, King of Sweden: 63
Vasa, House of, Karl X Gustav, King of Sweden: 66
Vasa, House of, Władysław IV, Tsar of Russia, later - King of Poland: 64, 67
Vasa, House of, Zygmunt III, King of Poland and King of Sweden: 63, 64, 65, 66, 67, 68

W

Wagner, Mieczysław, Officer Cadet (Res.): 204
Walter-Janke, Zygmunt, Major: 322
Wąsowski, Czesław, Corporal: 193, 196
Weil, Simone: 20
Wejtko, Władysław, General: 110
Werblan, Andrzej: 363
Wettin, House of, August II the Strong, King of Saxony and King of Poland: 77
Wettin, House of, August III, Prince of Saxony and King of Poland: 77, 78
Więcek, Julian: 236
Wierusz, Witold, Second Lieutenant (Res.): 228
Winnicka, Wanda (niece of Witold Pilecki's mother): 97
Wiśniewski, Jerzy, Second Lieutenant (Res.): 227
Wiśniewski, Kazimierz, General: 352
Włodarkiewicz, Jan, Major: 170, 171, 172, 174, 176, 177, 178, 180
Wojtyła, Cardinal Carol, later John Paul II, currently Saint John Paul II: xi, xii
Wolańska, Wacława: 350, 355, 360
Wolfówna, Maria: 351
Woźniak, Antoni, Sergeant: 200, 217
Wysocki, Stefan "Jeż", Lieutenant: 319

Z

Zabawski, Edmund: 234, 344
Zacharewicz, Mieczysław "Zawadzki", Captain: 332
Zagner, Roman: 192
Zaturski, Eugeniusz, Lieutenant: 170
Zieja, Jan, Father: 172
Zujewicz, Mikołaj, Sub-Capitan: 110

Ż

Żeligowski, Lucjan, General: 117
Żółkiewski, Stanisław, Grand Hetman of the Crown: 67
Żórawska, Flawia, Witold Pilecki's paternal grandmother: 101

BIBLIOGRAPHY

Abramow-Newerly, Jarosław, 'Lwy mojego podwórka', *Gazeta Wyborcza*, 2000, http://wyborcza.pl/1,75517,136040.html

Acton, Lord, 'Nationality,' *Essays on Freedom and Power*, Peter Smith, Gloucester, 1972.

à Kempis, Thomas, *The Imitation of Christ*, The Bruce Publishing Company, Milwaukee, 1940.

Aleksandrowicz, S., *Zarys historii wojennej 13 Pułku Ułanów Wileńskich*, Warszawa, 1929.

APMA-B, D-Aul-2/27, *Sterbebuch* (Auschwitz official death records).

APMA-B, Materiały obozowego ruchu oporu, v.37.

APMA-B, Zespół Materiały, v.92, (M. Leciejewska, *Biografia Witolda Pileckiego*, Wyższa Szkoła Pedagogiczna, Słupsk).

APMA-B, Zespół Materiały, v.220 (Tomasz Serafiński's statement).

APMA-B, Zespół Materiały, v.223, k.24-7 (the list, by Pilecki's hand, of all soldiers he had under his command during the Warsaw Uprising), also other materials, at kk.1-23.

APMA-B, Zespół Oświadczenia, v.27 (statements by former Auschwitz inmates)

APMA-B, Zespół Oświadczenia, v.54 (statement by Andrzej Harat)

APMA-B, Zespół Oświadczenia, v.74, kk.45-7 (Juliusz Gilewicz's biography, by Zygmunt Mianowski).

APMA-B, Zespół Oświadczenia, v.179 (statement by Eleonora Ostrowska).

APMA-B, Zespół Wspomnienia, v.75 (former Auschwitz inmate Edward Pyś's recollections).

APMA-B, Zespół Wspomnienia, v.98 (former Auschwitz inmates' recollections).

APMA-B, Zespół Wspomnienia, v.122 (former Auschwitz inmate Bolesław Giertych's recollections).

APMA-B, Zespół Wspomnienia, v.125 (Ludmiła Serafińska's statement).

APMA-B, Zespół Wspomnienia, v.130, k.1 (Andrzej Możdżeń's statement).

APMA-B, Zespół Wspomnienia, v.130 (Witold Pilecki's report).

APMA-B, Zespół Wspomnienia, v.172 (former Auschwitz inmate Zenon Ławski's recollections).

APMA-B, Zespół Wspomnienia, v.172 (former Auschwitz inmate Rudolf Diem's recollections).

APMA-B, Zespół Wspomnienia, v.179 (Eleonora Ostrowska's recollections).

APMA-B, Zespół Wspomnienia, v.203 (letters to the Auschwitz-Birkenau Museum).

APMO, Zespół Wspomnienia, *Wspomnienia W. Deringa*.

APMO, Zespół Wspomnienia, *Wspomnienia Eleonory Ostrowskiej*, k.179.

APMO, *Zaświadczenie Edmunda Galinata* [Edmund Galinat's testimony], Wilno, 21.06.1926, v.223c.London

Asnyk, Adam, 'Miejcie nadzieję'.

ASS MON, Akta sprawy, vv.1,2,4,5 [documents from the 1947-8 Pilecki pre-trial investigation, and the subsequent trial].

Atholl, Duchess of, *The Tragedy of Warsaw and its Documentation*, London, 1945.

Auer, Stefan, *Liberal Nationalism in Central Europe*, Routledge, London, 2004.

AUOP, Sygn. 1768/III/2: operational files concerning Witold Pilecki and seven others, k.186, recollections by Witold Pilecki from June 1946.

Baranowski, Z. *Niech złożą mandaty*, 'Nasz Dziennik', 2009, no.88.

Bardach, Juliusz, Leśnodorski, Bogusław and Pietrzak, Michał, *Historia państwa i prawa polskiego*, Państwowe Wydawnictwo Naukowe, Warszawa, 1987.

Bartoszewski, W., *Mój Auschwitz*, Znak, Kraków, 2010 (an interview by P.M.A. Cywiński and M.Zając).

Baszkiewicz, J., *Polska czasów Łokietka*, Wiedza Powszechna, Warszawa, 1968.

Bauer, Krzysztof, *Uchwalenie i obrona Konstytucji 3 Maja*, Wydawnictwa Szkolne i Pedagogiczne, 1991.

Benedict XIV – *Heroic Virtue: A Portion of the Treatise of Benedict XIV on the Beatification and Canonization of the Servants of God* (*De Servorum Dei Beatificatione et Beatorum Canonizatione*), Vol.1, Thomas Richardson and Son, London, 1850.

Besala, Jerzy, and Biedrzycka, Agnieszka, *Polski Słownik Biograficzny*, 2004-2005.

Bethell, Nicholas, *Zwycięska wojna Hitlera. Wrzesień 1939*, Instytut Wydawniczy PAX, Warszawa, 1997.

Bideleux, Robert, Jeffries, Ian, *A History of Eastern Europe: Crisis and Change*, Psychology Press, 28 January 1998.

Biskupski, M.B., *The History of Poland*, Greenwood Publishing Group, Westport Conn., 2000

Bober, M. 'Nazywał mnie swoją generałką' (an interview with Zofia Pilecka-Optułowicz, and her grandson, Krzysztof Kosior), *Nasz Dziennik*, 5.12.2009.

Bohlen, Charles E., *Witness to history, 1929–1969*. Weidenfeld and Nicolson, London, 1973.

Bohun, Tomasz, *Moskwa 1612*, Bellona, Warszawa, 2005.

Borah, William, 'Defiant Peace Bid Hurled By Hitler', *The Pittsburgh Press*, September 19, 1939.

Braudel, Fernand, *Civilisation & Capitalism: The Perspective of the World*, Harper and Row, New York, 1984.

Brym-Zdunin, Z., Żelazna Reduta. Kompania Zdunina w Powstaniu Warszawskim Zgr. *'Chrobry II'*, London, 1992.

Bryce, James, *The Holy Roman Empire*, The MacMillan Company, London, 1913.

Brzezinski, Richard, Vukšić, Velimir, *Polish Winged Hussar 1576–1775*, Osprey Publishing, Oxford, 2006.

Burnham, Robert, 'Somosierra: The Charge of the Polish Light Horse', http://www.napoleon-series.org/military/virtual/c_somosierra.html

Butler, J.R.M., *History of the Second World War. United Kingdom Military Series, Grand Strategy*, Vol. II, September 1939 – June 1941, Her Majesty's Stationery Office, London, 1957.

Butterwick, Richard, *Poland-Lithuania's Last King and English Culture: Stanisław August Poniatowski, 1732–1798*, Oxford University Press, 1998.

Bystrzycki, P. 'W sprawie odbicia przez AK więźniów obozu masowej zagłady w Oświęcimiu', *Wojskowy Przegląd Historyczny*, 1966, no.1.

Catholic Encyclopedia, 'Humility', newadvent.org

CAW, *W. Pilecki, Wniosek awansowy*, nr 2944 [*Witold Pilecki: Promotion Proposal*, Central Military Archive, File No 2944].

Centek, J., *Hans von Seeckt. Twórca Reichsheer. 1866-1936*, New Avalon, Kraków, 2006.

Chodurski, Michał, *Nikt tak nie ograbił Polski jak Szwedzi*, Polish Radio webpage, 31.08.2012.

Churchill, Winston S., *The Second World War*, Vol. 6, Chapter IX, 'The Martyrdom of Warsaw', Cassel, 1955.

Ciesielski, E., *Wspomnienia oświęcimskie*, Wydawnictwo Literackie, Kraków, 1968.

Collins Cobuild English Language Dictionary, London 1987.

Collins English Dictionary, London 2012.

Conquest, Robert, Preface to: *The Great Terror: A Reassessment: 40th Anniversary Edition*, Oxford University Press, USA, 2007.

Corwin, Lewinski, Edward Henry, *The Political History of Poland*, Polish Book Importing Company, New York, 1917.

Cyra, Adam, 'Raport Witolda', *Biuletyn Towarzystwa Opieki nad Oświęcimiem*, 1991, no.12

Cyra, Adam, *Rotmistrz Pilecki. Ochotnik do Auschwitz*, RM, Warszawa, 2014.

Czajkowski, A., 'Po dwakroć na barykadach Warszawy', [in:] *Udział kapelanów wojskowych w drugiej wojnie światowej*, Warszawa, 1984.

Czech, D., *Kalendarz wydarzeń w KL Auschwitz*, Oświęcim, 1992.

D'Abernon, Edgar Vincent 1st Viscount, *The Eighteenth Decisive Battle of the World, Warsaw 1920*, Hyperion Press, Westport Conn., 1977.

Dallas, Gregor, *1945: the war that never ended*, Yale University Press, 2005.

Datko, A.' 'Kult maryjny– jego tradycja i znaczenie', *Przegląd Powszechny*, 1982, nr 1-2.

Davies, Brian L., *Warfare, State and Society on the Black Sea Steppe, 1500-1700*, Routledge, London, 2007.

Davies, Norman, *Europe: A History*, Oxford University Press, 1996; also: Harper Collins, 1998.

Davies, Norman, *God's Playground, a History of Poland: The origins to 1795*, Columbia University Press, 1982, also 2005.

Davies, Norman, *Rising '44. The Battle for Warsaw*, Viking, New York, 2004.

Dębski, Sławomir, Kornat, Marek, 'Polska nie była bierna. Siedemdziesiąta rocznica paktu Ribbentrop-Mołotow', *Gazeta Wyborcza*, 21 August 2009.

Diem, R., 'Wspomnienia lekarza więźnia z Oświęcimia', *Przegląd Lekarski* 45(1), pp. 134-147.

Domańska, R., *Pawiak. Więźniowie Gestapo, Kronika 1939-1944*, Książka i Wiedza, Warszawa, 1978.

DZ PMA-B, file TA-201 (statement by fomer Auschwitz inmate Tadeusz Stulgiński).

Encyklopedia wojskowa, PWN and Bellona, Warszawa, 2007.

Evans, R.J.W., and von Strandmann, Hartmut Pogge, eds *The Revolutions in Europe 1848–1849*, Oxford University Press, 2000.

Fejkiel. W., *Więźniarski szpital w KL Auschwitz*, Muzeum Oświęcim-Brzezinka, 1994.

Fieldorf, M., Zachuta, L., *Generał 'Nil' August Emil Fieldorf. Fakty, dokumenty, relacje*, Instytut Wydawniczy PAX, Warszawa, 1993.

'Five of the most notable defections', Telegraph.co.uk. 27 July 2010.

Foreign Relations of the United States 1939, Washington 1956 vol.1 General, p. 342, document 465.

Frost, Robert I., *After the Deluge. Poland-Lithuania and the Second Northern War, 1655-1660*, Cambridge Studies in Early Modern History, Cambridge University Press, 2004.

Frost, Robert I., *The Northern Wars 1558–1721*, Pearson Education Limited, Harlow, 2000.

Garliński, J., *Oświęcim walczący*, Volumen, Warszawa, 1992.

Gawron, Wincenty, *Ochotnik do Oświęcimia*, Calvarianum, Oświęcim, 1992.

Getty, J. Arch, Rittersporn, Gábor, T., Zemskov, Viktor, N.,'Victims of the Soviet Penal System in the Pre-War Years: A First Approach on the Basis of Archival Evidence', *The American Historical Review*, Vol. 98, No. 4 (Oct. 1993).

Gieysztor, Aleksander *et al.*, *History of Poland*, PWN, Warsaw, 1979.

Gilbert, Martin & Gott, Richard, *The Appeasers*, Weidenfeld & Nicolson, London, 1967.

Goclon, J.A., *W obronie Europy. Wojna z bolszewicką Rosją w 1920 r.*, Toruń, 2006.

Goldman, Stuart D., *Nomonhan, 1939: The Red Army's Victory That Shaped World War II*, Naval Institute Press, 2012.

Goldman, Wendy Z., *Inventing the Enemy: Denunciation and Terror in Stalin's Russia,* Cambridge University Press, New York, 2011.

Grossfeld, L., *Polska a stosunki niemiecko-sowieckie 1918-1939*, Warszawa, 1988.

Gruszka, T., *W Murnau*, London 1994.

Herbermann et al. (Editors), *The Catholic Encyclopaedia*, 1910, Vol. 7.

Herwarth, Hans von, *Między Hitlerem a Stalinem. Wspomnienia dyplomaty i oficera niemieckiego 1931–1945*, Bellona, Warszawa, 1992.

Hubatsch, Walther, *Albrecht von Brandenburg-Ansbach. Deutschordens-Hochmeister und Herzog in Preußen 1490–1568*, Grote, Köln/Berlin, 1965.

Hunt, Lynn, Martin, Thomas R., Rosenwein, Barbara H., Smith, Bonnie G., *The Making of the West: Peoples and Cultures*, Volume C, Bedford/St.Martin's, Boston/New York, 2012.

Ihnatowicz, I., Landau, Z., Mączak, A., Zientara, B., *Dzieje gospodarcze Polski do roku 1939*, Wiedza Powszechna, Warszawa, 1988.

Isacson, Claes-Göran, *Karl X Gustavs Krig*, Lund, 2002, Historiska Media.

Jasienica, Paweł, *Polska anarchia*, Wydawnictwo Literackie, Kraków, 1988.

Jasiński, T., 'Złota Bulla Fryderyka II dla zakonu krzyżackiego z roku rzekomo 1226', *Roczniki Historyczne*, 1994.

Jędruch, Jacek, *Constitutions, elections, and legislatures of Poland, 1493–1977: a guide to their history*, EJJ, New York, 1998.

Johnson, Lonnie R., *Central Europe: Enemies, neighbours, Friends*, Oxford University Press, 1996.

Johnson, Samuel, *A Dictionary of the English Language*, 1755 ('Honour').

Karski, Jan, *Wielkie mocarstwa wobec Polski: 1919-1945 od Wersalu do Jałty*, PIW, Warsaw, 1992.

Kawalec, T., *Związek Bezpieczeństwa Kraju*, Harcerska Spółka Wydawnicza, Wilno, 1922.

Kisielewicz, D., *Oflag VII A Murnau, Łambinowice-Opole*, Uniwersytert Opolski, 1990.

Kledzik, M. 'Reduta rotmistrza Pileckiego', *Tydzień Polski*, London, 1994, no.3.

Kirchmayer, J., *Kampania wrześniowa*, Czytelnik, Łódź, 1946.

Klimecki, Michał, *Polsko-ukraińska wojna o Lwów i Galicję Wschodnią 1918-1919*, Wolumen, Warszawa, 2000.

Klubówna, Anna, *Zawisza Czarny w historii i legendzie*, Ludowa Spółdzielnia Wydawnicza, Warszawa, 1979.

Kłoczowski, Jerzy, *A History of Polish Christianity*, Cambridge University Press, 2000.

Kłodziński, S., 'Rola kryminalistów niemieckich w początkach obozu oświęcimskiego'. *Przegląd Lekarski*, 1974, no.1.

Komski, J., Listy do Redakcji, *Kultura*, Paris, 1963, No.7-8

Korman, Sharon, *The Right of Conquest: The Acquisition of Territory by Force in International Law and Practice*, Oxford University Press, 1996.

Kownacki, A. 'Jerzewski', *Jak powstało i walczyło zgrupowanie "Chrobry II"*, Warszawa, 1993.

Krajewski, Andrzej, 'Polskie Termopile, czyli cud pod Wizną', *Polska the Times*. 2009-09-04, 207 (575), pp.16-17.

Langbein, Hermann, *Menschen in Auschwitz*, Europa Verlag GmbH, München, 1995.

Lauteinann, *Geschichten in Quellen*, Bd.6.

League of Nations Treaty Series, vol.19.

Leopold, Cz., Lechicki, K., *Więźniowie polityczni w Polsce 1945-1956*, Gdańsk 1981.

Lewis, John E., *The Mammoth Book of True War Stories*, Carroll & Graf Publishers, New York, 1999.

Liddell, H. G., Scott, Robert, *An Intermediate Greek-English Lexicon: Founded Upon the Seventh Edition of Liddell and Scott's Greek-English Lexicon*, Benediction Classics, October 2010.

Lindsay, J. O.,*The New Cambridge Modern History*, Cambridge University Press, Cambridge, 1957.

'Lista straconych w więzieniach PRL w latach 1944-1956', *Wokanda*, 1990, nos 1-4.

Lukas, Richard C., *Forgotten Holocaust. The Poles under German Occupation 1939-1944*, Hippocrene Books, New York, 1997.

Lukas, Richard C., *Out of the inferno: Poles remember the Holocaust*, University Press of Kentucky, 1989.

Łojek, Jerzy, *Agresja 17 września 1939. Studium aspektów politycznych*, PAX, Warsaw, 1990.

Macleod, Roderic, & Kelly, Denis (eds), *Time Unguarded: The Ironside Diaries, 1937-1940*, Constable, London. 1962.

Macpherson, William (editor), 'Chapter CXXXIII Annals of France, from the Accession of Louis XV, to the Period following the Peace of Aix-la-Chapelle', *Encyclopaedia Metropolitana Volume XIII: History and Biography Volume 5* B, Fellowes, London, 1845.

Malinowski, K., *Tajna Armia Polska. Znak. Konfederacja Zbrojna. Zarys genezy, organisacji i działalności*, PAX, Warszawa, 1986.

Manteuffel, Tadeusz, *Historia Powszechna. Średniowiecze*, PWN, Warszawa, 1999.

Manvell, Roger, Fraenkel, Heinrich, *Heinrich Himmler: The SS, Gestapo, His Life and Career*, Skyhorse Publishing Inc., New York, 2007.

Marácz, László Károly, *Expanding European unity: Central and Eastern Europe*, Rodopi, Amsterdam, 1999.

Markiewicz, Barbara, 'Liberum veto, albo o granicach społeczeństwa obywatelskiego' [in:] *Obywatel: odrodzenie pojęcia*, Wydawnictwo Naukowe Scholar, Warszawa, 1993.

Masters, B. A., Ágoston, G., *Encyclopedia of the Ottoman Empire*, Facts on File Infobase Publishing, New York, 2009.

Mączyński, Z., 'Zbrodnicza Temida', *Prawo i Życie*, 1991, no.7.

Merriman, John, *A History of Modern Europe: From the French Revolution to the Present*, W.W. Norton and Co., New York, 1996.

Michaud, Claude, 'The Kingdoms of Central Europe in the Fourteenth Century', in: Michael Jones, *New Cambridge Medieval History vol. VI. c.1300 – c.1415*. Cambridge: CUP, 2000.

Mickiewicz, Adam, *Pan Tadeusz, czyli ostatni zajazd na Litwie. Historia szlachecka z roku 1811 i 1812 we dwunastu księgach wierszem*, published by Aleksander Jełowicki, Paris, 1834.

Możejko, Beata, Szybkowski, Sobiesław, Śliwiński, Błażej: *Zawisza Czarny z Garbowa herbu Sulima*, WiM, Gdańsk, 2003.

Mueller, Gordon H., 'Rapallo Reexamined: A New Look at Germany's Secret Military Collaboration with Russia in 1922,' *Military Affairs*, 1976, 40#3, pp.109-117 (inJSTOR)

Murphy, David E., *What Stalin Knew: The Enigma of Barbarossa*, Yale University Press, 2006.

New Testament.

Nagielski, Mirosław, 'Stanisław Żółkiewski herbu Lubicz', in: *Hetmani Rzeczypospolitej Obojga Narodów*, Bellona, Warszawa, 1995.

Nathanson, Stephen, *Patriotism, Morality, and Peace*, Rowman & Littlefield, Lanham Md, 1993.

Noakes, J. and Pridham, G. (eds) *Nazism 1919-1945*, Vol. 3, *Foreign Policy, War and Racial Extermination*, University of Exeter Press, 2010.

Nowak, Andrzej,'Polacy na Kremlu', *Wprost*, Nr 1182 (31 lipca 2005).

Nowak, Andrzej, 'The Russo-Polish Historical Confrontation', *The Sarmatian Review*, January 1997, Volume XVII, No 1.

Nowak, Jan, *Kurier z Warszawy*, Znak, Warszawa-Kraków, 1989.

Old Testament.

Oppenheim, Heinrich Bernhard, *The Right of Conquest: The Acquisition of Territory by Force in International Law and Practice*, Oxford University Press, 1996.

Orr, James, M.A., D.D. (General Editor), *International Standard Bible Encyclopedia*, 1915, ('Humility').

Ostrowska, E. 'Wspomnienia', *Czas* (Canada), 18 August 1984.

Oświęcim w oczach SS: Rudolf Höss, Pery Broad, Johann Paul Kremer, Oświęcim 2001

'Partitions of Poland', Encyclopædia Britannica Online, 2008.

Pasterak, Anna, *Przywileje szlacheckie*, Uniwersytet Pedagogiczny w Krakowie, 2004.

Pawłowicz, Jacek, *Rotmistrz Witold Pilecki 1901-1948*, Instytut Pamięci Narodowej, Warszawa, 2008.

Perrie, Maureen, and Pavlov, Andrei, *Ivan the Terrible (Profiles in Power)*, Longman, London, 2003.

Phillimore, Sir Robert, *Commentaries Upon International Law*, T. & J. W. Johnson, 1854.

Pilecka, Maria, *Dzieje rodu Pileckich (Saga)* [manuscript], Poznań, 1983.

Pilecki Andrzej, his letter, of 8 December 2014, to this author.

Pilecki, Witold, his entry into a Kazimiera Dacz's album, now in the private collection of a Vilnian, Ryšard Maceikianc.

Pilecki, Witold, his letter to Kazimiera Dacz, written in Lida, dated 13 June 1924.

Pilecki, Witold, his letter to Kazimiera Dacz, written in Vilnius, dated 22 December 1924.

Pilecki, Witold, his letter to Kazimiera Dacz, dated 31 March 1925.

Pilecki, Witold, his letter to Kazimiera Dacz, written in Vilnius, dated 6 October 1925.

Pilecki, Witold, his letter to Kazimiera Dacz, written in Sukurcze, dated 22 September 1926.

Pilecki, Witold, an undated letter to Kazimiera Dacz.

Pilecki, Witold, *Wspomnienia*.

Piłsudski, Józef, *Pisma zbiorowe*, v.V, Warszawa, 1937.

Piotrowski, Tadeusz, *Poland's Holocaust: Ethnic Strife: Collaboration with Occupying Forces and Genocide in the Second Republic, 1918–1947*, Jefferson NC, 1998.

Pipes, Richard, Brandenberger, David, Fitzpatrick, Catherine A., *The unknown Lenin: from the secret archive*, Yale University Press, New Haven, Connecticut, 1999.

Piwowarski, W. '*Kościół ludowy a duszpasterstwo*' ed. W. Piwowarski, in: *Religijność ludowa. Ciągłość i zmiana*, Wrocław 1983.

Plutarch, *Demosthenes*, 75 A.C.E.

Płużański, Tadeusz M., *Bestie. Mordercy Polaków*, 3S MEDIA, 2011.

Płużański, Tadeusz M., 'Inaczej niż w 'Przesłuchaniu'', *Gazeta Polska*, 2010, no.21.

Płużański, Tadeusz M., *Z otchłani*, Kolory, 2014.

Pobóg-Malinowski, Władysław, *Najnowsza historia polityczna Polski*, Vol. 3, Wydawnictwo Władysław Pobóg-Malinowski, Londyn, 1960.

Podhorodecki, Leszek, *Sławne bitwy Polaków*, Mada, Warszawa, 1997.

Podlewski, S., *Przemarsz przez piekło*, PAX, Warszawa, 1957.

Polska Wielka Księga Historii (eds. Andrzej Nowak, Monika Karolczuk, Piotr Budny, Zuzanna Dawidowicz, Henryk Głębocki, Agnieszka Pałac, Anna Śledzikowska), Kluszczyński, Kraków, 2012.

Polskie Siły Zbrojne w II wojnie światowej, v. 1, '*Kampania wrześniowa*', cz. 1 and 2, Polish Chief Staff's Historical Commission, General Sikorski Historical Institute, London, 1954.

'Pospolite ruszenie', WIEM Free Encyclopaedia.

Przemyski, A., *Ostatni Komendant generał Leopold Okulicki*, Wydawnictwo Lubelskie, Lublin, 1990.

Pseudo-Apollodorus, *Bibliotheke* ii. 5; Hyginus, *Fabula* 31.

Ragsdale, Hugh, *Imperial Russian foreign policy*, Cambridge University Press, Cambridge, 1993.

Rees, Laurence, *Auschwitz: A New History*, Public Affairs, New York, 2005.

Report W. KL Auschwitz. 1940-1943 (the original version of Witold Pilecki's report from Auschwitz translated into English by Adam J. Koch), Melbourne, 2013.

Riasanovsky, Nicholas V., *Old Russia, the Soviet Union and Eastern Europe*, American Slavic and East European Review, Vol. 11, No. 3. (Oct. 1952).

Ripley, Tim, *The Wehrmacht. The German Army in World War II 1939-1945*, Routledge, New York, 2013.

Roberts, Geoffrey, 'The Soviet Decision for a Pact with Germany', *Soviet Studies*, Vol. 44, No. 1, 1992.

Rodríguez, Pedro, *Camino* (ed. critica), Rialp, Madrid, 2004

Rosik, Stanisław, Wiszewski, Przemysław, *Wielki poczet polskich królów i książąt*, Wydawnictwo Uniwersytetu Wrocławskiego, Wrocław, 2006.

Rotfeld, Adam D., Torkunow, Anatolij W. (ed.), *Białe plamy – Czarne plamy. Sprawy trudne w relacjach polsko-rosyjskich (1918-2008)*, PISM, Warszawa, 2010.

Rzepecki, J., *Wspomnienia i przyczynki historyczne*, Warszawa, 1956.

Saint Augustine, *De patientia*, 426-428.

Sanford, V, *Katyń and the Soviet Massacre of 1940: Truth, Justice And Memory*, Routledge, London, New York 2005.

Scott, Hamish M., *The Emergence of the Eastern Powers, 1756–1775*, Cambridge University Press, 2001.

Sedlar, Jean W., 'Law and Justice', in: *East Central Europe in the Middle Ages, 1000-1500*, University of Washington Press, Seattle, 1994.

Seidner, Stanley S., *Marshal Edward Śmigły-Rydz Rydz and the defence of Poland*, New York, 1978.

Seidner, Stanley S., 'Reflections from Rumania and Beyond: Marshal Śmigły-Rydz Rydz in Exile', *The Polish Review* Vol. XXII, no. 2, 1977.

'Seven Years War?', *TIME Magazine*, 2 October 1939.

Shirer, William, *The Rise and Fall of the Third Reich*, Simon and Schuster, New York, 1960.

Siciński, Antoni, 'Z psychopatologii więźniów: Ernst Krankemann', *Przegląd Lekarski*, 1974. No.1

Sikorski, J., 'Farmaceuci – pierwsi więźniowie Oświęcimia', *Farmacja Polska*, 1973, no.6.

Siwek, Tadeusz, *Statystyczni i niestatystyczni Polacy w Republice Czeskiej*, website of Wspólnota Polska.

Sobieski, Wacław, *Trybun ludu szlacheckiego*, PIW, Warszawa, 1978.

Solovyov, Sergey, *History of the Downfall of Poland*, Moscow, 1863.

Sopicki, Stanisław, *Krzyż i Orzeł Biały*, London, 1966.

SPP, No.1785/III,3/2/BI, Witold Pilecki's statement.

SPP, Zeszyt Ewidencyjny Witolda Pileckiego.

Stawicki, R., *Rotmistrz Witold Pilecki 1901-1948*, Kancelaria Senatu, Biuro Informacji i Dokumentacji, Dział Analiz i Opracowań Tematycznych, opracowanie tematyczne OT-540. June 2008.

Steinbacher, Sybille, *Auschwitz: A History*, Verlag C. H. Beck, Munich, 2005.

Stone, Daniel, *The Polish-Lithuanian State, 1386-1795*, University of Washington Press, 2001.

Strzembosz, T., *Saga o* 'Łupaszce', Rytm, Warszawa, 1996.

Subtelny, Orest, *Ukraine. A History*, University of Toronto Press, 1994.

Szejnert, M., *Śród żywych duchów*, London, 1990.

Szelągowski, Adam, *Wzrost państwa polskiego w XV i XVI w. Polska na przełomie wieków średnich i nowych*, B. Połoniecki, Lwów, 1904.

Szyndler, Bartłomiej, *Tadeusz Kościuszko, 1746–1817*, Bellona, Warszawa, 1991.

Śluby króla Jana Kazimierza i Stanów Rzeczypospolitej zaprzysiężone imieniem narodu przed cudownym obrazem N. P. Łaskawej w Katedrze Lwowskiej a dotyczące polepszenia doli ludu pracującego oraz czci Najśw. Panny jako Królowej Korony Polskiej do wykonywania których to ślubów każdy miłujący Boga i Ojczyznę przyczyniać się winien, Lwów, 1887.

Taylor, A.J.P., *A History of World War Two*, Octopus Books, London, 1974.

The Auschwitz Volunteer: Beyond Bravery (contains the third, complete, version of Witold Pilecki's Auschwitz report, translated by Jarek Garliński), Aquila Polonica, Los Angeles, 2012.

The Holy Roman Empire, Heraldica.org.

The President of the Republic of Poland's Decree of 15 October 1943 replacing the President of the Republic of Poland's Decree of 24 November 1937 concerning Military and Navy Emblems, DzURP 1943, 22 October, No. 10, item 27.

The text of the Nazi-Soviet Non-Aggression Pact of 23 August 1939, Fordham.

Tippelskirch, Kurt von, General a.D., *Geschichte des Zweiten Weltkriegs*, Athenäum Verlag, Bonn, 1956.

Tracki, Krzysztof, *Młodość Witolda Pileckiego*, Sic!, Warsaw, 2014.

Treaty of Versailles, original text.

Trial of the Major War Criminals before the International Military Tribunal, 14 November 1945- 1 October 1946, v.15, Nuremberg, 1947.

Tucker, S.C., *A Global Chronology of Conflict*, Vol.2, ABC-CLIO, LLC, Santa Barbara, 2010.

Tuttle, Herbert, Adams, Herbert Baxter, *History of Prussia*, Houghton, Mifflin and Company, 1883.

Van Norman, Louis E., *Poland: The Knight Among Nations*, Fleming H. Revell Company, Grand Rapids, 1907.

Varvounis, M., *Jan Sobieski*, Xlibris, Bloomington, In., 2012.

Waligóra, B., *Zajęcie Wilna przez generała Lucjana Żeligowskiego*, Warszawa, 1930.

Wandycz, Piotr Stefan, *The lands of partitioned Poland. 1795-1918*, University of Washington Press, Seattle, 1974.

Wandycz, Piotr Stefan, *The Price of Freedom: A History of East Central Europe from the Middle Ages to the Present*, Routledge, New York, 2001.

Watt, Richard M., *Bitter Glory: Poland and Its Fate, 1918-1939*, Simon & Schuster, New York, 1979.

Weil, Simone, *Myśli*, choice by Aleksandra Olędzka-Frybesowa, Instytut Wydawniczy PAX, Warszawa 1985.

Weinryb, Bernard, *The Jews of Poland. A Social Economic History of the Jewish Community in Poland from 1100 to 1800*, Philadelphia, The Jewish Publication Society of America, Philadelphia, 1972.

Wejtko, W., *Samoobrona Litwy i Białorusi: szkic historyczny*, Warszawska Oficyna Wydawnicza, Warszawa, 1930.

Werblan, Andrzej, *Stalinizm w Polsce*, Warszawa, 1991.

Wiktorzak, A., 'Polskie Termopile', *Głos Weterana* No 1997/9.

Wimmer, Jan, *Wojna polsko-szwedzka 1655-1660*, Warsaw, 1973.

Wisner, Henryk, *Król i car: Rzeczpospolita i Moskwa w XVI i XVII wieku*, Książka i Wiedza, Warszawa, 1995.

Wontor-Cichy T., 'Więzień KL Auschwitz Franciszek Kolbe no. 127600', *W nurcie franciszkańskim*, 2007, no.16, p.127.

Woźniczka, Z., 'Polskie podziemie niepodległościowe (1945-1951)', part II, *Mówią Wieki*, 1991, no.4.

Wójcik, Zbigniew, *Jan III Sobieski. Poczet królów i książąt polskich*, Czytelnik, Warszawa, 1978.

Wright, M., *The World at Arms*, Readers Digest, London, 1989.

Wróbel, P., *Historical Dictionary of Poland 1945-1996*, Routledge, London, 2014

Wysocki, Wiesław Jan, *Rotmistrz Witold Pilecki 1901-1948*, Rytm, Warszawa, 2012.

Wyszczelski, Lech, *Wilno 1919-1920*, Bellona, Warszawa 2008.

Wyszczelski, Lech, *Wojna o Kresy Wschodnie 1918-1921* Bellona, Warszawa, 2011.

Yunis, H., *Demosthenes: On the Crown*, Cambridge, 2001.

Zamoyski, Adam, *The Polish Way: A Thousand-Year History of the Poles and Their Culture*, New York, Hippocrene Books, 1994.

Zawadzki, Hubert, Łukowski, Jerzy, *A Concise History of Poland*, Cambridge University Press, 2001.

Zawadzki, M., *Materials by Durham University Polish Society*, Durham University, 2007.

Zawadzki, W. H., *A Man of Honour: Adam Czartoryski as a Statesman of Russia and Poland, 1795–1831*, Oxford University Press, 1993.

Zieliński, Henryk, *Historia Polski 1918-1939*, PWN, Warsaw, 1984.

Zimmerman, Volker, *Die Sudetendeutschen im NS-Staat. Politik und Stimmung der Bevölkerung im Reichsgau Sudetenland (1938-1945)*, Klartext, Essen, 1999.

The author of this book thankfully acknowledges the generous provision to him of various unpublished archive materials on Witold Pilecki by the Institute of National Remembrance, Warsaw, Poland.

Endnotes

1. To be pronounced *VEEtold*, and *PeeLETSkee*, respectively.
2. To respectfully acknowledge Witold Pilecki's unassuming nature, and his evident lack of interest in career concerns, this author chooses to refer to him in this book as Captain Pilecki, even though the Captain was, in 2013, posthumously promoted to the rank of Colonel.
3. Its title is *Report "W"*.
4. They were: Soviet-occupied eastern part of Germany, since 1949 known as the German Democratic Republic (on October 3, 1990, it merged with West Germany to form the current Federal Republic of Germany), Albania, Austria (which after the conclusion of WWII got divided into four occupation zones controlled by the Soviet Union, the United States, Great Britain and France; the country regained its independence on May 15, 1955); Bulgaria, Czechoslovakia; Hungary, Romania and Yugoslavia. Except for Austria, the other countries, together with Poland, formed the so-called Eastern Bloc, a Soviet-controlled entity which existed until 1989. For Albania and Yugoslavia, the extent of that control soon diminished; Yugoslavia broke with the Soviet Union in 1948, and Albania, from 1956, fell under the influence of the People's Republic of China and became Maoist; from 1978, Albania started moving away from the latter alliance.
5. With Great Britain's and the United States' acquiescence at the Yalta conference in February 1945, the formerly independent countries of Estonia, Latvia and Lithuania were annexed by the Soviet Union and became, as its 'republics', parts of the Soviet Union's territory.
6. The original Polish term is 'żołnierze niezłomni'; they are also referred to in Poland as 'żołnierze wyklęci', the latter Polish term relates to their vilification by the early communist propaganda, and their barring from public memory in the communist Poland.
7. Adam Cyra, *Rotmistrz Pilecki. Ochotnik do Auschwitz*, Wydawnictwo RM, Warszawa, 2014, Jacek Pawłowicz, *Rotmistrz Witold Pilecki 1901-1948*, IPN, Warszawa, 2008, Krzysztof Tracki, *Młodość Witolda Pileckiego*, Sic!, Warszawa, 2014, Wiesław Jan Wysocki, *Rotmistrz Witold Pilecki 1901-1948*, Rytm, Warszawa, 2012.
8. *The Auschwitz Volunteer: Beyond Bravery*, Aquila Polonica, California, 2012, page XVII (that book contains a translation by Jarek Garliński of the final, more comprehensive, version of his Auschwitz report). Witold Pilecki worked on this report when at the headquarters of the Second Polish Army Corps in Ancona, Italy, during the 1945 summer.
9. Simon Weil, *Gravity and Grace*, Taylor & Francis e-Library, 2003, p.70.

10 Between 1772 and 1795, acting in collusion with the Kingdom of Prussia and the Austrian Empire, Tsarist Russia annexed, in three instalments, large chunks of the Commonwealth's territory. All three powers seized the rest of what had been remaining of the Commonwealth's territory in 1795. And so, Poland disappeared from the map of Europe in that year. The country that was the largest and one of the most powerful European countries only two and a half hundred years prior to that, and at the same time one of the most populous at the end of the sixteenth century, ceased to exist as a separate, and sovereign, entity.

11 Betrayed in February 1945 at the Yalta conference by its wartime allies, United States and Great Britain, Poland was handed over to Stalin, a ruthless butcher of his own nation, and a foresworn enemy of Poland, as their gift of sorts. It was a gift that Stalin very much coveted, for he sought vengeance on the Polish nation for its defeat of the Red Army in August 1920 called 'the miracle on the Vistula,' one of the most significant battles in all human history (see: Edgar Vincent, 1st Viscount D'Abernon, *The Eighteenth Decisive Battle of the World: Warsaw, 1920*, Hyperion Press, Westport, Conn., 1977). This victory saved Western Europe from becoming, in the wake of the October 1917 revolution, another conquest of Lenin's Russia (which was to be later re-named the Soviet Union), as he sought to convert his vision to spread communism across all Europe, and then the entire globe, into reality. His plan of vengeance on the Polish nation for this defeat, Stalin started implementing a few years before the Second World War. The so-called Polish Operation carried out by the NKVD, Stalin's secret police ('NKVD' was short for *Narodnyy Kommisariat Vnutrennikh Del*, 'National Home Security Committee') targeted, in 1937 and 1938, purported Polish agents in the Soviet Union. For NKVD, this action in reality targeted 'absolutely all Poles.' This campaign resulted in 139,835 Poles being convicted and 111,091 of them being executed (see: Wendy Z. Goldman, *Inventing the Enemy: Denunciation and Terror in Stalin's Russia*, Cambridge University Press, New York, 2011, p. 217). Many of those Poles lived in the westernmost parts of the Soviet Union, all of those being territories that used to be a part of the Commonwealth of the Kingdom of Poland and of the Grand Duchy of Lithuania. Persecution and extermination of Poles in the Soviet Union continued well after 1938. In March 1940, Stalin ordered the Katyń massacre of about 22,000 Polish officers, all of whom were prisoners of war who obeyed their command's order to surrender to the Soviets after they treacherously attacked Poland from the east on September 17, 1939, as the Polish Army fought the superior power of Germany's Wehrmacht and Luftwaffe advancing from the west. At that time, Germany was the Soviet Union's ally.

12 Hopes are still alive for his remains to be one day found buried in an unmarked grave somewhere within the "Łączka" sector of the Powązki Cemetery in Warsaw. By coincidence, it was within that very sector that Zofia Pilecka buried, in 1958, her baby daughter; at that time, that sector was still under development; it is possible that somewhere there, not far away from his granddaughter, there rest her heroic grandfather's remains.

13 Introduction to Norman Davies, to *The Auschwitz Volunteer: Beyond Bravery*, Aquila Polonica, California, 2012, page XIII.

14 This author very much hopes that the circumstances of his life, most significantly thirty years he has already spent as a migrant in Australia, a country where so many diverse cultures can be observed on a daily basis, have put him in a good stead whenever he needed to look at Poland's history and culture in a broader context, often through outsiders' eyes.

15 Contents of this chapter are not a comprehensive discussion of Polish history. It is not this author's intention, by presenting his outlook on how the knowledge of his country's history would have impacted on Witold Pilecki's values and life's objectives, to enter into debate with scholars from the respective areas of historical studies. The sole purpose of this chapter is to make it possible for readers less familiar with the history of Poland to gain a better insight into it, so as to help them better understand the motives behind Witold Pilecki's actions and decisions.

16 The Polish Legions' song beginning with the phrase '*Jeszcze Polska nie zginęła, póki my żyjemy...*' ['Poland has not died as long as we live...'] became in 1927 the new hymn of independent Poland. It is known as *Dąbrowski Masurka*, after General Jan Henryk Dąbrowski, the Legions' founding father. The words of this hymn remind all Poles of their duty to treasure, and be ready to fight for the freedom of their country.

17 The Austro-Hungarian Empire was formed as a dual monarchy of Austria and Hungary according to the treaty signed between its two parties in 1867; in effect, Austria and Hungary had until 1918 the same monarch, but separate two governments, parliaments, justice systems and law systems. The new monarchy replaced its forerunner, the Austrian Empire, one of the countries that took part in the partitioning of the Commonwealth of Poland and Lithuania.

18 In 1871, Germany became one state after it integrated almost all German-speaking smaller states, including Kingdom of Prussia, one of three countries that at the end of the eighteenth century partitioned the Commonwealth of Poland and Lithuania. The only German-speaking state that remained a separate entity was the Austro-Hungarian Empire. Until November 28, 1918, the day on which the last Hohenzollern ruler Wilhelm II abdicated, Germany had an Emperor as its head of state.

19 Stanisław Sopicki, *Krzyż i Orzeł Biały*, Londyn, 1966, p. 15.

20 Abraham ben Jacob (or: Ibrahim ibn Jacob), a tenth-century traveller, probably a merchant; excerpts from his memoirs covering his journeys have been preserved for posterity in works of various authors. His is the first reliable description of the Polish state under Mieszko I.

21 The name of Bohemia refers to the western and central parts of the territory of today's Czech Republic while the Czech Republic's easternmost part has for thirteen centuries been known under the name of Moravia.

22 Jerzy Kłoczowski, *A History of Polish Christianity*, Cambridge: Cambridge University Press, 2000, pp. 10–13.

23 Stanisław Sopicki, *Krzyż i Orzeł Biały*, Londyn, 1966, p.11.

24 Juliusz Bardach, Bogusław Leśnodorski and Michał Pietrzak, *Historia państwa i prawa polskiego*, Państwowe Wydawnictwo Naukowe, Warszawa, 1987, pp. 53–54.

25 Louis E. Van Norman, *Poland: The Knight Among Nations*, New York: Fleming H. Revell Company, Grand Rapids, 1907, p. 18. The phrase *antemurale christianitatis* was coined, and for the first time used, in 1519 by Pope Leo X in reference to Croatia, on whose soil the advancement of the Ottoman Empire was stopped shortly before.

26 *Śluby króla Jana Kazimierza i Stanów Rzeczypospolitej zaprzysiężone imieniem narodu przed cudownym obrazem N. P. Łaskawej w Katedrze Lwowskiej a dotyczące polepszenia doli ludu pracującego oraz czci Najśw. Panny jako Królowej Korony Polskiej do wykonywania których to ślubów każdy miłujący Boga i Ojczyznę przyczyniać się winien*, Lwów, 1887.

27 The English translation – '*Paradise for Jews.*'

28 His exact statement in Polish is reported as: '*Jeśliby Bóg nie dał Żydom Polski jako schronienia, los Izraela byłby rzeczywiście nie do zniesienia*', see: Bernard Weinryb, *The Jews of Poland. A Social Economic History of the Jewish Community in Poland from 1100 to 1800*, Philadelphia: The Jewish Publication Society of America, Philadelphia, 1972, p. 166.

29 The unification document states, among others, this (in translation into English): '*Kingdom of Poland and the Grand Duchy of Lithuania form one inseparable body, and it becomes one uniform Commonwealth of two states and nations, that become one.*' To avoid any misconceptions, one needs to explain here that in the sixteenth century, a nation usually meant a political entity and not an entity that shared common customs, language and culture. People who lived outside this Commonwealth would generally identify its entire nation as Polish. This does not mean that all Commonwealth residents would at that time identify themselves as Poles. Many Commonwealth residents at that time spoke German, Russian, Lithuanian, or Yiddish. Apart from Catholicism, many other religions could be found on Polish soil. Some people were Russian Orthodox, some Jewish, some Lutheran, some Calvinist, some - Muslim. In 1569, the Commonwealth of Poland and Lithuania included also four fief territories: Duchy of Prussia, Duchy of Courland, and two tiny principalities at its north-western perimeter, namely, Lębork and Bytów (*Polska Wielka Księga Historii* (eds. Andrzej Nowak, Monika Karolczuk, Piotr Budny, Zuzanna Dawidowicz, Henryk Głębocki, Agnieszka Pałac, Anna Śledzikowska), Krakow: Kluszczyński, 2012, p.242).

30 See: http://www.jewishmuseum.org.pl/en/wystawy-wystawa-glowna-galerie/paradisus-iudaeorum

31 The Yotvingians were a Baltic tribe with close cultural ties to the Lithuanians and Prussians. As a separate distinctive ethnic entity, the tribe ceased to exist in the sixteenth century.

32 Four centuries later, when the merger of the Margravate of Brandenburg with Ducal Prussia was accomplished (a few relevant details are provided later), the new state of Prussia, a core of the later Germany, developed further aspirations. A century after that, such aspirations culminated in Prussia becoming one of the three countries to partition the Commonwealth of Poland and Lithuania.

33 Jean W. Sedlar, 'Law and Justice', in *East Central Europe in the Middle Ages, 1000-1500,* University of Washington Press, Seattle, 1994, p. 328.

34 An excerpt from a letter by the Archbishop of Gniezno, Jakub Świnka, to the Pope (Sopicki, op.cit. p. 49).

35 A resolution reached by the synod of Łęczyca in January 1285 (Sopicki, op.cit., p. 49).

36 J. Baszkiewicz, *Polska czasów Łokietka,* Wiedza Powszechna, Warszawa, 1968.

37 Later in this chapter, there is a brief mention of the plans, made as early as the late fourteenth century by some of Poland's then most aggressive neighbours, to annex the entirety of Poland's territory.

38 *Polska Wielka Księga Historii*, op.cit., pp.136-138.

39 *Polska Wielka Księga Historii*, op.cit., pp. 154-156.

40 This matter is referred to, in some detail, in the subchapter below titled 'Wars against the Teutonic Knights Order.'

41 Its official Latin name is: *Ordo domus Sanctæ Mariæ Theutonicorum Hierosolymitanorum.*

42 This Order exists to this day. Today, however, it is a purely religious Catholic order.

43 *Polska Wielka Księga Historii*, op.cit., p.87

44 The Crusader Kingdom of Jerusalem was established in 1099, and survived until 1291, even though Jerusalem was lost for Christians already in 1244; afterwards, the Kingdom's capital was moved to Akka; whilst the Teutonic Knights Order retained its presence in the Holy Land until 1291, its main final stage place of residence was the castle of Montfort, the construction of which commenced in 1227-8 (see: Tadeusz Manteuffel, *Historia Powszechna. Średniowiecza,* PWN, Warszawa, 1999).

45 'The Jerosolimitan' meaning - 'of Jerusalem'.

46 The king famously explained his decision with these words: 'The Teutonic Knights on the Hungarian soil are like a fire in your breast, a mouse in your rucksack, a viper in your lap!', *Polska Wielka Księga Historii*, Kluszczyński, Cracow 2012, p.87).

47   The Holy Roman Empire was a multi-ethnic complex of territories in central Europe that was established during the Middle Ages and continued until its dissolution in 1806. The core and largest territory of the empire was the Kingdom of Germany; over long periods the Empire also included other territories, such as the Kingdom of Italy, the Kingdom of Bohemia, the Kingdom of Burgundy, as well as many other ones. The emperor's supreme power was seen as the continuation of the position previously held by the emperors of ancient Rome. While all Holy Roman Emperors were elected, elections were usually controlled by various dynasties. The German prince-electors who were the highest ranking noblemen of the empire usually elected one of their peers as 'The King of the Romans'; he would later be crowned Emperor by the Pope; the tradition of papal coronations was however discontinued in the sixteenth century. This Empire had never been truly unified; instead, it evolved into a decentralised, limited elective monarchy composed of virtually hundreds of principalities, duchies, counties, Free Imperial Cities, and other types of domains. While princes, lords, and kings of the empire were vassals and owed the Emperor their allegiance, they also enjoyed certain privileges that afforded them *de facto* sovereignty over their territories (see: James Bryce, *The Holy Roman Empire*, The MacMillan Company, London, 1913; *The Holy Roman Empire*, Heraldica.org.; Tadeusz Manteuffel, *Historia Powszechna. Średniowiecze*, PWN, Warszawa, 1999).

48   In fact, this papal Bulla was issued in 1235 but was, at the Order's request, backdated by the Emperor to 1226 (see T. Jasiński, "Złota Bulla Fryderyka II dla zakonu krzyżackiego z roku rzekomo 1226', *Roczniki Historyczne*, 1994).

49   Livonia is the mediaeval name of the territory of contemporary Latvia; it lies north of Prussia; and it was Christianised earlier than Prussia.

50   Later, its German name became - Danzig.

51   *Polska Wielka Księga Historii*, op.cit., p.132; the castle's German name is – Marienburg.

52   Sigismund of Luxemburg (1368 – 1437) was Prince-Elector of Brandenburg from 1378 until 1388 and, from 1411 until 1415, King of Hungary and Croatia from 1387, King of Bohemia from 1419, and Holy Roman Emperor for four years from 1433 until 1437. He was also King of Italy from 1431, and of Germany from 1411. In 1392, he presented to his allies a plan to divide Poland between the German Reich, the Teutonic Knights Order, Hungary and Moravia. His plan, interestingly, was not accepted by the Teutonic Knights Order, at that time his close ally. In 1410, shortly after the decisive battle of Grunwald, in which Poland routed the Teutonic Knights Order army, King Sigismund's army made an incursion into southern Poland. This forced some Polish army units which were moving north aiming to capture all Teutonic Knights castles, and bring their entire state under Poland's control, to be hurriedly redirected south. As a result of that incursion, Poland was not able to achieve in 1410 its strategic objective of regaining the possession of the entire territory which had been taken over by the Teutonic Knights Order in defiance of their agreements with Dukes of Masovia (see: Claude Michaud, 'The Kingdoms of Central Europe in the Fourteenth Century', in: Michael Jones, *New Cambridge Medieval History, Vol. VI. c.1300–c.1415*. Cambridge: CUP, 2000, pp. 735–63).

53 Nearly four hundred years later, the Kingdom of Prussia (which can be thought of as a transformed, and much larger, version of the Teutonic Knights' former state), was able to subdue Poland, aided in doing so by Russia and Austria, and to partition its territory.

54 The League's main purpose was to protect its own economic interests and diplomatic privileges in the cities and countries of that region, as well as along shared trade routes. In addition to having its own legal system, the League kept its own army of soldiers for protection and mutual aid.

55 *Polska Wielka Księga Historii*, op.cit., p.161.

56 Albrecht was born in Ansbach in Franconia, as the third son of Friedrich I, Margrave of Brandenburg-Ansbach. His mother was Sophia, daughter of Kazimierz [Casimir] IV Jagiellończyk, King of Poland and Grand Duke of Lithuania, and Elisabeth of Austria. Polish King Zygmunt I the Old was Albrecht's maternal uncle.

57 Albrecht died in 1568, having ruled for fifty-eight years; because of his great success in that role, he is regarded by many as the father of the Prussian nation, for without his contribution the unification of Germany in 1870 would not have possible in the form it then took (see: Walther Hubatsch, *Albrecht von Brandenburg-Ansbach. Deutschordens-Hochmeister und Herzog in Preußen 1490–1568*, Köln/Berlin: Grote, 1965).

58 Bromberg's Polish name is Bydgoszcz.

59 Their Polish geographic names are '*ziemia lęborska i bytowska*' (names derived from their respective main towns of Lębork and Bytów).

60 Wars against these three foreign powers had very different origins. In the case of the Ottoman Empire, Poland was simply defending its territory against the expanding Moslem Empire which sought to conquer new territories in Central and South-Eastern Europe, and introduce Islam there as the ruling religion. In the case of Sweden, the warfare had two causes: first, the Polish monarchy's claim to the Swedish throne (Zygmunt III Vasa had, from 1594 to 1599, been King of Sweden - then, his Catholicism made him unacceptable to his predominantly Lutheran Swedish subjects); second, Sweden had at that time very ambitious plans to annex territories it faced across the Baltic Sea. In the case of Russia, Poland grew concerned about Russia's growing power, its very considerable ambitions and dangerous foreign alliances; Russia claimed to be representing the interests of Orthodox minorities within predominantly Catholic Poland, minorities particularly dominant in the Commonwealth's eastern regions.

61 *Polska Wielka Księga Historii*, op.cit., p.247.

62 Under the Statutes issued by the King Kazimierz III the Great, the service in the Polish military was obligatory for all knights-landowners under the penalty of land confiscation. More wealthy knights provided a lances fournies unit (known in Poland as *kopijnicy*) while the less prosperous ones served as light horseman, or even infantryman. They were obliged to take arms and defend the country, as well as to participate in wars fought in foreign lands. *Pospolite ruszenie* could have been called by the king, or in his absence and when in dire need, from the 14th century, by the *starost* of the affected territory. As knights (later, the nobility - '*szlachta'*) were accumulating more and more privileges, the rules for the *pospolite ruszenie*. changed (for more details, see: Juliusz Bardach, Bogusław Leśnodorski, and Michał Pietrzak, *Historia państwa i prawa polskiego*, Państwowe Wydawnictwo Naukowe, Warsaw, 1987, p.113-114; *ibidem*, p.91-92).

63 Adam Szelągowski, *Wzrost państwa polskiego w XV i XVI w. Polska na przełomie wieków średnich i nowych*, B. Połoniecki, Lwów, 1904, pp. 318–321.

64 Brian L. Davies, *Warfare, State and Society on the Black Sea Steppe, 1500-1700*, Routledge, London, 2007.

65 *Polska Wielka Księga Historii*, op.cit., p.241.

66 Krzysztof Bauer, *Uchwalenie i obrona Konstytucji 3 Maja*, Wydawnictwa Szkolne i Pedagogiczne, 1991, p.9.

67 Polish parliament's official name is *Sejm*.

68 *Jure uxoris* is a legal term in Latin that means 'by right of [his] wife.' It usually refers to a man whose wife holds a royal title and in her own right rules over a territory. According to the principle of *jure uxoris*, husband of an heiress to throne becomes a co-ruler of all of her kingdom's territories. *Jure uxoris* monarchs are not to be confused with king's consorts, who are not co-rulers.

69 His full regal title was: 'Stephen, by God's grace King of Poland, Grand Duke of Lithuania, Duke of Ruthenia, Prussia, Masovia, Samogitia, Kiev, Volyn, Podlachia, Livonia and Transylvania.'

70 Jerzy Besala and Agnieszka Biedrzycka, 'Stefan Batory', in: *Polski Słownik Biograficzny*, 2004-2005, XLIII, pp. 118-119.

71 Daniel Stone, *The Polish-Lithuanian State, 1386-1795*, University of Washington Press, Seattle, 2001, p. 125.

72 Jerzy Besala and Agnieszka Biedrzycka, op.cit., p. 119.

73 Ibidem, p.124.

74 Jerzy Besala and Agnieszka Biedrzycka, op.cit., p. 124.

75 Jerzy Besala and Agnieszka Biedrzycka, op.cit., p. 120.

76 Ibidem, p. 119; Muscovy was the name used until the mid-sixteenth century for the state ruled by Grand Dukes; after it increased its territory several times under Ivan the Terrible, it assumed today's name of Russia, and its ruler acquired the title of a tsar. Accordingly, Russia's first tsar was Ivan.

77 Maureen Perrie, and Andrei Pavlov, *Ivan the Terrible (Profiles in Power)*. Longman, London, 2003.

78 In 1562, in Vilnius, Katarzyna married Swedish Crown Prince Jan, Prince of Finland. In 1569, Jan and Katarzyna were crowned King, and Queen, of Sweden (for more details see: Stanisław Rosik, Przemysław Wiszewski, *Wielki poczet polskich królów i książąt*, Wydawnictwo Uniwersytetu Wrocławskiego, Wrocław 2006, s. 923).

79 His full regal title was: 'Zygmunt III, by the grace of God, king of Poland, grand duke of Lithuania, Ruthenia, Prussia, Masovia, Samogitia, Livonia, and also hereditary king of the Swedes, Goths and Vandals.'

80 See: Mirosław Nagielski, "Stanisław Żółkiewski herbu Lubicz', in: *Hetmani Rzeczypospolitej Obojga Narodów*, Bellona, Warszawa, 1995, pp. 135-136, and Leszek Podhorodecki, *Sławne bitwy Polaków*, Mada, Warszawa, 1997.

81 See: Henryk Wisner, *Król i car: Rzeczpospolita i Moskwa w XVI i XVII wieku*, Warsaw: Książka i Wiedza, 1995.

82 See:Tomasz Bohun, *Moskwa 1612*, Bellona, Warszawa, 2005 and Andrzej Nowak, 'Polacy na Kremlu', *Wprost*, Nr 1182 (31 July, 2005).

83 Young Polish Crown Price Władysław ruled as Russia's Tsar from 1610 till 1612; the title of Tsar of Russia he used however till 1634, even though Russia since 1613 had Mikhail I, the first from the Romanov dynasty, as its Tsar; *Polska Wielka Księga Historii*, op.cit., p.277.

84 Andrzej Nowak, "The Russo-Polish Historical Confrontation', *The Sarmatian Review*, January 1997, Volume XVII, No 1.

85 *Poradlne* was subsequently reduced from twelve to two *grosze* for one *feud*, leading to a dramatic reduction in the Crown's revenue. More and more, the Crown came to depend on the Sejm allocating funds required for the upkeep, modernisation and enlargement of the Polish army.

86 After 1569, his (short) title became 'King of the Commonwealth of Poland and Lithuania.'

87 The first such contract was signed by King Henryk Walezy at his 1573 election; according to it, the king was to:
- pay for 100 Polish noblemen's education in Paris,
- pay off the debts left by King Zygmunt August,
- preserve the Polish-French alliance,
- provide several thousand infantrymen for the war against Ivan the Terrible,
- bring eminent overseas scholars to the Jagiellonian University (called at the time *Akademia Krakowska*),
- from its own estate, provide each year 450 thousand ducats to pay for the Commonwealth's needs,
- dispatch French warships to patrol the Baltic Sea,
- rebuild the Polish Fleet, and
- to renovate *Akademia Krakowska*.

88 The preamble of the *Nihil novi sine communi consensu* Bill [*Nothing new without everyone's consent*] stipulates (the following is an English translation of the original Latin): 'Whereas general laws and public acts pertain not to an individual but to the nation at large, wherefore at this General Sejm held at Radom we have, together with all our kingdom's prelates, councils and land deputies, determined it to be fitting and just, and have so resolved, that henceforth for all time to come nothing new shall be resolved by us or our successors, without the common consent of the senators and the land deputies, that shall be prejudicial, or onerous to the Commonwealth [or "Republic"], or harmful and injurious to anyone, or that would tend to alter the general law and public liberty.'

89 This high percentage is a result of a very large numbers of Poles having been knighted in reward for gallantry when defending their country; this is a testimony to the gallantry of Poles, and it also reflects the multitude of wars Poles had to fight, largely - as a result of the geopolitical location of their country. In 1576, the right to ennoble, except at wartime, was transferred from the King onto the Sejm. (Robert Bideleux; Ian Jeffries, *A History of Eastern Europe: Crisis and Change*, Psychology Press, 28 January 1998, pp. 146–148).

90 Their original term in Polish: '*Artykuły henrykowskie*.'

91 Zygmunt II August was the only exception from this rule - he was elected as the next king of Poland in 1529, as his father Zygmunt I the Old was still alive, and ruled; this came about because of his mother Queen Bona Sforza's insistence on their son's *vivente rege* election.

92 See: Juliusz Bardach, Bogusław Leśnodorski and Michał Pietrzak, *Historia państwa i prawa polskiego*, Państwowe Wydawnictwo Naukowe, Warszawa, 1987, pp. 216–7; *Artykuły henrykowskie*, Trybunał Konstytucyjny, Wszechnica Konstytucyjna, and Jacek Jędruch, *Constitutions, elections, and legislatures of Poland, 1493–1977: a guide to their history*, EJJ, New York,1998, pp. 84–86.

93 Wacław Sobieski, *Trybun ludu szlacheckiego*, PIW, Warszawa, 1978, p.60.

94 Paweł Jasienica, *Polska anarchia*, Wydawnictwo Literackie, Kraków, 1988; the *viritim* election was finally abolished in 1791, a mere four years before the final partition of Poland by three absolute powers takes place.

95 See: Juliusz Bardach, Bogusław Leśnodorski, and Michał Pietrzak, *Historia państwa i prawa polskiego*, Państwowe Wydawnictwo Naukowe, Warszawa 1987, p.223; Norman Davies, *Europe: A History*, Harper Collins UK, 1998, p. 659; Paweł Jasienica, *Polska anarchia*; Jacek Jędruch, *Constitutions, elections, and legislatures of Poland, 1493–1977: a guide to their history*, EJJ Books, New York, 1998, pp. 117–119; Barbara Markiewicz, "Liberum veto, albo o granicach społeczeństwa obywatelskiego" [in:] *Obywatel: odrodzenie pojęcia*, Wydawnictwo Naukowe Scholar, Warszawa, 1993; Piotr Stefan Wandycz, *The price of freedom: a history of East Central Europe from the Middle Ages to the present*, Routledge, New York, 2001, pp. 103–104.

96 *Polska Wielka Księga Historii*, op.cit., p.249.

97 Anna Pasterak, *Przywileje szlacheckie*, Pedagogiczny Uniwersytet, Kraków, 2004.

98 Robert Bideleux and Ian Jeffries, *A History of Eastern Europe: Crisis and Change*. Psychology Press, 28 January 1998, pp. 146–154.

99 Fernand Braudel, *Civilisation and Capitalism: The Perspective of the World*, Harper and Row, New York, 1984, p.54.

100 Robert Bideleux and Ian Jeffries, op.cit., pp. 146–154.

101 *Polska Wielka Księga Historii*, op.cit., p.381.

102 S. C. Tucker, *A Global Chronology of Conflict*, Vol.2, ABC-CLIO, LLC, Santa Barbara, 2010, p.657

103 M.Varvounis, *Jan Sobieski*, Xlibris, Bloomington, IN., 2012, p.129.

104 S.C. Tucker, op.cit., pp.656-659.

105 S.C. Tucker, op.cit., p. 660.

106 N. Davies, *God's Playground, a History of Poland: The origins to 1795*, Columbia University Press, 1982, p. 487.

107 The exact Polish Order of Battle and Strength Reports, as of August 1, 1683, cited after http://en.wikipedia.org/wiki/Battle_of_Vienna

108 B. A. Masters, G. Ágoston, *Encyclopedia of the Ottoman Empire*, Facts on File Infobase Publishing, New York, 2009, p.584.

109 S.C. Tucker, op.cit., p. 660.

110 M.Varvounis, op.cit., p. 152.

111 S.C. Tucker, op.cit., p.661.

112 S.C. Tucker, op.cit., p.661.

113 This phrase has since been used when referring to swift and conclusive victories.

114 S.C. Tucker, op.cit., p.661.

115 Each of its signatories had a black eagle as its state symbol.

116 Corwin, Edward Henry Lewinski, *The political History of Poland*, Polish Book Importing Company, New York, 1917.

117 Herbert Tuttle, and Herbert Baxter Adams, *History of Prussia*, Houghton, Mifflin and Company, Boston, 1883, pp. 369–371.

118 Aleksander Gieysztor *et al.*, *History of Poland*, PWN, Warsaw, 1979, p. 244.

119 László Károly Marácz, *Expanding European unity: Central and Eastern Europe*, Rodopi, Amsterdam, 1999, p.134

120 Corwin, Edward Henry Lewinski, op.cit., p.286-288.

121 Hugh Ragsdale, *Imperial Russian foreign policy*, Cambridge University Press, Cambridge, 1993, pp. 32–33.

122 Corwin, Edward Henry Lewinski, op.cit., p.286-288.

123 William Macpherson (editor), 'Chapter CXXXIII Annals of France, from the Accession of Louis XV, to the Period following the Peace of Aix-la-Chapelle' *Encyclopaedia Metropolitana Volume XIII: History and Biography Volume 5* B, Fellowes, London, 1845, p. 144.

124 J. O. Lindsay, *The New Cambridge Modern History,* Cambridge University Press, 1957, p. 205.

125 Corwin, Edward Henry Lewinski, op.cit., p.286-288.

126 J. O. Lindsay, op.cit., p. 205.

127 Hamish M. Scott, *The Emergence of the Eastern Powers, 1756–1775*, Cambridge University Press, 2001, pp.181-182.

128 Richard Butterwick, *Poland-Lithuania's Last King and English Culture: Stanisław August Poniatowski, 1732–1798*, Oxford University Press, 1998, p.169.

129 Hamish M. Scott, op.cit., pp.181-182.

130 "Partitions of Poland", Encyclopædia Britannica Online, 2008.

131 It was the first Department of Education ever established in Europe.

132 *Polska Wielka Księga Historii,* op. cit., p.397.

133 *ibidem*, p.395.

134 Andrzej Tadeusz Bonawentura Kościuszko (*Andrew Thaddeus Bonaventure Kościuszko* (February 4 or 12, 1746 – October 15, 1817) - famous Polish military engineer, general, and a national hero of both the Commonwealth of Poland and Lithuania, and of the United States. Kościuszko was born in February 1746 in the Polish–Lithuanian Commonwealth, in a village which is now in Belarus. In 1768, he moved to France in 1769 to pursue further studies. He returned to Poland in 1774, two years after the First Partition. In 1776, he moved to North America, where he took part in the American Revolutionary War as a colonel in the Continental Army. An accomplished military architect, he designed and oversaw the construction of state-of-the-art fortifications, including those at West Point. In recognition of his outstanding service, the Continental Congress promoted him in 1783 to the rank of Brigadier General. In 1784, he returned to Poland. In 1789, he received a Major-General commission with the Polish–Lithuanian Commonwealth Army. Two years after the Polish–Russian War of 1792 which had brought the Second Partition of Poland, in March 1794, he called for an uprising against Russia. Severely wounded in the Battle of Maciejowice in October 1794, he was taken prisoner of war, and later imprisoned at Sankt Petersburg. In 1796, following the death of Tsaritsa Catherine the Great, Kościuszko was pardoned by Tsar Paul I. Subsequently, he migrated to the United States. A close friend of Thomas Jefferson with whom he shared human rights ideals, Kościuszko wrote a last will in which he dedicated all his American assets to the purpose of providing education, and to the freeing all US slaves. He eventually returned to Europe and lived in Switzerland until his death in 1817 (see: Bartłomiej Szyndler, *Tadeusz Kościuszko, 1746–1817,* Bellona, Warszawa, 1991).

135 *Polska Wielka Księga Historii,* op.cit., p.439.

136 The official Russian position (e.g.: Sergey Solovyov, *History of the Downfall of Poland*, Moscow, 1863) and Nicholas V. Riasanovsky,'*Old Russia, the Soviet Union and Eastern Europe*', *American Slavic and East European Review*, Vol. 11, No. 3. (Oct., 1952), pp. 171–188) was that partitions of the Commonwealth were justified, since the Polish-Lithuanian Commonwealth had allegedly irreversibly degenerated as a result of the prolonged *liberum veto* abuse, making any thorough financial and social reform virtually impossible. Russians emphasised historical interconnections between Belarus, Ukraine and Russia as former parts of the mediaeval Russian state, where the dynasty of Rurikids reigned (Kievan Rus).

Many nineteenth-century contemporaries from Western Europe held different views: British jurist Sir Robert Phillimore (*Commentaries Upon International Law*, 1854 T. & J. W. Johnson, p. 819) considered these partitions a violation of international law; German jurist Heinrich Bernhard Oppenheim (*The Right of Conquest: The Acquisition of Territory by Force in International Law and Practice*, Oxford University Press, 1996, p.101) represented a similar view. The legality of the Commonwealth's partitions was challenged by, among others, French historian Jules Michelet, British historian and politician Thomas Babington Macaulay, 1st Baron Macaulay, and (earlier) Edmund Burke. Burke regarded these partitions as immoral (Sharon Korman, *The Right of Conquest: The Acquisition of Territory by Force in International Law and Practice*, Oxford University Press, 1996).

Others (eg. Norman Davies, *Europe: A History*, Oxford University Press, 1996, p.661) claim that the second and third partition took place after the Commonwealth started showing signs of recovery, and that they were undertaken with a clear intention to prevent the Commonwealth from recovering its former position of a regional power.

137 *Polska Wielka Księga Historii*, op.cit., p. 445.

138 See: Lonnie R. Johnson, *Central Europe: Enemies, Neighbours, Friends*, Oxford University Press, 1996, pp.127-128, and Piotr Stefan Wandycz, *The Price of Freedom: A History of East Central Europe from the Middle Ages to the Present*, Routledge, New York, 2001, p.133.

139 W. H. Zawadzki, *A Man of Honour: Adam Czartoryski as a Statesman of Russia and Poland, 1795–1831*, Oxford University Press, 1993, p.330, and Stefan Auer, *Liberal Nationalism in Central Europe*, Routledge, London, 2004, p.60

140 Jan Henryk Dąbrowski and Karol Kniaziewicz are two best-known commanders of these Legions.

141 During the Congress, Great Britain supported the idea of restoration of an independent Polish state (*Polska Wielka Księga Historii*, op.cit., p. 452).

142 In Polish – *Wiosna Ludów*.

143 Hungary was then placed under ferocious martial law; Kossuth and Bem both went into exile, which in Kossuth's case lasted for more than four decades; and the Austrian government was restored with full powers, which were vested in the young Emperor Franz Josef. Passive resistance of the Hungarian nation after the revolution's failure would eventually lead to the Austro-Hungarian Compromise (1867) and the birth of the Austro-Hungarian, as opposed to the purely Austrian, Empire.

144 They all had five common factors: widespread dissatisfaction with political leadership; demands for more participation in government and democracy; demands for freedom of press; the demands of the working classes; the upsurge of nationalism; and finally, the regrouping of the reactionary forces based on the royalty, the aristocracy, the army, and the peasants (R.J.W. Evans and Hartmut Pogge von Strandmann, eds. *The Revolutions in Europe 1848–1849*, 2000, pp. v. 4). See also: Lynn Hunt, *The Making of the West*: Volume C, pp. 683–684.

145 Norman Davies, *Europe: A History*, Oxford University Press, 1996, p. 828.

146 Piotr S. Wandycz, *The lands of partitioned Poland. 1795-1918*, University of Washington Press, Seattle, 1974.

147 Great War was the original name of World War I. It broke out on July 28, 1914, after the assassination by Serbian students in Sarajevo of Archduke Franz Ferdinand of Austria.

148 The now legendary First Cadre Company (its Polish name: *Pierwsza Kompania Kadrowa*) was a forerunner to the Polish Legions of the Great War, and became the core of their First Brigade.

149 Central Powers included: Germany, Austria-Hungary, the Ottoman Empire (since August 2,1914, and Bulgaria (since September 6, 1915).

150 *Polska Wielka Księga Historii*, op.cit., p.590.

151 *Polska Wielka Księga Historii*, op.cit., p.591.

152 Richard Pipes, David Brandenberger, and Catherine A. Fitzpatrick, *The Unknown Lenin: From The Secret Archive*, Yale University Press, New Haven, Connecticut, 1999, pp. 6-7.

153 Richard M. Watt, *Bitter Glory: Poland and Its Fate, 1918-1939*, Simon & Schuster, New York City, 1979, p.126.

154 Its Lithuanian name is: Nemunas, its Byelorussian one is Nioman, its Russian one is Neman, and its German one is Memel.

155 Lech Wyszczelski, *Wojna o Kresy Wschodnie 1918-1921*, Bellona, Warszawa, 2011.

156 The value of this reparation is expressed bearing into account the exchange rate of ruble in 1921.

157 Thomas à Kempis, *The Imitation of Christ*, The Bruce Publishing Group, Milwaukee, 1940, p.13.

158 *Leliwa* is one of the most widely held coats of arms among the Polish nobility; many of these families originated from the region of Lesser Poland (Polish: Małopolska); later, this coat of arms was also held by many from the nobility who lived in Lithuania; among them were Mickiewicz and Sienkiewicz families from which came one of the greatest Polish poets, Adam Mickiewicz, and the first Polish Nobel Prize laureate in literature, Henryk Sienkiewicz.

159 In the Kingdom of Poland, voivodes were governors of provinces. Castellans, in turn, governed castles, their power often extending upon the inhabitated territory surrounding the castle, even entire towns. Starosts in Poland were appointed by Kings as administrators of crown land territories or districts.

160 Pilica is a river in central Poland. It is the longest left tributary of the Vistuls river.

161 He was sent to Tomsk, then moved to Tobolsk, finally – to Wiatka (pronounced *Vyatka*) from where he was finally released and allowed to return to Warsaw; see: Krzysztof Tracki, op.cit., pp.31-2.

162 Ibidem, p.33.

163 Ibidem, p.37.

164 According to K. Tracki, this date of Witold Pilecki's birth is the most likely of all that appear in various available documents, by no means, though, a certain one.

165 Krzysztof Tracki, op.cit., p.46.

166 Ibidem, p.48.

167 M.Pilecka, op.cit., pp. 34 and 36.

168 Krzysztof Tracki, op.cit., p.59.

169 Ibidem, p.62

170 Krzysztof Tracki, op.cit., p.52; as reported by Wacław Szukiewicz.

171 Ibidem, p.51. *Trilogy*'s parts are: *With Fire and Sword*, *The Deluge*, and *Wołodyjowski, Esq.*

172 Henryk Sienkiewicz (1846-1916) is best known outside Poland for his Nobel-winning 1896 novel *Quo Vadis*.

173 Ibidem, p.53.

174 Maria Pilecka, *Dzieje rodu Pileckich (Saga)* [manuscript], Poznań, 1983, p.26

175 Ibidem, p.27.

176 *Wspomnienia Eleonory Ostrowskiej*, APMO, v.179, p. 146.

177 Maria Pilecka. op.cit. 27.

178 Krzysztof Tracki, op.cit., p.62

179 Maria Pilecka, op.cit., p.47.

180 Ibidem, p.63

181 Ibidem, p.64

182 Maria Pilecka, op.cit., p.65.

183 Ibidem, p.66.

184 Translated into English: Polish Scouts Association.

185 August 1, 1907 is recognized as the date the worldwide Boden-Powell Scout Movement commenced.

186 Maria Pilecka, op.cit., p.69.

187 Ibidem, pp. 70-1.

188 Ibidem, p.71.
189 Ibidem, p.72.
190 Maria Pilecka, op.cit., p.74-5.
191 Maria Pilecka, op.cit., p.85.
192 Maria Pilecka, op.cit., p.88.
193 Krzysztof Tracki, op.cit. p.89.
194 Henryk Zieliński, *Historia Polski 1918-1939*, PWN, Warszawa, 1984, pp. 84–88.
195 L.Wyszczelski, *Wilno 1919-1920*, Bellona, Warszawa 2008, pp. 44-6.
196 Krzysztof Tracki, op.cit. p.92-3.
197 Ostra Brama, also known as Medininkai Gate, was built in the early sixteenth century as a part of Vilnius fortifications at the time the city was the capital of the Grand Duchy of Lithuania. It owes its name to its shape ('ostra' is a Polish word for 'sharp'). Today, it is the only remaining gate there: the other gates were destroyed by the Russian occupant at the end of the eighteenth century. The famous Chapel at Ostra Brama still houses the miraculous icon of the Blessed Virgin Mary. For several centuries the icon has been an object of veneration by both Roman Catholics and Orthodox. One of the greatest Polish poets, Adam Mickiewicz, in his *Sir Thaddeus'* Invocation, entrusts himself to the Blessed Virgin Mary of Ostra Brama.
198 W. Pilecki, *Wspomnienia*, v.179, p.2.
199 W. Pilecki, op.cit., p.2.
200 W. Wejtko, *Samoobrona Litwy i Białorusi*, p.44.
201 W. Wejtko, op.cit., p.55.
202 T. Strzembosz, *Saga o 'Łupaszce'*, p.22.
203 *Wspomnienia Eleonory Ostrowskiej*, APMO, v.179, p.147.
204 Uhlan was a soldier of Polish light cavalry formation popular at that time.
205 S. Aleksandrowicz, *Zarys historii wojennej 13 Pułku Ułanów Wileńskich*, Warszawa, 1928, pp.14-15.
206 The then official name of the German Army.
207 L.Grossfeld, *Polska a stosunki niemiecko-sowieckie 1918-1939*, Warszawa, 1988, p. 5; J. Centek, *Hans von Seeckt. Twórca Reichsheer. 1866-1936*, New Avalon, Kraków 2006, p.64.
208 May 3 was proclaimed, in 1919, a Polish national holiday, one to memorize the proclamation of the 1791 Constitution, on May 3 of that year.
209 Witold Pilecki, *Wspomnienia*, p.2.
210 Maria Pilecka, op.cit., p.73.
211 An excerpt from Witold Pilecki's letter to Kazimiera Dacz, written in Sukurcze, dated September 22, 1926.

212 J.A. Goclon, *W obronie Europy. Wojna z bolszewicką Rosją w 1920 r.*, Toruń, 2006, p.174.

213 M. Pilecka, op.cit., p.88; B. Waligóra, *Zajęcie Wilna przez generała Lucjana Żeligowskiego*, Warszawa, 1930, pp. 14-15, 17, 39 and 47-8.

214 W. Pilecki, op.cit., p.5.

215 Krzysztof Tracki, op.cit., p.137.

216 These final exams had the usual format of *matura*, which is a written and, sometimes also an oral exam in Polish and Mathematics, and, additionally, in one elective subject, selected by the student.

217 In late 1918, one American Dollar was buying about eight Polish marka, in late 1923, just before the Grabski currency reform, it was buying 6,375,000 Polish marka. On April 1, 1924, the marka was replaced by the zloty. The Grabski reform was named after Władysław Dominik Grabski, twice Poland's Prime Minister during the 1920s.

218 W.Pilecki, op.cit., p.6.

219 M.Pilecka, op.cit., pp.87-8.

220 At that time, by the terms of the Treaty of Riga, central Lithuania was joined with Poland, whereas western and eastern Lithuania formed a separate country, the country we now know as Lithuania, and one that was in the USSR's sights well before the tragic events of 1940.

221 T. Kawalec, *Związek Bezpieczeństwa Kraju*, Harcerska Spółka Wydawnicza, Wilno, 1922, pp. 8 and 17.

222 *Zaświadczenie Edmunda Galinata* [Edmund Galinat's testimony], Vilnius, 21.06.1926, APMO, v.223c, card 4.

223 See: Pilecki's letter of 22.12.1924, written in Vilnius, and addressed to Kazimiera Dacz.

224 From his letter, which was written in Lida, on 13.06.1924.

225 From his letter of 6 October 1925 to Kazimiera Dacz; it was written in Vilnius.

226 From Witold's letter of 31 March 1925 to Kazimiera Dacz.

227 In their number, there are Prawocheński, Winnicki, Mikołajczyk, Protaszewicz, Bagiński, Świackiewicz, Klecki, Jamontt, Jeśmian, Połowiński, Trzeciak and Jankowski families (see: Krzysztof Tracki, op.cit., p. 172).

228 An entry to Kazimiera Dacz's album, now in the private collection of a Vilnian, Ryšard Maceikianec (see Krzysztof Tracki, op.cit., p. 175, footnote 400).

229 Witold's undated letter to Kazimiera Dacz (Krzysztof Tracki, op.cit., p. 175-6).

230 Witold's letter of September 22, 1926 to Kazimiera Dacz.

231 Krzysztof Tracki, op.cit., p. 188.

232 This fragment from Pilecki's poem *Sukurcze* appears in '*Nazywał mnie swoją generałką*' a video from the interview by M. Bober, of Zofia Pilecka-Optułowicz, and her grandson Krzysztof Kosior, which was published in *Nasz Dziennik*, on 5.12.2009. As a complete poem, in Polish, it can be found in: Krzysztof Tracki, *Młodość Witolda Pileckiego*, Sic !, Warszawa, 2014, on pages 215-226.

233 The latter has been included at the end of this book, as Exhibit 58.

234 M.Pilecka, op.cit., pp.93-6.

235 *W.Pilecki, Wniosek awansowy*, CAW nr 2944 [*Witold Pilecki: Promotion Proposal*, Central Military Archive, File No 2944].

236 E. Ostrowska, *Wspomnienia* [Recollections], p.4.

237 Ibidem.

238 W. Pilecki, *Wspomnienia*, p.7.

239 M.Bober, op.cit.

240 Ibidem.

241 Ibidem.

242 M.Bober, op.cit.

243 From Witold Pilecki's letter of July 14, 1929, written in Baranowicze, to Kazimiera Dacz.

244 Marshal Edward Śmigły-Rydz ['ɛmigwɨ 'rɨdz] (March 11, 1886 – December 2, 1941), before 1922 known as Edward Rydz, from 1922 onward, after adding his WWI nom-de-guerre 'Śmigły' in front of his family surname, as Edward Śmigły-Rydz, a Polish Army commander during the Polish-Soviet War 1918-1920, in 1935 appointed General Inspector of the Polish Armed Forces, and in 1936 a Marshal of Poland. He was Commander-in-Chief of Poland's armed forces during the September 1939 campaign. Left Poland on September 17, 1939, together with President Ignacy Mościcki [pronounced *Mostitski*], and became interned in Romania. Also known as a gifted amateur painter, and a poet..

245 Adam Cyra, op.cit., p.27.

246 Its name in Polish was '*Rzeczpospolita Polska*', as is that of the current Polish state (1989-); these two can be distinguished by their numerals: the former is referred to as The Second Republic (*Druga Rzeczpospolita*), the latter – as The Third Republic (*Trzecia Rzeczpospolita*). *Rzeczpospolita* is a literal translation of the Latin term *Res publica* into Polish; *Commonwealth* signifies a political community of states which have either common history, or wish to want to more closely coordinate their future policies, in particular – the foreign ones; such communities are for the common good of all their member entities; in this book, we use the term of '*Commonwealth of Poland and Lithuania*'. The Polish term '*Pierwsza Rzeczpospolita*' is in common use whenever one refers to the Commonwealth of Poland and Lithuania, even though it was in fact a monarchy (*Królestwo* – in Polish).

247 The Treaty was signed on June 28, 1919, after five months of negotiations, and was ratified on January 10, 1920

248 See: *Treaty of Versailles, Articles 231, 232-5.*

249 Lauteiann, *Geschichten in Quellen*, Bd.6., p.129.

250 *League of Nations Treaty Series*, vol.19, pp.248-252.

251 Gordon H. Mueller, "Rapallo Reexamined: a New Look at Germany's Secret Collaboration with Russia in 1922." *Military Affairs* (1976) 40#3 pp.109-117 (inJSTOR).

252 *Polska Wielka Księga Historii*, op.cit. p. 631.

253 *Ibidem*, p.672.

254 *Ibidem*, p. 672.

255 In his book *The Rise and Fall of the Third Reich* William Shirer argues that Czechoslovakia would have been able to offer significant resistance to the German army. Shirer also believes, that Britain and France would have been able to quickly win the war against Germany had they launched it already in 1938. When visiting the Czech-built border fortifications in early October 1938, Hitler is reported (see: Joseph Goebbels diary, 2 Oct 1938, p. 2) as having remarked to his propaganda minister: *'we would have shed here a lot of blood'* and that *'it was fortunate that there had been no fighting'* between Germany and Czechoslovakia.

256 Martin Gilbert & Richard Gott, *The Appeasers*, Weidenfeld & Nicolson, London, 1967, p.178.

257 Tadeusz Siwek, *Statystyczni i niestatystyczni Polacy w Republice Czeskiej*, Wspólnota Polska.

258 Slovakia's three infantry divisions and other Slovak military units participated later, in September 1939, in Hitler's invasion of Poland.

259 William Shirer, op.cit.

260 M.Pilecka, op.cit., p. 96.

261 This foreknowledge gave an immensely significant military advantage to the Allies, as the outcome of the war would prove. Everything about this operation was long kept a secret from the general public. Not for three decades after the war would the existence of Enigma, and of the code-breakers, become popularly known.

262 David E. Murphy, *What Stalin Knew: The Enigma of Barbarossa*, Yale University Press, 2006, p.23.

263 In this address, Hitler said: (…) *'Destruction of Poland is our first objective. It is not about reaching a pre-determined line: it is about annihilating their army. Even if a war was to break out [later] in the West, the destruction of Poland is our first task. For the propaganda purposes, I will provide a cause for this war, never mind if it is going to be credible, or not. Nobody asks the victor if he told the truth, or not; in all matters to do with starting and running a war it is not the law but the victory that decides. Be ruthless, be cruel'* (see: Natalia Siergiejewna Lebiediewa, "Inwazja Armii Czerwonej: IV rozbiór Polski", in: Adam D. Rotfeld, Anatolij W. Torkunow (ed.) *Białe plamy – Czarne plamy. Sprawy trudne w relacjach polsko-rosyjskich (1918-2008)*, Warszawa, 2010, p.266.

264 This pact made it possible for both Germany and the Soviet Union to pursue their aggressive objectives. It made starting the war in 1939 a feasible and attractive territorial expansion option for both countries. It also decided the fate of all other countries it concerned, even beyond WWII. This pact provided Hitler an ally he needed to win his *Blitzkrieg* campaign and obliterate the Polish Army within weeks. On the other hand, it provided the Soviet Union with an opportunity to once again annex the same eastern territories of Poland that its predecessor, the Tsarist Russia, had annexed and controlled between 1795 and 1918. This pact made also the annexation by the Soviet Union of several other neighbouring countries possible. According to an American diplomat Charles Bohlen, as confirmed by the now de-classified correspondence between the Moscow US embassy and the then Secretary of State, Cordell Hull, the contents of the pact's secret protocol were known to the US government already on August 24, 1939 (see: Charles E. Bohlen: *Witness to history, 1929-1969*. Weidenfeld and Nicholson, London, 1973; *Foreign Relations of the United States 1939*, Washington 1956 vol.1 General, p.342, document 465); they were made available to the US ambassador to Moscow, Laurence Steinhardt, by the secretary of the German embassy in Moscow, Hans von Herwarth (see: Hans von Herwarth, *Między Hitlerem a Stalinem. Wspomnienia dyplomaty i oficera niemieckiego 1931-1945*, Bellona, Warszawa, 1992, p.260). The American government immediately passed on this information to the British Foreign Secretary, Lord Edward Halifax, who in turn promptly passed in on to the French Foreign Affairs Minister, Georges Bonnet. By the time the latter received this information, the French government had already obtained it, a day before, from a source close to Hans Lammers, the then Head of the Reich's Chancellery (see: Sławomir Dębski, Marek Kornat, "Polska nie była bierna. Siedemdziesiąta rocznica paktu Ribbentrop-Molotow", Gazeta Wyborcza, 21 August 2009),

265 *The text of the Nazi–Soviet Non-Aggression Pact of 23 August 1939*, Fordham.

266 M.Pilecka, op.cit., p.97.

267 Roger Manvell, Heinrich Fraenkel, *Heinrich Himmler: The SS, Gestapo, His Life and Career*, Skyhorse Publishing Inc. New York, 2007, p.76.

268 It is uncertain if, and to what extent, the German High Command's campaign length estimate took into consideration the military assistance promised by the Soviet Union under the Ribbentrop-Molotov pact; the date the Soviet Union would be able to attack Poland from the east was at that time still uncertain as to the Soviet-Japanese Molotov-Togo ceasefire agreement was signed over three weeks later, on 16 September 1939; one is inclined to assume that the main reason for the discrepancy between these two German estimates of the duration of the Polish campaign was the Soviet participation factor; see: H.R.Knickerbocker, *Is Tomorrow Hitler's? 200 Questions on the Battle of Mankind*, Reynal & Hitchcock, 1941, pp. 29–30.

269 The date for the full mobilisation of the Polish Army was changed from August 30 to August 31, under considerable pressure from the French and the British who appeared to be fearful of provoking Hitler; as a result, most of the Polish military units that were mobilised on August 31 could not reach their points of deployment, as per the order of the defence campaign, before the hostilities started; see: Paweł Wieczorkiewicz, *Historia polityczna Polski 1935-1945*, Ed. II, KiW, Warsaw 2006, p. 76.

270 A.J.P. Taylor, *A History of World War Two*, Octopus Books, London, 1974, p.35.

271 Stanley S. Seidner, *Marshal Edward Śmigły-Rydz Rydz and the defence of Poland*, New York, 1978, p.162.

272 At the Nuremberg Trials, German Field Marshal Alfred Jodl will reveal this: *'If we did not collapse already in the year 1939, this was due only to the fact that during the Polish campaign, approximately 110 French and British divisions in the West were held completely inactive against the 23 German divisions.' Trial of the Major War Criminals before the International Military Tribunal, XV*, Nuremberg, 1948. p. 350.

273 This decision by the French and British Prime Ministers turned out to be a monumental error of judgment on the part of these two Poland's allies. Rather than attack Germany when it was at its most vulnerable, unable to put up any significant resistance to a full-scale joint land attack by the French and British armies, they instead allowed Hitler more time in which to conquer most of the Europe in a piecemeal fashion, occupy most of France, launch ruthless sea and air warfare against Great Britain and, finally, attack the Soviet Union.

274 MI6 – United Kingdom's Secret Intelligence Service carries out covert overseas collection and analysis of intelligence.

275 NKVD: Narodnyy Komissariat Vnutrennikh Del (English: National Commissariat of Internal Affairs) was the interior ministry of the Soviet Union; its successor was KGB: Komitet Gosudarstvennoi Bezopasnosti (English: Committee for State Security). In 1963, Philby defected to the Soviet Union.

276 *Polskie Siły Zbrojne w II wojnie światowej*, V. 1, 'Kampania wrześniowa', Part 1, p. 94.

277 Nicholas Bethell, *Zwycięska wojna Hitlera. Wrzesień 1939*, Instytut Wydawniczy PAX, Warszawa. 1997, pp. 139-143.

278 W. Pilecki, *Wspomnienia*, k.8-9.

279 W. Pilecki, *op.cit.*, k.9.

280 W. Pilecki, *Wspomnienia*, k.9.

281 J. Kirchmayer, *Kampania wrześniowa*, Czytelnik, Łódź, 1946, p.106.

282 Kurt von Tippelskirch, *Geschichte des Zweiten Weltkriegs*, Athenäum Verlag, Bonn, 1956.

283 Stanley S. Seidner, "Reflections from Rumania and Beyond: Marshal Śmigły-Rydz Rydz in Exile', *The Polish Review* Vol. XXII, no. 2, 1977, pp. 29–51.

284 The author was unable to establish the first name of this officer.

285 Geoffrey Roberts, "The Soviet Decision for a Pact with Germany', *Soviet Studies*, Vol. 44, No. 1, 1992, pp. 57–78.

286 Stuart D. Goldman, *Nomonhan, 1939: The Red Army's Victory That Shaped World War II*, Naval Institute Press, 2012, pp. 163-4.

287 Tadeusz Piotrowski, *Poland's Holocaust: Ethnic Strife: Collaboration with Occupying Forces and Genocide in the Second Republic, 1918–1947*, Jefferson NC, 1998.

288 Stanley S. Seidner, "Reflections from Rumania and Beyond: Marshal Śmigły-Rydz Rydz in Exile', *The Polish Review* Vol. XXII, no. 2, 1977, pp. 29–51.

289 George Sanford, *Katyn and the Soviet Massacre of 1940: Truth, Justice And Memory*, Routledge, London, New York 2005, pp. 20-4.

290 "Seven Years War?', *TIME Magazine*, 2 October 1939.

291 Stanley S. Seidner, *Marshal Edward Śmigły-Rydz Rydz and the defence of Poland*, New York, 1978, pp.289–91.

292 W. Pilecki, op.cit., k.13.

293 W.J. Wysocki, *Rotmistrz Pilecki*, Rytm, Warszawa, 2012, p.32.

294 W. Pilecki, op.cit., k.13-14. Already in early 1940, Pilecki learned that Maria, showing understandable caution, had left Sukurcze with her children soon after the Soviets invaded eastern Poland. For some time, she and they hid in a secret refuge in nearby Krupa; and there she also continued, for as long as she could, her work as a schoolteacher. During the 1939-1940 Winter War, she was told her name was on a Soviet National Home Security Committee list of Poles who, if captured, would be sent to Siberia. Having learned about this, she left Krupa with the children and went to live with her sister, who was at Wołkowysk (pronounced *Volkovisk*). Afterwards, having been helped by family members to come closer to the Soviet-German demarcation line, she was eventually able to cross that line – with children in tow – on April 7, 1940. From there, she only needed only to travel a mere seven kilometres to her parents' home in Ostrów Mazowiecka.

295 See: Jan Karski, *Wielkie mocarstwa wobec Polski: 1919-1945 od Wersalu do Jałty*, PIW, Warsaw, 1992, p. 281, also: J.R.M. Butler, *History of the Second World War. United Kingdom Military Series, Grand Strategy*, Vol. II, September 1939 - June 1941, Her Majesty's Stationery Office, London, 1957, pp. 10-12, 55-56, 81. British liaison officer, Gen. Edmund Ironside, was very well acquainted with the French military plans of that time yet he found nothing there to indicate a plan by the French High Command to launch an early attack on the German Siegfried [defence fortifications] Line. When at Warsaw, he learned about the French assurances to Poles. He knew, they would not be carried out into reality. In his diary, he wrote then: '*The French lie to the Poles when they say they will attack* [Germans]. *There is no such a concept at all.*' He did not share this knowledge with his Polish colleagues, though. Maybe because he likewise had serious doubts about Great Britain's immediate readiness for war (see:*Time Unguarded: The Ironside Diaries, 1937-1940*, ed. Roderic Macleod & Denis Kelly, Constable, London 1962, pp. 78–85).

296 Władysław Pobóg-Malinowski, *Najnowsza historia polityczna Polski*, Vol. 3, Wydawnictwo Władysław Pobóg-Malinowski, Londyn, 1960, p. 51, note 40.

297 *Encyklopedia wojskowa*, PWN and Bellona, Warszawa 2007, pp. 405-406 (vol. 1).

298 Tim Ripley, *The Wehrmacht. The German Army in World War II 1939-1945*, Routledge, New York 2013, p.50-67.

299 Some circumstances of this air catastrophe are still not known. The full report from this catastrophy is still a top secret British document.

300 Gregor Dallas, *1945: the war that never ended*, Yale University Press, 2005, p. 79; Norman Davies, *God's Playground: 1795 to the present*, Columbia University Press, 2005, p. 344.

301 Its Polish name: *Armia Krajowa*.

302 W. Pilecki, op.cit., k.14; the shooting incident was reported by his sister-in-law, Eleonora Ostrowska, see: E.Ostrowska, Rozmowa...; W.J.Wysocki, op.cit, p.33.

303 John E. Lewis, *The Mammoth Book of True War Stories*, Carroll & Graf Publishers, New York, 1999, p.389.

304 The Polish name of this regiment was *Pułk Ułanów Zasławskich*.

305 APMA-B, Zespół Wspomnienia, v.179, k.2-3, *Wspomnienia Eleonory Ostrowskiej*.

306 *Wspomnienia W. Deringa*, APMO, k.1.

307 M. Pilecka, op.cit., p.104.

308 W. Pilecki, op.cit., k.14.

309 W. Pilecki, op.cit., k.15.

310 E. Ostrowska, "Wspomnienia', *Czas* (Canada), 18 August 1984.

311 ASS MON, *Akta sprawy*, v.1, k.96 (Pilecki's testimony of June 26, 1947, which he gave when interrogated prior to his trial in 1948); also, M. Sieradzki's testimony of July 5, 1947, v.2, k.189.

312 APMA-B Zespół Wspomnienia, v.179. k.147 (Eleonora Ostrowska'a recollections).

313 K. Malinowski, *Tajna Armia Polska, Znak. Konfederacja Zbrojna. Zarys genezy, organisacji i działalności*, PAX, Warszawa,. 1986, p.85.

314 Information obtained by Adam Cyra directly from Pilecki's children, Zofia and Andrzej, when he met them on April 20, 1991 (see: Adam Cyra, op.cit. p.43).

315 M.Bober, op.cit.

316 Ibidem.

317 Kazimierz Malinowski, op.cit.

318 Richard C. Lukas, *Out of the inferno: Poles remember the Holocaust*, University Press of Kentucky, 1989, p. 5. ZWZ existed from November 13, 1939 until February 14, 1942.

319 Jan Nowak, *Kurier z Warszawy*, Znak, Warszawa-Kraków 1989, pp.37-38.

320 W. Dering, *Wspomnienia*, k.1.

321 Ibidem, k.2-3.

322 In English: *Union of Armed Struggle*.

323 K. Malinowski, op.cit., p.100.

324 ASS MON, *Akta sprawy*, v.1, k.74 (Pilecki's testimony of 18 June 1947, when interrogated in preparation for his trial in 1948).

325 W. Pilecki, op.cit., k.15.
326 Ibidem, k.15.
327 Sybille Steinbacher, *Auschwitz: A History*, Verlag C. H. Beck, Munich, 2005, p.89.
328 Ibidem, p.94.
329 Sybille Steinbacher, op.cit., pp.100-1.
330 Laurence Rees, *Auschwitz: A New History*, Public Affairs, New York, 2005, pp.168-9.
331 Ibidem, p. 298.
332 auschwitz.org, *Escapes and Reports*
333 Polish WWII underground intelligence was able to obtain an advance information about occupant planned street round-ups.
334 K. Malinowski, op.cit., p.101; the extraordinary courage of Pilecki's decision to get, as a volunteer, into the Auschwitz camp was officially recognised on November 11, 1941, when he was promoted to the rank of Lieutenant; at the same time it is a proof that his decision was entirely voluntary. His promotion to Lieutenant would not have been possible at the time when he still was an Auschwitz inmate, for this would have been against the pertinent Polish military promotion regulations.
335 M.Bober, op.cit.
336 ASS MON, *Akta sprawy*, v.5, kk.219-220 (an excerpt from Pilecki's unsuccessful clemency plea to President Bolesław Bierut, of 7 May 1948).
337 APMA-B Zespół Wspomnienia, v.179. k.148 (Eleonora Ostrowska'a recollections differ from the version of events as testified by Witold Pilecki in 1947; one needs to be mindful, though, that Pilecki needed to protect the identity of the people who provided him with secret accommodation during World War II).
338 R. Domańska, *Pawiak. Więźniowie Gestapo, Kronika 1939-1944*, Książka i Wiedza, Warszawa 1978, p. 95. The name of this prison where many thousands were incarcerated, and died in during the German occupation, is derived from the name of the street where it operated – Pawia Street.
339 APMA-B Zespół Wspomnienia, v.130. k.1 (Witold Pilecki's 1945 report).
340 *Kapos* were inmates whom the Auschwitz SS had given special assignments and privileges.

341 This chapter does not offer detailed descriptions of Pilecki's, often very confronting and graphic, experiences during his 31-month stay at Auschwitz. This is so, because later in this book readers will be able to acquaint themselves with Pilecki's original report from the Auschwitz camp (*Raport W*) which this author translated, and published, in 2013; those interested in learning even more about Pilecki's stay in this death camp may want to additionally read *The Auschwitz Volunteer: Beyond Bravery,* a book published by Aquila Polonica in 2012 in the USA. That book contains a translation by Jarek Garliński of the more comprehensive version of his Auschwitz report which was written by Witold Pilecki two years later, in 1945, while at the headquarters of the Second Polish Corps in Ancona, Italy; that book won, so far, two US literary prizes: the 2012 Prose Award for Biography and Autobiography, and the Silver Award for Autobiography/Memoir at the 2013 Benjamin Franklin Awards.

342 Based mainly on two sources: Adam Cyra, *Rotmistrz Pilecki. Ochotnik do Auschwitz*, RM Warsaw, 2014, and Pilecki's *Report W.*

343 Whenever a number appears in this chapter next to an inmate's name, it is his official Auschwitz inmate number, the most reliable way to positively identify an Auschwitz inmate.

344 Antoni Kocjan (1902-1944), a renowned Polish glider designer, and a Polish World War II underground movement hero who after his release from Auschwitz helped locate the supersecret German V-2 rocket testing site at Peenemünde so that it could then be annihilated by heavy RAAF bombing; he has worked out the technical secrets of that 'wonder weapon' of Hitler's. The Gestapo murdered him on August 13, 1944 together with a group of the last forty prisoners of Pawiak during the Warsaw Uprising. (see: http://en.wikipedia.org/wiki/Antoni_Kocjan)

345 Władysław Bartoszewski, born in 1922 in Warsaw. After his release from Auschwitz, he took part in the 1944 Warsaw Uprising. After the war, he was for many years involved in anti-communist activities, and got imprisoned for these by the Polish communist government. After 1989, he was (twice) Republic of Poland's Foreign Affairs Minister. He died in 2015.

346 W. Bartoszewski, *Mój Auschwitz*, Znak, Krakow, 2010 (an interview by P.M.A. Cywiński and M. Zając), p.22.

347 APMA-B Zespół Wspomnienia, v.130. k.7 (the 1945 Witold Pilecki's report).

348 Polish physicians were forbidden by German authorities to work at the camp as doctors.

349 Adam Cyra, *Rotmistrz Pilecki. Ochotnik do Auschwitz*, p. 49.

350 Adam Cyra, op.cit., p.50.

351 The identity of this wartime allied intelligence operative is unknown to this author.

352 J. Garliński, *Oświęcim walczący*, Volumen, Warszawa, 1992, p.51 and pp. 288-9.

353 Ibidem, p.52.

354 APMA-B Zespół Wspomnienia, v.130. k.25 (contains Witold Pilecki's report written in 1945).

355 Mariusz Bober, op.cit.

356 A. Cyra, op.cit., p.52.

357 APMA-B Zespół Wspomnienia, v.130. k.29 (1945 Witold Pilecki's report).

358 S. Kłodziński, 'Rola kryminalistów niemieckich w początkach obozu oświęcimskiego,' *Przegląd Lekarski*, 1974, no.1. pp.123-4. *Kapos* and Oberkapos were assigned at German camps various supervision and control tasks in respect of camp inmates. *Kapos were* prisoners themselves, so they also were at the mercy of their SS overseers. The word *Kapo* is of unknown origin; it might, or might not, have been derived from the German noun *Kameradschaftpolizei*, literally 'comrade police force.'

359 From an unpublished archive material from the Pilecki file (IPN BU 0259/168 v.6, p. 312) made available to the author of this book in early 2013 by the Institute of National Remembrance, in Warsaw, Poland.

360 Thomas à Kempis, *The Imitation of Christ*, The Bruce Publishing Group, Milwaukee, 1940, p.30.

361 W. Pilecki, *Raport W*, pp.79-80.

362 Captain Triebling's sister, Irena, was Franciszek Kolbe's wife; Franciszek Kolbe was a brother of Rajmund Kolbe, the latter being a Franciscan friar known in his order under assumed names of Maksymilian Maria. An Auschwitz martyr, he was in 1982 canonised by Pope John Paul II. (T. Wontor-Cichy, "Więzień KL Auschwitz, Franciszek Kolbe, no.127600', *W nurcie franciszkańskim*, 2007, no.16, p.127).

363 W. Gawron, *Ochotnik…*, pp. 73.

364 APMA-B Zespół Wspomnienia, v.130. k.37 (the 1945 Witold Pilecki's report).

365 APMA-B Zespół Wspomnienia, v.183. k.79 (the key to the name that appear in *Report W*).

366 *Rapportführer* was a mid-level SS officer's rank.

367 APMA-B Zespół Wspomnienia, v.130. k.38 (the 1945 Witold Pilecki's report).

368 A. Cyra, op.cit., p,58.

369 APMA-B Zespół Oświadczenia, v.27, kk.37 and 41d (statement provided by former inmate Kazimierz Rawicz).

370 W. Pilecki, *Raport W*, p.80.

371 APMA-B Zespół Wspomnienia, v.130. k.41 (1945 Witold Pilecki's report).

372 W. Pilecki, *Raport W*, pp.31, 76, 83.

373 APMA-B Zespół Oświadczenia, v.27, k. 41f (statement provided by former inmate Kazimierz Rawicz).

374 APMA-B Zespół Oświadczenia, v.27, kk. 41f and g (statement provided by former inmate Kazimierz Rawicz).

375 APMA-B Zespół Wspomnienia, v.130. k.51 (Witold Pilecki's report from 1945).

376 J. Sikorski, 'Farmaceuci - pierwsi więźniowie Oświęcimia', *Farmacja Polska*, 1973, no.6, pp.555-6.

377 APMA-B Zespół Wspomnienia, v.75. kk.164, 170-1 (recollections by former inmate Edward Pyś).

378 APMA-B Zespół Wspomnienia, v.130. k.79 (1945 Witold Pilecki's report).

379 APMO, Zespół Wspomnienia, *Wspomnienia W. Deringa*, k.28.

380 Ibidem, k.30.

381 APMA-B Zespół Wspomnienia, v.130. k.22 (1945 Witold Pilecki's report), also: APMA-B Zespół Wspomnienia, v.122. kk.18-20 (recollections by former inmate Bolesław Gierych).

382 W. Pilecki, *Raport W*, p.93.

383 R. Diem, *Wspomnienia lekarza*, p. 141.

384 APMA-B Zespół Oświadczenia, v.84, k. 16 (statement provided by former inmate Henryk Bartosiewicz).

385 APMA-B Zespół Oświadczenia, v.84, kk.46-8 and 57 (statement provided by former inmate Karel Stransky).

386 W. Pilecki, *Raport W*, p.116.

387 APMA-B, D-Aul-2/27, *Sterbebuch*, v.4/1942, p.382.

388 APMA-B Zespół Oświadczenia, v.84, k. 16 (statement provided by former inmate Henryk Bartosiewicz).

APMA-B Zespół Oświadczenia, v.11, kk.5 and 8 (statement provided by former inmate Tadeusz Lucjan Chróścicki).

389 APMA-B Zespół Oświadczenia, v.27, k. 41h (statement provided by former inmate Kazimierz Rawicz).

390 P. Bystrzycki, 'W sprawie odbicia przez AK więźniów obozu masowej zagłady w Oświęcimiu', *Wojskowy Przegląd Historyczny*, 1966, no.1, p.429.

391 J. Ciechanowski, "AK w Oświęcimiu', *Zeszyty Historyczne*, no.34, Paris 1975, p.219.

392 APMA-B Zespół Oświadczenia, v.74, kk.45-7 (Juliusz Gilewicz's biography, by Zygmunt Mianowski).

393 W. Pilecki, *Raport W*, p.102.

394 APMA-B Zespół Wspomnienia, v.75. k.171 (recollections by former inmate Edward Pyś).

395 DZ PMA-B, file TA-201 (statement by fomer Auschwitz inmate Tadeusz Stulgiński).

396 D.Czech, *Kalendarz wydarzeń w KL Auschwitz*, Oświęcim, 1992, p.239.

397 APMA-B Zespół Wspomnienia, v.130. kk.63-4 (the 1945 Witold Pilecki's report).

398 APMA-B Zespół Wspomnienia, v.130. kk.84-5 (the 1945 Witold Pilecki's report).

399 Dering, Wspomnienia...kk. 86, 163-4.

400 APMA-B Zespół Wspomnienia, v.130. kk.75-6 (the 1945 Witold Pilecki's report), also: APMA-B Zespół Wspomnienia, v.83, kk.30-1 (statement by former inmate Artur Karpik).

401 *Reichsdeutsch* category applied to all citizens of the Third Reich, while *Volksdeutsch* applied to the Third Reich's non-citizens who had German ancestry.

402 D. Czech, *Kalendarz*..., p.328; the exact number of ZOW members killed in that execution is something that we will almost certainly never know, because Pilecki – thanks to the rules of conspiracy which he himself conceived and applied – had very limited information about the Lower Five cells of the ZOW membership.

403 D.Czech, Kalendarz..., pp.367-9 and 392-3.

404 APMA-B Zespół Wspomnienia, v.130. k.83 (the 1945 Witold Pilecki's report).

405 APMA-B Zespół Wspomnienia, v.130. kk.83-4 (the 1945 Witold Pilecki's report).

406 J. Garliński, *Oświęcim*..., pp.144-5.

407 J. Komski, Listy do Redakcji, *Kultura*, Paris, 1963, No.7-8. s.228.

408 APMA-B Zespół Wspomnienia, v.172, k.161 (Rudolf Diem's recollections), v.54, k.57 (Andrzej Harat' statement), v.154, k.148 (former inmate Zenon Ławski' recollections).

409 APMA-B *Zespół Wspomnienia*, v.130. k.74 (The 1945 Witold Pilecki's report).

410 W. Pilecki, *Raport W*, p.106.

411 Ibidem, p.107.

412 *Arbeitsdienstführer* was a labour service leader at the Auschwitz camp.

413 E. Ciesielski, *Wspomnienia oświęcimskie*, Wydawnictwo Literackie, Kraków 1968, p.105.

414 W. Fejkiel, *Więźniarski szpital*..., p.156.

415 E. Ciesielski, op.cit., p.219.

416 W. Pilecki, *Raport W*, p.109.

417 A far more detailed description of their escape can be found later in this book, in his *Report W*..

418 After September 1939, the Nazi Germany authorities revised the pre-war German-Polish boundary, moving it eastwards, sometimes by a few hundred kilometres, into the pre-war Polish territory. In October 1939, they established an entity which they called the *Generalgouvernement* [General Governorate; Polish: *Generalna Gubernia*], an occupied area of the Second Republic of Poland which until January 1945 remained a quasi-colony under direct Nazi rule, rather than – as occurred in Norway, Slovakia, Croatia, Romania, and other lands – rule through a surrogate local administration. In 1941 (after the German attack on its former ally, the Soviet Union), this entity included much of the central and southern pre-war Poland, with most notably, three major cities: Warsaw, Cracow, and Lvov. Its administration consisted entirely of Germans, and at its head was Hans Frank, a Hitler appointee hanged at Nuremberg in 1946.

419 APMA-B Zespół Wspomnienia, v.130, k.101 (the 1945 Witold Pilecki report).

420 APMA-B Zespół Wspomnienia, v.125, kk.177-8 (Ludmiła Serafińska's statement).

421 Its English translation, by the same author, is provided to the readers of this book, as its next chapter.

422 APMA-B Zespół Materiały, v.220, k.48 (Tomasz Serafiński's statement).

423 APMA-B Zespół Wspomnienia, v.130, k.1 (Andrzej Możdżeń's statement).

424 APMA-B Zespół Wspomnienia, v.125, kk.179 (Ludmiła Serafińska's statement).

425 APMA-B Zespół Wspomnienia, v.125, kk.177-8 (Ludmiła Serafińska's statement).

  APMA-B Zespół Materiały, v.220, k.48 (Tomasz Serafiński's statement).

426 APMA-B Zespół Materiały, v.220, k.49 (Tomasz Serafiński's statement).

427 One should be mindful of the very specific, and difficult circumstances, in which *Report W* was written, further - of the limited circle of its intended readers and, last, that its form had to conform to the requirements of conspiracy in wartime. To assist readers, 'Explanatory Notes from the Translator of *Report W*' are provided at the end of this report.

428 The original typewritten *Report W* contains a large number of phrases, even entire paragraphs, where words are deliberately spaced out, to signal author's particular emphasis on them; in this book, all such phrases, or larger fragments, are written in bold letters instead, since spacing them out would render reading this document more difficult.

429 Pilecki was able to bring together a number of eminent pre-war Polish politicians incarcated at Auschwitz (their names are listed underneath) to work together in an exemplary and constructive way as members of ZOW's political cell. Prior to the war they represented political options which were fiercely opposing each other.

430 A *Lagerältester* was a Kapo who bore the responsibility for enforcing discipline upon the camp's inmates. Usually he had been a criminal convicted before the war.

431 It was in April 1943 that news of the 1940 bloodbath in Katyń Forest and environs had reached the outside world. Goebbels announced it on Nazi-controlled radio during that month. Prime Minister Sikorski, still in London exile, called for an International Red Cross investigation into the killings. Only three months later Sikorski perished in a Gibraltar plane crash under circumstances that, three-quarters of a century later, are still mysterious.

432 Inmates in WWII German concentration camps could be sent, for a period of time, to a penal work unit (in German: Strafkompanie - SK) in punishment for disobeying their superiors, violating camp discipline, or any other reason which according to camp authorities merited such a punishment; inmates in those divisions had to work harder, and longer hours than other concentration inmates (e.g. in a quary), they were given less food, and were often savagely maltreated; they also lived in barracks which were isolated from other camp barracks. For more related details, see: auschwitz.org

433 Correct spelling of that name is: Alois.

434 Maria Szelągowska, born in 1905 in Lwów, daughter of Adam Szelągowski, a well-known historian, professor at the Lwów University. By profession a chemical engineer, she worked together with Captain Pilecki in the AK underground [organisation] in Warsaw, and in summer 1945 - in Italy, typewriting secret materials and reports by Pilecki relating to his various experiences and to the underground military activity at KL Auschwitz. She was arrested in 1947, and found guilty in the same trial that condemned Witold Pilecki, though in her case without a capital sentence. She died in 1989.

435 These have been prepared by either Dr. Adam Cyra, or the translator of *Report W*, to clarify certain events covered in this report.

436 ASS MON, Akta sprawy... v.1, kk. 8 and 75.

437 W. Pilecki, *Report W*, p.117.

438 E. Ciesielski, *Wspomnienia...*, p.178; also: APMA-B Zespół Wspomnienia, v.98, kk.91, 94-6.

439 W. Pilecki, *Report W*, pp.75-6.

440 APMA-B. Zespół Wspomnienia, v.172, kk.113 and 159-160 (statement of former inmate Rudolf Diem).

441 J. Garliński, *Oświęcim...*, p.193.

442 M. Fieldorf, L. Zachuta, *Generał 'Nil' August Emil Fieldorf. Fakty, dokumenty, relacje*, Instytut Wydawniczy PAX, Warszawa, 1993, pp.104-5.

443 ASS MON, Akta sprawy... v.2, k.264 (statements by Witold Pilecki during an interrogation on June 18, 1947, ahead of his trial).

444 SPP, Zeszyt Ewidencyjny Witolda Pileckiego.

445 M.Fieldorf, L. Zachuta, op.cit., p.114.

446 Ibidem, pp.117-8.

447 ASS MON, Akta sprawy... v.1, kk.63 and 75 (statements by Witold Pilecki during an interrogation on June 18, 1947, ahead of his trial).

448 APMA-B, Materiały obozowego ruchu oporu, v.37, k.46. While attending to his Auschwitz surveillance and intelligence collection tasks, Stefan Jasieński was shot, and badly wounded near the camp's perimeter by Auschwitz Gestapo functionaries. He was then taken to the camp's inmates hospital and brutally interrogated; later, he was put into the Death Block and presumably died there in early January 1945 (the exact date of his death being unknown), two or three weeks before this camp's liberation by the advancing Soviet and Polish military units.

449 M.Bober, op.cit.

450 Ibidem.

451 The advances by the Soviet Army over 1943 on the Eastern Front had outstripped, by far, the progress the Western Allied powers had made over the same year, after their invasion, first of Sicily (July 9, 1943), and then of the Italian mainland (September 3, 1943); the decisive Western Front landing operation on the beaches of Normandy commenced on June 6, 1944, in other words, at a time when the Soviet Army had already 'liberated' swathes of Poland's pre-war territory.

452 Norman Davies, *Rising '44. The Battle for Warsaw*, Viking, New York, 2004, pp.204-6.

453 Norman Davies, *Rising '44. The Battle for Warsaw*, Viking, New York, pp.206-8.

454 Winston S. Churchill, *The Second World War*, Vol. 6, Chapter IX, 'The Martyrdom of Warsaw' (London: Cassel, 1955).

455 Duchess of Atholl, *The Tragedy of Warsaw and its Documentation*, London, 1945.

456 Norman Davies, *Rising '44. The Battle for Warsaw*, pp.232.

457 ASS MON, Akta sprawy, v.5, k.220.

458 SPP, No.1785/III,3/2/BI, Witold Pilecki's statement, p.1.

459 S. Podlewski, *Przemarsz przez piekło*, PAX, Warszawa, 1957, p.131.

460 SPP No.1785/III,3/2/BI, Witold Pilecki's statement, p.1.

461 M. Kledzik, 'Reduta rotmistrza Pileckiego', *Tydzień Polski*, London, 1994, no.3; A. Kownacki 'Jerzewski', *Jak powstało i walczyło zgrupowanie 'Chrobry II'*, Warszawa, 1993, p.60.

462 SPP No.1785/III,3/2/BI, Witold Pilecki's statement, p.4.

463 A. Kownacki, op.cit., p.60.

464 Z. Brym-Zdunin, Żelazna Reduta. Kompania Zdunina w Powstaniu Warszawskim Zgr. *'Chrobry II'*, London. 1992, p.83.

465 SPP No.1785/III,3/2/BI, Pilecki's statement, p.5.

466 E. Ciesielski, op.cit. pp-178-9.

467 APMA-B. Zespół Wspomnienia, v.203, k.83, letter of 14 August 1997 from J. Mierzanowski to the Auschwitz-Birkenau Museum.

468 APMA-B. Zespół Materiały, v.223, k.24-7 (the list, by Pilecki's hand, of all soldiers he had under his command during the Warsaw Uprising).

469 ASS MON, Akta sprawy, v.1, k.8 (Pilecki's interrogation on May 8, 1947, before his trial.)

470 W.J. Wysocki, op.cit. pp.101-2.

471 APMA-B. Zespół Oświadczenia, v.179, k.152, (statement by Eleonora Ostrowska).

472 J. Rzepecki, *Wspomnienia i przyczynki historyczne*, Warszawa, 1956, pp.283-4.

473 A. Kownacki, op.cit., p.140-3. Murnau's official German name was Oflag VII-A

474 D. Kisielewicz, *Oflag VII A Murnau, Łambinowice-Opole*, 1990, pp.150-1; T. Gruszka, *W Murnau*, Hove, London 1994, pp.64-7.

475 APMA-B. Zespół Wspomnienia, v.203, k.84, letter of 19 August 1997 from J. Mierzanowski to the Auschwitz-Birkenau Museum.

476 D. Kisielewicz, op. cit., p.170.

477 APMA-B. Zespół Materiały, v.223, kk.1-23.

478 M. Fieldorf, L.Zachuta, op.cit., p.141.

479 A. Przemyski, *Ostatni Komendant generał Leopold Okulicki*, Wydawnictwo Lubelskie, Lublin, 1990, pp.206-33.

480 M. Fieldorf, L. Zachuta, op.cit., pp.138 and 142.

481 AUOP. Sygn. 1768/III/2: operational files concerning Witold Pilecki and seven others, k.186: recollections by Witold Pilecki from June 1946.

482 D.Kisielewicz, op.cit. pp.172-3.

483 Ibidem, p.173.

484 APMA-B. Zespół Wspomnienia, v.203, k.85, letter of 19 August 1997 from J. Mierzanowski to the Auschwitz-Birkenau Museum.

485 Copies of both texts are archived in APMA-B, Zespół Wspomnienia, vv.130 and 179.

486 APMA-B. Zespół Wspomnienia, v.203, k.85, containing a letter of 19 August 1997 from J.Mierzanowski to the Auschwitz-Birkenau Museum.

487 Polish military units in Western Europe were subordinated to the Republic of Poland's Government-in-Exile, which never recognised the Soviet Union's de facto occupation and control of Poland, this occupation being a result of the Roosevelt-Churchill-Stalin agreement at Yalta in February 1945.

488 APMA-B. Zespół Wspomnienia, v.203, k.88, letter of 19 August 1997 from J.Mierzanowski to the Auschwitz-Birkenau Museum.

489 AUOP.Sygn. 1768/III/2, k.185.

490 ASS MON, v.1, k.65, Pilecki's pre-trial testimony from June 10, 1947.

491 ASS MON: v.1, k.160, Maria Szelągowska's pre-trial testimony from June 27, 1947 and v.1, k.65, Witold Pilecki's testimony from June 10, 1947.

492 ASS MON, v.1, k.79, Pilecki's pre-trial testimony from June 18, 1947.

493 ASS MON, v.1, k.220, Tadeusz Płużański's pre-trial testimony from June 10, 1947.

494 ASS MON, v.5, k.220, Pilecki's plea to Bolesław Bierut for clemency, of May 7, 1948.

495 ASS MON, v.1, kk.174-180, Tadeusz Płużański's pre-trial testimony from May 7, 1947.

496 ASS MON, V.1, k.70, Pilecki's pre-trial testimonyfrom June 10, 1947.

497 ASS MON, v.1, k.194, Makary Sieradzki's pre-trial testimony from July 9, 1947, and ASS MON v.1, k.70, Pilecki's pre-trial testimonyfrom June 10, 1947.

498 ASS MON, V.1, k.76, Pilecki's pre-trial testimony from June 18, 1947.

499 ASS MON, v.1, k.41, Pilecki's pre-trial testimony from May 24, 1947.

500 ASS MON, v.1, k.81, Pilecki's pre-trial testimony from June 18, 1947.

501 ASS MON, v.1, k.81, from the indictment document of January 23, 1948.

502 ASS MON, v.2, kk.155-158, Witold Różycki's pre-trial testimony from June 11, 1947, and ASS MON, v.1, kk.100-102, Pilecki's pre-trial testimonyfrom June 27, 1947.

503 ASS MON, Documents filed, v.3, k.118, photocopies of the plenipotentiary letter by General Anders of 28 Aprik 1946

504 This information was obtained by Adam Cyra from Maria Pilecka during his interview of her on April 20, 1991.

505 ASS MON, v.1, kk.84-5, Pilecki's pre-trial testimonyfrom June 20, 1947.

506 A. Czajkowski, 'Po dwakroć na barykadach Warszawy', [in:] *Udział kapelanów wojskowych w drugiej wojnie światowej*, Warsaw, 1984, pp.414-428.

507 ASS MON, v.1, kk.29-31, Pilecki's pre-trial testimony from May 19, 1947.

508 ASS MON, v.2, kk.231-238, Wacław Alchimowicz's pre-trial testimony from October 10, 1947.

509 Researchers of this subject (A. Cyra, *Rotmistrz...*, pp.167-8, W.J. Wysocki, *Rotmistrz...*, pp.133-139; T.M. Płużański, *Z otchłani (...)*, p.166) have found that Leszek Kuchciński, the person with whom the older Płużański shared a flat, was an informer to MBP, and a provocateur. In his recent book, *Bestie. Mordercy Polaków*, Tadeusz M. Płużański, son of Pilecki's courier, additionally unravels details of Alchimowicz's involvement in the Soviet-controlled communist activity during the concluding years of World War II and argues that it was more likely Alchimowicz, who after the war worked with the MBP, and not – Kuchciński, who should take the main responsibility for the betrayal, and the subsequent death, of Captain Pilecki. The matter still awaits a final resolution.

510 M. Bober, op.cit.

511 ASS MON, v.1, k.10, Pilecki's pre-trial testimonyfrom May 8, 1947.

512 According to a 1993 study, a total of 1,053,829 people died in the Gulag from 1934 to 1953 (see: Getty J. Arch, Rittersporn, Gábor T., Zemskov, Viktor, N., 'Victims of the Soviet Penal System in the Pre-War Years: A First Approach on the Basis of Archival Evidence', *The American Historical Review*, Vol. 98, No. 4 (Oct. 1993), pp. 1017-1049). When one accounts for the practice of releasing Gulag prisoners who were either suffering from incurable diseases or were about to die, the actual Gulag death toll was likely to be far higher, about 1.6 million deaths between 1929 and 1953. Some present estimates of the total number of inmates who died in Gulag camps are higher still, and exceed a staggering ten million victims (see: Robert Conquest, Preface, *The Great Terror: A Reassessment: Fortieth Anniversary Edition*, Oxford University Press, USA, 2007. p. xvi).

513 Piotr Wróbel, *Historical Dictionary of Poland 1945-1996* (London: Routledge, 2014), p. 1885.

514 His words were: '*Ja zostanę, wszyscy nie mogą stąd wyjechać, ktoś musi tu trwać bez względu na konsekwencje.*' see: Wiesław J. Wysocki, op.cit.

515 M.Bober, op.cit.

516 A. Cyra, op.cit. p.168.

517 Ibidem, p. 169; the dates of three further arrests related to this case, and namely those of Fr Antoni Czajkowski, Tadeusz Szturm de Sztrem and Wacław Alchimowicz, are not provided in the available prosecution and court files.

518 ASS MON, Akta sprawy .,, t.1, kk.172-3, Tadeusz Płużański's testimony from May 6, 1947.

519 ASS MON, Akta sprawy ,,, t.2, k.193, Makary Sieradzki's testimony from July 9, 1947.

520 On May 14, 1947, Pilecki sent a poem to Colonel Różański, in which he unambiguously asked that he and he alone be assigned all the blame for the operation of the network which he had established (Wysocki, *Rotmistrz...*, pp.124-5).

521 AUOP Sygn. 1768/III/1, Akta operacyjne Witold Pileckiego i siedmiu inych osób, k.74.

522 Cz. Leopold , K.Lechicki, *Więźniowie polityczni w Polsce 1945-1956*, Gdańsk 1981, pp.36-7.

523 ASS MON, Akta sprawy..., v.4. k.240, Witold Pilecki's act of indictment dated December 4, 1947.

524 ASS MON, Akta sprawy..., v.4. kk.212-239 (odpisy wyroków WSR w Warszawie); 'Lista straconych w więzieniach PRL w latach 1944-1956', *Wokanda*, 1990, nos 1-4.

525 M. Bober, op.cit.

526 Andrzej Werblan, *Stalinizm w Polsce*, Warszawa, 1991, p.66.

527 Z. Mączyński, 'Zbrodnicza Temida', *Prawo i Życie*, 1991, no.7.

528 ASS MON. Akta sprawy, v.5, kk.22-105, main trial's protocol.

529 APMA-B, Zespół Wspomnienia, v.179, k.156, Eleonora Ostrowska's recollections from the trial.

530 Ibidem, k.155

531 ASS MON. Akta sprawy..., v.5, kk.25-6, from the main trial's protocol.

532 Those accused in the Stalinist era political trials would often mention to the court that they were 'too tired' to read interrogation protocols before signing them; in fact they did not read them for they knew that it would not matter, anyway; if they indeed found and reported any inaccuracies in the protocol they would be rewarded with extra-savage beatings; even more beatings and other tortures were awaiting them if they later admitted to the court that fear of beatings had influenced their failure to read the protocols.

533 ASS MON. Akta Sprawy..., v.5, kk.26-41; the main trial's protocol.

534 Ibidem, v.5, kk.107-117, Warsaw Military District Court verdicts of March 15, 1948.

535 Ibidem.

536 See: Pseudo-Apollodorus, *Bibliotheke* ii. 5; Hyginus, *Fabula* 31.

537 APMA-B, Zespół Wspomnienia, v.203, k.87, J. M. Mierzanowski's letter of August 19, 1997, to the Auschwitz-Birkenau Museum.

538 APMA-B, Zespół Oświadczenia, v.125, kk.181-182, reported by Ludmiła Serafińska.

539 Jarosław Abramow-Newerly, 'Lwy mojego podwórka', 2000, http://wyborcza.pl/1,75517,136040.html

540 ASS MON. Akta Sprawy..., v.5, kk.179-182.

541 Ibidem.

542 ASS MON. Akta Sprawy..., v.5, k.194.

543 ASS MON. Akta Sprawy..., v.5, k.223.

544 T. M. Płużański, 'Inaczej niż w 'Przesłuchaniu'', *Gazeta Polska*, 2010, no.21; both of them will several years later be released from prison.

545 Z. Woźniczka, 'Polskie podziemie niepodległościowe (1945-1951)', część II, *Mówią Wieki*, 1991, no.4.

546 M. Bober, op.cit.

547 M. Szejnert, Śród żywych duchów, London, 1990, p.132.

548 M. Leciejewska, *Biografia Witolda Pileckiego*, Wyższa Szkoła Pedagogiczna, Słupsk, p.75 [APMA-B, Zespół Materiały, v.92].

549 Pedro Rodríguez, *Camino* (ed. critica), Rialp, Madrid, 2004, point 622.

550 New Testament, *1 Corinthians 13:4-8 (English Standard Version)*.

551 M.Bober, op.cit.

552 M.Bober, op.cit.; (Pilecki's own words: '...*będziesz dziedziczką świeżego powietrza*').

553 From Andrzej Pilecki's letter, of December 8, 2014, to this author.

554 R.Stawicki, *Rotmistrz Witold Pilecki 1901-1948*, Kancelaria Senatu, Biuro Informacji i Dokumentacji, Dział Analiz i Opracowań Tematycznych, opracowanie tematyczne OT-540. June 2008.

555 Z.Baranowski, *Niech złożą mandaty*, 'Nasz Dziennik', 2009, no.88.

556 M.Bober, op.cit. Zofia's exact words were: '*Trwa sztafeta pokoleń.*'

557 According to the doctrine of the Catholic Church, a person presents heroic virtues when at least in some regards he, or she follows Jesus' example, and seeks to imitate Him. Heroic virtue is a habit of good conduct that became a man's second nature; it enables its owner to perform virtuous actions with uncommon promptitude, ease and pleasure, from supernatural motives and without human reasoning, with self-abnegation and full control over his natural inclinations (see: Heroic *Virtue: A Portion of the Treatise of Benedict XIV on the Beatification and Canonization of the Servants of God (De Servorum Dei Beatificatione et Beatorum Canonizatione)*, Vol.1, Thomas Richardson and Son, London, 1850, pp. 1-44). When the Holy See formally recognises someone's heroic virtues, it means that the Church is of the view that that person exhibited the theological virtues of faith, hope and charity as well as the cardinal virtues of prudence, justice, fortitude and temperance to a heroic degree.

www.ingramcontent.com/pod-product-compliance
Lightning Source LLC
Chambersburg PA
CBHW031505080526
44588CB00019B/2724